Piety, Politics, and Power

Piety, Politics, and Power
Lutherans Encountering Islam in the Middle East

DAVID D. GRAFTON

◆PICKWICK *Publications* · Eugene, Oregon

PIETY, POLITICS, AND POWER
Lutherans Encountering Islam in the Middle East

Copyright © 2009 David D. Grafton. All rights reserved. Except for brief quotations in critical publications or reviews, no part of this book may be reproduced in any manner without prior written permission from the publisher. Write: Permissions, Wipf and Stock Publishers, 199 W. 8th Ave., Suite 3, Eugene, OR 97401.

Pickwick Publications
A Division of Wipf and Stock Publishers
199 W. 8th Ave., Suite 3
Eugene, OR 97401

www.wipfandstock.com

ISBN 13: 978-1-60608-130-3

Cataloging-in-Publication data:

Grafton, David D.

    Piety, politics, and power : Lutherans encountering Islam in the Middle East

    xiv + 298 p. ; 23 cm. Includes bibliographical references and index.

    ISBN 13: 978-1-60608-130-3

    1. Evangelical Lutheran Church in America—Missions. 2. Mission to Muslims. 3. Christianity and other religions—Islam. 4. Islam—Relations—Christianity. 5. Lutheran Church—Missions. I. Title.

BV2540 G75 2009

Scripture quotations are from the New Revised Standard Version Bible, copyright © 1989 National Council of the Churches of Christ in the United States of America. Used by permission. All rights reserved.

Manufactured in the U.S.A.

To the innocent victims of Taba (2004)

Contents

List of Illustrations / ix

Preface / xi

1. Introduction / 1
2. Luther and "the Turk" / 20
3. The Lutheran Pietists in the Middle East / 59
4. National Missions in the Holy Land / 107
5. Early American Lutheran Views of Islam and Mission in Persia / 147
6. The American Lutheran "Conversation" with Islam / 182
7. Conclusion: An American Lutheran View of Islam in the Middle East in *"Pax Americana"* / 237

Appendix: American Lutheran Personnel in the Middle East (1950–2003) / 257

Credits / 263

Bibliography / 265

Index / 285

Illustrations

Figure 1 Matthias Gerung Woodcut / 23
Figure 2 LOM Staff, Arbil, Iraq, 1950 / 171
Figure 3 LCMS Personnel, Beirut, Lebanon, 1973 / 191
Figure 4 Bruce Schein, LCA Personnel, Larnaca, Cyprus, 1982 / 205
Figure 5 Harold Vogelaar and Mark Swanson, LCA Personnel, Larnaca, Cyprus, 1982 / 230
Figure 6 ELCA personnel, Larnaca, Cyprus, 1992 / 235

Preface

CHRISTIAN-MUSLIM RELATIONSHIPS CAPTURE THE attention of the world today. Many of us wish this attention focused upon creative interfaith initiatives through which one-half of the human community (2.1 billion Christians and 1.3 billion Muslims) could cooperate in promoting the reconciliation of the human family and the transformation of human lives. Tragically, more often than not, the attention focuses upon "the other" as the feared enemy. Portions of the Muslim world live in dread of neo-colonial "Christian" powers whose terrorizing military might has totally surrounded them for centuries, whose economic power has dominated them, and whose materialistic culture impacts their societies through television, movies and music.

In spite of the fact that the "Christian" West has thousands of nuclear weapons that could annihilate the entire world population innumerable times, many Americans tremble because it might be possible for a few militant Muslims to successfully carry out a second 9/11. Within this twenty-first century context approximately 40 percent of the U.S. population sees Islam as a possible threat, the violent enemy, an alien religion.

Dr. David D. Grafton's volume, *Piety, Politics and Power: Lutherans Encountering Islam in the Middle East*, is an excellent resource for Lutherans and other Christians living within this context. Dr. Grafton's research develops a lively narrative that vividly describes the Lutheran story as imbedded in centuries of Christian-Muslim engagement. The narrative begins with Luther and the origins of the Reformation. Surprising for many will be the revelation that the German Reformation was actually miraculously saved by the Muslim Turk Suleiman "the Magnificent," sultan of the Ottoman Empire. Again and again the Holy Roman Emperor, Charles V, and the Roman pope were stymied from moving against Luther. They wanted Luther eliminated but they needed the military power of the German princes to prevent the collapse of Europe before the forces of a Muslim empire. These circumstances molded Luther's views of "the terrible Turk." Luther saw the forces of Suleiman as the judgment of God calling Christians to repentance, and as a sign of the end of the world because "The Turks" were the Gog and Magog of Biblical prophecy (Ezek 38–39 and Rev 20:8). This militant context led Luther to make numerous pejorative comments about the Turks, Islam, and Muhammad. This original Lutheran context is in many ways similar to our contemporary context where Islam is symbolized not as the "Terrible Turk" but as the "Muslim terrorist."

Grafton's narrative focuses upon American Christian-Lutheran engagement with Islam in the Middle East; however, it traces the Lutheran narrative through Martin Luther, German Pietism, European national churches, and then through American Lutheran presence in the Middle East, culminating in the work of the Evangelical Lutheran Church in America. Grafton's account portrays the integral relationship that often existed between Christian missions and western colonialism. This fusion of imperialism and Christian missions has created deep suspicions of the gospel among Muslim peoples.

Grafton's narrative describes a multiplicity of historical contexts, analyses, and visions of Christian-Muslim engagements. For example, Muslims have been seen as the enemy or a competing inferior religious force. They have also been viewed as potential partners in struggles for justice and peace, as the religious "other" who needs to be known and understood as a fellow member of the human family, or as a religious community touched by God and created in God's image. Dr. Grafton is an excellent guide through this religious, political, historical maze as it is traced through five centuries. The journey introduces the reader to the wisdom and obstinacy of those involved in the journey. The book offers innumerable possibilities for new insights that may enable contemporary Christians to walk more faithfully and sensitively through the twenty-first century Christian-Muslim journey.

Dr. Harold Vogelaar, whose creative and sensitive contribution to Christian-Muslim relationships is described in Grafton's book, has related an encounter with a young Muslim artist near Cairo, Egypt. While visiting a Muslim home Dr. Vogelaar saw an unusual painting of a Muslim who held a "peace dove" in one hand and a sword in the other. Dr. Vogelaar asked for the symbolism of the painting. The artist replied that the young man represented Islam, which is always an advocate for peace and struggles for peace in the world. However, Muslims are also aware of forces that threaten their peace and security. Therefore it is necessary to use the sword to defend the community. Dr. Vogelaar then asked whether it was possible for him to paint a figure who carried the dove with two hands. The young artist thought for a long time before replying, "I think I would have to paint a picture of Jesus."

I have often wondered how we as the Christian community might witness more clearly and boldly to the Prince of Peace who eternally carries the dove with two hands. We are claimed by the kingdom of God concretized in Jesus. Jesus embodies the kingdom of God as a vulnerable Jewish prophet who rejects violence as a means of imposing God's will but walks faithfully in God's path in spite of violent opposition and crucifixion. Can this "two-handed carrying-a-dove" Jesus inspire us to a more intense Christian-Muslim journey? Is it possible for Muslims to be introduced to Christ as the Suffering Servant rather than Christ, the Crusader? Dr. Grafton in a concluding chapter writes: "It is imperative that the church dialogue with Muslims who have 'misheard' the Christian witness to . . . Jesus Christ through the language of 'crusade' rather than 'crucifixion.'"

—Dr. Mark Thomsen
Visiting Professor of Mission
Lutheran School of Theology at Chicago

1

Introduction

AMERICANS HAVE ALWAYS HAD a unique relationship with the Middle East. From the early days of the new colonies the New Promised Land of North America was seen as the incarnation of the ancient Eastern Promised Land. With newly arrived immigrant communities in the New World, settlements sprang up throughout the wilderness recalling their ancient biblical heritage: Mt. Zion, Hebron, Bethlehem, etc. This was a new Promised Land for a new Promised People. But as the communities in the wilderness flourished and thrived socially and economically, and looked westward, many Americans pined for their spiritual roots in the biblical East. Evangelical preachers began looking back over their shoulders toward the true lands of the Bible. It was only a matter of time before the idea sprung forth that if the New Zion could be conquered through the hard work and zeal of a new chosen nation, certainly the true lands of biblical heritage could be reclaimed just the same.

Encouraged by the developments of the Evangelical Great Awakening in Britain, Americans began to imagine new spiritual quests. While the European powers sought commercial exploits and the new American republic carved out its own niche within the web of international relationships, American Evangelical Christians began to take seriously the opportunities of a new land and its riches, by sending out is best and brightest to carry an American Enlightenment to the East. From Mount Ararat in the North to Mount Sinai in the South, American Evangelicals drove eastward into the Middle East to reclaim their biblical heritage for Christ. And yet, although Americans did have a unique perspective of the Holy Lands quite different from their European cousins, their views of the Middle East and its people rested upon very long tradition of past images.

From antiquity Western written accounts and artistic portrayals provided a wide variety of images of the lands of the Middle East, which has come to be known as the "Orient." From these records the "Orient" has always carried a sense of fascination of the mysterious unknown: its people, their customs, and their religions. No area of this mysterious land was more intriguing than "Arabia." The ancient Greek historian Herodotus in the fifth century BCE described "Arabia" as an exotic place filled with spices and aromas, and populated by great snakes. By the first century BCE the Roman Empire came into closer contact with the people of the Middle East primarily for commercial purposes. Records and images of Arabs became more frequent. The Roman historian Strabo in the first century CE painted a picture of the people of Arabia as uncultured desert nomads who engaged in the trade of exotic spices.[1] The Aramean peoples of the Near East had also known of the Arabs as traders. An eighth century BCE. Assyrian record of Sargon II states that he received from "Samsi, queen of Arabia," a tribute of "gold, products of the mountain, precious stones, ivory, seed of the maple, all kinds of herbs, horses, and camels."[2] These descriptions found their ways into the sacred writings of both Jews and Christians, reflecting the ancient records of the desert nomads who provided the civilized world with luxury items of "gold, frankincense, and myrrh" (see 1 Kgs 10:15; Isa 60:6–7; Jer 25:24; Ezek 27:21–24; Matt 2:1–11 [Ps 72: 10–11]).[3] In the seventh century, however, a series of events occurred that would dramatically alter Western views of the Orient. A group of people from the Arabian Peninsula, the place of the great "snakes" and spices, burst forth from the arid lands on the edge of the Byzantine Empire, overrunning everything in their path. Within only a hundred years the Arabs were at the gates of France, only to be turned back by Charles Martel at the Battle of Tours in 732. The Arabs, these ancient Bedouin traders, were now known by a new identity, being led by their prophet Muhammad, known pejoratively as "Mohamet" in Western medieval literature. Middle Eastern Christians who had previously lived under both an alien Chalcedonian Christian Roman Empire and a Zoroastrian Persian Empire were now forced to live under the Arab

---

1. Herodotus, *Histories*; Strabo, *Geography* 16.4.3–4.
2. Hitti, *History of the Arabs*, 38.
3. For some very helpful and interesting works about the "Orient" and its relations to the Old and New Testament, see Montgomery, *Arabia and the Bible*; and the more recent work by Yamauchi, *Persia and the Bible*. For a more recent argument about the Arabs in Scripture, see Tony Maalouf, *Arabs in the Shadow of Israel* and "Were the Magi from Persia or Arabia?"

Muslims. These "Oriental" Christians described their new overlords in a variety of manners, some positive while others negative. Some were impressed by their religious tolerance, as opposed to Byzantine "oppression" against non-Chalcedonian heretics—the Armenians, Chaldeans, Copts, and Syrians. Others were offended by the Arabs' lack of culture and their cruelty. Regardless of these initial reactions, however, the Christians of the Middle East had the opportunity to develop first hand experiences of the "believers" [*muʿaminīn*], as they would call themselves—Muslims, as we have come to know them.

However, across the Dardanelles in Constantinople and further west in Rome, European Christians developed their own perceptions of Muslims from afar. The political borders of empires at war prohibited honest first-hand spiritual encounters, what Jean-Marie Gaudeul calls a dialogue "from across the Borders."[4] Information about Muslims was often limited to what was expressed through political propaganda and the bravado of kingly pronouncements, or what information could be smuggled across enemy lines. Thus, most of the images and information of this "Other" was second or third hand. There were some attempts throughout the eleventh and twelfth centuries by Latin missionaries, the Dominicans especially, to come to some sort of accurate intellectual understanding of Muslims and their religion. These Christian missionaries traveled across the Mediterranean to live in the Muslim world and began a serious attempt at learning its language, cultures, and religion. However, their writings were usually guided by the tenor of the times, the tragic military and economic confrontations between Eastern and Western communities during the Crusades. During this medieval period the term "Saracen," the Latinized Greek word meaning "tent-dweller," came to signify not only the "primitive" cultural background of the Arabs but their new religion as well, Islam. The famous eleventh century medieval *Song of Roland* recalled the gallant fight of Charles Martel's army against the invading "Saracen" hordes across the Pyrenees. The song became a classic reference for European views of Muslims. The "Saracen" became the new barbarian. Whereas ancient Rome had previously faced the barbarian hordes of the Huns and the Goths, now the new Holy Roman Empire was facing the challenge of these "Saracens." European literature quickly associated the word "Saracen" with all followers of the religion of Islam, regardless of

---

4. Gaudeul, *Encounters and Clashes*.

the ethnic background. While the Moors of Spain were ethnically different than the Arabs of the Levant or the Turks of Eastern Anatolia, they were all called by the derogatory term "Saracen."[5] By 1453 the Ottoman Turks, another ethnic community that had converted to Islam, managed to conquer much of the Muslim Middle East and expanded their empire up to the very gates of the ancient Byzantine capital of Constantinople. In an earth-shattering event, the Turks scaled the ramparts of the capital of Eastern Christendom, the seat of the Ecumenical Patriarch of Constantinople, and conquered the last holdout of the Byzantine Empire. Eventually they would turn the cathedral church of the Hagia Sophia into a mosque. The fall of Constantinople was burned into Western memory through song, poetry, and painting, lamenting this catastrophic date. But the threat did not end there. By the seventeenth century the Turks were at the gates of Vienna, the center of Renaissance European culture. The image of the "Arab" or the "Saracen" was replaced by that of the "Terrible Turk." Faced with a Muslim threat, which was seemingly turning the European world upside down, Christians began to interpret the Muslim threat within the framework of biblical apocalyptic imagery provided by the twelfth century mystic Joachim of Fiore. One could be consoled that the rampaging Turks were merely a sign of the end times predicted by Christ in the little Apocalypse of Mark. These apocalyptic images were quite common as Martin Luther began his career as a young monk. As we will see in the first chapter of this book, for Luther the "Terrible Turk" served as a cultural reference point, which emerged from the international politics of the day. The frightening public image of the Turk contributed to his own biblical and theological hermeneutic, and helped to further the cause of Lutheranism. Luther, like other apocalypticists, saw the Turk as only one manifestation of the end time, not its cause.

Jumping forward nearly half a millennium, American images of Islam have followed a similar vein as the Medieval European tradition of the cultural denigration of Muslims. As a result of the 1973 October War between Egypt, Syria, and Israel, the Organization of Arab Petroleum Exporting Countries (OAPEC) enacted an oil embargo on the allies of Israel. The embargo created an energy crisis in the United States as the price of a barrel of oil skyrocketed. As Americans felt the impact of having their daily activities restricted due to the reduction in the availability of

---

5. See Tolan, *Saracens*, 10–12.

gasoline, negative images of the Arab Bedouins appeared in American media. Cartoons, advertisements, and lyrics in pop culture appeared, decrying the dagger totting, greedy oil sheikh riding a camel in the desert.[6] The greedy sheikh was quickly replaced by the "mad Ayatollah" after the Iranian hostage crisis of 1979, in which Iranian students in Tehran held 66 Americans hostage for 444 days. During the Lebanese Civil War throughout the 1980s, Americans were bombarded with pictures of Western hostages as radical Muslim groups utilized the media to instill fear for political purposes. Most recently, the tragedy of 9/11 has been followed by horrible and gruesome images on the Internet of radical Muslims beheading innocent victims. According to one of the leading North American Christian Dispensationalist authors, these actions "perfectly d[escribe] the nature and genetic characteristics of Ishmael and his descendents, the Arabs."[7] Like the apocalypticists before him, this author interprets the actions of "the Arabs" as ushering in the End. These are the images of Islam and the Middle East to which Americans are currently subjected.

Western culture, both in its European and North American forms, has for the most part developed images of Muslims "from across the Borders."[8] By this I mean that these images have developed from afar, across not only political boundaries, but also cultural, geographic, and religious boundaries. Images of the "Other" have developed from within the safe confines of our own geographic and cultural safe havens. And thus, these images have easily been based upon imagination and caricatures. Naturally, this goes both ways. Middle Eastern Muslims have developed their own images of the West from within the boundaries of their own prejudicial religious and cultural borders as well.[9] The sudden and dramatic realization of the presence of American Muslim communities within the "homeland" after 9/11 has prompted a great deal of curiosity, interest, fear, and anxiety about the presence of the enemy in our midst, even though "the enemy" has been residing with us since the early days of the Republic!

Throughout history, however, there have been records of those who have crossed the boundaries to view first hand the culture and religion

---

6. See Shaheen, *Reel Bad Arabs*.
7. Lindsey, *Everlasting Hatred*, 59.
8. Gaudeul, *Encounters and Clashes*.
9. See, for example, El-Cheikh, *Byzantium Viewed by the Arabs*.

of the "Other." Throughout the medieval period the Dominicans and Franciscans traveled to the lands of Islam. Venetian merchants carried on significant ongoing trade and conversation with their Muslim counterparts in Middle Eastern cities and ports. By the seventeenth century curious European travelers began to publish records of their personal journeys to "the Orient," referring to its people in a variety of ways.[10]

The Western missionary movement that emerged at the end of the eighteenth century, resting on Continental Pietism and reveling in the throes of the British Great Awakening, began a new encounter with Muslims in the Middle East. These missionaries brought with them many images from their own culture of a backward and deplorable Muslim Orient. As the missionaries settled down in the Middle East or in the Asian subcontinent and came into daily contact with Muslims, they began to develop a wide variety in their own first hand views and images of Islam. Interestingly enough, they found not only what they believed to be a Muslim community in need of being raised from the pits of spiritual despair, but Jewish and Oriental Orthodox communities caught in a deplorable state of "petrification" as well. In 1812, one of the earliest Protestant reports by the American Board of Commissioners of Foreign Missionaries (ABCFM) wrote:

> The whole mingled population [of the Middle East] is in a state of deplorable ignorance and degradation—destitute of the means of divine knowledge, and bewildered with vain imaginations and strong delusions.[11]

Before the European powers—and long before the United States—became interested in the Middle East for imperial interests, Western Protestant missionaries began to engage Middle Eastern communities out of an eager desire to bring the whole Orient into the modern age through the light of the Gospel. According to Rufus Anderson, general secretary of the ABCFM, "Protestant ideas of truth, of liberty, of conscience, of progress, are spread far and wide, and are convulsing these nations" thanks to the work of the Western missionaries.[12] This was the American Enlightenment *par excellance!*

---

10. See J. Smith, "Old French Travel Accounts" and "French Christian Narratives"; as well as the classic 1960 text by Daniel, *Islam and the West*.

11. Khalaf, "Protestant Images of Islam," 211.

12. Vander Werff, *Christian Mission to Muslims*, 112.

By the nineteenth century, American missionaries, carrying with them European images of "the Orient" and their own cultural perspectives about the "light" of American Evangelical religion, began to engage with the people of the Middle East and share their experiences with their constituents back home. These individual missionaries, like the merchants before them who lived among the peoples of the Middle East, had the opportunity to engage them, not across the political and geographic boundaries of the world, but as neighbors. Certainly, there was always a cultural divide between the indigenous peoples and the foreigners, but those that stayed for any length of time had the opportunity to reflect more deeply about the culture of their neighbors; that is, until the national interest of the missionaries' home country interrupted the relationship.

Lutheran missionaries, including some Americans, guided by their own beliefs in the gospel and by the Lutheran confessions came to the Middle East to proselytize among the Jews, to reform the Oriental Orthodox Christians, and to convert the Muslims. These missionaries were able to engage in conversations with the Muslims of the Middle East in a direct fashion rather than across the borders. In some cases, direct contact challenged pre-conceived notions of the role of the gospel in society; in most cases it reminded the missionaries that these Muslims were real people who had a long tradition of the presence of God in their midst. While there have been numerous works published about Anglican, Catholic, Presbyterian, and Reformed missions to the Middle East, to date there has not been a specific history of American Lutheran missions to the Middle East. This book aims to review the basic narrative of American Lutheran engagement in the Middle East. How did American Lutherans come to the Middle East? What was the purpose of their mission? What was the result? Did the Lutherans offer something unique in their mission? Who did they engage and why?

Lutheran mission societies followed many other European and American mission agencies to the Middle East. In fact, Lutheran mission agencies (be they independent or denominational) were quite late in throwing their missiological hats into the ring of the Middle East. Ironically, however, individual Lutherans were some of the first missionaries appointed by other inter-denominational mission societies or non-Lutheran agencies to work in the Middle East, the most prominent being the Church Missionary Society (CMS) of the Anglican church. While American Lutheran immigrant communities did take part in the growing missionary fever of the late eighteenth and nineteenth centuries by sending out their own missionaries to India, Papua New Guinea, Madagascar, and other parts of Africa, they were slow in coming to the Holy Lands. American Lutherans did not arrive on the shores of the eastern Mediterranean until the middle of twentieth century!

This work seeks to provide a narrative of that American Lutheran encounter in the Middle East, focusing primarily on how American Lutherans developed an engagement with Muslims of the Middle East. Several themes have been drawn out within this narrative: *piety*, *politics*, and *power*. Aside from a nice alliteration, these realities have been very much present in the story of Lutheran missions in the Middle East. In the first part, Lutheran engagement in the Middle East was driven by a sincere faith in the God of Jesus Christ, "whom God raised from the dead." Missionaries have historically been individuals with a spiritual *piety* that has driven them to leave their homeland and seek people of other cultures to carry the gospel message of salvation in Christ. This faith manifested itself over time in a particular piety that has driven them to share this faith with either those "perishing" from the lack of knowledge, or to share this experience of God in dialogue with others who may have had a different experience of the Divine. Second, mission in the Middle East has *always* involved *politics*. The specific cultural underpinnings of the Middle East, be it Jewish, Christian, or Muslim, has tended to wrap spirituality within social and familial networks. One cannot think of an "individual" spirituality within the Middle Eastern context, at least in the same way as North Americans have always known that. Thus, one's religion—one's faith—is always tied to that of one's communal identity, and one's role in that particular community. Faith, therefore, is a political issue. To engage in matters of faith, is always a matter of messing with politics, the *polis*—the "city," and the organization of society. Even though Evangelical missionaries have tended to decry politics in their ministries, one can never truly divorce spirituality from communal identity in the Middle East. There is no such thing as a separation between religion and politics in the Middle East. Lastly, politics always has to do with the pursuit and maintenance of *power*. International politics—relations between "cities"—is a story of power; whether one is trying to get power, keep power, or protect power—it is all about power. In the sixteenth century, the Holy Roman Empire was engaged in a power struggle with the German princes, Spain, the Vatican, and the Ottomans. In the nineteenth century, German involvement in the

Middle East was about establishing national power in the face the demise of the Ottoman Empire. In the twenty-first century, U.S. dominance in the Middle East has largely been about protecting "national interests"—oil and security. In each and every case, nations have sought power (for either good or ill). Christian missionaries, by virtue of their nationality, have always been both perpetrators and victims of these power plays. To ignore the issue of power is to put not only one's self and one's mission, but even the proclamation of the gospel itself into great jeopardy. Thus, whether the missionaries liked it or not they were never only engaging in a purely "spiritual" exercise to save souls, they were engaged in power politics. This is been the story of all Christian mission to the Middle East, whether it be intended or not, whether it be admitted or not. This is the nature of society in the Middle East.

METHODOLOGY

Much of the original research in this work has been drawn from archives and records of the Lutheran Orient Mission (LOM), the Lutheran Church—Missouri Synod (LCMS), and the Evangelical Lutheran Church in America (ELCA) and its predecessor church bodies, the American Lutheran Church (ALC) and Lutheran Church in America (LCA). These records include formal reports, board minutes, denominational handbooks, newsletters, press releases, and personal correspondence. Many of the mission personnel involved in this narrative who are still living have been contacted, interviewed, or corresponded with. In addition, I have been guided by the Anglican, Presbyterian and Reformed missiological histories within the Middle East. Rufus Anderson's *History of the Missions of the American Board of Commissioners for Foreign Missions* (1875), Eugene Stock's classic *History of the Church Missionary Society* (1899), and Andrew Watson's *American Mission in Egypt* (1904) have been invaluable assets to the narrative of Protestant mission in the Middle East. Other works that have added to this field have been Lewis Scudder III's history of *The Arabian Mission* (1998) of the Reformed Church in America, and Heather Sharkey's *American Evangelicals in Egypt* (2008). Lastly, numerous historical studies have been utilized, including, most prominently, A. L. Tibawi's *British Interests in Palestine, 1800–1901* (1961) and *American Interests in Syria 1800–1901* (1966). To date there has been no comprehensive history of the Lutheran presence in the Middle East in English. However, several general works of previous Lutheran mission narratives have been utilized, including Preston A. Laury's *A History of Lutheran Missions* (1905), and those of the German missiologists Julius Richter, *A History of Protestant Missions in the Near East* (1910), and Gustav Warneck, *Outline of the History of Protestant Missions* (1884). (The works of these last two scholars have drawn criticisms for their particular pro-German biases; nevertheless, they have proven to be extremely valuable records over the years.) It is our hope that this work will add to a body of literature that has been lacking up till now.

This work is framed by two important dates. It begins in 1518, the year of Luther's reference to the "Turk" in his *Ninety-Five Theses*, and concludes in 2003 with the U.S.-led invasion of Baghdad, the beginning of American military occupation in the Middle East. Thus, the reader will note the distinct political atmosphere in which Christian-Muslim, and in this case specifically Lutheran-Muslim, relationship and conversation has taken place.

Chapter 1 describes the social-political landscape of Germany at the time of the Holy Roman Empire and its relationships with the Muslim Ottoman Empire during the sixteenth and seventeenth centuries. Although much has been written about Martin Luther's views of Islam, chapter 1 will seek to serve as a necessary point of departure for the Lutheran experience in the Middle East.[13] Luther's investigations of Islam were undertaken only in so far as they fit into his own concerns of God's wrath and punishment because of the church's lack of repentance. In other words, he was first and foremost concerned about the pastoral problems of his community. He was not concerned about world evangelization! Islam was part of a larger context that was threatening to undo European Christian society because of its own refusal to repent. For Luther, all of humanity was under God's wrath and in need of repentance: the secular powers, the institutions within society, the church, the Jews, and even the Turks. Because of its refusal to repent, society was being punished from within and without. Thus, the office of the pope and the image of the Turk stood

---

13. Two very recent works on Luther and Islam are Francisco, *Martin Luther and Islam*; and Choi, "Martin Luther's Response to the Turkish Threat." Francisco argues that Luther actually engaged in a systematic apologetic against Islam, while Choi argues that Luther was primarily concerned about pastoral matters, and Islam was only treated in relation to all other issues and problems facing the Christian community in Germany. In this work we agree with Choi's approach. Although Francisco's work is very detailed and well-researched, it seems that his view of Luther's apology to Islam is overstated.

together as icons for the downfall of Christian society. The two are often found together in many of Luther's writings as examples of the refusal to do God's will, spiritually and temporally.

Chapter 2 will look at the first Lutherans who journeyed to the Middle East and engaged its people in both cultural and religious conversation for the sake of preaching the *evangelical* gospel. It is important to remember that the earliest Lutheran generation was consumed with supporting and defending the Augsburg Confession against the Roman papacy. Thus, the first Lutheran missionaries intended to provide a necessary counterweight to the Latin Catholic missionary endeavors that were already well under way in the region through the *Congregatatio de Propaganda Fide*, attempting to bring the Oriental churches under the fold of Rome. After this initial thrust, Lutherans felt the need to preach to the Jewish community of the Holy Lands. Only then did Lutherans begin to engage Muslims.

Chapter 3 will focus on the development of the German Lutheran presence in Palestine. Guided by the context of social-political realities of the nineteenth century, a strong Lutheran presence in the Middle East was carved out of the imperial politics. Even though Lutheran missionaries often had little or no interest in helping to create national identities, their work was aided, fostered, and in some cases curtailed by various national political forces working either in their favor or against them. As England and Germany developed strong imperialistic designs throughout the world, their cooperation in Jerusalem in establishing the joint Anglican-Lutheran bishopric could not have taken place outside of court politics. Those Lutheran missionaries who had no need for worldly orders also saw them as a necessary function of God's ordering of the world. Thus, even though they may not have intended to comply with imperialist structures they were pulled into their orbits.

Chapter 4 will narrate the origin of the American Lutheran presence in the Middle East. It begins with one of the earliest American Lutheran reflections on Islam as a "missionary problem." While American Lutheranism was still trying to organize its own immigrant communities into effective synods during the middle of the nineteenth century, there were a few independent mission organizations that had grown out of the European context of independent missions that began to think about work in the Middle East. Following the great fervor of the 1910 Edinburgh Missionary Conference, American Lutherans committed themselves to work among the Kurds and Nestorians in northern Persia. The work in Persia was ultimately the catalyst that drove American denominations to engage fully.

Chapter 5 is the heart of this study. It will focus on the origin of the work of the LCMS and the predecessor bodies of the ELCA, the LCA and ALC. It was during the end of the twentieth century, prior to the Iranian revolution of 1979 and the growth of Islamic radicalism, that American Lutheran missions focused specifically on an engagement with Islam and "conversation with Muslims" in one form or another. The denominational American engagement centered on three cities: Beriut, Jerusalem, and Cairo.

In the Conclusion, we will briefly survey the most recent issues related to the ELCA and the Middle East. Our focus will be, once again, on placing the relationships of American missions in the Middle East in the broader framework of the international context—where mission is done. We hope to draw out further questions for the next level of engagement. For example, in the current *"Pax Americana"* of the Middle East, with the U.S. military occupying a foreign country, and in the midst of a worldwide conservative and often radical Islamist atmosphere, how are American Lutherans to move forward with a faithful and life-giving witness to the gospel among the people of the Middle East?

LIMITATIONS OF THE WORK

In order to tackle the topic at hand I have made specific choices to limit the scope of the work. The study is aimed at American Lutheranism in the Middle East. As some readers will find, there are significant gaps in the history reviewed here. It does not, for example, cover the history and work of the Lutheran church in Denmark, Norway, or Sweden. (The Danish Missionary Society and its predecessor, the Danish Church Mission, was very active in Aden, Yemen from 1903 until 1965, and in Syria from 1906 until 1927, and had a great impact on Christian-Muslim relations.)[14] I have specifically focused on the German Lutheran-Reformed Pietist tradition, which set the tone and direction for the contemporary American mainline Lutheran church experience in the Middle East. The ultimate aim of the work is to narrate the story primarily of the work of the ELCA and its predecessor bodies, and origins of the work of the LCMS.

---

14. See Hansen, *Blandt muslimern I Kamalun.*

DEFINITIONS

Another important limitation to the work has been the determination of the geographic area to be included and the terminology to be utilized. The general area of the world called "the Middle East" was known during the seventeenth, eighteenth, and nineteenth centuries as the Orient. It was not until 1902 that the term "Middle East" was coined in the United States to denote the particular geographic area of southwest Asia, as opposed to the Far East. With the collapse of the Ottoman Empire after World War I, the Middle East became an area of various newly recognized nation-states. Sometimes this geographic area is now called the heart of the "Muslim world" or even the "Arab world." Although all of these definitions do overlap and describe much of the same region and groups of people, they have particular, different meanings.

The "Arab world" describes the twenty-two nations of the world that are comprised of native Arab speakers. This is a linguistic definition, not geographic, nor even religious. The Arab world stretches from West Africa (Morocco and Mauritania) to the horn of Africa (Somalia and Djibouti), and as far as the Indian Ocean (Comoros Islands). Recent statistics show that the Arab world includes 280 million people.[15] The Arab peoples have a wide variety of cultures, although Islamic culture does predominate—albeit in different forms. Many Arab countries are comprised of significant populations of non-Muslim Arabs (specifically, Christians, animists, Jews, and Mandeans), and even populations of non-Arab minorities (i.e., Berbers, Kurds, Turkmen, etc.). Because many Arab countries do not have official census figures taken, the number of non-Muslim Arabs is always difficult to ascertain. Depending on the statistics that are utilized and who has gathered the information, Egypt alone has anywhere from four to twelve million Arab Christians, mostly Coptic Orthodox.[16] Lebanon

---

15. UN Development Programme, *Arab Human Development Report 2002*, 35. It is important to note that there are trends among both Copts and Lebanese Maronites who argue that their communities are not ethnically Arab, but rather ancient Egyptian and Phoenician, respectively. However, in this work I am utilizing the contemporary sociological definition of "Arab," based on language.

16. Courbage and Fargues cite that Egyptian Christians make up 5.7 percent of the Egyptian population (*Christians and Jews under Islam*, 209). The CIA *World Fact Book* estimates 6 percent of the population (CIA, "Egypt"). The *World Christian Encyclopedia* estimates that Christians make up 15.1 percent of the population ("Egypt," 1:250). The U.S. Copts Association estimates the figure at 16 percent ("Guide: Christians in the Middle East").

and Syria also include significant Arab Christian populations: Orthodox, Catholic and Protestant. According to Phillipe Fargues, in 1995 there were over 6.5 million Arab Christians living in the Middle East, making up a total of 6.1 percent of the population of the Arab world.[17] It is often surprising for many Americans to learn that Arabs have been important members of both the Jewish and Christian faiths (even though Acts 2: 5–11 clearly records both).

The term "Muslim world" has been very much misunderstood in the recent years. Although the center of the Muslim world is in Arabia (Mecca and Medina), and much of the formative periods of Islamic philosophical and theological development have taken place in present day Egypt, Iraq and Syria, Arabs comprise only about 18–20 percent of the total Muslim population of the world.[18] The top four most populous Muslim countries in the world are Indonesia, Pakistan, Bangladesh, and India. In fact, there are more Muslims in India alone than in all the Arab world. These Muslim communities are not ethnically or linguistically Arab. Thus, the Muslim world encompasses a global dimension of Muslim communities (including Muslims in the United States). The "Muslim world" is a religious definition, uniting people who follow the same religious beliefs centered on the belief in one God, as revealed in the Qur'ān via the prophet Muhammad.

Within the Muslim world there are "denominational" differences, if we might dare to call them that. The Sunni community is the largest Muslim branch, comprising nearly 90 percent of all Muslims. The Shi'a, who broke from the Sunnis in 661 based upon a disagreement over the selection of a legitimate political representative after the death of Muhammad, have become the dominant Muslim confession in Azerbaijan, Bahrain, and Iran. They also comprise a significant community in Afghanistan, Lebanon, Iraq, Oman, and parts of Saudi Arabia. Different Shi'a communities are labeled for the different leaders they accept as the legitimate spiritual successors of Muhammad: 'Alawi (the ruling family of Syria), Alevi, Ismailis (or Seveners), and Ja'faris (or Twelvers), for example. In addition, there are several quasi-Muslim sects, in that, although they follow many of the beliefs and practices of orthodox Islam, the majority of Sunnis consider them heretical. These would be the Ahmadiyya, Druze, Ibadi, and the Yazidis.

---

17. Fargues, "Arab Christians of the Middle East."
18. Esposito, *Islamic World*, 1:43.

Muslims may be of Arab, Afghani, African-American, Berber, Chinese, Indian, Persian, Turkish, or even Russian descent. They may all be able to recite portions of the Qur'ān in Arabic, but their native tongues and cultures may be very different. Even within the definition of the "Muslim world" we find a great deal of diversity that defies the attempt to paint the picture of a monolithic civilization.

The "Middle East" is a geographic term. It covers a vast territory stretching from Egypt to Iran, and from Turkey to northern Sudan. This is a territory that comprises not only Arabs but also a wide assortment of ethnic groups. Armenia, Iraq, Iran, Israel, Lebanon, Syria, and Turkey all include non-Arabs—who may be Muslims, Christians or Jews. It is important to remember that Iranians, although 99 percent Muslim, are not Arabs. They are ethnically Persian. (In contemporary American-Iranian relations it would be helpful to remember this; Persians do not see themselves as Arabs.) In addition, there is a sizable Armenian Christian population in Iran. Turkey, as well, is over 99 percent Muslim, but ethnically Turkish. Israel, Lebanon and Syria all include significant Christian populations of non-Arabs. Israel is made up significant numbers of western immigrant Jews from Europe, most recently from Eastern Europe and the Russian states, and North America. Lebanon has a large Armenian population and is the site of the Armenian Apostolic Catholicos of Cilicia and the Armenian Catholic Patriarch. The small Republic of Lebanon, with its population of six million people, includes seventeen different confessional groups, all legally represented in the government. Iraq and Syria also reflect interesting dynamics, as significant numbers of citizens are ethnically Armenian, Chaldean, Circassian, and Kurd, as well as Arab. The war in Iraq, however, has dramatically altered the ethnic landscape of the country, and currently it is impossible to determine the percentage of these communities due to the massive numbers of displaced persons.

The Arabs themselves represent a wide assortment of religious persuasions. The Arab Muslims of Syria make up approximately 89 percent of the population, but are made up of Sunni, Shi'a, 'Alawi, Druze, and Yazidi. The Arab Christians of Iraq and Syria consist of a mixture of Christian communities from contemporary Western Evangelical transplants to ancient Oriental Orthodox churches tracing their roots back to the first apostles. Iraq even included a very old sect of Mandeans, a Gnostic Christian sect tracing its roots back to the second century. Latest reports, however, indicate that due to the violence of the war in Iraqi this community is now nearly extinct.[19] Thus, it is clear in this brief survey that the Middle East is made up of a variety of peoples and religions and is anything but a monolithic Arab Muslim society.

The term "Middle East" then, has been specifically chosen in this work to describe the peoples of the region stretching from Egypt to Iran and from Armenia to northern Sudan. The Middle East encompasses a wide assortment of ethnic groups and a great array of religious persuasions. (This definition, then, would exclude Afghanistan, Pakistan and the northern "stans," designating these as belonging to Central Asia.) The religious communities of the Middle East include Christians (Oriental and Eastern Orthodox, all seven Catholics rites, and Protestants of a wide variety), Jews (of Sephardic and Ashkenazi traditions), Muslims (of Sunni, Shi'a, and other variant sects), Mandeans and Zoroastrians![20] We have chosen this definition to work with here specifically to underline the diversity of peoples in the region, as well as to recognize the historical reality that the object of Lutheran missionary endeavors over the years has been to a variety of different groups of people. Lutherans have explicitly aimed their missions at Jews, Christians, and Muslims; Arabs, Assyrians, Persians and Sudanese—depending on the time and place.

Although it may seem redundant to some readers, it is necessary to say something of the term "Lutheran" as it is used here. For those non-Lutherans interested in either mission history or Western relations with the Middle East, or generally interested in Christian-Muslim relations, the continual references to Lutheran identity will probably seem redundant. For this the author apologizes. Lutherans have always been known to "navel gaze" and overanalyze their own importance. So be it. Those interested in a Lutheran history or a Lutheran perspective will probably be a bit frustrated by the loose sense of Lutheran identity used in this work, for the Lutheran tradition utilized here bounces between Free and Confessional (recognized by the several Lutheran synods or mission agencies included in the narrative), and also includes those individuals or groups from the Reformed branch of the Protestant family. Lutherans have always argued amongst themselves over who is really "Lutheran enough." For Confessional Lutherans the inclusion of the Moravians

---

19. Taneja, *Assimilation, Exodus, Eradication*.

20. A helpful review of the complexity of both ethnicity and religion in the Middle East can be found in Bengio and Ben-Dor, *Minorities and the State in the Arab World*. For further information on the variety of peoples of the Middle East, see their Appendix I.

will seem quite a stretch. Yet those from the Lutheran-Reformed United Church tradition will wonder why the author is spilling ink on the topic in the first place. The author merely wishes to point out, realizing the danger of being charged with "navel gazing," that the Lutheran historical record has something important to say in this matter. If we can justify such an approach here, for the purposes of clarity, it should suffice that we are including those persons and communities that saw Luther as their spiritual forbearer and the Augsburg Confession as a faithful understanding of Christian belief (even if they did not hold to the *Augustana* solely).

A few words about Lutheran Pietism are also now in order. Philipp Jacob Spener (1635–1705), a pastor from Strasbourg, published his famous work *Pia Desideria* in 1675.[21] This book helped to galvanize a movement of individuals and small intentional communities who engaged not only in spiritual revival but foreign missions as well. Lutheran Orthodoxy, with its traditional focus upon *catechesis*, held firmly to the foundation of "salvation by faith alone" as a response to the preaching of the Word. The communally proclaimed Word was the primary focus; and thus faith was built on that external Word. This has often been called *fides quae creditor* [faith that is believed]. Therefore, developing a right belief in repentance to the Word *was* the mission of each Christian. The Pietists, however, saw the necessity of some kind of moral or spiritual response to the Word that was publicly visible, often in the form of a testimonial of conversion. This is *fides qua creditor* [that by which faith is believed]. Because of the focus on individual regeneration rather than "right belief" or even adherence to a particular theological confession, the Pietist movement cared little for the formal ecclesiastical distinctions. Spener played down the differences between the Lutheran and Reformed branches, and in some cases even the Anabaptist branch, of the Reformation.[22] This would be especially true after the unification of the Lutheran and Reformed branches of the church by Prussian King Frederick William III (1770–1840) in 1817. This Pietist movement affected not only some of the early Lutheran missionaries to the Middle East, but the overall culture of the German-speaking missionaries who came to the Middle East. The teachings of Auguste Francke (1663–1727) at Halle, Johann Albrecht Bengel (1687–1752) in Württemberg, and Zinzendorf (1700–1760) in Moravia had a direct

---

21. See Stein, *Philipp Jakob Spener*.
22. See Feuerhan, "The Roots and Fruits of German Pietism."

impact on the work of Lutherans in the Middle East. The followers of these three charismatic leaders would become the primary Lutherans engaged in mission in the Middle East. The graduates of the seminary at Halle would provide many of the earliest missionaries who journeyed to the Middle East, especially with Anglican mission societies. The Pietism of Württemberg was especially important, as in the words of F. Ernest Stoeffler, "it became a genuine grass-roots movement, in which the butcher, the baker, and the candlestick-maker had a real stake" in the work of mission.[23] More Württemberg Pietists would engage Jews, Orthodox and Muslims in the Middle East than any other group of Lutherans throughout the history of Lutheran Middle Eastern mission. And lastly, Zinzendorf's legacy, although never really engaging large numbers of Germans, can be traced to the contemporary Mennonite engagement in the Middle East, especially in Egypt and Palestine.

By the middle of the nineteenth century, a general movement among like-minded Protestants created the Evangelical Alliance. This association provided the groundswell of support for ecumenical endeavors, associations, and relationships.[24] For the Pietists, confessional lines between Anglicans, Lutherans, and Reformed were often blurred, being considered *adiaphora* (that is, of secondary importance to the message of the gospel). The theological institutes at Basel and Hale, and the numerous mission societies reviewed here, were made up of members of the Anglican, Lutheran, and Reformed churches of Europe.

In putting this narrative together we have had to make judicial decisions on what material to include and present here. Although there is much more that could be written on this matter, for the sake of time and energy—and the reader's limits—we have had to pull out the most important issues germane to the ultimate point; an American Lutheran engagement with the Middle East, leading specifically to an encounter with Middle Eastern Muslims. There certainly are many more individuals and events that could have been recorded here. There have been hundreds of individuals, formally trained missionaries and casual student researchers, who have all in many ways had an impact on the Lutheran presence in the Middle East. It is simply impossible to do them all justice here. Thus, the omission of both important events and people must rest solely

---

23. Stoeffler, *German Pietism*, 129. Stoeffler's work is an extremely valuable contribution to the knowledge of Lutheran Pietism as related in this work.

24. See Railton, *No North Sea*.

on the author's shoulders. A small token of recognition is intended by the inclusion of formally appointed individuals by the American Lutheran denominations of the twentieth century in Appendix I. Even with this small note, numerous individuals served or lived in the Middle East in many non-formal capacities. They, unfortunately, are not listed. What can be said with clear affirmation is that the author holds in high esteem the individuals and families who have been part of this story. Like most other missionaries, they have had to endure the challenges of living in another culture and the often-difficult circumstances of economic, social, and political turmoil. They have been caught in the middle of mass riots, demonstrations, bombings, and wars. They have had to endure being searched and interrogated by "security." They have been caught in curfews, airlifted and relocated. They have witnessed the death of friends and family, and in several cases have actually given of their own lives. The story told here would not have been possible except for the lives of these apostles who went out, their hearts on fire, in order to teach, preach, heal, live with, and learn from the people of the Middle East; Jews, Christians, and Muslims all. And yet, in the midst of this, they would all recognize and be quick to add that their "sacrifice" (if that word can be used) was nothing compared to the sacrifices of the people with whom they have lived and worked, for whom the region of the Middle East is truly home.

2

Luther and "the Turk"

[To] fight against the Turk is the same as resisting God...

—Martin Luther, 1518

OUR JOURNEY INTO THE American Lutheran engagement in the Middle East, and with Islam in particular, must start at the beginning—with Luther himself. The late medieval image of "the Turk" played a considerable role in Luther's concept of Islam. Even though there has been considerable work done on Luther and Islam, it is necessary to review not only Luther's engagement with the Islamic material he was able to acquire and review, but the general atmosphere of Christian-Muslim relations during the early sixteenth century. Putting Luther's writings on Islam into the social-political context of the turmoil between the Holy Roman and Ottoman Empires of the sixteenth century, as well as within the intra-Christian struggles of various European principalities, will help to provide a sound basis to interpret Luther's views of Islam, as well as provide insights for Christian-Muslim relations in the early twenty-first century, specifically, American Lutheran-Middle Eastern Muslim relations. In this chapter we will look at Luther's view of "the Turk" as a sociological phenomenon and place his writings into the appropriate historical context to which he was responding.

Both the Holy Roman Emperor Charles V and the Ottoman Sultan Suleiman "the Magnificent" were crowned rulers over their respective empires in 1520. These coronations brought about new complications to the European social-political context. In the words of Bernard Lewis, the "Ottoman and Hapsburg armies faced each other in central Europe in a struggle that would determine the fate of the entire continent."[1] Lewis's

---

1. Lewis, *Islam and the West*, 74.

comment is a reminder that the role of "the Turk" had a large impact on Luther's world, thought, and the development of Lutheranism itself.² Certainly, imperial politics between the Holy Roman and Ottoman empires were much more complicated than a simple monolithic "clash of cultures." Intra-European and intra-Christian struggles were just as important to Christendom, if not more important, than Christian-Muslim struggles. For example, King Francis I of France's numerous negotiations with Suleiman to provide unhindered access for Turkish ships to the western Mediterranean and Atlantic, in order to harass Spanish shipping, demonstrates the complexity of seventeenth century international politics. We might also highlight Venetian and Genoese economic treaties with the Ottomans that disregarded papal prohibitions in dealing with the Turks. In any case, within the complexity of international politics the Turkish contribution to the rise of Lutheranism is certainly noteworthy, but often overlooked.

Many of the important popular works on Luther in English have not done justice to the Turkish problem as an important factor in the early success of the Reformation.³ Roland Bainton's *Here I Stand* (1950) and Erik Erikson's classic *Young Man Luther* (1958) set much of the tone for the modern focus on the personal spiritual turmoil and theological outlook of Luther.⁴ Martin Marty's most recent biography on Luther, however, does help to put the role of "the Turk" back into the proper sociological perspective. Recalling a common sixteenth-century Austrian saying, "the Turk is the Lutheran's lucky star," we are reminded that the success of Lutheranism was in part due to the Islamic threat of the Ottoman Empire and the fear of the "Terrible Turk."⁵ George Forell sums up well the relationship between Luther, Lutheranism, and the "Terrible Turk":

> Instead of fearing the Turks, Luther had every reason to be grateful to them. It was the constant danger of a Turkish invasion that had

---

2. Contra G. Miller, "Luther on the Turks and Islam."

3. For example see Friedenthal, *Luther*; Oberman, *Luther* (the original German work was written in 1982); and Loewenwich, *Luther's Theology of the Cross*. The problem of the "Turk" is only briefly mentioned in Nestingen, *Martin Luther*, a companion to the 2003 film *Luther*. Two exceptions to this would be Kittelson, *Luther the Reformer*, esp. 279–80; and Lohse, *Martin Luther*, 4. This point of the problem of the "Turk" lacking in Lutheran studies has also been made recently by R. Smith, "Luther, the Turks, and Islam."

4. Bainton, *Here I Stand*; Erikson, *Young Man Luther*.

5. Marty, *Martin Luther*, 165, see also 151–52, 163–69.

kept the Emperor from taking severe measures against Luther's reformation. The empire needed the help of the Evangelical princes in the war against the Turks and therefore had to postpone its plans to destroy Luther. From the point of view of realistic power politics, the safety of the Reformation depended upon the strength of the Turkish armies.[6]

THE "TERRIBLE TURK" IN POPULAR IMAGERY

The fall of Constantinople, the heart of eastern Christendom, in 1453, prompted a genre of responses in art, song and literature portraying the "Terrible Turk."[7] By 1522 the last bastion of the Knights of St. John on the island of Rhodes fell to the Ottomans, and Hans Sebald Beham, an artist from Nuremberg, carved an engraving of the event. The scene, looking more akin to southern Germany than the eastern Mediterranean, was intended to strike fear into the hearts of its audience, including the illustration of an unfortunate Christian impaled upon a stake.[8] A similar woodcut by Matthias Gerung from the 1540s depicted Turks slaughtering Christians (Figure 1).[9]

Another artist, Erhard Schoen, provided Germany with many images of the Turk through his artistic carvings, such as *Siege of Vienna* (1529), *Siege of Budapest* (1541), and the most graphic *Ravages of the Turks* (1532). Schoen also drew other images for the European imagination, including *Turkish Procession* (1532), in which the Turks are burning homes and churches. These popular portrayals were available to the general public, especially the illiterate. They became the peasants' view into international politics, and created a "visual political narrative."[10] Depictions of peasant families being led away as captives with their children skewered on pikes could not but create horror and revulsion in the general public. Luther certainly was affected by such common political commentaries.

---

6. Forell, "Luther and the War against the Turks," 259–60.

7. Egil Grisilis provides an extensive bibliography of German and English works reviewing this image in "Luther and the Turks," 191 n. 33.

8. Wheatcroft, *Infidels*, 280.

9. Strauss, *German Single-Leaf Woodcut*, 305.

10. See Leuthold, "The Book and the Peasant."

FIGURE 1: Matthias Gerung Woodcut

> How abominably the Turks kill, spear, hack to pieces so many people, children, women, young, and old, who have done them no harm. They act as if they were the wrathful devil in person.[11]

> He puts your house and home to the torch, takes your cattle and fodder, money and possessions, stabs you to death (if you are so well), rapes or kills your wife and daughter before your eyes, hacks to pieces your children and impales them on your fence-stakes.[12]

> When I hear that the Turks are venting their rage on Christian blood in a most cruel manner, that they are impaling little children on stakes, that they are abusing women for purposes of unmentionable disgrace, it certainly becomes me to groan, and the human heart cannot help being deeply moved at such monstrous behavior.[13]

After the first Turkish assault on Vienna in 1529, reports spread about the Turks massacring those captives who could not keep up with the army on its withdrawal down the Danube. Luther too contributed to the spreading of these reports. He wrote, "[T]hose that can walk are led away like cattle, dragged, tied together, and driven. Those that cannot walk are immediately stabbed to death, regardless of their age."[14]

Aside from fearful images of captivity, there was also various first hand reports from prisoners who had managed to escape. One of these was Oluf Eigilsson, a Lutheran pastor from Iceland, who was captured by Muslim corsairs and sent off to Algiers. Eventually he bought his freedom and returned to Iceland and wrote a book about his experiences.[15]

After the siege of Vienna, the common image of the "Terrible Turk" only grew stronger and became part of European lore. Shakespeare incorporated much of mid-sixteenth century views of the "Turk" in his plays, especially *Othello*. The play is centered around the fall of the island of Rhodes in 1522, where the governor of Venice sends Othello to Cyprus to protect Venetian interests against "'a malignant and a turban'd Turk.'"[16] By the middle of the sixteenth century the famous Florentine poet Dante had been immortalized through his epic *Divine Comedy*, which was by then

11. *WA* 30/2:162.
12. Ibid.
13. *LW* 6:253; *WA* 44:188, as cited in Choi, 175.
14. *WA* 30/2:162.
15. Lewis, *Islam and the West*, 74.
16. Act 5, scene 2.

circulating in new editions.[17] Included in Dante's sojourn through hell was Muhammad and Ali, his son-in-law and fourth rightly-guided caliph. There in the eighth circle of hell, Muhammad and Ali spend all eternity walking in circles and being cloven in half by a devil, their wounds healing until they return, only to be struck again.[18] In addition to artistic commentary, the increasing use of the popularized *fliegenschrift* [printed pamphlet] in Germany helped drive home this fear of "the Turk" in what Kenneth Setton calls "pamphlet warfare."[19] The popular *Türckenbüchlein, A Little Book about the Turks*, attempted to describe the tales of terror and atrocities of the Turks[20] went through four editions, demonstrating general consumption.[21]

Throughout his life Luther only wrote six works dealing specifically with the Turks or Islam. This is not particularly a huge amount of material, given Luther's voluminous output of material throughout his active career as a theologian and scholar. That being said, "the Turk" does figure prominently throughout all of his works. His view of the Turk was primarily fed by popular descriptions available both in art and literature. He makes constant reference to "the Turk" throughout all his writings, and especially in his "table talks" (conversations at his dinner table that were recorded by his students). During 1529–30 and 1541–43, when a Turkish invasion of Germany was generally feared, "the Turk" figured prominently in Luther's sermons. However, the focus was never on Islam per se, but Luther utilized these images and fears to remind his followers that the

---

17. Originally completed by 1373, it received critical acclaim and became an instant classic. It was the Italian edition of 1555, however, that provided the title *Commedia*. For further influence of the "Turk" on European literature see Salem, "The Elizabethan Image of Islam"; and Patrides, "'The Bloody and Cruell Turke.'"

18. "Who could find words, even in free-running prose, for the blood and wounds I saw, in all their horror—It would be nothing to equal the mutilation I saw in that Ninth chasm. No barrel staved-in and missing its end-piece ever gaped as wide as the man I saw split open from his chin down to the farting-place, and from the splayed trunk the spilled entrails dangled between his thighs... And Ali goes weeping before me—like me, a schismatic, and cleft: Split open from the chin along his face up to the forelock. All you see here, when alive, taught scandal and schism, so they are cleavered like this. A devil waits with a sword back there to carve each of us open afresh each time we've gone our circuit round this road, where while we grieve our wounds close up before we pass him again..." (Alighieri, *Inferno*, 295–97).

19. Setton, "Lutheranism and the Turkish Peril," 137.

20. *LW* 46:157 n. 5.

21. Bohnstedt, *Infidel Scourge of God*; as in Wheatcroft, *Infidels*.

evils and dangers of the world are at hand primarily to drive us into the arms of Christ. Luther, as pastor, was always focused on reminding his flock that only Christ could save them from both their own sin and the troubles of the world. And, in the case of the "Terrible Turk," he was God's temporal punishment in a world gone awry. The only thing that could save them was prayer, repentance, and renewed faith in Christ.[22]

From a civic perspective, Luther believed that the Turks undermined the three estates of society: the church, the government, and the Christian home. First, Luther's central Christocentric theology led him to understand that by denying Jesus's divinity, "Mohammed's Koran . . . leaves almost nothing of Christian truth remaining."[23] Second, Luther explains Islam's danger to European government and social order. He wrote, "there is much glorification of the sword" in the Qur'ān. Christ's "office" or station of love is supplanted by Muhammad's "office" of the sword, which would destroy all "temporal government"—at least all European "Christian" government.[24] Thus, the Turk is a murderer and robber, subverting the natural nominalist order of creation. "The Turkish faith, then, has not made its progress by preaching and the working of miracles, but by the sword and by murder, and its success has been due to God's wrath."[25] Like Christian heretics, Arians, Donatists, the radical Thomas Müntzer—and even the pope—Islam utilized murder and violence to perpetuate their beliefs. The "pope, along with his followers, wages war, commits murder, and robs not only his enemies, but he also burns, condemns, and persecutes the innocent, the pious, the Orthodox, as a true Antichrist."[26]

The third danger to European society was that Islam sought to destroy the Christian home by devaluing the institution of marriage. "Mohammed's Koran thinks nothing of marriage, but permits everyone to take wives as he will. It is customary among the Turks for one man to have ten or twenty wives," and women are "bought and sold like cattle."[27] This threatens the bedrock of Christian community, the estate of marriage, based upon

---

22. Choi, "Martin Luther's Response," 184. Choi notes that out of the 153 recorded sermons between 1529 and 1530, the Turk is mentioned in 70, and of the 16 recorded sermons between 1541 and 1543, the Turk is mentioned in 9 (see esp. 112–13, 166–67).

23. *LW* 46:176, 181

24. *LW* 46:196, also 178.

25. *LW* 46:179.

26. *LW* 46:180.

27. *LW* 46:181.

Genesis 3:24, and subverts the natural order of creation. In his *Appeal for Prayer against the Turks* (1541) Luther rails against the desecration of marriage due to the practice of polygamy. (This critique of gender roles within Muslim communities continues to be put forward in contemporary Christian-Muslim conversations.) However, Luther's venom is just as strongly directed toward the church hierarchy as toward Islam.

> In all history we do not read of such desecration and destruction of marriage as in the papacy and among the Turks. The pope, under the pretense of chastity, has forbidden marriage and condemned it as sinful; the Turk tears man and wife apart and sells the women as though they were mere cows or calves. I have written about these and other related matters in my sermon which I preached to the army. In brief, both the papacy and the Turkish kingdom are doing nothing else than destroying the authority of home, city, and church.[28]

LUTHER'S APOCALYPTICISM

The image of "the Turk" in popular European potrayal contributed much to Martin Luther's own overarching belief in apocalypticism, that Europe was nearing the end times as revealed in the Scriptures. Fear of the Turk—*Türkenfurcht*—was, in the words of Gordon Rupp, "an eschatological and apocalyptic portent."[29] He often made reference to "the Turk" and the apocalypse in his works, especially his personal letters, table talks, biblical commentaries, and sermons.

In a sermon on the Gospel of John he preached:

> For Christ declares: "This is the judgment which has come over the world and over this city because they love false doctrine and a sinful life. Therefore, they will perish more ignominiously than Sodom and Gomorrah." Aye, rumor has it that the Turk is ready to march on Germany. The country is ripe for judgment; it flows with the blood of poor Christians who have been murdered. Our ungrateful people fairly devour their pastors. Therefore I fear—although I prophesy.[30]

---

28. *LW* 43:239.
29. Rupp, "Luther against 'The Turk,'" 260.
30. *LW* 22:390.

Interestingly, in his *Commentary on Genesis* (chapter 41) we catch an unmistakable glimpse of Luther's "A Mighty Fortress," which paints the image of the reality of war with the Ottoman Turks:

> No matter how much the world and its prince rage in the pope and the Turk, nevertheless they will not drive out of me confidence in God, once it has been attained. Satan shall not make things so sour for me, much less the Turk. To be sure, they can take away this life or property, wife and children, likewise good health; but I will hope in God forever.[31]

Lastly, one of Luther's most popular hymns was written in the face of Turkish fear. "Lord Keep Us Steadfast in Thy Word" was a fervent prayer for protection in such troubling times:

> *Lord keep us steadfast in thy Word*
>   *And curb the Turks' and Papists' sword*
> *Who Jesus Christ, thine only Son*
>   *Fain would tumble from off thy throne.*[32]

The words of the hymn were eventually changed to be less offensive. The current *Evangelical Lutheran Worship* hymnal provides a more benign Luther:

> *Lord, keep us steadfast in your word;*
>   *curb those who by deceit or sword*
> *would rest the kingdom from your Son*
>   *and bring to naught all he has done.*

Thus, we see that Luther fit the popular image of "the Turk" into his own theological perspective. For Luther, the decay of the ordered world clearly pointed toward the end times and Christ's return. It was none other than the pope who was besieging the spiritual realm, and "the Turk" who was attacking the temporal realm who would bring about the final apocalypse. Luther wrote in his *Appeal for Prayer against the Turks* in 1541,

> the two kingdoms, that of the Turk and that of the pope, are the last two plagues of the wrath of God, as the Apocalypse calls them. They are the "false prophet" and "the beast" and both must be bound and cast into the "lake of fire."[33]

---

31. *LW* 7:132.
32. *LW* 53:305; *WA* 35:468.
33. *LW* 43:238.

In his exegesis of the book of Ezekiel that same year, Luther saw clear markers of scriptural doom in contemporary events:

> For Scripture prophesies to us about two terrible tyrants which on the eve of the Last Day will lay waste and destroy Christendom—the one spiritually with false and poisonous teaching and worship, that is the Pope with all his Popery—the other with his sword in a bodily and outward fashion . . . as Christ tells us in Matthew 24, of a tribulation such as the earth hath never seen before, and that is the Turk.[34]

In the dedication of his translation of the book of Daniel to Prince John Frederick in he wrote:

> Grace and peace in Christ Our Lord—the world is running faster and faster, hastening towards its end, so that I often have the strong impression that the Last Day may break before we have turned the Holy Scriptures into German!
>
> For this is sure: there are no more temporal events to wait for according to the Scriptures: it has all happened, all has been fulfilled—the Roman Empire is finished, the Turk has come to the peak of his power, the power of the Pope is about to crash—and the world is cracking to pieces as though it would tumble down . . . for if the world were to linger on, as she has been hitherto, then surely all the world would go Mohammedan or Epicurean, and there would be no more Christians left, as Christ said.[35]

By the beginning of the sixteenth century the world was falling apart. At least, this was the general perception of the local population in Germany. "Everybody had been seized by fear: fear of the plague, fear of the new regime [in Rome], and fear of the Turks."[36] In a letter to Wenceslas Link in 1529 he wrote:

> Concerning the apparitions of which one hears in Bohemia, nothing is certain; many [people] deny [that they have occurred]. It is certain, however, that the northern light, which has been [seen] here and which I, too, have seen on the Saturday after Epiphany at eight in the evening, has been seen in many places, even as far away as the ocean. In addition Doctor Hess writes that in December the sky above the cathedral of Breslau was fiery during the night, and

---

34. As cited in Rupp, "Luther against 'The Turk,'" 258.
35. Ibid., 257.
36. Friedenthal, *Luther*, 353.

> that on another day two flame-like roof frames were seen with a burning broom in the midst of them. I think that through these fires it is signified that the Last Day may be at hand. Rome falls, kings fall, popes fall, and obviously the world will tumble, just as a big house which is about to collapse usually begins its decay with little cracks. Only the Turk, the final Gog and Magog, is to glory in his supreme victory and is [then] to perish, together with his companion, the pope.[37]

In a table talk with his companions, Luther was recorded as saying:

> All things in Scripture have now been fulfilled. Only Daniel 12 remains. Daniel and the Revelation of St. John fit together well. I think Rome is the holy place between two seas. There sits the pope in the temple of God. But if the Turks go there everything is ruined. There is nothing left but the day of judgment. Then the world will come to its end.[38]

It was this worldview to which Luther was responding. As the pastor in Wittenberg, Luther reacted to the social-political issues that dominated the lives of his parishioners, over which they had no control, and the images that dominated their fears.

In 1529 the Ottoman army was marching to Vienna and threatening Europe. Luther was encouraged by his followers to provide some pastoral remarks about the coming disaster. He had already written his treatise *On War against the Turk* in the fall of 1528; now, as the pastor in him was wont to do, he began preparing a sermon. In the *Army Sermon against the Turk*, Luther found the book of Daniel and Revelation speaking to him.[39] Like many apocalypticists before him, Luther saw the Turk through the lens of apocalyptic prophecy. In Daniel 7 he interpreted the fourth beast with ten horns as a prophecy about Islam.

> I saw in the visions by night a fourth beast, terrifying and dreadful and exceedingly strong. It had great iron teeth and was devouring, breaking in pieces, and stamping what was left with its feet. It was different from all the beasts that preceded it, and it had ten horns. I was considering the horns, when another horn appeared, a little one coming up among them; to make room for it, three of the earlier horns were plucked up by the roots. There were eyes like

---

37. *LW* 49:217.
38. *LW* 54:27, no. 332.
39. *WA* 2:160–97.

human eyes in this horn, and a mouth speaking arrogantly. (Dan 7:7–8)

Common medieval interpretation associated the four beasts of Daniel as the Assyrian, Persian, Greek and Roman Empires. The Turks, by first plucking up Constantinople in 1453, then Assyria in 1514, and now threatening Rome, were seen as the newly grown horn on the fourth beast. This last horn was none other than Muhammad, "speaking arrogantly" against Christ and Christianity. This last horn presents the culmination of the wrath of God in the Last Judgment. "Daniel says that after the Turks there will immediately follow judgment and hell," he wrote.[40] Luther described the Ottoman Empire as the "Gog" of Ezekiel (chapters 38–39) and Revelation (20:8). Throughout the rest of his life Luther would continue to see the geo-political landscape through this apocalyptic lens. In his *Appeal for Prayer against the Turk* (1541) and in his *Preface to Revelation* (1545), written near the end of his life, Luther saw "the last two plagues of the wrath of God" (Rev. 15:1) as the pope and the Turk, as the "false prophet" and "the beast" (Rev 20:10).[41]

Luther was not the first, nor the last apocalyptic preacher to look at Islam from such a frame of reference. Throughout the medieval period there was a whole corpus of prophetic material warning of the coming of Islam. This material gained in popularity after the crisis of 1453 when Constantinople fell to Mehmed II. Johann Hilten from Eisenach had prophesied that by 1600 the Turks would rule over all of Italy and Germany. Other Western authors had prophesied Mohammad as one of the false prophets of Matthew 24:11, as well as the second beast from Revelation 13.[42] Thus, Luther rests on a long tradition of medieval apocalypticism reading Islam into the texts.[43]

---

40. *Heerpredigt wider den Türken*, WA 30/2:162. See also Grislis, "Luther and the Turks," 184–85.

41. *LW* 43:238. See also Luther's *Preface to Revelation*, where he writes, "After the Turks, the Last Judgment follows quickly" (quoted from C. Wolf, "Luther and Mohammedanism," 163).

42. Setton, *Western Hostility to Islam*, 42 n. 51, and 10–11, respectively. Setton's work is an invaluable resource for reviewing medieval prophecies; see esp. 29–46.

43. Arguably, Luther's reference for such an interpretation was the Franciscan Johann Hilten, who lived in Eisenach, where Luther grew up as a student. Hilten was himself influenced by Joachim of Fiore, the twelfth century apocalyptic preacher who saw the "Saracens" as the antichrist. Joachim relied upon even earlier Christian apocalyptic thought coming out of Spain in the ninth century. One such writer, Paul Alvarus, was

This long-standing medieval apocalyptic tradition was utilized by many of Luther's contemporaries. Justus Jonas and Philipp Melancthon, two of Luther's closest friends, as well as Ulrich Zwingli and Martin Bucer, all received this particular apocalyptic tradition. (A notable exception to the Reformers in this regard is John Calvin.)[44] Melanchthon wrote *De origine imperii Turcorum* [The Origin of the Turkish Peril], in which he reviewed the prophesies of the coming of Islam. His source was the work of Bartholomaeus Georgievicz, a soldier who was captured at the battle of Mohacs in 1526 and lived as a slave under Turkish rule for nearly ten years.[45] In his *Commentary on Daniel* (1543), Melanchthon stated, like Luther, that the Turk and the pope were the Gog and Magog of Ezekiel and Revelation.[46] He developed his particular biblical interpretation even further, however, arguing that according to Scripture Muslims were descendents of Esau, who was born red (Gen 25:25) and sold his birthright for some "red" porridge (Gen 25:30). Therefore these descendents of the tribe of Edom were the cousins of the Israelites, the "red Jews" (Gen 36:1, 8).[47] Martin Bucer also argued that Muslims descended from Esau and the tribe of Edom, and thus bore "divine judgment that sanctioned an identification of the Edomite Mohammed as a son of perdition."[48] A generation after Luther, his own *Sermon against the Turk* was being utilized as a source. In 1663 Michael Wendt published *Doctor Martin Luthers Erschreckliche Türcken Propheseyung*, a compendium of statements Luther made about his interpretation of Islam.[49] But what does Luther say of Islam, the religion of the Turks? What did Luther know of the beliefs of "the Turk"?

---

the first documented Christian writer to associate Islam with the beasts of Daniel and Revelation. In his work *Indiculus Luminosus*, Alvarus argued that Muhammad had died in the year 666 (the mark of the beast) of the "era of Spain" (Southern, *Western Views of Islam*, 25). For the influence of this movement on Christian Missions see Cutler, "9th Century Spanish Martyrs' Movement."

44. See Slomp, "Calvin and the Turks."
45. Setton, *Western Hostility*, 29–46.
46. Williams, "Erasmus and the Reformers," 352.
47. Ibid.
48. Ibid., 354.
49. Setton, *Western Hostility*, 41.

LUTHER'S VIEWS OF ISLAM

Luther did demonstrate on several occasions his desire to learn more about the religion of the Turks. In 1529 he acquired a *Tract on the Religion and Customs of the Turks*, written by George of Hungary in 1481, who spent nearly twenty years in captivity under the Turks.[50] The text provided both positive and negative examples of Turkish society. Because of this even-handed approach, Luther felt that it was the most dependable work on the religion of the Turks that he had so far come across. He wanted to publish the tract to help the Germans understand the people who had been God's left hand of punishment. Thus, after the crisis of Vienna in 1529 Luther felt that it was important to republish the *Tract* in a new Latin translation with a preface, which he would ultimately do in 1530.[51]

However, Luther did not see Islam in its own right. He placed the work within the context of his own confrontation with Rome. Reading George's report, which conveyed some aspects of Muslim popular piety in the Ottoman Empire, he found many similarities between Islamic practices and the problems of Roman Catholic teachings. The Turks held to a faith that was "beautiful, effective, and [a] robust show of ceremonies, good works, and false miracles."[52] Several years later, in his *On the Psalms* (1532–33), Luther wrote: "[The Muslims] seek faith through certain merits and works so that they prescribe certain rules of dress, dietary regulation, fastings and so forth, like the righteousness of Papist and Turk which consists solely in such externals."[53]

Ultimately, after reading the *Tract*, Luther came to the conclusion that the Turks relied on the same form of religion as Rome—outward works and ceremonies. The big difference, however, between the two religions was that the Turks were faithfully following their own religion of outward works while the pope had subverted the true gospel of Christ. The Muslims were far more "splendid in ceremonies . . . even including that of the religious or all of the clerics."[54] In fact, he went so far as to charge Rome with discouraging the study of Islam because Rome would have to admit that the Muslims were far better believers than the Roman

---

50. See Francisco, *Martin Luther and Islam*, 24–29.
51. Heinrich and Boyce, "Martin Luther—Translations," 258–59.
52. Ibid., 260.
53. C. Wolf, "Luther and Mohammedanism," 172.
54. Heinrich and Boyce, 259.

Catholics themselves! The *Tract* pointed out to Luther that at least the Muslims were sincere in their faith, albeit misguided. In a similar and consistent view regarding the role of public religion and its structure within society, Luther was able to use Islam as an example of how European Catholic society had been mislead in its own faith.

At least one year prior to his reading of George's *Tract*, Luther had acquired a Latin text of the *Confutatio Alcorani* [Refutation of the Qur'ān] written by Ricoldo De Montecroce (1243–1320), as well as the *Cribatio Alcorani* [Critique of the Qur'ān] by Nicolas of Cusa (1401–64). Both works included portions of the Qur'ān translated into Latin; Ricoldo's for apologetic purposes and Nicolas's for dialogical ones. Luther had hoped to publish a copy of the Qur'ān in German, but he abandoned the project at the time. Perhaps he found the quality of the translations too poor, or he found Montecroce's claims about the Qur'ān too incredulous.[55] However, by 1542 he had decided to translate the *Refutation* into German, so that "those who are now or in the future under the Turks might protect themselves against Muhammad's faith, even if they are not able to protect themselves against his sword."[56]

It is clear that Luther did not have access to any other material on the life of Muhammad, especially the biography of the Prophet [Sira], other than that of Montecroce and Cusa.[57] These two works, along with George of Hungary's *Tract*, formed the core of the sources that Luther utilized in learning about Islam. It was not until 1542, when he did get a hold of a recently published edition of the Qur'ān in Latin by the Swiss Reformed scholar Theodore Bibliander (1504–64), that he was able to read more of the Turks' sacred book. He felt it worthy of being translated into German "to read the writings of the enemy in order to refute them more keenly, to cut them to pieces and to overturn them, in order that they might be

---

55. WA 53:272. See Heinrich and Boyce, "Martin Luther—Translations," 262.

56. WA 53:392. For a detailed analysis of this see Francisco, *Martin Luther and Islam*, 175–210.

57. Heinrich Knaust, a student in Wittenberg, gathered some material on the life of Muhammad in 1542. In addition, Bibliander produced a large work of translated Islamic texts in 1543. However, there is no indication that Luther had read these or utilized the information (see Francisco, *Martin Luther and Islam*, 55–56, 99). Luther did note, however, that he had read the work *De orbis terrae Concordia*, by his younger contemporary Guillame Postel in 1544, but again there is no evidence it provided further information than *Cribatio* and *Refutatio*. In fact, Francisco argues that Luther did not think much of Postel's work (ibid., 99).

able to bring some to safety, or certainly to fortify our people with more sturdy arguments."[58] A younger Luther, driven by the same youthful zeal as that of some of his greatest works of the 1520s, might have been able to produce a commentary on the Qur'ān as he had wanted to do. However, that was not to be. Luther was in ill health the last few years of his life and much of his energy was taken up in writing his commentaries. This is quite unfortunate, given the fact that by 1543 new translations of the Qur'ān were starting to appear on the market, and Luther's keen mind could have offered something to this field of study.

The first translation of the Qur'ān into a Western language appeared in the twelfth century when the Englishman Robert of Ketton made a Latin translation at the request of Peter the Venerable, the abbot of the Cluny monastery (1092–1156). Ketton's translation would serve as the basis of most Western study on Islam until the time of the Renaissance, when French and English replaced Latin as the *lingua franca* of Europe.[59] With the advent of the printing press access to the medieval material was now made more accessible.[60]

Theodor Bibliander, professor of theology at Zurich, made a Latin revision of Ketton's translation of the Qur'ān, as noted above. However, while the edition was going to print, the authorities in Basel banned the printing and threw the printer, Johannes Oporin, in jail, seeking charges against him and Bibliander for providing easy access to heretical books with the possibility of leading the people astray.[61] Luther and numerous other Reformers wrote to the Basel authorities and convinced them to release the offending parties, to not destroy the imprints of the book, and finally to allow it to be published. Luther then wrote a preface for the text,

---

58. Heinrich and Boyce, "Martin Luther—Translations," 266.

59. Two other early Latin translations of the Qur'ān were done, one by Mark of Toledo in 1210 and another by John of Segovia in 1458. Johannes Terrolensis completed a copy in 1518, but to date there is no evidence of its use. See Gaudeul, *Encounters and Clashes*, 148.

60. The first Italian translation appeared in 1547 by Andrea Arrivabene. Andre du Ryer made the first French translation in 1647. Alexander Ross then translated this edition into English in 1649. Another English edition was made by George Sale in 1734, and yet another by Claude Savay in 1783. A German translation was made by Solomon Schweigger, at about the same time as du Ryer, and was used as the basis of an anonymous Dutch translation in 1641. The first Arabic text published in the West was that of Lodovico Marriacci, in 1698. See Pearson, "al-Kur'ān".

61. Williams, "Erasmus and the Reformers," 349.

which was finally published in Basel in 1543.⁶² He convinced the powers in Basel that it would be better for Christianity to be able to refute Islam by reading its own text than to be ignorant about its views.

Based on his previous reading of Montecroce, as well Bibliander's assessment of the origins of Muhammad's views, Luther followed a common medieval Christian view, which held that Muhammad utilized what Western theology considered non-orthodox Christian sources:

> All history shows that Mohammed came from the Arians, the Macedonians and the Nestorians, in which he was situated from the very beginning for some time.⁶³

In other words, for Luther it was easy to see how Muhammad had come up with his views about God and Jesus, as he was surrounded in Arabia by Jews, Arians—who held that Jesus was created, and not "one with the Father," and Nestorians—who held that Mary was not the "God-bearer." In one table talk Luther stated, "Nestorians and Jews have certainly helped compose the Koran. Nestorians have become Arians who believe that Christ is not God, but is nevertheless a Great Lord."⁶⁴

Following his sources, Luther was convinced that Muhammad created a hodgepodge of a new religion from Judaism and eastern Christianity, "a new belief that dissents from the prophets and apostles."⁶⁵ According to Luther, Muhammad repudiated not specifically the Old Testament, but more importantly the New Testament, and the finality of Christ as the savior and Son of God. In his early reading of his sources in 1528 he wrote:

> In the first place, he [Muhammad] greatly praises Christ and Mary as being the only ones without sin, and yet he believes nothing more of Christ than that he is a holy prophet, like Jeremiah or Jonah, and denies that he is God's Son or true God. Furthermore, he does not believe that Christ is the savior of the world who died for our sins, but that he proceeded to his own time and completed his work before his death, just like any other prophet.⁶⁶

---

62. The text was officially titled *Machumetis Sarracenorum principis vita ac doctrina omnis, quam & Ishmahelitarum lex, & Alcoranum dicitur.*
63. WA 54:160, as cited in C. Wolf, "Luther and Mohammedanism," 166.
64. C. Wolf, "Luther and Mohammedanism," 167.
65. Heinrich and Boyce, "Martin Luther—Translations," 264.
66. LW 46:176.

Later, in his reading of Bibliander's translation, he would pick up again on the concept of propitiary sacrifice for sin as anathema for Islam.

> The church of God by necessity embraces the prophets and apostles; Muhammad rejects their teaching. In the church of God from the very beginning this voice of the gospel has always been handed on: that the eternal Father willed that the Son of God become a sacrifice for sins; Muhammad scorns this sacrifice and propitiation.[67]

Orthodox Islam removes the need for salvation and the work of a Savior, primarily because it would be unjust for God not to allow each individual to rest upon the balance of their own good and bad deeds. Salvation, or election, in Islam is built upon the faithful following of the path of the prophets and the law of God as revealed in the Qur'ān [*sharī'a*]. Due to his strong christocentric frame of reference Luther saw Muhammad as departing from the consistent message of the prophets.

Another important observation that Luther would make from his reading of the Qur'ān was its criticism of the Trinity. In a table talk during the spring of 1543 Luther stated:

> The Turk has just one argument, and this is: Cursed be all those who worship more than one God; the Christians do this; therefore [cursed be the Christians]. I concede the minor premise because Christians believe in God the Father, the Son, and the Holy Spirit. No matter how one tells the Turks, they can't believe that three are one.[68]

Even earlier, in a sermon for Trinity Sunday in 1528, Luther would correctly assess one of the major theological disputes between Christianity and Islam:

> The Jews, Turks, heathen must consider such teaching [on the Trinity] as the worst error and highest heresy, and say that we Christians are silly and foolish when we make three Gods, since it is unreasonable that there be more than one God.[69]

His assessment strikes to the heart of two prominent *ayāt* [verses] of the Qur'ān.

---

67. Heinrich and Boyce, "Martin Luther—Translations," 266.
68. *LW* 54:454–55.
69. C. Wolf, "Luther and Mohammedanism," 169.

> *O people of the Scripture! Do not exaggerate in your religion nor utter aught concerning Allah save the truth. The Messiah, Jesus son of Mary, was only a messenger of Allah, and His word which He conveyed unto Mary, and a spirit from Him. So believe in Allah and His messengers, and say not "Three." Cease! (It is) better for you! Allah is only One God. Far is it removed from His transcendent majesty that he should have a son. His is all that is in the heavens and all that is in the earth. And Allah is sufficient as Defender* (4:171).

> *And when Allah saith: O Jesus, son of Mary! Didst thou say unto mankind: Take me and my mother for two gods beside Allah? he saith: Be glorified! It was not mine to utter that to which I had no right. If I used to say it, then Thou knewest it. Thou knowest what is in my mind, and I know not what is in Thy mind. Lo! Thou, only Thou art the Knower of Things Hidden.* (5:116)

The christocentric Luther was correct in his assessment of the major theological differences between Islam and Christianity: the different understandings of the revelation of God's "self" or "will." In Islam, God revealed his "will" in giving of the Qur'ān. In Christianity, God reveals God's very "self" in the giving of his Son—a very part of his own essence.

Despite this negativity, Luther did detect some positive aspects of the adherents of Islam. Having read about the popular Sufi brotherhoods, Luther could not help but be impressed:

> The Turks, so I have heard, have priests and pious men who do many things in ecstasy. They are seized and are sometimes thrown prostrate insensible, where, on coming to themselves they speak sublimely and wonderfully. The common folk view these things, and seeking the great men there, of course they think them to be of a special holiness.[70]

It must be recognized, however, that Luther never looked at Islam as a solitary entity to be studied or understood. It was rather part of a larger threat toward the church. The problems of the world were not solely the fault of Muslims and their ways. Rather, the ultimate problems of European society stemmed from within, from within the church and from within German society. As stinging as some of Luther's barbs could be toward Muhammad and Islam, this polemic could not match up to what he would throw at the pope or what he directed to his own German

---

70. See "Disputation against the Anti-Nomians," in *WA* 39, as cited in C. Wolf, "Luther and Mohammedanism," 173.

people! The state of affairs in Europe was not the fault of Muhammad, Islam, or the Turk. Writing to Joachim of Brandenburg in 1532 he stated:

> I beg that those on our side may not place their reliance on the Turk's being altogether wrong and God's enemy while we are innocent and righteous in comparison with the Turk, for such presumption is also vain. Rather it is necessary to fight with fear of God and reliance on his grace alone. We too are unrighteous in God's sight. Some on our side have shed much innocent blood, have despised and persecuted God's word, and have been disobedient, and so we cannot take our stand on our merits, no matter how righteous or unrighteous the Turks may be.[71]

In the end, Islam for Luther was similar to all other human attempts at justification; just as the laws of the Jews and the decretals of the pope. One can easily see how Luther fit his critique of Islam directly into the scope of his criticism of the Roman Catholicism of his day, where both the pope and Muhammad created a "doctrine of works."[72] Luther recognized in Islam a similar religious framework to Judaism and contemporary Rome. In *On the Psalms* (1532) Luther wrote that Muslims "seek faith through certain merits and works, so that they prescribe certain rules of dress, dietary regulation, fastings and so forth, like the righteousness of the Papist . . . which consists solely in such externals."[73] As a religion of rites, then, it subverted faith in God and the work of Christ. Their laws were barriers to true faith in God. (This is quite ironic, however, as Muslims have long distanced themselves from any sacramental faith of Christianity, arguing that Islam does not have a priesthood or accept any mediation of God through individuals or sacraments. Rather all individuals have direct petitionary access to God.) Yet, on the other hand, Luther was able to speak more highly of the religion of Islam than that of Rome. At least the Muslims were being true to their own faith, while Rome was wallowing in hypocrisy.

SULEIMAN AND THE HAPSBURGS

In 1517, the same year Luther nailed his *95 Theses* to the door of the castle church at Wittenberg, under the rule of Selim "the Grim" the Turks had

---

71. *LW* 43:216.
72. Ibid.
73. C. Wolf, "Luther and Mohammedanism," 172.

overrun Syria, the Hijaz (portions of the Arabian Peninsula), and Egypt, claiming complete mastery over the Arab Middle East. By 1520 Selim was dead, however, and the reins of the empire were turned over to his son Suleiman. Unlike his father, Suleiman was a ruler of great learning and self-discipline. He would be known as Suleiman "the Great" and Suleiman "the Lawgiver." An Italian emissary to the new sultan's court described him as

> tall, but wiry, and of a delicate complexion. His neck is a little too long, his face thin, and his nose aquiline ... a pleasant mien, though his skin tends to pallor. He is said to be a wise lord, fond of study, and all men hope for good from his rule.[74]

This is not the description of a fearsome, "Terrible Turk." In fact, most European rulers scoffed at Suleiman's coronation, assuming that the days of the Turks were now over; that the young ruler would not have the stomach for empire building. Suleiman, however, was still his father's son. His father having conquered most of the Middle East, Suleiman turned his eye westward. He would extend the borders of the Ottoman Empire from horizon to horizon.

Throughout much of the early sixteenth century there was a three-way power struggle in Western Europe. The struggle centered on the rivalry between Charles I, the Hapsburg king of Spain, and Francis I, the king of France. Caught between the two was the bishop of Rome. Both sovereigns desired to be crowned as the Holy Roman Emperor. For this they wanted the support and blessing of the Roman pontiff. Pope Leo X, unfortunately, decided to back the wrong horse, the pious king of France, Francis I. However, Charles was too experienced a politician and too shrewd a diplomat to be simply out chosen. With money in his own treasury he managed to gain support from the nobility of the empire, pressuring Leo to recognize his right to the throne. Charles V was crowned the Holy Roman Emperor in 1520, ironically the same year that Suleiman the Magnificent came to power.

Throughout his reign as emperor, Germany was a constant arena of political trouble for Charles. His problem ultimately focused on the young Augustinian monk Martin Luther. Rome saw Luther as a Hussite heretic. The papal legates were convinced that the problematic monk needed to be silenced. Charles also saw Luther as a nuisance to his overall political

---

74. Jason Goodwin, *Lords of the Horizons*, 80–81.

agenda. Luther's criticisms of the papacy regarding the sale of indulgences and corruption in 1517 and 1518 were taken to heart by some of the German princes, who saw an opportunity to assert their own power. This was the last thing Charles needed; a nationalist uprising within his empire the very moment he needed a solid front against Suleiman in the East and Francis in the West. Charles called the Germans together at the provincial town of Worms for a diet (an assembly of German princes and nobility) on January 27, 1521. The diet would be a four-month-long consultation to address the important issues of organizing the Holy Roman Empire.[75] It was not until April, however, that Luther was summoned to stand before the diet to answer to the charges of his "heretical" writings. Roland Bainton, in his classic work *Here I Stand*, describes the meeting:

> The scene lends itself to dramatic portrayal. Here was Charles, heir of a long line of Catholic sovereigns—of Maximilian the romantic, of Ferdinand the Catholic, of Isabella the orthodox—scion of the house of Hapsburg, lord of Austria, Burgundy, the Low Countries, Spain, and Naples, Holy Roman Emperor, ruling over a vaster domain that any save Charlemagne, symbol of the medieval unities, incarnation of a glorious if vanishing heritage; and here before him a simple monk, a miner's son, with nothing to sustain him save his own faith in the Word of God. Here the past and the future were met.[76]

In the midst of this social and religious turmoil, Charles attempted to assert his authority as the "defender of the faith" over against France in the West, the Turk in the East, and this heretic from among the rebellious and uncouth Germans. Luther was, in the eyes of Charles, expendable in the great scheme of international politics. The Emperor formally declared Luther a heretic and an outlaw. He told the diet:

> After having heard yesterday the obstinate defense of Luther, I regret that I have so long delayed in proceeding against him and his false teaching. I will have no more to do with him. He may return under his safe conduct, but without preaching or making any tumult. I will proceed against him as a notorious heretic.[77]

---

75. Durant, *Reformation*, 359.
76. Bainton, *Here I Stand*, 141.
77. Ibid., 144.

The day after Charles condemned Luther, Hieronymus Balbus, an emissary from Louis II of Hungary, rose to speak to the assembly to seek reinforcements against an approaching army of Turks in the East. The emissary stated that they desperately needed their German brethren to aid and assist them. But Luther had stolen the show at Worms. After the two-day debate over Luther and his writings, the princes had no further taste for politics. There was neither energy nor will left in the diet. For the Germans princes it was Luther and German pride that was at stake, not fears of the "Terrible Turk."

Charles, although a Hapsburg with familial lands being threatened by Suleiman in Hungary, was at heart a Spaniard. He was at that time really more concerned by the problems with France over his own private residences in Spain. He left the diet and Germany, not to return for almost ten years. The Hungarians were thus left to their own devices. Rather than shoring up support in the face of Suleiman's advancing army, Hungary was left wide open to Turkish invasion. It was too late. Belgrade fell and the Balkans were now in Suleiman's hands. But this was only the beginning.

In April 1526, just as the new campaign season was underway, Suleiman the Magnificent and his army marched forth from the gates of Istanbul, once again heading toward Hungary. News of this movement certainly must have reached the ears of Charles, but as during the threat of 1521 Charles was more concerned about events in the West. Francis I had managed to convince Pope Clement VII and the cities of Venice and Milan to throw in their lot with him and sign a pact, known as the *League of Cognac*. If this wasn't enough, Charles received word that Francis had also managed to get Suleiman to agree to a treaty wherein the two sovereigns would work in tandem against the interests of the Holy Roman Empire: Suleiman agreed to keep up Turkish naval pressure in the Mediterranean along the coast of Spain and to continue his march through Hungary and ultimately threaten Italy. Faced with this new threat, Charles needed to reign in his rabble Germans in order to deal with Francis. Thus, the German princes were summoned to the city of Speyer for another diet. This time, however, Charles himself would not be present at the diet, but would send his brother Ferdinand as his official representative. In preparation for this meeting the German princes, primarily John of Saxony and Philip of Hesse, who had been feeling pressure from Rome to enforce the ban on Luther proclaimed at Worms, pledged themselves to fight against the emperor, if necessary.

By July of 1526 Charles was apparently worried enough about this situation to rethink his designs on Germany. Charles wrote his brother Ferdinand, telling him to take a more delicate approach with the princes rather than enforcing the ban of Luther at the Diet of Worms. He desperately needed the princes' support to defend the empire from Suleiman's advance in the East.[78] Thus, the diet met at Speyer and the emperor's party agreed to postpone discussion of enforcing the ban on Luther until such a time at which the atmosphere was more congenial to such matters. As a compromise, the emperor agreed to allow each prince the right to govern his own territory in regards to churchly matters as they saw fit.[79]

While the diet was meeting, Suleiman was marching north along the Danube. With the German princes and territories otherwise occupied with imperial politics, the Hungarians were once again on their own. Only two days after the diet was adjourned, Louis II, king of Hungary, was slain on the fields of Mohacs. By early September Budapest fell. All of Hungary was now in Suleiman's hands and Vienna, further up the Danube River, was in great peril. Suleiman was now face to face with his next opponent, Ferdinand, duke of Austria—brother of Charles V—whom he called the "little man of Vienna." Sending an envoy to Ferdinand he said, "Tell him that I will look for him on the field of Mohacs, or even in Pest, and if he fails to meet me there I will offer him battle beneath the walls of Vienna itself."[80] Satisfied with his booty, however, Suleiman returned to Istanbul, leaving his newly acquired territory in the hands of his generals. He would not return for another three years.

Without the Turkish threat in the East, the German princes would have been forced to submit to the emperor's wishes to ban Lutheran teaching, or face war. Fortunately for the Lutherans, the Turks provided the opportunity for some breathing space in order for their movement to gain momentum and solidify. The Turk truly was Luther's lucky star.

---

78. See excursus by Gottfried G. Krodel in *LW* 49:155.

79. We see here the origins of the Peace of Westphalia (1628): *cuius regio eius religio* [to each ruler goes the religion], meaning that the religion of a particular principality was determined by the religion of the ruler.

80. Goodwin, *Lords of the Horizons*, 87.

THE SIEGE OF VIENNA

During the winter of 1526–27 the Holy Roman Emperor Charles V continued to plan for his overall strategy in response to the *League of Cognac* (the alignment of Italian city-states, the pope, England, and France). He ultimately decided that there was no other alternative than to beat his enemies into submission. Thus, as the winter of 1527 broke, Charles did the unthinkable. His imperial troops moved on Rome. In a scandalous decision by the "defender of the faith," he sacked Rome to regain control of the Italian city-states. It would take another two years for the conflict to end, but by June 1529 Charles would force the pope to capitulate to his political power. By August, Francis I was humiliated and signed a treaty with Charles. Thus, Charles had managed to establish his undisputed authority as the Holy Roman Emperor on the continent. All this occurred just in time as Suleiman once again ventured forth from Istanbul.

As the spring campaign season of 1529 began, Suleiman made ready to march out of Istanbul in order to head up the Danube through the Balkans. His sights were set on Vienna—a prominent symbol of European culture—and it seemed at the time as if nothing could stop him. Charles was consumed by his struggles with the *League of Cognac* and so was not attending to the eastern part of his empire. Charles thought that if he could gain the support of the German princes he would be able to set up a wall of defense against the Turkish threat. He would then be able to continue to focus upon his troubles with France. However, Charles underestimated both the German princes and Suleiman.

Charles sent out his imperial vice-chancellor, Balthasar Merklin von Waldkirch, to read the riot act to the German princes.[81] Thus, another diet was called at Speyer in March of 1529. The Second Diet of Speyer would become the politically defining moment for the rebel movement. Whereas the First Diet at Speyer left the religious issues of each estate up to the decision of each German prince until such a time as was convenient for him to call a new council, Charles now felt the time was right for stricter enforcement of his own religious beliefs. He sent his brother Ferdinand to enforce the ban on Luther (enacted at the Diet of Worms in 1521) and to shore up the eastern defenses of the empire against the oncoming threat from Suleiman. Yet once again, when push came to shove, Charles felt that the stakes were too high to allow Luther to undercut the necessary German support from

---

81. *LW* 49:222.

defending the empire. He changed his tactics and decided on a softer approach. Charles's official letter to the diet—rather than the originally intended heavy-handed enforcement of Worms—ended up being an olive branch. Ferdinand, however, had not received the letter from his brother and proceeded to lay down the gauntlet to enforce the ban of Worms.

It is at this moment that the Protestant Reformation officially began as a social-political movement. The delegates of the cities of Nürnberg, Ulm, and Strasbourg signed a protest and officially presented it to the imperial viceroy, Ferdinand. The princes and delegates of these rebel cities took it upon themselves the right to preach the evangelical doctrines of the faith as outlined by the Reformers. They sent a copy of the protest with a delegation to Charles. He would, however, have none of it. It was then that Charles realized the time for soft tactics had passed. Charles threw the delegation in prison and demanded the withdrawal of the protest.[82] The German "protestants," primarily John of Saxony, Margrave George of Brandenburg, and Philip of Hesse, all began to plan for an imperial attack on their territories. It appeared as if the Holy Roman Empire was headed toward war.

Once again, however, Suleiman incited a different outcome. By April 1529 the new campaign season was under way and the Turks were preparing for their campaign up the Danube. As if that was not cause enough for concern, rumors were traveling throughout eastern Germany that the Turks were not acting alone but in coordination with the Venetians, who now had a formal ambassador to the court of Suleiman. Luther even stated to his friends that the pope himself was aiding the Turks![83]

Ferdinand needed to rush back to Vienna from Speyer in order to attend to the oncoming Turkish advance. There would be no attack on the rebel Protestant cities by the empire. Rather, the empire needed to be defended from the "Terrible Turk." Fortunately for Ferdinand—and Charles—Suleiman's gamble at Vienna would not pay off. The Turkish army arrived at Vienna in September, too late in the campaign season. Excessively heavy summer rains had slowed the advancing army and prompted them to leave numerous heavy guns behind, stuck in the mud. Thus, by the time the Ottomans had arrived at Vienna they were not in

---

82. *LW* 49:244.
83. *LW* 49:220 n. 9.

the best position for a long, drawn out siege. In October they lost heart and retreated.

By the autumn of 1529 Charles V was in a much more comfortable situation than he had been three years previous. Throughout the summer he had managed to control the German princes and the free towns, sign a treaty with Francis I, and be crowned emperor by Clement VII. By October not only were the internal disputes within the Holy Roman Empire settled, but also Suleiman had been turned back from Vienna. Thus, feeling secure in his position, Charles once again began preparing to solidify his rule in Germany. In December of 1529 he called for another imperial diet. This time the diet was to meet at Augsburg in the spring of 1530, and Charles intended on being present. The young monk who had stood up to the emperor at the Diet of Worms almost ten years before would not, however. Augsburg was an imperial city and Luther was still under the ban of Worms. He could not travel to the diet lest he be arrested. However, Luther would be represented by a host of supporters and fellow Reformers who would provide defense for their Reformist views. Charles was willing to hear their views on religious matters, but he wanted to respond to the issue on his own terms—but it was not to be.[84]

On June 25, 1530 the Lutherans presented to the emperor the *Augsburg Confession*. This document would become the official statement of faith for the Reformers. The Roman legates who were present responded to this confession with their own rebuttal several weeks later. Upon hearing the official Roman Catholic response, the emperor declared that the Protestants had been successfully refuted and ordered them to respond. Philip Melancthon, Luther's closest companion, immediately set to work on *The Apology of the Augsburg Confession*, which was finished on September 22. Melanchthon presented the document, however, the emperor never allowed it to be read at the diet.

In the end, the Diet of Augsburg was a compromise. The emperor had officially declared his belief in the truth of the Roman Catholic faith and decried the evangelical views of the "Lutherans." However, Luther and his views were given a further six-month grace period. The emperor was willing to wait until Clement VII organized a pontifical council to make a final ecclesiastical decision on Luther's theological views. He did not feel it within his authority to pass doctrine and declare Luther's views hereti-

---

84. *LW* 34:5.

cal, but would only suggest that the head of the church do so. Ultimately, Clement did give approval for such a council but he never organized it.[85] Charles' six-month grace period would, however, once again be waylaid by the Turks.

By the spring of 1532 Suleiman was ready to have another try at Vienna. He and his army marched from Istanbul at beginning of the campaign season in May, heading straight for the gates of Vienna. As we will see below, Luther was blamed for the Turkish advance, especially by the Roman Catholic bishop of Vienna.[86] On this occasion, Charles V would not take the threat so lightly and would attend to matters himself.

This time Charles would personally faced off with Suleiman the Magnificent from behind the walls of Vienna. He sent out reinforcements to the city of Guns, about seventy miles southeast of Vienna. Bad weather prohibited a timely journey toward Vienna, and Suleiman arrived at Guns later than expected. Reluctant to take on Suleiman's army of three hundred thousand men directly on the field, Charles was satisfied with waiting out a siege at Guns. Seeing a long and dreary siege in front of him, Suleiman decided the city was not worth it. After only nineteen days he retreated down the Danube.[87] The summer rains had washed away the advance to conquer Vienna—much to the chagrin of Francis I. This would be the closest that Suleiman would personally ever get to Vienna.

Charles V, the "defender of the faith," Holy Roman Emperor, had successfully defended central Europe from "the Turk." Through political skill, and a little bit of luck, he managed to deal with one political opponent after another and hold together an empire. While Charles abided within the bosom of the one true church and its faith, his political ambitions and intuitiveness allowed him make decisions based upon *realpolitik*, rather than theological premises. He did fight for the idea of Christendom, but Christendom was more than Rome. For Luther, however, defense of the homeland was never about Christendom or its ideal.

---

85. It would not be until 1545 that the Roman Catholic Church would organize the Council at Trent.

86. *LW* 54:27, no. 206.

87. Goodwin, *Lords of the Horizons*, 88.

LUTHER AND THE CRUSADE

Throughout the late Middle Ages, the papacy had continued to call for a crusade against Islam. But ever since the fall of the last crusader outpost at Acre in 1291, Europe was hard pressed to muster its forces to take the cross and lead the charge to the Holy Land. With the capture of Constantinople by the Turks in 1453, Europe was faced with the reality that they could no longer take the fight to the Muslims; rather, the Muslims would now bring the fight to them on European soil. In 1459 Pope Pius II called a council urging the powers of Europe to take up a crusade against the Turks. This was not to be, however, as France, Spain, and the Italian city-states were far more interested in their own political problems. Pius had even taken it upon himself to write to the Turkish sultan, inviting him to Christianity. The letter was a polite epistle, appealing to both the power of Christian Europe and the heights of Renaissance rationalism.

> A very little thing can make you the greatest, the most powerful, the most famous person of your time . . . It is to be found all over the world—a little water with which you may be baptized . . .[88]

Frustrated with the lack of support he found among the sovereigns in Europe, Pius II resolved to organize and lead the next crusade himself. Shortly after departing Rome he died, leaving his crusaders leaderless and without a specific plan.[89] In 1514, Cardinal Bakocz of Hungary called for a new crusade to beat back the infidels. His call must have been half-hearted, for he abandoned his newly formed army upon hearing of Pius's death in order to campaign in Rome for his own election to the papacy, leaving fifty thousand peasants, to ravage the countryside.[90] When Leo X came to the papal throne, he continued the call for crusade, sending letters to European sovereigns to take the cross. Leo's successor, Adrian VI, did likewise. These papal pronouncements found their way into public consumption through pamphlets that were published and distributed throughout Europe. One pamphlet, *A Call for a Crusade against the Turks and All Who Are Opposed to the Christian Faith*, was a popular resource in Germany. Another, written by a contemporary of Luther, Ulrich von

---

88. Text as found in Gadaeul, *Encounters and Clashes*, 1:213–14. See also Southern, *Western Views of Islam*, 98–103; and N. A. Weber, "Pope Pius II." There is disagreement regarding the actual dating of the letter and the interpretation over its importance.

89. N. A. Weber, "Pope Pius II."

90. Friedenthal, *Luther*, 408.

Hutton, was called the *Exhortation to the German Princes*.[91] Even Erasmus of Rotterdam, in *Utilissima consultatio de bello Turcis inferendo*, called for the rulers of the day to take up arms.[92]

The call for a crusade had always been connected with the role of the sale of indulgences. When Pope Urban II proclaimed the first Crusade in 1095 he declared that those who took up the cross would receive, not forgiveness of sin, but remission of penalties in purgatory. Those who could not actually go on crusade could participate in their own way by paying a simple fee, in lieu of physical service. The concept of crusade was applied not only to those going to the Holy Land to fight the "Saracens" or the "Turks," but to those fighting heretics, the enemies of the pope and the church as well. By Leo's time, with the expansion of the "Eternal City," with all of its monumental architectural enterprises, the sale of indulgences developed into an elaborate payment system for the reduction of individual penalties which would help build up the glory of the church in Rome. Those living far from the centers of Renaissance Rome, however, had little emotional attachment to Leo's vision. The financial support for the Eternal City meant little to their daily medieval life. Thus, the indulgences that were offered began to be seen as taxes to Rome, rather than as participation in the crusade or even the building up of the kingdom against the forces of evil.[93]

As Pastor Luther witnessed the continuing growth of the sale of indulgences, he was mortified that money was being utilized as a method of excusing the Christian from God's just judgment. Given Luther's predisposition toward the apocalyptic, he came to see "the Turk" not simply as the enemy, but as God's left hand of judgment on an immoral European church. In his explanation to the *95 Thesis* he wrote:

> [P]lagues, wars, insurrections, earthquakes, fires, murders, thefts, as well as the Turks, Tartars, and other infidels; none but a poor Christian would fail to recognize in these the lash and rod of God. ... Many, however, even the "big wheels" in the church, now dream of nothing else than war against the Turk. They want to fight, not against iniquities, but against the lash of iniquity and thus they would oppose God who says that through that lash he himself

---

91. *LW* 46:157–58; see *WA* 30/2:84. For a translation see Housely, *Documents on the Later Crusades*.

92. Setton, "Lutheranism," 155.

93. *LW* 48:82.

punishes us for our iniquities because we do not punish ourselves for them.[94]

Luther's medieval worldview, and his own struggles with the demonic, played an important role in his view that the world was being threatened by temporal forces from without and spiritual forces within. The Turk, then, was God's deserved judgment on society for its waywardness. In very crude and cutting language he pulls no punches:

> Antichrist is at the same time the pope and the Turk. A living creature consists of body and soul. The spirit of Antichrist is the people, his flesh the Turk. One attacks the Church physically, the other spiritually.[95]

Luther regarded Rome's attempt at self-glorification as leading the church and all of civilization into hell.

> It is a scandal how the pope has all this time led us by the nose with this war against the Turks. He has used it to make off with our money, destroy many Christians, and cause much misery. When will we learn that the pope is the devil's most dangerous tool? Was it not the pope who incited the good King Ladislas of Hungary and Poland, and many thousand Christians, to make war upon the Turks . . . Yet what misery has recently come to Hungary as a result of this same war against the Turks, which was begun with a Roman indulgence. But we remain blind as far as the pope is concerned.
>
> . . . God does not demand crusades, indulgences, and wars. He wants us to live good lives. But the pope and his followers run from goodness faster than from anything else, yet he wants to devour the Turk. This is the reason why our war against the Turk is so successful—so that where he formerly held one mile of land he now holds a hundred. But we still do not see it, so completely have we been taken in by this Roman leader of the blind.[96]

In his *Explanation to the Ninety-Five Thesis* (1518) Luther had written that to "fight against the Turk is the same as resisting God . . ."[97] Pope Leo X took this statement personally and declared Luther *persona non gratta*. His *Exsurge Domino* (1520) lambasted Luther for being a traitor to the faith and to the Holy Roman Empire. Because of his outspoken views against

---

94. *LW* 31:91–92.
95. *Table Talk*, in WA 3, as cited in Setton, "Lutheranism," 151.
96. Luther, "Defense against All the Articles," in *LW* 32:89–91.
97. *LW* 31:91.

the pope and the church's crusade against the Turks, Luther was blamed by Rome for the coming of the Turks and for the defeat of the Hungarians at Mohacs in 1526. A pamphlet that circulated after the defeat, entitled *Why the Turks Defeated the Hungarians,* laid the blame at Luther's feet for refusing to support the holy war against the infidels.[98] The papal nuncio in Germany, Francesco Chieregati, said, "We are occupied with the negotiations for the general war against the Turk, and for that particular war against that nefarious Martin Luther, who is a greater evil to Christendom than the Turk".[99] It was not until the siege of Vienna in 1529, however, that Luther finally responded to his critics. Like his other works, Luther did not write as a politician, providing political values or platforms. He wrote as a pastor, to those who needed guidance in how to respond to the coming Turks. Luther's primary concern was not to help people understand Islam or Muslims, but to clarify the proper reason for which Christians should defend themselves against Suleiman's advancing army.

His treatise *On War against the Turk* (1529) was a response to his critics over his refusal to support a crusade against the invading Turks. He also refused the charge that he invited such an invasion.[100] In the international crisis of an impending attack on Vienna (and possibly Germany) Luther responded to the criticism that he was being "unpatriotic." His objection to the idea of crusade was two-fold. First, in his view, Rome was simply utilizing the call for crusade for its own greed. Luther argued that Rome simply wanted to use Germans for their own purposes, for filling the coffers of Rome with German ducats. Second, it was not the role of the pope to defend Christian political territory; that was the right of the emperor. Bishops calling for crusade and actually taking part in the fight were confused in their roles, argued Luther. It "is not right for the Pope, who wants to be a Christian, and the highest and best Christian preacher at that, to lead a church army, or army of Christians."[101] So, setting quill to parchment, Luther set about to clarify his position vis–à–vis the issue at hand and encouraged the Germans to make "wise and serious preparation" for war.[102]

98. *LW* 46:158 n. 9.
99. Setton, "Lutheranism," 147.
100. *LW* 46:157–205.
101. *LW* 46:168.
102. *LW* 46:203.

Luther had recognized that large amounts of popular material being published was polarizing, telling people either to go to war as a crusade against the Turks or that good Christians should be pacifists—some even spoke about how much better they would all be under Turkish rule, including Thomas Müntzer and Sebastian Franck.[103] Earlier in 1526 Luther spilt no small amount of ink in his *Instructions for the Visitors of Parish Pastors in Electoral Saxony* attempting to clarify his position on crusade.

> Some preachers clamor recklessly about the Turks, saying we should not oppose the Turks since Christians may not avenge themselves. This is seditious talk which should not be permitted or tolerated. For the government is given the power of the sword and commanded to punish all murder and pillage. Therefore it is obligated to wage war against those who start an unjust war and are responsible for pillage and murder. This vengeance is not forbidden. For Paul says in Rom. 13[:4] that government executes the vengeance of God, which means that it is instituted and commanded of God and given help by God in time of need. . .
>
> Some say that we should not defend the faith with the sword, but should suffer like Christ, or the apostles, etc. Undoubtedly it is true that they who do not bear rule should each in his place be willing to suffer and not defend himself, as Christ did not defend himself. For he had no worldly authority or rule, and did not wish any, as in John 6[:15] he would not allow the Jews to make him a king.
>
> The government, however, must protect its subjects against unjust powers whether such unjust power be exercised on account of faith or for some other reason.[104]

In the late medieval worldview it was understood that God created specific functions for each person in society for the benefit of the whole order. In order for society to function properly people needed to faithfully discharge the roles in which they had been placed. Those who held temporal offices should discharge their duties as civic leaders. Those who held churchly offices should administer those duties. According to Luther, Christians could and should fight in the cause of the emperor, kings, and princes to defend their lands, but under the authority of the "secular" rulers—as subjects. Thus, Luther does not deny that there is an

---

103. *LW* 46:161. See Bohnstedt, *Infidel Scourge of God*; Francisco, *Martin Luther and Islam*, 44–48.

104. *LW* 40:305.

evil enemy to be opposed, but that the war against the Turk is simply under the jurisdiction and office of the worldly rulers.[105] This is not a part of the church's role. Christians can take part in the war but only under the authority of the emperor, not the bishops or the pope.

In previous documents—*The Freedom of a Christian* (1520) and *Temporal Authority: To What Extent It Should Be Obeyed* (1523)—Luther had outlined what has come to be known as the doctrine of the two kingdoms. In these two treatises he explains that the church carries out God's charge of preaching, teaching, and administering the sacraments. Through God's "right hand," an individual is driven to Christ through repentance and then freed from the judgment of God through the grace of Christ. The rulers of the world, however, function as God's "left hand," providing the very judgment of God or the protection of God in social-political terms. God functions in two ways in the world: through the church and its office, and through the powers of the world and their office.[106]

In *On War against the Turk* we see the "two kingdoms" ethic clearly being applied. As a pastor, Luther continued to underline his position that he was neither a pacifist nor a crusader. He begins his treatise by defending his pervious statements against crusade.

> The popes had never seriously intended to wage war against the Turk; instead they used the Turkish war as a cover for their game and robbed Germany of money by means of indulgences ... They undertook to fight against the Turk in the name of Christ, and taught and incited men to do this[107]

There is a sense here in which, recognizing both the criticism labeled against him and the reality of a clear Turkish threat to Vienna, Luther realized the gravity of the situation. This was no longer 1517, when he was simply exchanging barbs with the pope. Times had changed. The ominous and threatening image of "the Turk" was now a reality. By 1529 he was responding to a new pastoral and national crisis. *On War against the Turk* reflects this change. Although Suleiman was still "Gog and Magog"

---

105. *LW* 46:200.

106. The association of the political powers with the law, and the church with the gospel, is not really an accurate explanation of Luther's "two kingdoms"; for God works both condemnation and forgiveness in both kingdoms, just in different ways. For a helpful review of the "two kingdoms" doctrine see Braaten, *Principles of Lutheran Theology*, 123–40.

107. *LW* 46:164–65.

and part of the coming apocalyptic judgment, Luther was no fatalist. It was not simply a matter of the Turk playing the part of God's left hand and that there was no alternative course but to suffer the wrath to come. Rather, Luther exhorts Christians to first purge themselves of their own sin, confess, and then fight—not a crusade, but a necessary and just war to ward off the evils of the world.

> Since the Turk is the rod of the wrath of the Lord our God and the servant of the raging devil, the first thing to be done is to smite the devil, his lord, and take the rod out of God's hand.[108]

If Christians attended to matters of their own spiritual well-being they would then be in a much better position to undertake their own particular civic duty to defend themselves under the authority of the emperor who was given the responsibility of their protection.[109] In response to a Christian soldier who wrote him to ask whether it was proper for him to take part in the war, Luther's first word of advice was for the soldier to confess his sins and then to "hew away" at the Turks.[110]

Again, in this letter to Elector Joachim of Brandenburg in 1532 he wrote:

> I beg that those on our side may not place their reliance on the Turk's being altogether wrong and God's enemy while we are innocent and righteous in comparison with the Turk, for such presumption is also vain. Rather it is necessary to fight with fear of God and reliance on his grace alone. We too are unrighteous in God's sight. Some on our side have shed much innocent blood, have despised and persecuted God's word, and have been disobedient, and so we cannot take our stand on our merits, no matter how righteous or unrighteous the Turks and we may be.[111]

Luther's *Appeal for Prayer against the Turks*, then, has more to do with his lamentation of the state of German society than his response to the threat from Istanbul. The *Appeal* is a pastoral epistle, providing a liturgy of psalms and prayers to be used in times of national crisis.

Even though Germany was now deserving of punishment because of its immorality and lack of holding to the Word, Christians might fight

---

108. *LW* 46:170.
109. See Forell, "Luther and the War," 256–71.
110. *LW* 43:216.
111. *LW* 43:216.

with a clear conscience, knowing that they were defending their own families and children, towns, and country from the Turkish invader. The Christians again are not fighting a holy war but "a just war."[112]

LUTHER'S FINAL APPEAL FOR PRAYER AGAINST THE TURKS

In 1540 a dispute over the throne to Hungary prompted Suleiman to strike central Europe once again.[113] King John Zapolya of Hungary (1526–40), whose throne had been tacitly supported by Suleiman after King Louis II had been slain in a battle at Mohacs, died in June of 1540. Nine days before his death, however, Queen Isabella gave birth to an heir to the throne. Archduke Ferdinand of Austria, seeing an opportunity now to extend the Hapsburg family grip on eastern Europe, sought to find support for his own claim to the throne of Hungary. Given the political reality of the day, both parties tried to gain Suleiman's support, sending emissaries to Istanbul in order to gain some kind of political backing from the real power of the day. Suleimain saw this as an opportunity. He saw an opportunity to extend his empire even further over eastern Europe and solidify his hold on its lands. This is exactly what he did. He moved forces into Hungary, annexed the territory, and turned the cathedral of Buda-Pest into a mosque.

A new wave of fear swept across eastern Germany. John Frederick, the elector of Saxony, sought out Luther for spiritual guidance. He petitioned Luther to once again take his pen in hand and provide a message—an "appeal for prayer"—to the German people that God would stem the Turkish tide. Luther responded quickly, writing his *Appeal for Prayer against the Turks*. The pamphlet was extremely popular, going through ten different editions between September 1541 and 1542.[114] The appeal apparently worked, for Suleiman ultimately withdrew his forces from Hungary after hearing that the French had decided to break their alliance with the Ottoman's and that Constantinople was now exposed with its army so far from home.

The *Appeal* provides little further information about Luther's views of the Turks. We find much of the same rhetoric of the *Army Sermon* written twelve years earlier. Luther, once again, focuses primarily upon

---

112. LW 43:238.
113. See Francisco, *Martin Luther and Islam*, 36–38.
114. WA 51:585–625.

the lack of faith and morality among the German people rather than the religious rhetoric of crusade and the "infidel." The aging Luther exerts most of his energy in the *Appeal* by chastising German society for being "ripe and bursting with sin against God."[115] No one is spared from his cantankerous ravings about the state of immorality: "the religious leaders (both Catholic and Reformers alike), "peasants and businessmen . . . nobles, counts, dukes and lords . . . townsmen . . . servants, maids and hired men . . . lawyers . . . The imperial court! . . . I almost forgot to mention the banker . . ."[116] For all have sinned and fallen short!

This is classic Luther. There is a constant railing against sin, the driving toward repentance, and the assurance of forgiveness in the face of a gracious God. After hammering away at the Law, Luther then goes on to provide gracious pastoral resources for a community in anxiety. He outlines a short service as well as Psalm readings for an afflicted people. In the midst of this service we find this repentant prayer:

> Thou, who are a gracious Father to us and a stern Judge over our enemies, take this matter into thy hands. For they are more thine enemies than ours. When they persecute and oppress us, they persecute and oppress thee. . . . The Turk wants to put his Muhammad in the place of thy dear Son, Jesus Christ, for the Turk blasphemes him and asserts that Christ is no true Son of God and that Muhammad is a greater prophet than he. . . . Therefore arise, O Lord God, and sanctify thy name which they desecrate.[117]

After this, recalling some of the venom from the *Army Sermon*, Luther not only sought to bolster the faith of the offending German people, but to demonstrate once again that he does not advocate a fatalistic attitude of God's coming judgment through the Turk. On the contrary, he lays out a justification for taking up arms against the Turks.

> We are not fighting to win land and people, wealth and glory. Nor are we aiming to establish idolatry or extend it. Rather are we fighting to establish God's word and his church. Especially do we fight for our children, for the coming generations. We are fighting that the Turk may not put his devlish filth and the blasphemous Muhammad in the place of our dear Lord, Jesus Christ. That is the real reason and serious purpose for which we now fight, die,

---

115. *LW* 43:221.
116. *LW* 43:220–22.
117. *LW* 43:232–33.

or live. This is most certainly true. Therefore we are fighting a just war against the Turk and are Christ's holy saints and will die a blessed death.[118]

What is very clear in this late writing about Islam is that Luther sees the Turk and his religion as a threat to European life only in so much as European society is a threat to itself. It is a society completely corrupt and in need of rejuvenation. It is only a reformed European Christian society that would be able to "take the rod" out of God's hand and let the Christians face the Turks with clean hearts.

Following the fear of invasion in 1540, and the publication of Bibliander's translation of the Qur'ān in 1541, Luther decided it was time to go back and publish something on the religion of the Turks. It was at this time that he went back to one of his original sources: the Dominican Riccoldo Montecroce. He decided that it was time to translate Montecroce's *Refutation of the Qur'ān* into German, which he did very quickly. He wanted to provide some help for those Germans who would continue to be faced with the Turkish threat, especially for those taken away into captivity. He wanted to provide some kind of manual that would help bolster a Christian's faith when challenged by the tenants of Islam. In the end, Montecroce's apologetic method would be enough for Luther. For Luther, there was no dialogue with Islam, only a necessary knowledge of that which, like the pope's decretals, could subvert the gospel.

Throughout sixteenth century, the Lutheran Reformation in Germany was part of a large international event that involved the principalities of Europe and the Ottoman Empire. Martin Luther was a child of his age and therefore was affected by the social-political atmosphere and the predominant image of the "Terrible Turk." Because of his public pronouncements of God's judgment on Europe, Luther was blamed for the 1526 defeat of Mohacs that opened up Europe to Turkish invasion. He responded to this criticism by writing *On War against the Turk* (1529) and *Preface to "The Tract on Religion and Customs of the Turks"* (1530), as well as publishing his *Army Sermon against the Turk* (1529). It is important to remember that Luther's references to "the Turk" must be viewed within the social-political framework of the Holy Roman Emperor's attempt to stem the tide of the advance of the Ottomans into central Europe, as well as within his overall view of the coming apocalypse. The tales and images

118. *LW* 43:238.

of the "Terrible Turk" were part of the present fear of the world in the early part of the Renaissance, and more importantly, the fear of the wrath of God. The Turk was merely one event that fit into the larger scope of events that were challenging the church and its proper role in the pursuit of encouraging true repentance to Christ.

It was only near the end of his life, however, after he had written his *Appeal for Prayer against the Turk* (1541), that Luther turned toward publishing anything on the religion of the Turks. He returned to sources that he was given very early on in his career, specifically Montecroce's *Confutatio Alcorani*. He translated this into German and added a preface. Although he had always hoped to translate the Qur'ān into German, he never had the time, nor the resources to provide what he felt an accurate translation. Finally in 1542, during the controversy over the publication of a translation of the Qur'ān in Zurich, he did he write a preface to *Bibliander's Translation of the Qur'an* (1543). Overall, the religion of the Turk was nothing more than another human attempt at subverting the message of the gospel, by providing "decretals." The religion of the Turk and his way of life was part and parcel of a larger movement of the world toward the end times that included both Rome and the Holy Roman Empire.

Charles V's agreement with the Lutheran princes at the Diet of Augsburg had as much to do with his attempt to come to some political compromise with the Germans in order to shore up his defenses of the empire against the Turks as it did with the theological propositions of Lutheranism. In the end it was the Protestants who came out of the turbulent sixteenth century in Europe as winners. The threat of Turkish invasions forced Charles V to sue for a compromise with the Lutheran princes. He needed their support and, more importantly, their troops to be able to stem the tide of the advancing Turkish threat. In the words of George Forell, "Although the religious peace of Augsburg cannot be credited to the Turkish threat against the eastern possessions of the Hapsburgs, nevertheless the Ottoman threat . . . influenced the final outcome of the Protestant struggle."[119] From the very beginning, then, Lutheranism had a symbiotic relationship with Islam; the apocalyptic threat of the "Terrible Turk" was seen as part of God's wrath, and Protestant success was owed largely to the reality of that threat.

---

119. Fischer-Galati, "The Turkish Question," 310.

3

The Lutheran Pietists in the Middle East

(Seventeenth–Nineteenth Centuries)

> In truth the dim light of human reason can never guide man through the dark night of ignorance, amid the dense forests of doubt and the deep quagmires of error, so that he may safely reach his goal. The traveller along the narrow way that leads to God can hope to arrive at his rest only through the guidance of the light of the Sun of the Divine Word. And such a Revelation hath God in His mercy bestowed upon the sons of men, that by it they might learn what their reason alone could not discover. And in this Revelation the Most High has declared His Will regarding mankind, and revealed the way of salvation and the means of attaining to the knowledge of the Merciful Creator and eternal bliss. Thanks be to God for His unspeakable gift!
> —Karl Gottlieb Pfander, 1829

LUTHER AND THE EARLY Reformers have often been charged as lacking a theology of mission. Gustav Warneck, the nineteenth century Lutheran missiologist, wrote, "Painful as it is . . . we cannot disguise it—the great reformer's view of the missionary task of the church was essentially defective."[1] The charge that Luther and his associates failed in their evangelical task of being witnesses "to the ends of the earth," however, is to apply post-Reformation expectations regarding Christian missions that simply were not part of the worldview of the early Reformation era. This claim is an unfair assessment, which often applies mission theology of the nineteenth and twentieth centuries that sought to "evangelize the

---

1. Warneck, *Outline of the History of Protestant Mission*, 17. The late David Bosch also noted the indifference of the Reformers to foreign missions (*Transforming Mission*, 243). See also Stolle, *Church Comes from All Nations*; P. Peters, "Fruits of Luther's Mission-Mindedness"; and Valleskey, "Luther's Impact."

world within a generation." James A. Scherer points out that Luther certainly did not have a nineteenth century missiology. He did, however, see the *missio Dei* as an underling factor for all proclamation.

For Luther, the missionary/evangelical task was to overcome the "distortion of the gospel message [that] had led to the degeneration of the mission into ecclesiastical propaganda, forced conversions, crusades, and non-evangelical methods."[2] In addition, the Reformers of the *Augustana* were reared in a European ethnocentric view of Christendom and its subsequent understanding of mission. A predominant missiological view of the day was that the apostles had already fulfilled the Great Commission of Christ in Matthew 28. The world had been successfully evangelized and Europe, the center of the world, was now in the midst of a battle for the revival of Christendom. As the Reformation evolved from theological disputes into separatist "Protestant" communities, Lutheran leaders became "involved in a sheer battle for survival."[3] The sixteenth and seventeenth centuries moved from vitriolic diatribes against the papacy to violent battles between potentates, throughout the Thirty Years War. It was only with the signing of the Peace of Westphalia in 1648 that the religious wars of continental Europe concluded and mission-minded Protestants could think about directing their theological energies in other directions. It is important to remember, however, that the Roman Catholic Church had already had a long tradition of foreign missions by the seventeenth century, especially mission toward the Middle East.

The center of this Protestant missiological debate began just three years after the Peace of Westphalia, when the Lutheran faculty at the University of Wittenberg, the center of Lutheran orthodoxy, declared that only the apostles of Christ were given the command of the Great Commission, and they had successfully completed their mission by going, teaching, and baptizing! Under the agreed blueprint for European society, the peace of Westphalia had declared *cuis regio eus religio*—that it was the responsibility of each sovereign to propagate the gospel in his or her own territories.[4] Thus, the responsibility of preaching the gospel was wholly given over to the reforming potentate in his or her own particular territory and jurisdiction.

---

2. Scherer, *That the Gospel*, 6; see also idem., *Gospel, Church and Kingdom*.
3. Bosch, *Transforming Mission*, 245.
4. Ibid., 251; Mulholland, "From Luther to Carey," 90.

In response to the charge of failing to undertake the Great Commission to "go" outside of their own political boundaries, we must ask, where were the Reformers to direct their mission? In the late medieval worldview, the reign of Christ had been established on earth through the sovereign rule of his duly appointed monarchs—especially the kings of France, Spain, and the Holy Roman Empire. Outside these Christian kingdoms were the realms of Islam; to the East was Suleiman and "the Turk," to the south was the Moor, who had just been removed from the kingdoms of Seville and Granada through the grand Roman Catholic *Reconquista* in 1492. As we have already demonstrated, the predominate method of Christian proclamation to the Orient was through crusade. Although the mendicant orders (the Dominicans and Franciscans, for example) had a history of peaceful missionary enterprises toward Islam, they certainly were a minority. It was Peter the Venerable, who, in his desire to engage in direct dialogue with Muslims, wrote:

> I do not attack you—Muslims—as our people often do, by arms; but by words; not by force, but by reason; not in hatred but in love . . . the sort of love that should exist between those who worship Christ and those who turned away from Him, the sort of love that existed between our Apostles and the Gentiles of their time whom they were trying to draw to the law of Christ . . . In the same way, I, one of the innumerable servants of Christ, and the least of them, I love you; because I love you, I write to you; and since I write to you, I invited you to salvation . . . not a passing salvation, but a lasting salvation; not salvation which will end with this short span of life, but salvation lasting to eternal life.[5]

In addition to Peter, St. Francis (1181–1226) has come to be seen as the most explicit example of loving Christian witness to Islam. The story of Francis's encounter with the Egyptian Sultan Kamil across the front lines at the battle of Damietta in Egypt has become legendary, and the basis for contemporary models of dialogue.[6] Many other Dominicans took up the call to engage in missions across the borders of the medieval period. Armed with their belief in the superiority of the love of Christ, they sought to convince Muslim rulers of the "rationality" of Christianity.[7]

---

5. Gaudeul, *Encounters and Clashes*, 1:57.

6. See Hoeberichts, *Francis and Islam*.

7. One of the most important Dominican missionaries to Islam was certainly Raymond Lull. However, Lull saw military action by Europe as a necessary function to

Thomas Aquinas (1225–74) provided the Dominicans with a manual to help evangelize among Jews and Muslims in Spain and the Middle East: *Summa de veritate catholicae fidei contra gentiles*.[8] The rational arguments about the truth of the Christian faith in Aquinas's work would become the standard Christian apology toward Islam throughout the medieval period, as well as up into the nineteenth century Protestant missionary movement.[9]

By the seventeenth century, however, it was clear to Latin Catholic missions that Muslims were not the only people in need of evangelization. With the discovery of the New World, the Great Commission once again became an important theological concept. In 1622 Pope Gregory XV organized the *Sacred Congregation de propaganda fide*, whose function was to propagate the Christian faith in non-Christian lands. However, for many Protestants of the early Reformation era, the concept of carrying the gospel to the unknown corners of the world had not yet touched the imagination of their late medieval European worldview.

AGE OF DISCOVERY

Luther was only a boy when Christopher Columbus waded ashore on the sands of Hispaniola. With the discovery of the New World by Columbus and Magellan's circumnavigation of the globe, the world suddenly opened up for exploration—and conquest. Spain and Portugal were propelled into an arms race of acquiring new markets and territories to supply raw materials for their own expanding nations in the Americas. Also, by taking advantage of new routes around Africa they sought to bypass the expensive and unpredictable land routes through the Ottoman Empire. It was not until the combined British and Dutch fleet destroyed the Spanish Armada in 1588 that these new worlds were then completely opened to Protestant nations. As the Netherlands, Denmark, and later England began to invest in these foreign markets, the realization that much of the world was un-Christianized became a reality for these Protestant nations. As they colonized lands whose indigenous populations were not members

---

allow missionary endeavors to have a chance. See Zwemer, *Raymond Lull*; and Bonner, *Doctor Illuminatus*.

8. Aquinas, *Summa Contra Gentiles*.
9. See Pfander, *The Mîzânu'l Ḥaqq* ("Balance of Truth").

of any monotheistic faith—neither Jew nor Muslim, the question over the status of their "heathen" souls became an important theological issue.

While the concept of the New World and all of its new possibilities was taking shape in Western Europe at the beginning of the sixteenth century, it had yet to directly affect the Germans. They were far removed from the possibilities of transoceanic travel. The reality of the Age of Discovery was worlds away from the realities of Germany and Eastern Europe, and the concept of preaching the gospel to the pagans was not part of the central European worldview. Here the missionary evangelical mindset would not take root for nearly one hundred years. As we have already noted it was Roman Catholic mission that was directly impacted by the new discoveries in the Western Hemisphere and the expanding markets in the East. While Catholic conquistadors and the Jesuits came into contact with indigenous Americans and East Indians, the Reformers were busy clarifying their own theology through the development of Reformed/Lutheran communities and principalities. Luther and his central and eastern European colleagues lived in a world that was focused on European Christian life. The Reformation was aimed at the transformation of medieval Christian spiritual life and its subsequent communal reform. For all intents and purposes, this was the role of proclamation—true repentance of the individual toward Christ that would affect one's vocation within society, or in the case of Calvinism, would help to bring about a Christian community. For the Reformers, the closest non-Christian community was that of the Turk, and the "Terrible Turk" was beyond the bounds of God's grace.[10]

Luther's particular view of mission to Islam was primarily limited to the concept of providing pastoral support and encouragement to those Christians who found themselves captured and enslaved by the Turks. In his *Army Sermon* he provided helps for those on the frontlines or in the frontier zones who might find themselves taken into captivity. By holding fast to the Christian faith and through memorization of the Lord's Prayer, the Apostles' Creed, and the Ten Commandments, he wrote that

---

10. By the medieval age, Europeans had labeled all Muslims from the East "Sarcacens." This was the Latinized term of the Greek phrase *sara kenoi* utilized by Jerome in the fourth century. For Jerome, this label referred to the casting out of Hagar and Ishmael by Sarah; literally "cast out from Sarah." Thus, the descendents of Ishmael, according to later church fathers, were those "cast out" from God's promises. See Shahîd, *Rome and the Arabs*, 96.

a Christian could provide a witness to the Muslims under whose captivity lived.[11] Because "the Turk" stood as part of the overarching symbol of God's judgment on the world for Luther, there was never the need to develop a concept of missional "going." His apocalyptic views colored his attitude toward world history. The signs of the times clearly pointed toward Christ's imminent return.

EXTRA ECCLESIUM NULLAS SALUS

While the concepts of world evangelization were not a part of the general medieval Christian worldview, there had been scholastic debates regarding the status of those individuals outside the authority of the visible church. St. Augustine's classic work *The City of God* challenged the Western church with the particular problem of how to reconcile personal salvation with a visible connection to the Mother Church. Must one be a member in good standing within the Roman Catholic Church in order to be saved? The official doctrine of the Catholic Church has been summed up in the phrase *extra ecclesium nullas salus* [outside the Church there is no salvation]. In order for a person to be saved by the grace of Christ, he or she must partake of the Church's sacraments and adhere to the authority of its teachings.

By the sixteenth century, the Reformation had raised the theological issue of visible participation in the Catholic Church in a very real and critical way. During the medieval period scholastics had asked questions about the salvation of the great Greek moral philosophers who had lived before Christ but whose lives reflected what they felt to be the moral nature of God. Was it possible, for example, that Socrates or Cicero, who lived exemplary lives, had somehow received God's grace? By the sixteenth century, however, the issue of salvation outside the Church was not simply a theoretical issue about dead philosophers. By then participation in the visible Church was a critical issue, as large segments of Catholic society in Europe had withdrawn themselves from the fold of Rome. The invectives hurled at Luther by Pope Leo in his *Exurge Domine* of 1518

---

11. *WA* 30/2:192-95, 51:62-22; *LW* 43:239. Francisco argues that Christian witness by captives was the motivation for Luther to begin developing a Christian apologetic toward Islam (Francisco, *Martin Luther and Islam*, 9). We would argue, rather, that Luther's purposes were not apologetic but pastoral, equipping fearful Christians with tools necessary for their own faith life in captivity.

ensured that the traditional doctrine remained a solidly accepted Roman Catholic doctrine. If one broke with Rome, there was no salvation.

The Protestants responded to Roman claims of authority by arguing that the medieval church had abandoned its faith in Christ alone and in the Holy Scriptures (*sola fide* and *sola scriptura*) for a faith based upon human traditions and institutions. As the anathemas were being thrown back and forth, the age-old debate about the visible church was *ipso facto* resurrected. The humanist scholar Erasmus, although sympathetic with the Reformers, never broke with Rome. Ultimately, he would argue that "where the soul of Cicero dwells is perhaps not for human judgment to decide."[12] But the discovery of the New World had raised the issue of the status of the newly discovered "pagans." In 1533 Erasmus wrote:

> No one is obliged to know whether this one or that one is a member of the Church. It is enough to believe that there is on earth such a society of those predestined to [eternal] life which Christ by his spirit adhered to himself whether among the Indians, the inhabitants of Cádiz (*Gaditanos* = in general Moors), Hyperboreans, or Africans. It may well be that there are lands somewhere on the earth either islands or continents which have never been discovered by sailors or geographers in which nevertheless the Christian faith might flourish. It is for God alone to examine the recesses of the heart, whence it be that the judgments of many men are uncertain.[13]

By 1530 and the Diet of Augsburg, however, Erasmus had to think not only about the ancient Greeks, but contemporary schismatics who had voluntarily withdrawn themselves from the Roman Catholic Church. These new schismatics would be placed in a similar category with the ancient Orthodox churches which, although grounded in solid Christian tradition, refused to accept the primacy of the bishop of Rome. In addition to these Christians, there were those monotheists—Jews and Muslims—who not only refused to acknowledge the authority of the bishop of Rome, but Jesus Christ himself. Erasmus argued that perhaps the Jew and the Muslim, as monotheists, were participating in a *preparatio evangeli*; that their religion was preparing the way for a later faith in Christ. The categories of communities of the world reflected in Aquinas's

---

12. Williams, "Erasmus and the Reformers," 330.

13. Erasmus *Opera*, vol. 5, col. 1175A, as cited in Williams, "Erasmus and the Reformers," 333.

Contra Gentiles—the Jew, the Saracen, and the Pagan—would resurface in the seventeenth century as the world was confronted by new worlds and new peoples.

HUGO GROTIUS

Suleiman the Magnificent's bid to take Vienna in 1529 was truly the high water mark of the Ottoman Empire's expansion. After Suleiman's reign, the empire would slowly suffer from internal and external threats, ensuring that it would remain mostly on the defensive. From within, the empire suffered a series of breakdowns in the central administration, taxation, and the upheaval of both the professional military corps (*janissaries*) and the professional religious leaders ('*ulemā*'), which led to a continued leadership crisis.[14] From without, the empire was continually faced with European nations that began to develop sophisticated methods of modern warfare. Thus, by the end of the seventeenth century and throughout the beginning of the eighteenth century, the Ottoman Empire suffered a series of severe military failures that would remove the fearful image of the "Terrible Turk" from European imagination. In 1606 the Ottomans signed the treaty of Sitavatarok with the Hapsburgs, accepting a cease-fire in the war in the Balkans.[15] In 1699 the Russian Empire was threatening the Ottoman Empire from the north. With the Treaty of Carlowitz, the Turkish sultan was forced to relinquish Muslim territory to the Russian Christian potentate. And, with the Treaty of Küchük Kaynarja of 1774, the Russians not only mandated that the sultan hand over Ottoman territory, but stipulated that the Russian Orthodox Emperor would then have spiritual authority over all Christians living in the Ottoman Empire (Eastern Orthodox, Oriental Orthodox, and all Catholics of the various rites)!

In 1798, Napoleon's crushing defeat of the Mamluks in Egypt helped to bring about an end to the medieval Ottoman Empire. The death knell of Ottoman imperial power, however, came in 1827, when a combined British, French, and Russian fleet destroyed the Ottoman and Egyptian navy at Navarino Bay. As a result of these dramatic European victories, the empire would begin a series of military, political, and economic reforms to help right itself. Known as the *Tanzīmāt*, these new laws were attempts to help the empire keep pace with a modernizing Europe. The reforms

---

14. See Hourani, *Arabic Thought*, 34–66.
15. Bernard Lewis, *Middle Eas*, 120.

dramatically challenged the Ottoman state, moving it from a medieval empire to a modern nation.[16] Europe, however, had also begun to look upon the empire in a very different way as well.

The French Egyptologists and Orientalists of the *Societé d'Egypte* who accompanied Napoleon on his campaign to Egypt in 1798 began to depict a new illustration of the Middle East. The image of "Terrible Turk" was replaced instead by the portrait of an area of the world that became known as the "Orient," the place of mystery and mystique. Instead of woodcuts depicting slaves being impaled on poles or lead away as captives by "the Turk," the Orientalists began to create captivating portraits of the sultan's harem and the seductive and ancient East. Curiosity now replaced fear.

One individual who was important for the development of a Lutheran Pietist perspective toward Islam in the seventeenth and eighteenth centuries was the Dutch Reformed scholar Hugo Grotius (1583–1645). Often called the "Father of International Law" for his famous work *On the Law of War and Peace* (1625), Grotius almost single-handedly transformed the Protestant view of Islam from that of the religion of the invading "Saracen" to that of an "unreasonable religion." With the threat of Turkish invasion having receded, and with Europe transforming itself from a medieval society on the verge of a cataclysmic collapse toward an enlightened optimism, the continent could now afford to look upon Muslims with different lenses.

Grotius, in his work *The Truth of the Christian Religion* (1627), laid out an argument for how Christianity was the logical religion of the Creator. Writing from Paris, Grotius' work is a classic piece of Western rationalism, fully entrenched in the humanistic views of the developing Enlightenment. Utilizing Aquinas's categories of "pagan," "Jew" and "Mahometan" (Muslim), he stated that God had given each individual human a mind to reason and make rational choices. Some people, however, have a greater ability to make rational choices than others, he argued. Nevertheless, each person had some measure of reason. Thus, because of God's propensity to grant freedom—which is manifest through reason—

---

16. For a thorough review of the *Tanzīmāt* period see Davison, *Reform in the Ottoman Empire*; Hourani, *Arabic Thought*; Lewis, *Emergence of Modern Turkey*; and Ma'oz, *Ottoman Reform*.

it was clear that all other religions and their systems fall short of the ideal of Christianity.[17]

Recognized not only for its inductive quality to educate Christians about the "errors" of other religions, but for its missiological qualities as well, *The Truth of the Christian Religion* became an evangelistic tool. Grotius's ideas were carried to the far-flung corners of the known world. At a time when merchants, soldiers, and civil servants of burgeoning European imperialist machines set off for the "Orient" with copies of Grotius's work aboard their ships, his manual provided arguments for the Christian faith that were utilized by a wide variety of Europeans. The book was translated into numerous European languages from its original Latin, as well as into Turkish by an Englishman living in Turkey who saw the importance of the work as a method of evangelism among Muslims. By 1660, the great Anglican missionary Bishop Pococke had even translated the work into Arabic.[18]

For Grotius, Muslims had risen out of Arabia in the same manner in which the Huns had overrun the Roman Empire. Islam was, then, a religion of the uncivilized and the uncultured. He wrote:

> This religion, which was plainly calculated for bloodshed, delighted much in ceremonies, and would be believed, without allowing liberty to inquire into it: for which reason the vulgar are prohibited reading those books which they account sacred . . . It is true indeed, all men have not alike capacities for understanding everything; many are drawn into error by pride, and others by passion, and some by custom . . .[19]

According to Grotius, Islam was clearly of human devising, built upon "childish rudiments" to which the "perfect law" of Christ comes to supplant.[20] Following the custom of the Dominicans long before him, Grotius then sets out to refute the claims of Islam and argue for its inferiority and its unreasonableness compared to that of the rationality of Christianity. One hundred years after Luther's *On War against the Turk*, Grotius utilized the same medieval Dominican sources. The Latin translation of the

---

17. For an image of the frontispiece of the English edition of Grotius' work, which provides the categories of Christian, Jew, Mohametan, and Pagan, see Ernst *Following Muhammad*, 40–43.

18. Burigny, *Life of the Truly Eminent*, 262.

19. Grotius, *Truth of the Christian Religion*, 235–36.

20. Ibid., 243.

Qur'ān by Montecroce was still the most available copy, and the arguments of Nicholas of Cusa were still widely used. Grotius also utilized the record of Bartholomaeus Georgievicz, a Hungarian captured at the battle of Mohacs in 1526, who provided a first hand account of life under the Turks.

The importance of Grotius' work was not so much for its uniqueness; he did not advance any new critique of Islam that his predecessors had not already put forward. He was clearly knowledgeable of the previous dialogue between Christians and Muslims during the medieval period and raised the same issues put forward by the Dominicans in response to Islam, including the corruption of Christian scripture, the comparison of Jesus and Muhammad, the methods of propagating their respective faiths, the treatment of women, the divinity of Jesus, and finally the "absurd" fables in the Islamic tradition. In fact, his work demonstrates the lack of fresh thinking about Islam during the late medieval period. Yet, *The Truth of the Christian Religion* was important because of its wide circulation and availability. At a time when Europeans were beginning to travel eastward into the lands of the Turk, his manual provided information that was utilized by a wide variety of people. The underlying message was that the Turk and his religion was now no longer something to fear, or that was to bring about the wrath of God. Rather, it was merely one example of the "errors all mankind are prone to fall into."[21] The errors of Islam should be combated not by the sword or crusade, but by providing the clear and reasonable truth of Christianity. However, what is even more important about his work, for the purpose of our narrative, is Grotius's impact on the first Lutheran missionary to the Middle East, Peter Heyling.

PETER HEYLING

As the Thirty Years War raged in Europe during the first half of the seventeenth century, the most immediate danger to Protestant survival was not Islam, but Roman Catholic armies. Peter Heyling grew up in Lübeck, where the Hanseatic League of northern Germany was fully involved in the violence of the Thirty Years War. Heyling proved to be an ardent proponent of Luther and his works. He considered Luther his "spiritual father," and himself to be a messenger of the "Lutheran faith."[22] This con-

---

21. Ibid., 251.
22. Meinardus, "De Petro Heylingo," 145.

text provides us the opportunity to understand Heyling's later missionary impulse. It is quite telling that this first Lutheran missionary to the Middle East directed his energies not toward Islam, but to the Coptic Orthodox Church, in order to warn the Oriental Orthodox Church of the dangers of Roman Catholicism! In fact, Heyling apparently did not seem troubled by Islam at all. Following Grotius's arguments, he saw Islam as an inferior religion that would eventually collapse. Rather, he was more concerned about the "theological errors and corrupt practices of the [Coptic] Monks, especially the invocation of the Saints and the veneration of relics."[23] Thus, debating the dangers of "Popish" ways and refuting the Latin Catholic Capuchin monks who had been attempting to reunify the Coptic Church with Rome took up his energies.[24]

At the age of twenty Heyling left Lübeck to go to Paris to study law. It was here that he came under the influence of Grotius. The two became very close and would continue to exchange correspondence for most of Heyling's life. Under Grotius's tutelage, Heyling and six other colleagues formed an evangelical brotherhood of students who agreed to carry the gospel to the Orthodox churches of the East in order to rejuvenate them with the evangelical faith. Heyling's early biographer tells us that he was the one especially chosen by the group to share the Protestant message in Egypt, while Hieronymus von Dorne was to go to the Greek Orthodox community in Constantinople. The two friends would meet briefly in Jerusalem in 1634. Other than this reference, we know nothing more of the other collaborators.[25]

Heyling left Paris for Alexandria in the spring of 1633. Presumably with letters of introduction, he was accepted into the home of the French

23. Meinardus, "Peter Heyling, History," 310.

24. Under the orders of the *Congregatio de Propagande Fide*, which was organized in 1622, the Capuchin order was "charged to promote the union with Rome of the Oriental Christians (Slavs, Greeks, Syrians, Egyptians, and Abyssinians) [for the purpose of] the foundation of foreign seminaries, the printing of catechisms and similar works in many languages." The Capuchins arrived in 1630 and immediately approached the Coptic monasteries in Wadi Natrun for permission to live among the monks to learn Arabic. By 1741 several bishops of the Coptic Orthodox Church declared their allegiance to the bishop of Rome and formed the Coptic Catholic Church. See Benigni, "Sacred Congregation," n.p.

25 See Michaelis, *Sonderbarer Lebens-Lauff Herrn Peter Heylings, aus Lübec, und dessen Reise nach Ethiopien*. Much information about Heyling is found in Ludolphus, *New History of Ethiopia*; and Wansleben, *Brief Account*. I am deeply grateful to the late Dr. Otto Meinardus for his long conversations with me regarding Peter Heyling, and for sharing all his resources on the matter.

consul general in Alexandria until such a time as he was able to find passage up the Nile to the port of Bulaq at Cairo. Arriving in Cairo, he realized that the only effective way to communicate with the Copts was to learn Arabic. His French host suggested that he petition the monks at the monastery of St. Mecarius in Wadi Natrun, halfway between Alexandria and Cairo, to stay with them in order to learn Arabic. His request was granted. As it turned out, the request was not so unusual, as Latin Catholic missionaries would often request housing at the monasteries. The Franciscans and Capuchins had made it their policy to settle with the monks of Wadi Natrun, to both learn Arabic, either in preparation for their trips to Ethiopia, or to engage the Copts in dialogue about relations with Rome. Since 1630 the Capuchins had been organized in Egypt for the explicit purpose of attempting to reunite the Coptic Orthodox Church with Rome. After Heyling arrived in Wadi Natrun the Capuchin fathers began to see him as a threat. It is at this point that the unfortunate ill will between Lutherans and Catholics of the seventeenth century was brought to the fore. Heyling and the Capuchins, who were under the leadership of the Arabic scholar Agathange de Vendome, became involved in a bitter dispute debating the evils of Protestantism or Catholicism in front of the Copts. (Catholic historical sources claim that the bitter rivalry between Heyling and Agathange ultimately led to Agathange's martyrdom in Ethiopia at Heyling's bidding.)[26]

Heyling spent eighteen months in Wadi Natrun learning Arabic and engaging the Coptic monks in conversations about the "evangelical faith."[27] He returned to Alexandria there to engage in further theological disputations with Orthodox leaders. After befriending the Syrian Orthodox archbishop in Alexandria, Heyling received permission to return to Wadi Natrun to enter the monastery of the Syrians, only a short distance from the monastery of St. Mecarius, this time to learn Syriac. Here he continued to convince the monophysite monks the error of their ways through polite dialogue. He demonstrated that their prayers to the saints and the veneration of relics were unscriptural. According to the late Otto Meinardus, Heyling was always "considerate and moderate with regard

---

26. The sources which detail Heyling's malevolent intentions and "infernal machination" can be found in Wansleben, *Brief Account*; Lequien, *Oriens christianus*; Cocchia, *Storia delle missioni*; Detole, *Etiopia Francescana*; and Hess, "Capuchin Friars Minor."

27. Meinardus, "De Petro Heyling," 143.

to his opponents."²⁸ He became known among the monks as Mu'allim Butros [Peter the Learned].

After five months with the Syrian monks, Peter once again returned to Cairo where he this time befriended the Greek Orthodox leaders to explain the faith of the Augsburg Confession and to demonstrate the error of "Catholic heresies." Heyling then received permission to travel to Jerusalem with a caravan of Coptic and Syrian monks in order to meet with his old friend Hieronymus von Dorne, who had been working in Constantinople. Upon arriving in Jerusalem, Heyling visited the Coptic Orthodox archbishop in Jerusalem. He was then granted permission to spend eight days inside the Church of the Holy Sepulcher; probably the only Protestant ever to be given this opportunity by an Orthodox prelate!

In 1634 the new Ethiopian emperor Fasilides sent an embassy to Alexandria petitioning the Coptic patriarch to send a bishop to consecrate a new patriarch of Ethiopia as the previous one who had passed away.²⁹ This was a devastating event for Latin Catholic missions, as Fasilides's Father Susenyus had opened Ethiopia up to the Jesuits and had actually accepted the primacy of the bishop of Rome. Fasilides, however, had now reversed this policy and ordered all Roman Catholic missionaries out of the country. Both Heyling and Agathangelos, the head of the Capuchin order in Egypt, saw the need for a new Ethiopian patriarch as an opportunity to directly impact the confessional views of a whole nation. After several attempts to consecrate a new patriarch for Ethiopia, Agathangelos appealed to the Coptic patriarch Matthew III to consecrate Abba Markos, a friend of the Capuchins, and send him to take up the Episcopal seat.

However, Heyling, having once again received permission to travel, this time to Ethiopia, journeyed with the newly consecrated Abba Markos, patriarch of the Ethiopian Orthodox Church. By the time that Markos arrived in Ethiopia and had taken up his duties his view of Roman Catholicism, the Jesuits, and the Capuchins had been radically changed. In 1638 he had all Roman Catholic missionaries expelled or killed. We can only imagine that Heyling had something to do with Markos's changing

---

28. Meinardus, "Peter Heyling, History," 306. Meinardus notes that Heyling is the last European to record the actual presence of Syrian monks living at Deir al-Surian.

29. Since the sixth century, the Ethiopian Orthodox Church has taken its authority from the Patriarch of Alexandria, and considers itself to be in direct episcopal succession from St. Mark. Thus, the Ethiopian patriarch was usually chosen and consecrated by the successor to Mark in Alexandria.

views and the expulsion of the Catholic missionaries. It is also likely, however, that Emperor Fasilides, who had already been predisposed against the Catholic orders, was a main source of the persecution. Another Lutheran, Johan Michael Wansleben, had followed Heyling to Egypt with the intention of making it all the way to Ethiopia in order to evangelize among the Orthodox. However, at some point during his travels in Egypt he recanted of his reformed faith and became a Dominican. He accused Heyling of inciting Fasilides against the Catholic priests and charged Heyling with the responsibility of their martyrdom![30] Later Catholic records would also charge Heyling with the responsibility of the martyrdom of Agathangelos, who traveled to Ethiopia in 1638 to bring the Ethiopians back within the Roman fold.

After his arrival in Ethiopia with Bishop Markos, Heyling received a warm reception in Ethiopia, so much so that he remained in Ethiopia for seventeen years. He even married the daughter of Emperor Fasilides. Numerous historical sources give a positive record of Heyling's witness there, being recognized for living "a studious and solitary life," and for translating the New Testament into Amharic, a copy of which Samuel Gobat (who will be introduced to below) would later read.[31]

In 1656 Heyling received permission to travel back to Cairo from Fasilides. Passing through Suakin, Heyling was forced to stop and present himself to the Turkish governor. Upon meeting Heyling, the governor was not pleased with the missionary's status and wealth. (After seventeen years at the court of the emperor he had apparently become quite well off, which was the source of many accusations against him by the Catholic missionaries.) According to the story as it was heard by the Coptic monks in Cairo, the governor demanded that Heyling either submit to Islam or be killed. He answered: "I will never surrender my faith. Do with me as you will." Heyling was then martyred.

Peter Heyling's story is also a stark reminder that Catholic-Lutheran theological disagreements during the seventeenth century carried over into the Middle East. Roman Catholic historical records are not kind to Heyling. They are all unanimous that Heyling posed a physical danger to the Capuchin work in Egypt, and ultimately the status of Catholicism in Ethiopia. Other sources however, (including some Roman Catholic

---

30. Meinardus, "Peter Heyling, History," 314.
31. Ibid., 314–15; see 323 for a detailed list of historical references.

records) do speak highly of Heyling's learning and disposition in witnessing to the gospel. It is hard to imagine that a foreigner in Egypt or Ethiopia in the seventeenth century, raising questions about the traditions and practices of the ancient churches, would not either be quickly expelled or worse by the religious leaders or the Turkish governors acting at the bequest of the patriarchs. The fact that Heyling managed to ingratiate himself with the Coptic bishops, the Syrian, Greek Orthodox, and Ethiopian patriarchs, as well the monks with whom he lived, speaks well of both his ability to engage the Orthodox as well as to speak in a "considerate and moderate" manner in his theological dialogues. Thus, we can conclude that he was able to both assimilate into the local culture and to communicate himself effectively. Because of this, it is easy to imagine why the Capuchins would have seen Heyling as such a threat to their own missionary goals. Heyling's desire to witness to the evangelical faith among the Copts, Syrians, and Ethiopians was sidetracked by these Catholic-Lutheran struggles. Unfortunately, this would not be the last time Lutherans would become sidetracked by inter-denominational squabbles in the Middle East.

LUTHERAN SCHOLASTICISM, PIETISM, AND FOREIGN MISSIONS

The seventeenth and eighteenth centuries witnessed the rise of the Pietist movement among the Reformed and Lutheran communities in Europe. Pietism would come to have a huge impact not only on Lutheran missions in general, but on Lutheran missions in the Middle East in particular. Although the first missionaries sent out by the Lutheran church were attached to the state-church missions of Sweden (to the Laplanders) and Denmark (to Tranquebar in India), it was the Lutheran Pietists, working outside of the state church structures, who filled the needs of many of the early Anglican and Reformed mission societies—especially those that worked in the Middle East. There are at least three reasons why the Pietist movement proved a strong advocate and participant in global missions.

First and foremost, the Pietists reacted strongly against firmly rooted German scholasticism. Jacob Spener and Auguste Francke focused on individual conversion and "heartfelt" repentance in daily life, not simply orthodox belief.[32] This focus naturally lent itself to an active interest in

---

32. Cracknell, *Justice, Courtesy and Love*, 27.

mission, whereupon Pietists understood an active and external faith as part of one's life of sanctification. In many cases this active faith led one to journey abroad to share the good news. The proponents of scholasticism, on the other hand, were rather skeptical about "enthusiasts" who were interested in engaging in acts of conversion. Philip Nicolai (1556–1608), one of the most prominent early Lutherans to struggle with the issue of mission, stressed that it is God who undertakes mission (i.e., the *missio Dei*) and that, if we might paraphrase his views, "if God had wanted us to preach to the heathen he would have put us there!" Following the position of the faculty of Wittenberg, he held strongly to Luther's concept of vocation and argued that the duty and responsibility of Christians is to serve the neighborhoods in which they are found. There was no need to travel to the far corners of the unknown world.[33] God had already provided a mission for each Christian in his or her own community. For this reason Nicolai was a proponent of establishing relations with Eastern and Oriental Christians for the purpose of strengthening their Christian witness to the Turk.[34] In his view, God had placed the Eastern and Oriental Orthodox churches in their own context for that very task. Why not then accompany them in their mission? On the other hand, John Konrad Dannhauer (1603–66), a colleague of Nicolai's and a professor in Strassbourg, under whom Spener was taught, saw the importance of a training college of the church so that missionaries could be sent to the East to evangelize among the Turks and the Jews.

The most radical of detractors of global mission among the scholastic Lutherans, however, was John Ursinus, who argued that "God has not left himself without a witness" in any nation. If those nations had not already converted to Christianity it was because they had refused God's grace, were not capable of understanding God's message, or were not capable of rational choices.[35] This argument would become a mainstream missiological idea throughout the eighteenth and nineteenth centuries as the concept of mission as *civilatrice* (that is, the bringing civilization to the heathens) gained ground, especially in North America among those mission societies working among the Native Americans.

---

33. Bosch, *Transforming Mission*, 250.
34. Contra Bosch, *Transforming Mission*, 250.
35. Laury, *History of Lutheran Missions*, 33–34.

A second reason for the Pietists striking out on their own mission activities was due to their distrust of churchly order and institution. The scholars from the various Lutheran universities insisted that if there were to be any global mission of the evangelical church then it must be done according to good order. The Pietists insisted that, on the contrary, missions should have nothing to do with church order, as this would only create administrative nightmares and get bogged down in state politics. The scholastic Lutherans would also insist that missionaries be properly trained, which meant they had attend formal studies, and be duly ordained. In fact, some orthodox Lutherans called the early Lutheran Pietist missionaries sent out to India "false prophets" because they had not received a proper and duly recognized call from the church.[36] The Pietists were more prone to accepting fully committed laypersons with a passion for mission work than clergyman infected with the straightjacket of orthodoxy. (These various perspectives on mission continue to trouble the policy of all Protestant mission agencies.)

A third reason for the development of independent pietistic mission programs was the reaction to the constraints of the state church itself. The faculties of the traditional bastions of Lutheran orthodoxy, the University of Wittenberg in particular, had firmly stated it was the state's responsibility to provide for the preaching of the Word.[37] Therefore, according to official policy it was the state administrators' responsibility to make allowance for the proclamation of the gospel. As Protestant nations began to colonize the world, colonial administrators were then responsible for the oversight of the gospel among the "heathen." In reality, very few Lutheran kingdoms or principalities set aside funds or personnel for mission outside of their own particular territory. Duke Ernest the Pious of Gotha (1640–75), however, urged his fellow nobleman to take up the responsibility of foreign missions, to the East in particular. He wrote, "Those supreme governments and municipalities, which have the means and opportunity to bring the Christian doctrine by honorable, sacred and justified means into such lands, make themselves guilty when they refrain from doing this."[38] Gotha took this responsibility seriously and sent out two individuals to the East: Paul Flemming to Persia, and John Wansleben to Egypt

---

36. Warneck, *Outline*, 44.
37. Bosch, *Transforming Mission*, 251.
38. P. Peters, "Fruits of Luther's Mission-Mindedness."

(whom we have already met above). Other than Gotha, the German territories, however, had no existing unit for extending the church abroad.

Another German noble interested in mission beyond the bounds of the home territory—specifically to the East—was Baron Justinian Ernest von Welz (1621–68). In 1664 he wrote *A Christian and True-Hearted Exhortation to All Right-Believing Christians of the Augsburg Confession*. He also wrote *An invitation to the Approaching Great Communion, and a Proposal for a Jesus-Society of Christian Edification*. In these pamphlets he encouraged the German nobility to found a *collegium de propaganda fide* for the purpose of mission work in the Orient. He desired to instruct students in Eastern languages, the study of ecclesiastical history and the lives of the early church fathers, and methods of mission. The scholasticism common throughout German Lutheranism, however, created an institutional barrier prohibiting the growth of interest in foreign missions. Disappointed, he took matters into his own hands. He then went himself to Dutch Guiana as a missionary, where he quickly succumbed to illness and died.[39]

Denmark, on the other hand, had acquired territory in the East and West Indies during the seventeenth century. Under the leadership of King Frederick IV (1671–1730), a formal state missionary endeavor was undertaken in India. Two students of the Danish-Halle missionary school, Bartholomew Ziegenbalg and Heinrich Pluetschau, were enlisted and ordained by the state church of Denmark to carry the gospel to the Hindu Tamils and Muslims of India. They arrived at Tranquebar on July 9, 1706 and thus became the first Lutheran missionaries of a formal Lutheran mission. The Tranquebar missionary post was the mother of all Lutheran missionary endeavors, and functioned until 1808 when the British gained control of India. From 1808 until 1837 the mission struggled, as it was forced to work under the oversight of the Anglican church. In 1837 the Danish Lutherans turned over their properties to the Evangelical Lutheran Missionary Society of Dresden.[40]

Thus, the Pietists, driven by their own individual sense of responsibility, took up the call for foreign missions. Augustus Herman Francke, the friend and colleague of Spener, called for the development of a seminary of missions at Halle that would include an "Oriental college" to focus

---

39. Warneck, *Outline*, 25–27.
40. Laury, *History of Lutheran Missions*, 38–64.

on "awakening of the Greek and Eastern churches."[41] A number of individuals would be sent out through this college to work in Russia and the Caucasus among the Orthodox churches. It is to Auguste Francke and his work to which we now turn.

HALLE AND BASEL MISSIONS

Auguste Francke, one of the early Pietists and a professor at the University of Halle, secured the support of King Frederick IV to establish a mission institute. The King was a proponent of Christian mission abroad and thus supported evangelistic endeavors in the Danish territories. Francke was firmly convinced that the state church should not have any direct involvement in the work of missions, having a great distrust for church bureaucracy and state institutions. However, he did have to make some concessions to the king. The first missionaries of Halle were to be ordained under the orders of the Danish Lutheran church and its crown. After Ziegenbalg and Pluetschau had been sent out to India, Halle began training missionaries to go off into territories outside of the authority of the Danish crown, under the auspices of other Protestant mission agencies. This mission school would function for 130 years before it surrendered its property and holdings to the Leipzig Missionary Society in 1840. Between 1821 and 1840, however, the Halle institute functioned in coordination with another ecumenical missionary training center, the Basel Missionary Society in Basel, Switzerland.

Organized in 1815 by C. G. Blumhardt, the missionary training center at Basel would ultimately eclipse Halle as the premiere missionary training center for Lutheran and Reformed Pietists. The fact that the center drew its support from a variety of Protestant groups from Austria, England, Germany, and Switzerland, and had no formal ecclesiastical tie with any one church body, proved agreeable to the Pietists. In fact, many of the graduates of Basel from Lutheran backgrounds, reared in churches that accepted the Augsburg Confession, would go on to work under the auspices of the Church Mission Society, traditionally the low-church branch of the Church of England.[42]

After providing missionaries to fill the ranks of various mission organizations for several years, the Basel Mission felt confident enough to

---

41. Warneck, *Outline*, 43.
42. See Jenkins, "Church Missionary Society"; and Railton, *No North Sea*.

send out missionaries on its own accord. In 1820 a delegation of Swabian German immigrants in the Trans-Caucasus area of Tiflis approached Blumhardt about sending some missionaries to provide spiritual care for their colony. The Swabians were originally from Württemberg, a section of the Germany that was heavily influenced by Lutheran Pietism, and were, thus, aware of the work of the Basel Mission.[43] Blumhardt saw this as an opportunity to approach the Eastern Orthodox and Armenian churches as well as the Muslims of northern Persia. He saw this as a strategic opportunity to enter the region.[44]

The mission to the Swabians initially received support from the Russian emperor Alexander I. They were given, however, strict guidelines on what they could and could not do by the Russian Orthodox sovereign. It was understood that their primary task was to serve as chaplains to the German immigrant community. If they were to succeed in converting Muslims in the area, however, those Muslims would have to resettle in the Swabian communities and not mix with the Eastern or Oriental Orthodox. Proselytizing among the Russian Orthodox was, of course, off limits.

The first two graduates of Basel given this task in the East were A. H. Dietrich and Felician Zaremba. Zaremba, a young Polish nobleman, had given up his family title and fortune after his conversion experience and came to Basel in order to serve as a missionary. He was very knowledgeable of the Russian Empire and Blumhardt saw him as the perfect choice for this particular mission. His easy-going personality helped him to engage with the Armenians and Muslims. It is primarily a tribute to him and his abilities that the Trans-Caucasus mission was very successful. Shortly after commencing their work they were soon joined by a third, Johann Jacob Lang.

The missionaries began by utilizing the two great legacies of Luther—education and translation of the Scriptures into the vernacular. The Lutherans first set about opening schools in order to teach their communities to read. New converts learned to read the catechism first, and then the Bible. In translating the Bible, Dietrich and Zaremba's first task was to utilize translations of the Tartar and Armenian languages already developed by the Russian Bible Society (which had been organized in 1813). Zaremba also initiated a translation of the New Testament into

---

43. Jenkins, "Villagers as Missionaries."
44. Richter, *History of Protestant Missions*, 97.

Azerbaijani. The Lutherans worked for thirteen years before their mission became to be seen as a threat to the Orthodox community. It was then that the Czar closed them down and removed them from the Empire.

ZINZENDORF AND THE MORAVIANS[45]

One individual who was profoundly affected by Spener and Francke, and who influenced Protestant mission to the Middle East, was Nicolas Ludwig von Zinzendorf. His ideals and beliefs were instilled into a community of Protestants that took up the challenge toward foreign mission, including mission in the Middle East. It is important to briefly mention his background in order to demonstrate how his vision of Christian witness would be played out in the Middle East.

Zinzendorf was from Saxony and was sent as a young boy to Halle in order to study under Auguste Francke. Although deeply affected by Francke and the Pietist movement, he left Halle when he was sixteen to continue his higher studies among the Orthodox Lutherans at Wittenberg. The theological atmosphere could not have been more different than at Halle! The scholasticism of Wittenberg was strange to him, compared to the personalized spirituality at Halle. Zinzendorf found himself alone in his defense of Pietism, and his experience undoubtedly helped him to solidify his beliefs in response to the theological views he encountered at the university. After his education at Wittenberg he took a trip to France where he was shocked by both the atheistic tendencies of the Enlightenment thinkers and the loose morality of society, especially among the religious leaders. By the time he returned to his home in Saxony, Zinzendorf was thoroughly convinced for the need of an active faith grounded in a simple life of work, prayer, Bible reading, and public witness.

In 1722 Zinzendorf provided hospitality to a group of Hussite refugees fleeing Catholic persecution. He allowed them to stay on his estate in an area that came to be known as "Herrnhut." Because of his hospitality Zinzendorf garnered the reputation of providing a safe haven for theological dissenters and heterodox communities. Over time, more dissenters arrived at Herrnutt. It was in this context that he began to help shape a pietistic community that did not force adherence to any one set of Protestant theological doctrines (Lutheran, Reformed, or Anabaptist),

---

45. See Thompson, *Moravian Missions*; Kinkel, *It Started with Zinzendorf*; and Schattschneider, "Pioneers in Mission."

or the submission to any religious institution, but held only one thing in common: simple faith and unity in Jesus Christ. From this community Zinzendorf created the one of the most active Protestant missionary movements ever, the Moravians. Moravian missionaries would be sent out all over the world with a simple message in the salvation of Jesus Christ, a handful of whom them made their way to the Middle East.

In 1740 Arvid Gradin, a Swede, was sent to Constantinople and spent four months there meeting Muslims and attending prayers in the mosque.[46] He was politely received by the Greek Orthodox patriarch who declined to get too involved with the Moravian lest he upset the delicate relationship between the Roman Catholics and the Russian government. The Roman Catholics were seeking a bid at that time from the Russian emperor to serve as a channel for all Orthodox initiatives in the Ottoman Empire. Gradin, perhaps frustrated with the politics and complexities of the religious communities, eventually returned home.[47]

Two Moravian doctors, Frederick William Hocker and Rüffer, went to Persia in 1747 to minister to the descendents of the "wise men from the East," the magi of Matthew 2. Their three-year sojourn was beset with constant troubles and upheaval. At this time the Safavid empire was in its last days and Afghani tribesmen were overrunning Persia. For their own safety the two were forced to return back to Germany. Hocker would later return to the Middle East in 1752. Gralisch and Gruhl, who spent some time with the Tartar tribes in the Caucasus, undertook a similar mission. They did not stay long, however, given the difficulty of life in a tightly knit Tartar society.

Between 1752 and 1783 the Moravians came to Egypt to engage the Copts. Their mission was simple: settle among the Egyptians, provide for their own livelihood by their own skills (i.e., tent-making ministry), and witness to the Christian faith through a simple lifestyle. John Henry Danke came in 1753 to work as a carpenter. He presented his credentials to the Coptic patriarch Markos VII (1745–69) and was allowed to live and work in al-Bahnaa outside of Cairo. He remained there until 1761 when he returned home.

William Hocker, who had already attempted a mission in Persia, returned to the Middle East a second time this time to Egypt in 1752. A

46. Hutton, "Moravian Missions to Moslems," 126.

47. Hamilton, *History of the Mission*, 32, as cited in Shelley, "Beginnings of Protestant Missionary Activity," 4.

theology student, George Pilder, accompanied him. Their ultimate goal was to travel from Egypt to Abyssinia, just as Peter Heyling had, but they suffered a shipwreck en route. Eventually both made it back to Europe. These events would not deter Hocker, however. He came back to Egypt a third time in 1768; this time with John Antes, a watchmaker. They began their ministry in Cairo in and worked for fifteen years before they were forced to leave due to political instability of the late Mamluk period.

Whenever the Moravian missionaries set out for their respective fields, they were given guidelines for their work with the Oriental Christians:

> [They were] not to interfere with the ecclesiastical relations of the native Christians, nor to enter into discussion of polemical subjects; but in all their intercourse to endeavour to direct attention to the essence of Christianity, and to impart advice to such as listened to them according to the Scriptures and their own experience; and teach them how, by means of Jesus' merits, they might obtain rest for their souls, true holiness of life, and evangelical liberty, which leave the conscience unfettered by human tradition.[48]

Although not confessional Lutherans, the Moravians did accept the teachings of Luther and accepted the authority of the Augsburg Confession, albeit not exclusively. Ultimately they were not interested in the wholesale conversion of Orthodox, Jewish or Muslim communities. In fact, their Pietism dictated that they focus on individual encounters that would allow the Spirit to work in its own manner.[49] In the words of missiologist Kenneth Scott Latourette, "The Moravians never sought to bring all other Christians into their Church . . . [T]hey wished to be a leavening and transforming influence in other communions."[50] This simple method was well suited to the Middle East where strong communal identity creates a difficult atmosphere for public evangelism, which is often interpreted as an attack on any one specific community being targeted.

The Pietist tradition has often seen the hand of God at work outside of the institutional church. As the state churches of Europe struggled to come up with both theological and ecclesiastical methods for conducting mission in either newly formed colonies, or in territories outside of

---

48. Watson, *American Mission in Egypt*, 30–31. See also Hutton, "Moravian Missions."

49. Bosch, *Transforming Mission*, 253.

50. Latourette, *History of the Expansion of Christianity*, 3:48.

their sovereign jurisdiction, the Pietists were free from institutional entanglements to engage "the Jew, Turk, and pagan." With the dawn of the eighteenth century, however, European churches would begin forming independent mission agencies to undertake foreign missions. Lutheran and Reformed Pietists graduating from both the Halle and Basel training centers were eager candidates to serve in these new societies.

EARLY PROTESTANT MISSION SOCIETIES TO THE MIDDLE EAST[51]

During the eighteenth century England experienced a spiritual revival movement, which has come to be known as the Great Awakening. This religious resurgence within British society led to the development of numerous English mission societies, for the purpose of both domestic and foreign mission work. Several of these foreign mission societies were organized by Anglicans primarily for the purpose of the distribution of Christian literature and the Bible in the newly forming North American colonies; among them were the Society for the Propagation for Christian Knowledge (1699) and the Society for the Propagation of the Gospel (1701). These societies were instilled with a positive vision of the New World and motivated by new opportunities to preach the gospel to the Native Americans. The biography of the great missionary to the Delaware Indians, David Brainerd, written by Jonathan Edwards (1703–58), a prominent leader of the Great Awakening in America, spurred on the work of the SPCK and SPG.

However, it was the Baptists, dissenters from the Anglican church, who were actually the first to form their own organized mission society, the Baptist Society for the Propagation of the Gospel amongst Heathen (1792), for the purpose of sending missionaries. William Carey, often credited as beginning the modern era of missions, wrote *An Enquiry into the Obligations of Christians to Use Means for the Conversion of the Heathens* in 1786. Carey's work prompted a vast array of individuals moved by the Great Awakening to take up the cause of foreign missions and reopen the long-standing debate over the responsibilities of the church in fulfilling the Great Commission. A number of Anglican mission societies followed the Baptists' lead and drank from the well of spiritual revival;

---

51. For an excellent and brief summary of the development of Protestant missions to the Middle East, see Vander Werff, *Christian Mission to Muslims*, 97–183.

including the London Missionary Society (1795) and Church Missionary Society (1799), as well as the London Society for the Promoting of the Gospel amongst the Jews (LSPGJ, 1809), which began work among Jewish Egyptians in Alexandria. They were all organized as voluntary associations within the community of the Church of England. Each society organized its own funding and developed its own programs to send missionaries to the new worlds that were opening up due to the developments in technology and sea travel.[52]

The Scottish Presbyterians followed suit with their own independent societies as well. The Edinburgh and Glasgow Missionary Societies began work in 1796. These societies would ultimately unite to form the Church of Scotland Mission Society in 1835. The Scots began their work in the Middle East, however, like the Anglicans, not in an effort to convert Muslims but to convert the Jews. Scottish communities contributed heavily for the work of the LSPGJ and the London Jewish Society (LJS), organized in 1809 and 1820, respectively. The first LJS missionary to the Middle East was a German Jewish convert to Christianity, Joseph Wolf from Bavaria. Unlike the Moravian missionaries who settled in one locale, Wolf was a peripatetic, journeying throughout North Africa and the Middle East from 1821 to 1827; including Gibraltar, Alexandria, Cairo, the Sinai, Jerusalem, Beirut, Damascus, Aleppo, Baghdad, Irbil, and Busra.[53]

Lutheran Mission societies followed this interest in mission to the Jewish community as well. In fact, the first exclusively German mission societies were aimed at the Jewish communities in Europe. In 1835, The Society of Israel's Friends was created in Strasbourg, followed in 1836 by the Society for the Christian Care of the Jewish Proselytes in Berlin. By 1844 the Scandinavian Lutherans also began creating their own missions to the Jews. The Norwegians organized the Jewish Missionary Association in Stavanger, the Finns began the Jewish Missions of the Finish Missionary Society (which would become very active in Jerusalem), the Swedes the Society for Missions to Israel in Stockholm, and the Danes the Danish Lutheran Society for Missions to Israel, in 1844, 1863, 1876, and 1885, respectively. The LCMS would become the first American Lutheran synod to begin working among the Jews in its own country in 1881.[54]

52. For a thorough review of the history of these movements see Stock, *History of the Church Missionary Society*, vol. 1.

53. Gidney, *History of the London Society*, 101–11.

54. Lohse gives quite an extensive list of these societies in *Martin Luther*, 86–92.

A prominent figurehead of this movement of mission to the Jews among the Lutherans was Franz Delitzsch (1813–90), professor of Old Testament studies in Erlangen and Leipzig. He is most noted for his translation of the New Testament into Hebrew, primarily as a tool for evangelization among the Jews. In 1886 he revived the *Institutum Judaicum* in Leipzig. Originally founded in 1694 by John Henry Callenberg at Halle, its primary purpose was to train missionaries to convert the Jews. (The institute still functions today, now as a center for Judaic studies at Münster University and renamed the *Institutum Judaicum Delitzschianum*.)[55] In the same year that Delitzsch founded his *Institutum* in Leipzig, Hermann Stack, professor of theology, founded a similar institute in Berlin.[56]

What is intriguing about this interest in mission to the Jews is that although these societies saw the conversion of the Jewish people as an important ministry, and in some cases a necessary precursor to the second coming of Christ, they did not develop or absorb any European anti-Semitic theology. Unlike much of mainstream Western Christian anti-Semitism that claimed that Christ's death was on Jewish hands (Matt 27:25), these missionaries were quite to the contrary. In fact, many of the societies became involved in assisting Jewish families fleeing Europe from violent pogroms. By the late nineteenth century, many of the societies became involved in supporting political Zionism, and the relocation of Jews to Palestine. They saw the development of such a movement as the fulfillment of biblical prophecy. After the Six Day War of 1967, this stream of piety would evolve into a "Christian Zionism," which argues that supporting the modern day state of Israel is a Christian requirement, necessary in order to help bring about the second coming of Christ, and ultimately, the conversion of the Jewish people.[57]

The first European Protestant missionary to engage Muslims in the Middle East, however, was Henry Martyn (1781–1812). Officially a chaplain of the British East India Company, he was employed to serve British Christians living and working for the company in Calcutta. Martyn, however, not content with chaplaincy work, desired to engage Muslims. He

---

55. Lose, *Lutheran Foreign Mission*, 86. See the Institutum Judaicum Delitzschianum Website: http://egora.uni-muenster.de/ijd.

56. Gidney, *History of the London Society*, 434.

57. There is a growing abundance of works on Christian Zionism. See Merkley, *Politics of Christian Zionism*; Prior, *Christian Zionism*; Ruether and Ruether, *Wrath of Jonah*; and Sizer, *Christian Zionism*.

struck out on his own, heading to Persia where he engaged local Muslim leaders in apologetic dialogues before his untimely death at the age of only thirty.[58] Martyn's role in the development of Protestant mission to Islam is pivotal. He has been idealized and seen as the father of both Christian apologetic and dialogical models by both conservative and liberal missionary agencies to this day.[59]

Yet, it was William Jowett of the CMS who was the first missionary sent by a Protestant missionary agency to the Middle East for the explicit purpose of evangelizing among the indigenous population. He was sent under orders to research the feasibility of "the diffusion of Christian truth among Jews, Mahometans and pagans."[60] Jowett, who spent five years traveling the Middle East in order to determine the best location for a Protestant mission, ultimately settled in Malta where a printing press was established for the distribution of Christian literature. After he settled there in 1815 and sent back reliable information to the CMS board regarding the feasibility of opening up other mission posts, the CMS began sending personnel to Syra, Smyrna, and later Cairo. Because of Jowett's primary role, all other mission agencies would follow in his footsteps, heeding his advice and counsel, specifically the American Congregationalists and Presbyterians. Much more will be said of British missions in the Middle East in the next chapter. However, at this point it is sufficient to note the debt to which the early American missionary enterprise paid to the Anglicans, and especially to those Lutherans serving with the CMS and other mission societies.

Americans, moved by the evangelical preaching of Jonathan Edwards, began founding their own mission societies in the eighteenth century. As a result of North American evangelicalism in New England, the New York Missionary Society, the Massachusetts Missionary Society and the Connecticut Missionary Society were all formed to propagate the gospel to the whole world, while the Female Society for Promoting Christianity amongst the Jews followed the lead of its European counterparts. The largest of American missionary agencies, however, was the

---

58. See Padwick, *Henry Martyn*; and Vander Werff, *Christian Mission to Muslims*, 30–36.

59. For background of the history of the Henry Martyn Institute in Hyderbad, India and its transformation from a missionary training center to an institute for inter-faith dialogue, see D. D'Souza, "Evangelism, Dialogue, Reconciliation."

60. Tibawi, *British Interests in Palestine*, 12.

American Board of Commissioners for Foreign Missions (ABCFM), an ecumenical missionary society made up of Congregational, Presbyterian and Reformed congregations that came into existence in 1812. One of the earliest projects of the ABCFM was the desire to send missionaries to the Middle East and to "occupy" Jerusalem.

In his sermon delivered at the occasion of his departure to Palestine, Pliny Fisk clearly laid out the society's goals for the mission:

> Let the Mohammedans of Judea embrace Christianity, and they would with great ease diffuse it through the surrounding Mohammedan countries. Let the Jews of Judea embrace the Messiah, and they would with ease and efficacy make knowne to their brethren everywhere, that they had found Him of whom Moses in the law, and the Prophets did write. Let the Catholics of Judea learn the simplicity of the Gospel, and instead of rehearsing useless and unfounded traditions to pilgrims, who visit the church of the holy sepulcher, they will tell them the affecting story of the Savior's death; explain its design and efficacy; and send them away not laden with relic, and filled with superstitions, but melted to penitence, and excited to gratitude and obedience. Let the Greek and Armenian Christians add to what they now have of the true religion, such doctrines and feelings, as we may hope they will receive from reading the Bible, and hearing the Gospel.[61]

Levi Parsons and Pliny Fisk set out from Massachusetts in 1819 to ascertain the possibilities of American Protestant missions in Jerusalem, as it was "the centre of the world" for Jews and Christians, and as such deserved their best attempts.[62] After a brief meeting with the CMS missionary William Jowett in Malta, it was deemed unwise to focus on Jerusalem, as it was considered unsafe for foreigners and would be a difficult station to maintain. Jerusalem at the time was a small Turkish garrison. It had no easy access for supplies and had no foreign consulate for protection. Thus, they settled on opening a mission post in Smyrna. Smyrna, which had been a base of operations for American and British merchants, was well suited for receiving supplies and had a suitable infrastructure.

In 1820 the Greek War of Independence broke out, forcing Parsons and Fisk to abandon Smyrna and relocate to Malta and then, ultimately, to Beirut. Beirut, as a growing port city, became an ideal location for the

---

61. Davis, *Holy Land Missions and Missionaries*, 30.
62. Tibawi, *American Interests in Syria*, 21.

development of the earliest Western Protestant missionary accomplishments. Supported by the missiological concepts of Rufus Anderson, the director of the ABCFM, the Americans began setting up schools in order to help teach the Arabs and Armenians to read the Scriptures in their own languages. One of the most important enterprises was a new translation of the Bible into Arabic, begun under the direction of Eli Smith together with the Syrian Butrus al-Bustani and finally accomplished in 1865 by Cornelius Van Dyck. (The Van Dyck translation is still utilized today and considered the *textus receptus* of the Arab Protestant church today.)

This publication of the Van Dyck Bible is indicative of the Americans' overall strategy and view of mission. Salvation through Christ was only possible when one was able to ascertain the truths of Scripture by reading it and then pondering the power of the grace of God. The Americans did not, however, carry with them only a religious message of salvation, but particular American ideals of individual freedom and progress. In the words of the primary architect of the ABCFM's policy, Rufus Anderson, "Protestant ideas of truth, of liberty, of conscience, of progress, are spread far and wide, and are convulsing these nations."[63] American cultural perspectives would, naturally, color how the missionaries perceived Jews, Christians, and Muslims in the East. In deciding to open up a mission in the Middle East, the board noted in their minutes:

> In Palestine, Syria, the Provinces of Asia Minor, Armenia, Georgia and Persia, though Mohammedan countries, there are many thousand Jews, and many thousands of Christians, at least in name. But the whole mingled population is in a state of deplorable ignorance and degradation—destitute of the means of divine knowledge, and bewildered with vain imaginations and strong delusions.[64]

The Americans, through both the ABCFM and, after 1870, the Presbyterian church, began a very successful mission in the Middle East, primarily in Lebanon and subsequently in Egypt, which led to the establishment of numerous indigenous Middle Eastern churches.[65] They quickly discovered that due to legal restrictions and, more importantly, communal sensitivities, proselytizing among Muslims was not an easy

---

63. Vander Werff, *Christian Mission to Muslims*, 112.

64. Khalaf, "Protestant Images of Islam," 217.

65. For a review of the history of the ABCFM in the Middle East see ibid., 103–25. For a review of Presbyterian work see ibid., 126–52; and Elder, *Vindicating a Vision*.

task. Thus, they set about to reform the ancient churches, which they saw as mummified corpses, in order that those indigenous Christian communities would be witnesses to the Muslim communities. Anderson wrote:

> We may not hope for the conversion of the Mohammedans unless true Christianity be exemplified before them by the Oriental Churches. . . . Hence a wise plan for the conversion of the Mohammedans of Western Asia necessarily involved first a mission to the Oriental Churches.[66]

Henry Jessup (1832–1910), the longest serving American missionary of the ABCFM in Syria and Lebanon, was much more vitriolic in his description of the Eastern Christians:

> What makes it harder to work among the Moslems is, that they have seen the false, idolatrous parodies of Christianity in the East, so long, that they think one denomination claiming the name of Christ is just as bad as the rest. The Greeks and the Maronites worship pictures and images, and pray to the Virgin Mary and to saints, and the Moslems think all Christians do the same. But since they have been able to look into Protestant Churches, and see there no idols, and especially since they have heard the Word of God in simplicity preached and read in their own tongue, they have begun to think there is a difference.[67]

Unlike Henry Martyn, who undertook direct encounter with Muslim religious leaders, the Americans would undertake "indirect evangelism." They decided that the most effective method of proselytizing among Jews and Muslims was to revive the "nominal" Christians in the Near East, who would then become indigenous witnesses to the cause of world evangelization, where "Oriental Christianity and Islam were coupled as the two pillars of temporal and spiritual corruption."[68] The American response to the "ignorance" of the Middle Eastern Christians and Muslims, then, was education. By creating schools to teach the "Orientals" the basics of math and science, as well as the ability to read the Bible, these Christians—and subsequently the Jews and Muslims—would be raised out of the mire of

66. Vander Werff, *Christian Mission to Muslims*, 103–4.
67. Khalaf, "Protestant Images of Islam," 227.
68. Ussama Makdisi "Reclaiming the Land of the Bible: Missionaries, Secularism, and Evangelical Modernity," *American Historical Review* vol. 102, no. 3 (June 1997), 691 Tibawi, *American Interests*, 15. For a helpful review of the objectives and methods of Protestant missions among Muslims in the Middle East see Vander Werff, 101–3.

their own spiritual and social ignorance to see the truth. Thus the overall cure for Middle Eastern unbelief was religious education. For the early Protestant American missionaries from the pietistic tradition, the sanctification of one's soul had as much to do with the advancement of one's daily quality of life as it had to do with one's spiritual life. The two were intertwined. In the American mind, to raise the standard of living naturally would bring about a spiritual revival as the pinnacle of human spiritual achievement.

The collapse of the Ottoman military was only indicative of the collapse of the state administration itself. This was what Usama Makdisi calls the "transitional times" for the Ottoman Empire, between the military defeats that began with the Treaty of Carlowitz in 1699 and ended with the reform period which began in 1839 and culminated in 1876.[69] While the Ottomans had preserved power and authority in their empire only through direct rule in the major urban areas, they had ruled indirectly in the rural areas—including most of what is now Lebanon and Syria. The lack of a strong central government meant that imperial services were almost non-existent. Local law enforcement, taxation, and other government services were dependent upon local nobility who acted on behalf of their own interests. There was no systematic imperial school system. The only schools that did exist were organized through the local mosques and Orthodox churches. Education in this vein was focused on religious indoctrination through rote memory from either the Qur'ān or the Bible. Otherwise, the vast majority of people were illiterate. Thus, the Protestant missionaries to the Middle East walked right into a context where their cultural-religious background enabled them to provide a method of engagement with the society at large. They found themselves settling in cities without direct Ottoman rule, and thus were initially able to develop their schools free from the eyes of the local Ottoman governor.

The American missionaries' view of education went hand in hand with the development of "literary-evangelism." Their belief in *sola scriptura* assumed a level of education in which a believer could access the Scriptures for themselves. The American missionaries saw the educational process—the bettering of one's self—as a part of one's sanctification. Thus, the American Protestant missionaries set themselves to the task of edu-

---

69. Makdisi, "Reclaiming the Land," 684. For further information on the decline and then reform of the Ottoman Empire see Davison, *Reform in the Ottoman Empire*; Hourani, *Arabic Thought*; Lewis, *Emergence of Modern Turkey*; and Ma'oz, *Ottoman Reform*.

cating the indigenous people by creating a system of small schools in order that they might be able to read the Scriptures in their own languages, be educated, and thus raise themselves out of the despair of poverty and superstition.

The Protestant mission schools were open to members of all religious communities throughout the Ottoman Empire, including Muslims, in order to educate the local populace. The crowning achievements of the Presbyterian educational activity were the establishments of what were later to become known as the American University in Beirut in 1866 and the American University in Cairo in 1914. George Herrick, a Presbyterian and one of the leading missionaries serving under the ABCFM during the late nineteenth century, summed up the American cultural perspective of missions in the Middle East:

> The leading and controlling purpose of missionary endeavour in our day is not, as it was in the inception of foreign missions a century ago, to snatch a soul here and there as a brand from the burning. It is the enlightenment, and education, by the power of Christian civilization, of Christian education, by the persistent use of all the forces and accessories of Christian philanthropy. The impetus and motive is found in our Lord's summing up the second table of the law, "Thou shalt love thy neighbor as thyself."[70]

The concept of American evangelical mission to the Middle East, both among the Congregationalists and the Presbyterians was built on the American ideal of enlightenment. Education, centered on the concept of reading the Bible in the vernacular, would raise people to the possibility of a virtuous life, and therefore, the possibility of salvation. However, the "virtuous life" included the American ideals of individualism, equality, and progress. Some Arab Christians have argued that the American methods of "literary-evangelism" and education led to a renaissance in Arabic literature known as *al-Nahda* [The Renaissance], which laid the foundations for the development of Arab nationalism in the early twentieth century.[71] Others, however, have argued that the American missionary endeavor was "cultural imperialism."[72] (We will return to this issue of American cultural imperialism in the conclusion.)

---

70. Vender Werff, *Christian Mission to Muslims*, 124.

71. George Antonius, *Arab Awakening*, 35–60, and Hourani, *Arabic Thought*. See also Abu-Ghazaleh, *American Missions in Syria*.

72. For example see Barber, Jihad vs. McWorld; and Khalaf, Cultural Resistance. A very helpful review of Arabic anti-missionary literature is Sharkey, "Arabic Antimissionary

Another American Protestant missionary endeavor, which took a different missiological approach in the Middle East, was that of the Arabian Mission of the Reformed Church in America (RCA-AM). Begun in 1889 by James Cantine and Samuel Zwemer as a step-child of the Presbyterian work in the Middle East, the Dutch Reformed Americans explicitly set out to "occupy the Cradle of Islam," Arabia. Zwemer's explicit missiology was to engage Muslims directly in the Arabian Peninsula primarily through medical missions and the development of dispensaries and hospitals. Stanley Mylrea, one of the prominent RCA missionaries wrote:

> The profession of medicine carries with it in Arabia, as in most countries, a certain distinction. There is an Arab proverb which places medicine above religion. The very word, doctor, becomes in the Arab's mouth, Hakeem the Wise Man. And so it is that in Arabia, the medical man is one whose advice is asked for and listened to, whose influence counts in the community and in whose hands lie many opportunities to mold public opinion and to lay the foundations for Christian progress in a quiet unobtrusive way, disarming alike to religious fanaticism and racial prejudice. Given the right personality, the Christian doctor's potentiality for good in a country like Arabia is almost limitless.[73]

The RCA-AM stands as an important lesson for the modern Christian missionary endeavor in the Middle East. First and foremost, the Arabian Peninsula was outside of the general authority and control of the Ottoman Empire—under the "indirect rule" previously mentioned. Because it was working in the remote areas of the Ottoman Empire, the RCA-AM removed itself from the issues of the "Eastern Question" and the international politics of the day. They were not involved in the complexities of international support for religious minorities that plagued the early German Pietists in areas under control of the Russian Orthodox Church. They did not become involved in complaints to the Ottoman authorities by the Armenian or Greek Orthodox bishops, nor did they have to engage in Protestant-Catholic debates. Second, the United States had no vested interest in the region of the Persian Gulf. While the British

---

Treatises." The most widely utilized source in the Arab world that conflates Protestant missionary activity with imperialism and colonialism is Khālidī and ʿUmar Farrūkh, al-Tabshīr wa'l-istiʾmār fī al-bilād al-ʾarabiyya [Evangelism and imperialism in the Arab world].

73. Scudder, *Arabian Mission's Story*, 256.

utilized both Aden and Busra as naval ports for their fleets, the United States had no economic imperial designs at that time. Thus, throughout the nineteenth century up until the 1920s when petroleum was discovered, the Americans could not be charged with having colonial interests. This would change dramatically, however, with the discovery of "black gold." The RCA-AM missionaries are remembered fondly in the peninsula specifically because of their altruistic intentions that were devoid of questions relating to political power. The Arabian Mission is remembered as the one organization that came before oil and stayed. Third, the RCA-AM was one of the only Protestant agencies to undertake "direct evangelism" with Muslims in the Middle East. (The other agency would be the LOM, to which we will turn in chapter 4.)

And yet, even though the RCA-AM specifically kept itself apart from any foreign political authority and worked explicitly with local Arab sheikhs, the work of the RCA-AM would come to be known among the Arabs of the gulf as the "American Mission"—rather than the "Arabian Mission." They would ultimately be designated by the nation, or *millet*, from which they came. Although the RCA-AM mission personnel worked hard to maintain their distance from any political affiliation or association throughout the years, in the end the peninsular Arabs labeled them as they labeled all people—according to the particular community to which they belonged. This underlines the importance of communal identity in the Middle East and the constraints under which foreign missionaries are continually subjected. Personal identity is ultimately located in the nature of belonging to a particular community or confession. Religion and communal organization (be it political or social) are intimately tied together. Thus, an individual is recognized as a person by virtue of the family, clan, or tribe to which they belong.

Lutheran involvement in the Middle East during this period was intimately tied to the Anglican missionary societies, both the LJS and CMS. Throughout the early nineteenth century, the Great Awakening in England had led to a widespread ecumenical mission movement. In the late summer of 1846, over 900 individuals from England, the European continent, and North America gathered in London to charter the Evangelical Alliance. This ad-hoc grouping of evangelical leaders from different denominations was the impetus for the support of interdenominational mission.[74] (It would also become the foundation for the early twentieth century Student Volunteer Movement.)[75] Of this multi-national gathering, Germans, from both the Lutheran and Reformed churches, were the largest European contingent.

Despite their initial ability to organize and finance mission programs, the Anglicans had a difficult time finding personnel from within their own constituency to serve abroad. Thus, they began to draw missionaries from both the Halle and Basel seminaries.[76] Of the twenty-four missionaries sent out by the CMS during its first fifteen years, seventeen were Germans. And, eleven of the first fifteen missionaries of the LSPGJ were Germans.[77] By the end of the fourth decade of the nineteenth century, seventy CMS missionaries were German Lutherans trained at Halle or Basel.[78]

The movement of the Evangelical Alliance had created a multitude of relationships between the Lutheran and Reformed churches in Germany, the Netherlands, and England. They found that, although they came from different historical churches and traditions, their piety was in many ways very similar. The low church Anglicans and these Lutheran Pietists held similar views regarding the church as an institution: it was a necessary structure to be tolerated in the march toward world evangelization. Thus, these low-Anglicans were often willing to accept Lutheran pastors who had not been ordained in the historical episcopate of the Anglican church; and, for their part, the Lutheran Pietists were willing to put up with Episcopal supervision and bureaucracy.[79] Ultimately, however, the issue of the rite of ordination in the historical episcopate would undo the Anglican-Lutheran partnership in the Middle East, not because of

---

74. Railton, *No North Sea*, xvi–xvii.

75. See Showalter, *End of a Crusade*.

76. The Anglicans also tapped other German Pietist seminaries, such as the Berlin Missionary Seminary. In 1804 Melchior Renner and Peter Hartig were sent out by the CMS to Sierra Leone. See Tibawi, *British Interest*, 18.

77. Railton, *No North Sea*, 152.

78. Gensichen, "German Protestant Missions," 182.

79. This would not be the case, however, among American Lutherans. On several occasions American Lutheran missionaries in the General Synod, the Mission Society of the Ministerium of Pennsylvania, and the Missouri Synod, left the CMS, ABCFM, and the German Hermannsburg Mission, respectively, over confessional and doctrinal issues. See L. Wolf, *After Fifty Years*, 30–32; F. Dean Lueking, *Mission in the Making*, 207; and E. Wolf, *Lutherans of America*, 499.

theological issues but primarily due to political ones, as we shall see in the next chapter. In any case, German Lutheran and Reformed Pietists actually supplied the manpower for much of the early Anglican missions.

When the CMS decided to open up further mission posts in the Middle East they turned to the Lutherans. The first CMS missionaries sent to Egypt in 1825 were the Lutherans J. R. T. Lieder and W. Kruse, who worked among the Copts. F. A. Hildner was sent to the island of Syra in 1828, and J. Zeller and Peter Fjellstedt to Smyrna in 1830 to work among the Greek Orthodox.[80] Fjellstedt is a good example of one of the early Lutherans trained at the ecumenical mission institutes who were sought out and commissioned by the Anglican Church. For most Lutheran Pietists of the eighteenth and nineteenth centuries, the CMS of the Anglican Church provided a perfect outlet for their desire to serve abroad.

PETER FJELLSTEDT

Peter Fjellstedt grew up on a family farm near the Norwegian border on the shores of Lake Vänern in Sweden. From an early age he was recognized as an extremely bright young man. Through the help of his pastor, Fjellstedt was enrolled at a school in Karlstad, Germany where he began his education in the Bible, German, French, Latin, Hebrew and Greek before he moved on to study at the missionary training center in Basel, Switzerland. Throughout his time in Germany, Fjellstedt demonstrated the skill of a linguist, adding Icelandic, Italian, Spanish, Portuguese, Arabic, Ethiopian, Amharic, Coptic, Persian, as well as learning to read Sanskrit and Tamil! This innate linguistic skill naturally helped him to fit right into the CMS policy of "literary-evangelism." During his time as a missionary he was able to translate the Anglican Book of Common Prayer into Turkish.

Fjellstedt was drawn toward foreign missions fairly quickly in his educational career. In 1828 he managed to establish the first Swedish mission society, *Svenska Missions Sällskapet*.[81] Even after he returned from work overseas in 1840 he continued to be directly involved in missions. He was asked to direct the Mission Institute at Lund, which would ultimately merge with the Swedish Missionary Society. During Fjellstedt's tenure at Lund, the Mission Institute was known for its rigorous theologi-

---

80. Richter, *History of Protestant Missions*, 96.
81. Eklund, *Peter Fjelldstedt*, 7.

cal training and for its high church orientation, which bothered many of the pietistic-minded pastors.[82]

Fjellstedt himself, however, was a Swedish Pietist heavily influenced by both the Moravians and the German Württemberg movement. Although he felt strongly about the necessity of one's personal relationship with Christ, he held fast to the importance of the church's role in guiding believers to Christ. He was thus able to combine both the individual devoutness of the Pietist movement with the Church of Sweden's institutional structure.[83] Like many other early Lutheran missionaries, Fjellstedt received his missionary training at the ecumenical training college in Basel and then received a call through the Anglican CMS. However, unlike most other Lutheran Pietists, Fjellstedt was ordained by his own state Church of Sweden. The fact that he received an Episcopal ordination would later become an issue for him dealing with the religious social system of the Middle East, and especially with the Orthodox.[84]

His original intention while studying at Basel was to go to Ethiopia, perhaps to follow in the footsteps of Peter Heyling or Johan Michael Wansleben. However, the unstable political situation in Ethiopia at that time prohibited him from attaining this goal. So, he and his newly married wife, Christiana, left for Madras, India where they served from 1831–36 with the CMS. Because of poor health, he and his family returned to England to re-evaluate their next step. It was at this point that he was asked to go to Izmir, Turkey to be part of the Mediterranean Mission. From 1836 until 1840 he served in Izmir and was part of the CMS program to "revitalize" the Eastern churches in order to indirectly witness to Muslims. Fjellstedt, having learned a number of the Eastern languages, was heavily utilized at the Smyrna missionary post. Some of his time was spent in coffee houses, engaging in dialogue with members of the educated Muslim community. However, he, like other Protestant missionaries in the Middle East, found a great deal of resistance from the Orthodox hierarchy. Ultimately, it was the Greek Orthodox Church that proved most troubling for him. The hostility of the archbishop of Ephesus toward Protestant activity caused him to question his own calling as a missionary. Uncertain as to why the Orthodox would not accept the simple concepts

---

82. Ibid., 12.

83. See Gritsch, *Born-Againism*.

84. Eklund, *Peter Fjelldstedt*, 66.

of the Protestant faith, especially given the fact that he himself had received an "apostolic" ordination, he left Smyrna to return to Europe, and within a year he accepted the post of fundraising chairman for the Basel Mission society.

During his time spent in the coffee houses in Turkey, Fjellstedt came to believe that Islam was not the harbinger of the antichrist, but rather a positive expression of human attempts to apprehend the divine. In fact, contrary to other nineteenth and early twentieth century Protestant missionaries who viewed Islam as theologically problematic—as a post-Christian tradition that had rejected Christianity—Fjellstedt argued that mission work among Muslims is merely different, not inherently problematic.[85]

Like Luther, Fjellstedt was a biblical apocalyptic who saw signs of the end times. And yet, unlike Luther, he did not see Islam as one of the protagonists to bring about the wrath of God. For him, Islam was not of the antichrist. On the contrary, it held some positive value as one aspect of the human attempt to seek out the universal God. Holding firmly to a strong Christology, Revelation 20:1–39 provided for him the basis of how the nations might come together under Christ's lordship. According to Fjellstedt, all peoples, with their own particular religious backgrounds, be they Hindu, Jewish, Muslim, or even neo-Platonic humanists, would be transformed by the Spirit of God during the millennium mentioned in Revelation 20.[86]

Following the early Renaissance debates centered on the question of the salvation of the pre-Christian Greek philosophers, Fjellstedt believed that the salvation of non-Christians could take place at the judgment seat. Death was not the final arbiter of salvation. Based upon his reading of 1 Peter 4:6, he held that non-Christians would have the opportunity to confess their faith in the Living God. In an essay entitled "Different Ways in Which God Reveals Himself to Humankind" Fjellstedt wrote:

> Those heathen who will be saved although they have not in this life learned to know Jesus, have nevertheless already been converted by God's Spirit as he is shown by the Apostle Paul . . . After death for the first time they will learn to know the ground of their salvation. They do not forego a proper conversion upon

---

85. Ibid., 9. For an example of this "problematic" perspective see Gairdner, *Reproach of Islam*.

86. Eklund, *Peter Fjelldstedt*, 90.

> which their salvation depends: they have already in their lives through their longing hearts turned to Christ even though they did not know him.[87]

Fjellstedt here appears to be closer to Erasmus's view of salvation than Luther's. In contemporary theological terms, we might see Fjellstedt's views as fitting in to the Christological debates of exclusivism and pluralism. His thoughts appear very similar to the views of the twentieth century Lutheran Theologian Carl Braaten and his eschatological inclusivism.[88]

Based upon his interpretation of Acts 14:17–18, Romans 1:18–22, and Psalm 19, Fjellstedt had a positive view of the ultimate salvation of non-Christians. He wrote the following in "Different Ways":

> Partly through the memory of the primordial revelation given to the ancestors of the human race by which knowledge was retained from generation to generation among the people of the earth, partly through the wonder of creation and nature, partly through the acts of Providence, and partly through conscience and once in awhile even through extraordinary ways God has revealed himself to the heathen in all times.[89]

Thus, God the Father creates and lays his "primordial" laws within the hearts of all of humanity. God the Spirit then comes to pry open those revelations which have been given in other religions in order to bring all to the realization of the salvation given through God the Son. In another essay entitled "Is There Any Way to Salvation for the Heathen Who Do Not Get to Hear the Gospel?" Fjellstedt grounded all religious thought and piety upon human "conscience." Therefore, those non-Christians who have been obedient to that divine law revealed within their consciences might in the end be saved.[90] Such a theology, naturally, provides a very positive view of other religions and its adherents. As one of the earliest Lutheran missionaries in the Middle East, his views provide a very interesting perspective on Islam, and certainly warrant more attention.

---

87. Ibid., 52.
88. See Braaten, *Apostolic Imperative*.
89. Elkund, *Peter Fjelldstedt*, 49.
90. Ibid., 51.

KARL GOTTLIEB PFANDER

Another important Lutheran Pietist who graduated from Basel and went out to serve in the Middle East was Karl Gottlieb Pfander. Originally Pfander was sent to Persia under the auspices of the Basel seminary and then later under the CMS in both India and Turkey. His book *The Balance of Truth*, an apologetic work against Islam, would become the most prominent piece of Protestant missionary literature utilized by Christian missions in the Middle East throughout the twentieth century.

Pfander was a prominent Lutheran Pietist from Württemberg. He was ordained under Lutheran orders from the state church in Wurttemberg and then sent to Shusha, now located in Azerbaijan, in 1825 until the Russian government expelled all Protestant missionaries in 1837.[91] Although the Armenian archbishop probably instigated a move to rid Shusha of the Protestant evangelists because of the Germans' attempts to proselytize among the Armenian Orthodox, it also is highly likely that Pfander's efforts to convert Muslims in the area may have been partly to blame. His work began to cause religious tension in the region.[92] It would not be the last time Pfander would be the center of such a controversy.

After Pfander and the missionaries were expelled from Shusha he was eventually called by the CMS to work in India, where he was re-ordained in the Anglican church. He served here for sixteen years, from 1841 to 1857 (at Agra and later Peshawar near the current Pakistan-Afghanistan border, the important site for the development of al-Qaeda at the end of the twentieth century). It was during Pfander's time in Agra that he distinguished himself as a missionary interested in developing apologetic material in response to Islam. He has been noted by Western evangelical missionaries as being the "the greatest of all missionaries to Mohammedans."[93] Because of threats to his life by the Muslim community, he was eventually relocated to Constantinople where he worked from 1858 to 1865. Once again, because of threats to his life in Constantinople, he was forced retired to England.[94]

Pfander, although a Pietist, managed to walk a balance between an evangelical piety and utilizing the concepts developed in German scho-

---

91. Bennett, "Legacy of Karl Gottlieb Pfander," 77.
92. Ibid.
93. Church Missionary Society, *One Hundred Years*, 78.
94. Vander Werff, *Christian Mission to Muslims*, 41.

lasticism. A gifted linguist, he wrote tirelessly in numerous languages. His apologies attempted to demonstrate through a systematic method that Christianity was a rational religion and that Islam could not stand up to such scrutiny. In the words of one scholar, he "wanted the Muslim to apply the methods of his historical criticism to the origin and development of Islam."[95] Although he was prepared to apply a Lockean method of philosophical inquiry to the validity of moral religion, he was not prepared for the effects of German historical-critical textual scholarship, developed from the very same scholastic ideas, being utilized in the field of biblical studies at that time.[96] Following on the heals of the Enlightenment, German scholars such as Hermann Samuel Reimarus (1694–1768), J. G. Eichorn (1752–1827), and D. F. Strauss (1808–74) were beginning to apply source critical methods to the Gospels, as well as study the transmission of the texts. This movement reached its height through the work of Rudolf Bultmann (1884–1976). Pfander, however, had graduated from Basel and was in Shusha, far from the hallowed halls of the German universities, during these new developments in biblical criticism. When he graduated from Basel the concepts of Lockean philosophy were basis of the intellectual methods employed on the mission field to demonstrate the superiority of the moral system of Christianity. This method fit well with the traditional logical pattern used by Thomas Aquinas and the Dominicans, who had written their apologies more than five hundred years earlier. Pfander, like other Pietists, was not prepared, however, to respond to source and textual criticism, not only from fellow Germans but most of all from Muslims!

Pfander's method of engagement was, first and foremost, through the publication of works and tracts, public preaching whenever the chance was provided, and occasionally direct engagement with Muslim mullahs. This method led to his public criticisms of Islam, Muhammad, and the Qur'ān; what ultimately led to threats on his life. Because of his insistence on using public discourse as a method of evangelism, it was necessary for him to continually relocate from place to place to escape danger. It was the publication of his most controversial work, *Mīzān al-ḥaqq* [The Balance of Truth], that proved to be his greatest legacy among Christian apologists, and his greatest downfall.

95. Ibid., 42.

96. For a review of Locke's influence see Locke, *Reasonableness of Christianity*; and Nuovo, *John Locke and Christianity*.

The Balance of Truth was written while Pfander was in Peshawar. It was the culmination of his public arguments with Muslim leaders. His missionary colleagues, convinced of the brilliance of his work, encouraged him to put the arguments down on paper. In 1829 he originally wrote the book in German, whereupon it was then translated into a variety of languages (Armenian, Persian, Hindustani, Arabic, Turkish, English, etc.). The work did not go unnoticed by Muslim scholars. Numerous Muslim sheikhs either attempted rebuttals or sought him out to refute his claims. The most famous encounter on record between Pfander and a Muslim scholar was his public debate with Rahmatullāh Ibn Khalīl al-'Uthmānī al-Kairānawī, a Shi'a scholar of Agra, Persia, in 1854. In this debate both scholars utilized reason and historical-critical methods to prove the superiority of their own religion and scripture over the other. At the end of the debate both sides claimed victory.[97]

Al-Kairānawī took Pfander's methods to task, utilizing the best of German scholarship to attack Christianity and the Bible. Quoting German scholastics that began to undermine the uniqueness of the Bible as a sacred religious text, al-Kairānawī quoted from David Freidrich Strauss's famous *The Life of Jesus*, with which Pfander was not familiar. In addition, al-Kairānawī utilized the best of German textual research, discussing textual variants and manuscript differences of the New Testament to prove the "corruptedness" of the Bible [*taḥrīf*]; that it was not the "Word of God" but rather the words of men.[98] The debate led al-Kairānawī to publish his response to *The Balance of Truth*, called *Iẓhār al-ḥaqq* [The Demonstration of the Truth].

This debate stands out as one of the most popular modern Christian-Muslim debates for both Christian and Muslim missionary communities, who have continued to utilize not only the same methods as Pfander and al-Kairānawī, but their books as well. *The Balance of Truth* and *The Demonstration of Truth* continue to line the shelves of the respective bookstores of those involved in public evangelism and *da'wah* [Muslim evangelism]. Pfander's works, including *Miftāḥ al-Asrār* [The Key of Mysteries], *Tarīq al-Ḥayāt* [The Way of Life], and *Remarks on the Nature*

---

97. Bennett clearly lays out the possible scenario that the Christians were bested in the debate and the CMS whisked Pfander out of Agra as a "diplomatic move" ("Legacy of Karl Gottlieb Pfander," 78, 80).

98. For a review of the Muslim concept of the corruption of the Christian Scriptures see Saeed, "Charge of Distortion."

of Muhammadanism, have been translated into numerous languages and are still distributed to Muslim communities. The works are utilized by evangelical missionary organizations, and can be found on the British evangelical Web site *Answering Islam*.[99] In response, the contemporary Muslim Web site *Answering Christianity*[100] offers opportunities for Muslims to review the "corrupted" texts of the Bible and to prove that the Bible is not God's revealed Word.[101]

What made *The Balance* so popular and intriguing to Muslims at its outset was Pfander's use of language and his knowledge of the Qur'ān and Muslim historical sources. The introduction of the book is given over to the use of Semitic poetry and proverbs. The descriptions of God as the "most high, the merciful, the gracious," the "eternal and unchangeable creator," and the "almighty, all-wise, and all-gracious" were taken from "the ninety-nine names of God" utilized in popular Muslim piety.[102] In addition, his Pietist conception of God as providing a moral path in which he "rewards the good and punishes the wicked" resonated with the Qur'ānic concept of God.[103] By the end of the Introduction, the Muslim had been provided an image of Allah that did not necessarily contradict that of Islam. Thus, the text draws the Muslim into its argument, intrigued that a Christian missionary would be utilizing Islam.

Pfander's overall argument, following John Locke's concepts of revelation and religion, states that that which is divine and truthful must lead humanity to live an ethical, upright, and moral life. Any religion claiming to be based upon true revelation, then, must be accessible through a logical system that can be known through the God-given human conscience. A divinely revealed text cannot contradict human conscience, which seeks to live the moral and ethical life. "It is not possible," wrote Pfander, "that the Word of God should contradict the conscience, which He has given us as our guide.... Thus, if a book which claims to be a divine revelation states that God is possessed of evil attributes, then we declare that such a book cannot be Divinely inspired."[104] Part III of *The Balance* then seeks to

99. http://www.answering-islam.org.

100. http://www.answering-christianity.org.

101. For a helpful review of the importance of this public debate see Shirrmacher, "Influence of German Biblical Criticism."

102. Pfander, *The Mîzânu'l Ḥaqq*, 18–20.

103. Ibid., 21.

104. Ibid., 30, 35.

provide the unethical or immoral attributes of the God of Islam. Naturally, this section is the most controversial section of the book, and has become the focus of debate between Christian and Muslim apologists.

An axiomatic argument utilized by Pfander is that the conscience and the human heart ultimately drives a person toward overcoming the "sinful" condition. Although the conscience provides the guidelines for morals, it cannot by itself overcome the barriers of the "sinful" human condition. Thus, the "desire for knowledge of the Truth" leads one to realize that one cannot attain the goal of a completely pure religious state. Because of this, one is led to seek "for pardon" or forgiveness; and then is ultimately brought into a state of "purification."[105]

From the Muslim perspective, the Christian argument has always been puzzling, as it interjects what Islam considers unnecessary. Islam understands true revelation as providing "guidance and mercy" to the human life. For Muslims this is a given in the form of the Qur'ān. The gift of "guidance" is sufficient because it ultimately relies on the "mercy" of God. The Christian assertion has always been that the condition of sin prohibits humanity from being able to follow the guide. The guide, in other words, is not enough. Thus, whereas both Islam and Christianity have "guides," (i.e., the Qur'ān and Christ, respectively) the purposes of these guides are very different. In the end for Pfander, "The question at issue is, 'Who is in our day the Saviour of the world: the Lord Jesus Christ, or Muhammad?'"[106] This is in essence a misplaced question for the Muslim. It is not a question Islam asks.

Also in Part III of *The Balance*, Pfander invites his Muslim readers to see with "courtesy and brotherly affection" "[w]hat proof is there . . . that Muhammad is the Apostle of God?" and subsequently, whether the Qur'ān is divine revelation.[107] He responds to Muslim claims that Muhammad is predicted in the Bible, and then puts forward his own criticisms of Islam; namely, that the Qur'ān was not a miracle and that Muhammad's conduct was unbecoming of a true religious leader. First, Pfander reviews numerous passages of the Old and New Testaments that historically Muslims have claimed refer to the coming of Muhammad, which proves the supercession of Islam over Christianity. The most prominent of these passages

---

105. Ibid., 26.
106. Ibid., 226, 368.
107. Ibid., 225.

include Deuteronomy 18:15, Isaiah 63:1-6, and John 16.[108] Traditional Muslim sources have argued that the "prophet" in Deuteronomy and the "comforter" of John were predictions by both Moses and Jesus of the coming of Muhammad. In response, Pfander takes each passage in turn and, utilizing exegetical methods, argues that the texts in and of themselves do not support such Muslim readings.

Pfander then turns to the Muslim claim that the Qur'ān is the miraculously revealed word of God. According to Islam, the Qur'ān itself is a miracle from God. Its recitation is peerless, the most elegant and eloquent of any book because it is God's very own speech. Although Muslims have long debated the status of the Qur'ān and its intrinsic relationship to God—much like the early Christian debates about the persons of the Trinity—most Muslim communities have come to accept the view of the uncreatedness of the Qur'ān. Before creation, God's speech was written on the golden tablet in heaven, and was revealed to the prophets throughout time.

Utilizing Islamic sources, traditions, and histories, however, Pfander highlights several examples that point out various passages of the Qur'ān that were lost from memory by the "reciters" and never collected into the full text.[109] In addition, using philological Oriental research, he makes the case that some of the words in the Qur'ān are words borrowed from other Semitic languages, including Ethiopic, Syriac and Persian.[110] Thus, he argues that the Qur'ān is a historical document influenced by seventh century Quraysh Arabia and the communities around it.

The meat of Pfander's attack on Islam, however, is relegated to a review of the content of Muhammad's life. Like Christian apologists before him, Pfander follows the arguments previously elicited in the early medieval document *The Apology of al-Kindī* and the twelfth century works of Peter the Venerable, abbott of the monastery at Cluny. These Christian apologies argued that the Qur'ān itself denies that Muhammad provided

---

108. Ibid., 227–52. The biblical references cited include: Gen 49:8-10; Deut 18:15, 18; 32:21; 33:2; Pss 45:5; 149:1–9; Song 5:16; Isa 21:7; 42:1–4, 10–12; 53; 54:1; 63:1–6; 65:1–6; Dan 2:45; Hab 3:3; Hag 2:7; Matt 3:2; 17:11; 20:1–16; 21: 33–44; Mark 1:7; John 4:21; 14:16, 17, 26, 30; 16:13; 1 John 4:2–3; Jude 14, 15; Rev 2:26–29. In addition, two Shi'i references include Gen 17:20 to the Twelve Imams, and Jer 46:10 to the martyrdom of Hussein.

109. Pfander, *The Mîzânu'l Ḥaqq*, 258–60.

110. Ibid., 263.

any miracles to prove his identity as a prophet, and that his lifestyle was contrary to the accepted morals of "revealed religion." The brunt of Pfander's argument falls on traditional Western critiques of Muhammad's moral character, especially in terms of his violent military activity and his involvement in polygamy.[111] "In other words, in what respect was his conduct, in moral matters, better than that of such conquerors as aim only at success in this world and enjoyment of sensual pleasures?"[112] According to Pfander, how could Muhammad be a prophet when he behaved in such a manner?

The Balance of Truth was and continues to be seen by Christian apologists and polemicists as an answer to the problem of evangelism among Muslims. In good Semitic style it provided many responses to Muslim claims about religion. However, the work would prove to undermine much of the CMS work in the Middle East. After the public debate in Agra, Pfander was moved to Peshawar for his own safety. In 1858 he was relocated to Istanbul, where he was put in charge of the new CMS mission, which included a bookshop. The shop stocked copies of *The Balance* in Turkish and sold it in the market next to the great Hagia Sophia Mosque. Once the contents of *The Balance* became known, riots ensued. The store was burned and the Turkish government shut down all CMS activities in Turkey. Pfander was forced to flee the country. He went to England where he died in 1865, waiting for another opportunity to return to the Middle East.

During the eighteenth and nineteenth centuries Islam ceased to be the great goliath of the late medieval period. The images of the Crusades and the struggles with the infidel Saracens and Turks gave way to the rise of Europe; economically, intellectually, and politically. During the Age of Discovery the race for supremacy began on the seas and in the newly discovered territories of the world. The medieval *Song of Roland* and its "clash of civilizations" gave way to Descartes, Newton, and Darwin and their mechanical view of the universe, in which natural

---

111. For a review of earlier Christian apologists, including *The Apology of al-Kindī*, Peter the Venerable, and others, see Gaudeul, *Encounters and Clashes*, vols. 1, 2, esp. 1:142–48, 2:246–48. A helpful resource for later Western Protestant views utilizing this same "morality" argument can be found in Khalaf, *Cultural Resistance*, 211–30. It is ironic that Christian critiques of the life of Muhammad have historically focused upon his immorality and violent disposition, whereas in Muslim piety, Muhammad has always been seen as the merciful and charitable parent, father, and leader.

112. Pfander, *The Mîzânu'l Ḥaqq*, 343.

law reigned supreme. The Enlightenment then paved the way for how European scholars, the Orientalists, and missionaries would begin to view Islam. Islam was subjected to scholarly critique, in which it was found to be interesting, intriguing, unreasonable, or—in the case of the missionaries—wanting. The fear of "the Terrible Turk" and his religion gave way to a smug amusement of Islam's faults, and ultimately its moral failures, as missionaries encountered a weakened infrastructure of the Ottoman Empire and a low point of Islamic philosophy, science, and education.

The Lutheran Pietists were some of the earliest Protestant Christians to take up the call for foreign missions. They supplied the manpower for many of the major inter-denominational mission agencies of the day. The fact that their own churches either frowned on foreign missions for theological reasons or were simply lukewarm to the idea, drove the Pietists into the arms of other denominational mission societies. As Jim Scherer states, "Pietism thus liberated Lutheranism from the crippling restraints of Orthodoxy and provided a theological and structural bases for human participation in the mission of God."[113] It was not, however, until international politics imposed itself on the region that German Lutheran missions developed due to the driving force of German National identity and pride. In the next chapter we will look at Lutheran missions in Palestine and its legacy.

---

113. Scherer, *That the Gospel*, 22.

4

National Missions in the Holy Land

We want to help our courageous people in Palestine . . . pioneers of German labour in the Orient who are faithful to their Fatherland and give it honour. . . We must not neglect these people. Our appeal is directed to all those who are prepared to act for Palestine and for German settlement.

—Society for the Promotion of the German Settlement in Palestine, 1899[1]

WHILE MANY DIFFERENT MISSION societies engaged in work in the Middle East, Lutheran mission societies were slow to get on board. American Lutherans were only beginning to organize themselves from immigrant communities on the fringes of American society. The European state-church Lutherans were still governed by the rules of Westphalia and subject to whether their rulers desired to engage in foreign mission. The Pietists were by now fully committed to numerous nondenominational mission societies. Thus, it was not until the later part of the nineteenth century that Lutherans began to organize their own mission projects for the Middle East. While Persia and Caucasus region became a very important area of mission for many mission societies, it was Palestine that proved to be the area in which the most visible Lutheran presence organized itself. In order to understand how Lutherans as a specific confessional body became involved in Palestine during this time, it is vital that we understand the background of the international politics of the day, and especially the role of the British Empire in Ottoman affairs.

During the middle of the nineteenth century, the Ottoman Empire was in its death throes. European states that had begun to develop their own national identities and desires for imperial projects saw the weaken-

---

1. Alex Carmel, "Political Significance," 64.

ing of the Ottoman Empire. They dubbed the empire the "Sick Man of Europe," as an opportunity for their own expansionist dreams. In 1830 the French landed troops in what is present-day Algeria, occupying parts of northern Africa up until 1962. The British, with their desire to connect the Mediterranean with the "Jewel of the Crown," India, via the Suez Canal, occupied Egypt in 1882 under the premise that they were protecting their financial and national interests. Yet the British, French, and Prussians understood that the Ottomans were an important buffer against Russian expansion in the Balkans, the Mediterranean, and even into Persia. And, while on the one hand each European nation was willing to expand its own territories at the expense of the Ottomans, on the other hand they did what they could to insure that the weakened empire did not collapse in order to prevent the other European nations from getting ahead in the imperial game. Like a gigantic game of *Risk*, this *realpolitik* of supporting the Ottoman Empire just enough to further one's own national and imperial benefits became known as the "Eastern Question." How was one to take advantage of the "sick man" without allowing other nations too many of the spoils? One of the ways European powers engaged the Ottoman Empire in this international intrigue to gain leverage over other nation-states was by supporting particular minority groups within the Ottoman Empire.

Whether or not they desired to be involved in the issues of international politics or church-state relations as patriots for their respective nations or "soldiers" of an advancing Christendom, Western missionaries (and their mission projects) became representatives of these particular international designs in the Middle East. It can be said clearly that the early Protestant missionaries were not imperialists. They had no designs for creating and supporting a European or American empire for economic gain. (In fact, the American missionaries arrived long before the U.S. as a nation found any "national interest" in the Middle East!) These missionaries truly intended to focus on what they considered the spiritual betterment of those they came to serve. But, as we have already argued, for the missionaries of the ABCFM especially, spirituality was manifested in an enlightened and progressive lifestyle. Thus, the transformation of the individual's soul would naturally yield to the transformation of the local culture, especially a culture that was Islamic through and through.

Whereas in most regions throughout the world missionaries were forced to work inside the administration of a European colony, work in the Middle East entailed working within the domains of another sovereign empire—a Muslim empire. Missionaries worked under the jurisdiction of an Islamic state in which the sultan was the supreme authority. Certainly, the Muslim authorities were not keen on these "Franks" preaching the gospel to Muslim communities; for them to do so was to risk deportation, imprisonment, beating, or even martyrdom. In some cases, such as with Pfander, the missionaries did upset the local Muslim sensibilities, which caused social unrest. Thus, mission activities could upset the carefully balanced local inter-confessional applecart. Orthodox bishops were not particularly happy to see their families being provided services through evangelical schools and dispensaries, and Sunni notables did not take kindly to local village Christian sheikhs being treated with too much pomp and circumstance by visiting foreigners. Maronite bishops invited the Jesuits into their villages to build schools in order to "compete" with the Protestant mission schools. The reality of Christian foreign mission work in the Ottoman Empire during the nineteenth century meant that the missionaries affected not only the target community they wanted to preach the gospel to, but also the delicate balance of inter-confessional relations in their area, as well as international relations abroad. Western missionaries may not have promoted their work with the support or funding from their own governments, but by the middle of the nineteenth century they were able to appeal to European and American consuls for protection. By the 1840s European nations began to utilize the enterprises of missionaries in order to gain some leverage over other European imperial interests. Each major nation established protection for a particular religious minority within the empire to support and defend their communal rights, and subsequently, the particular missionary enterprises of its fellow citizens who worked among those Ottoman minorities. When push came to shove, a Western presence could guarantee freedom for the "advancement" of evangelization over against local Ottoman rule. Time and time again European and American missionaries would appeal for protection against insurgent radicals (during the Druze-Maronite civil war in Mount Lebanon, against persecution of converts in Upper Egypt, and in Armenia during the Turkish massacres, for example). At other times they were very much against the imperial designs of their governments. CMS and LJS missionaries often clashed with the policies of their government, and especially with the Anglican church hierarchy, while American Presbyterians were very outspoken against the support of Jewish immigration and the American support for political Zionism in Palestine. In the end, it can be argued that while diplomats made decisions based on the national interests of their countries, the missionaries made decisions for what they understood was in the best interest of evangelizing their local targeted community. Sometimes these interests were mutual, sometimes they were at odds, and sometimes they intersected for different purposes. From reading through mission diaries and reports, it is clear that in their own way the missionaries had noble spiritual intentions. However, it cannot be denied that their presence and work did affect and contribute to the complicated web of social networks and international politics of Ottoman society. This was never purely a spiritual matter.

THE BREAKDOWN OF THE OTTOMAN MILLET SYSTEM

The Christians of the East within the Ottoman Empire, as under previous Islamic dynasties, were organized into legally recognized communities. Classical Islamic law recognized Christians and Jews not only as *People of the Book*, but also as *dhimmīs*. They were not only recognized as special religious communities, but had particular legal rights and responsibilities as well. Muhammad and the early Muslim community recognized that both Jews and Christians belonged to communities to whom God had previously sent prophets. And these prophets, *Musa* and *'Isā*, had brought books that contained the words of God; *al-Tawrāt* and *al-Injīl* [the Law and the Gospel]. Thus, followers of these prophets, perhaps misguided, still reflected God's will and were bound to live according to those books. The Qur'ān reflects this view in several places, two of the most prominent verses being:

> *And there are, certainly, among the People of the Book, those who believe in Allah, in the revelation to you, and in the revelation to them, bowing in humility to Allah . . . (3:199)*

> *Lo! Those who believe, and those who are Jews, and Christians, and Sabaeans–whoever believes in Allah and the Last Day and does what is right–surely their reward is with their Lord, and there no fear shall come upon them, neither shall they grieve. (2:62)*

And yet, these *People of the Book* were not Muslims. They had not completely come to accept Muhammad as the last prophet and the Qur'ān as the last revelation. According to Islamic social organization, then, there needed to be some kind of distinction between the Muslims, the *People of the Book,* and the polytheists who did not believe in the One God. The legal term, *dhimmī* was applied to the monotheists (as well as later to Zoroastrians in Persia and Hindus in India) to distinguish their rights and responsibilities from both the Muslims and the polytheists under Islamic law.[2]

Dhimmīs were formally recognized religious minority communities that were given certain rights, responsibilities, and prohibitions. They were allowed to continue to worship and organize their own lives as they saw fit, as long as they recognized the authority of the Islamic state, and as long as they did not disparage either Muhammad or the Qur'ān. This communal organization was both a blessing and a curse. On the one hand, classical Islamic law allowed for Christianity to continue, and in some cases thrive under Islam. On the other hand, since it was always subject to the whims of particular Muslim rulers, Christianity in the Middle East was forced to become an insular society, expending its energy for its own survival. The church became the institution that was not only the spiritual center of Christian community, but also the center of the national life of Eastern Christians. The church's primary role became to preserve the national identity of a particular Christian community, whether Armenian, Coptic, Greek, Syrian, or Maronite. This history of the traditional Christian communities of the Middle East has itself been a history of *dīn wa dawla,* or "religion and state," insofar as the "state" represented the particular social organization of indigenous Christian communities.

By the seventeenth century, Suleiman the Magnificent thoroughly organized this Qur'ānic classification into the *millet* system, whereby each religious community maintained its own religious leadership, worship, collection of taxes, and legislation of legal codes. To be recognized as a subject of the Muslim government required that one legally belonged to a specific religious community (i.e., Jewish, Greek Orthodox, Maronite, etc.). The religious leader for each community (i.e., the Chief Rabbi of

---

2. For a review of the rights and regulations of Christians as *dhimmīs* see the classic study by Tritton, *Caliphs and Their Non-Muslim Subjects*; as well as the listing of various editions of the "covenant" in Lewis, *Islam: From the Prophet,* 219–23. See also Yeor, *Dhimmi: Jews and Christians*; idem., *Islam and Dhimmitude*; Friedmann, *Tolerance and Coercion*; Hoyland, *Muslims and Others.* Yeor's works are extremely helpful for the listing of historical documents, but must be read with extreme care as the author "stacks" the documents up to so as prove the consistent persecution of Jews and Christians, which is overstated.

Istanbul, the Ecumenical Patriarch of Constantinople, the Coptic Patriarch of Alexandria, etc.) was a formal government official who represented that particular community to the caliph.³ This system is still utilized in Syria and Lebanon, and to some extent unofficially in Egypt, where one's religious community determines what kind of services will be rendered or received. In addition, according to these longstanding Islamic categories, foreigners who did not belong to these indigenous communities but were living within the empire were granted protection [*amān*], and were thus labeled as *musta'mīn*. These Islamic categories would become vitally important for the foreign missionaries who began working in the Ottoman Empire. However, as we will see below, with the growth of European economic, political, and military power, and with the weakening of the Ottoman state, these medieval categories would begin to break down.

There were three contributing factors to the ultimate breakdown of medieval Ottoman society. First there were internal administrative difficulties. Suleiman the Magnificant was a man ahead of his time. He propelled the Ottoman Empire to unparalleled heights. Unfortunately, his descendents could not keep pace with him. After Suleiman's reign there were a number of inept sultans who ruled. Under their watch the tax collection fell into shambles, and central authority lost its sway. In addition, an unintended result of Suleiman's reorganization of the traditionally independent religious class in the seventeenth century into formal governmental positions was the sudden breakdown of the nobility. Positions among the religious classes, the *'ulemā'*, were now not only the prerogative of aristocratic families, but open to any family that could get their sons into the requisite government positions—either by passing examinations, or more often than not, through their deep pockets! In addition, new government military schools also eroded the traditional sense among the aristocracy of their hold on the military and society. The disenchantment of the military and religious classes was only enhanced by the lack of any strong political leadership by successive sultans.⁴

The second factor, which opened the door for the collapse of the medieval Ottoman society, was the invasion of Palestine and Syria by Ibrahim Pasha of Egypt. This was the catalyst that set the ball rolling. During the end of the eighteenth century, the waning Ottoman Empire,

---

3. See Tibawi, *British Interests*, 29–30.

4. See Hourani, *Arabic Thought*, 34–66; Halil İnalcık and Kafadar, *Süleymân the Second*; and Imber, *Ebu's-Su'ud*.

the "Sick Man of Europe," was vulnerable and in search of a way to be able to keep pace with the ascending empires of Europe. In order to resurrect the dying empire, Sultan Selim III (1789–1807) invited the Western powers to send military experts to help train their officers in the ways of modern warfare by using advanced knowledge in trigonometry, geometry, physics, and geography. Selim's successor, Sultan Mahmud II (1808–39), followed suit and began a series of military, economic, and legal reforms called the *Tanzīmāt*, designed to remake the ancient medieval Muslim empire into a modern Western nation-state.[5] In addition, the sultans not only received foreign civil servants, but they sent their own government employees to foreign capitals to learn as much as they could about the culture of ascending Europe. During this period of weak central government, Muhammad Ali, the viceroy of Egypt, took advantage of the situation in order to bolster Egypt's standing by invading Palestine in 1831 and Syria in 1832. The Ottoman sultan was powerless to remove the Egyptians, and would ultimately need to rely upon European military intervention to once again to preserve the empire. In 1840, a combination of France, Britain, Prussia, and Austria helped to force Ibrahim to relinquish the Levant.

Ibrahim Pasha's short eight-year rule in the Levant dramatically transformed the social-political landscape, however. Supported by Egypt's desire to take advantage of the Lebanese silk trade and the customs taxes of those Muslims traveling the pilgrimage trail from Damascus to Mecca, Ibrahim Pasha utilized the best of what Egypt had learned through its own transformation into a modern state under his father. He introduced a modern social-political organization that would overturn the traditional medieval governmental structure of Palestine and Syria.[6] He organized a council system, called the *meçlis*, whereby important nobleman, merchants, and officials sat together to provide advice on administrative matters for the local governor. The new administrative system provided a firm basis for the revitalization of the economy as well as created a positive image of an enlightened Orient.[7] What is important about these councils was that they included the Christian leaders and merchants of each district.

5. See Kramers, "Tanzimāt."
6. Grafton, *Christians of Lebanon*, 67.
7. Ibid., 76–80.

Jerusalem would prove to be a different story, however. For much of the late Ottoman period Jerusalem was not a vital city. Taking advantage of the *millet* reforms that were being pronounced from Istanbul, however, the number of foreign civil servants, merchants, travelers, and missionaries began to grow. Jerusalem, once an administrative backwater, now became the center of foreign activity. The Egyptian invasion and the social-political changes instituted by Ibrahim Pasha, along with the *Tanzīmāt* legislations from the capital of the empire, proved to be changes from which the Ottomans could not backtrack. The LJS missionary John Nicholayson remarked, "Only when the Egyptian forces headed by Ibrahim Pasha first entered Palestine could I really settle down in Jerusalem . . . and therefore the permanent Protestant mission in Jerusalem proper could first be founded only in 1833."[8] Unlike the days when Pliny Fisk and Levi Parsons found Jerusalem to be too isolated and difficult to find suitable places to live, Jerusalem had now begun to attract people from all over the world. By 1838 Britain had appointed a vice-consul in Jerusalem to handle the growing number of British subjects in the city. The other European powers were soon to follow Britain's lead: Prussia in 1842, and France in 1843.[9] Nicholas I of Russia also sent a personal envoy to explore the situation in 1843.[10] Each of these diplomatic posts had indigenous Ottoman communities that they began to favor.

The Egyptian foray into the Levant proved to be the deciding factor in transforming Ottoman society and prompted the third factor that led to its breakdown: the interference of Western nations into the social structure of the empire by claiming the right to protect Ottoman minorities. In order to take advantage of a weakened Ottoman state, and in order to use the sultan for their own gains, Western powers intervened in the internal disputes of the empire by sending troops to oust Ibrahim Pasha. Western entrance into Ottoman affairs in the 1830s led to their support of particular minority communities in the 1840s and 1850s. The invasion and subsequent European pressure helped to create a social-political context in which diplomats, merchants, and missionaries could work and develop their own projects and programs.

---

8. Ibid.
9. Pittman, "Protestant Bishopric in Jerusalem," 7.
10. Masters, *Christians and Jews*, 153.

THE RISE OF NATIONAL AND CULTURAL MISSIONS

As early as 1535, Francis I of France and Suleiman II signed the first of many protocols, known as the *Capitulations*, in which foreign Latin Catholics were granted protection to live and work in the Ottoman Empire. This was initiated primarily for the Venetian and French Catholic merchants working in what is now Turkey, Lebanon, and Syria, as well as Egypt. Suleiman saw the importance of allowing these European merchants to carry on trade and commerce within his borders. However, as time went on the protocols were amended to include merchants, religious pilgrims, and chaplains serving the foreign Catholic community, and were ultimately extended to the indigenous Catholics of the Ottoman Empire![11] French support for the rights of Arab Catholics in Lebanon even ultimately led to the establishment of an Ottoman Catholic governor within the territory of Mount Lebanon.[12] Even though France was a secularist state after the 1789 revolution, Catholic missionaries served as important "surrogates for French diplomats" because of their knowledge of the region and its peoples.[13] Much like with the American cultural perspectives we reviewed in the previous chapter, the Jesuits became part of an overall francophone mission where the subtleties of French education introduced continental European cultural and philosophical issues among the Middle Eastern Catholics. French schools not only taught Catholic doctrine, but French philosophy, including Enlightenment thought, introducing the concepts of *dignité*, *eqalité*, and *liberté*.

By the late eighteenth century, other European nations began to vie for the protection of indigenous Middle Eastern Christians. The Treaty of Küchük Kaynarja of 1774 between Russia and the Ottoman Empire was the catalyst for this European cold war race for minority protection. The treaty, humiliating for the Ottomans, stated that the Russian czar was now the "protector" of all Orthodox Christians within the Ottoman Empire.[14] The importance of this treaty cannot be stated enough in terms of its effect on Middle Eastern society. (It is the equivalent of the Treaty of Westphalia and the U.S. Constitution in the development of church-state relations.) With the signing of this treaty hundreds of years of Islamic tradition were

---

11. Frazee, *Catholics and Sultans*, esp. 67, 79, 96, 102.
12. Grafton, *Christians of Lebanon*, 80–82.
13. Masters, *Christians and Jews*, 152.
14. See Hurewitz. *Diplomacy*, 1:92–101.

wiped away. The whole foundation of Islamic society was undermined. Before the ink was even dry on the parchment, the Islamic medieval concepts of *Dār al-Islām* [the House of Islam] and *Dār al-Ḥarb* [the House of War] were emasculated. The Russian potentate now claimed spiritual authority over all Orthodox subjects within the Ottoman Empire.[15] The provisions of the treaty would ultimately lead to Russian diplomatic projects to support and educate the Orthodox communities within the Ottoman Empire as well as to support for Orthodox pilgrims in Jerusalem. As a result, other foreign states began to claim the right not only to protect their own subjects within another sovereign empire, but also to dictate the laws that would apply to their own citizens on foreign soil. They then extended the same privileges of protection to the indigenous Ottoman communities with which they were associated. This would ultimately lead to war, as each empire supported its own surrogate's interests.

In a dispute between the Greek Orthodox and the Latin Catholics over property rights within the Church of the Holy Sepulchre in Jerusalem, Russia invoked its rights under the Treaty of Küchük Kaynarja and intervened on behalf of the Orthodox. The Ottomans had had enough of this interference and responded by declaring war on Russia in 1853. Britain and France joined the Ottomans in hopes of keeping Russian imperialist designs in check. The results of this international conflict, known as the Crimean War, would directly affect the future status of minorities within the Ottoman Empire. The Crimean War was a direct result of the politics of the "Eastern Question," where two Western nations fought as allies of the Ottoman sultan against another Western Orthodox empire.

By 1856 the Russians were defeated and had signed the Paris Peace Treaty. More importantly, however, several weeks before the conference the Ottomans issued a declaration known as the *Hattī Humāyūn*. This proclamation declared that the *millet* system was legally null and void and that all subjects of the empire held equal standing before the sultan.[16] This, and a previous decree in 1850 by the sultan recognizing the Protestants as a legal community, was seen by the missionaries of Britain, Germany, and the United States as a green light for their mission work, urging them on in their attempts to evangelize within the empire. The Russians continued to support their own projects as well. In 1857 a Russian Orthodox bishop

---

15. Grafton, *Christians of Lebanon*, 16. See also Hopwood, *Russian Presence*.
16. Grafton, *Christians of Lebanon*, 75.

was sent to Jerusalem to "advance Russian and Orthodox interests in the Holy Land."[17] The Franciscans also began to step up their educational activities. The British, however, were not to be left out of the competition for international influence of minorities within the Ottoman Empire. This disruption of the *millet* system whereby the foreign nations began "adopting" indigenous communities led to various European governments supporting their religious protégés over against the protégés of other governments, and thus, specifically national projects rather than purely spiritual ones. Bruce Masters puts the issue extremely well: "Unwittingly, the enthusiastic, if politically naïve, Protestant missionaries had set off a cultural war wherein European powers sought proxies in an escalation of the competition to influence the various religious communities of the empire."[18]

The Anglicans and Scottish Presbyterians had begun work in Palestine under the LSPGJ and LJS in 1808 and 1820, respectively. Their desire to convert the Jews was part of an overall dispensational theology that saw the establishment of a Jewish-Christian church on Mount Zion as a fulfillment of biblical prophecy.[19] While the dispensational evangelicals were interested in converting Jews to bring about the return of Christ, the British were in general more concerned with British standing in the East *vis-à-vis* other European nations. In the words of the Committee of the Church of Scotland for Promoting Christianity among the Jews, it was hoped that British involvement among the Jews in Jerusalem would result in "more extensive establishment of British influence."[20] Shortly after the British consul general was appointed in Jerusalem in 1838, the British Foreign Office directed the newly appointed consul to "afford protection to the Jews generally; and . . . take an early opportunity of reporting to His Lordship [Palmerston] upon the present state of the Jewish population of Palestine."[21] Missionaries of the LJS saw this as their golden opportunity to reap the benefits of the support and stability of the British government. However, their work among the Jews would place them in competition with the CMS, whose work was among the Orthodox communities.

17. Pittman, "Protestant Bishopric," 51.
18. Masters, *Christians and Jews*, 152.
19. Stock, *History of the CMS*, 2:142.
20. Tibawa, *British Interests*, 42.
21. Ibid., 33.

Early Anglican missionary endeavors outside Palestine were decidedly interested in evangelizing Muslims. William Jowett, the first CMS missionary to the Ottoman Empire, helped to set the future policy of the CMS in the Middle East: cooperation with the Eastern churches in order to bring about their evangelical revival for the purpose of converting Muslims. This would be done with the aid of the British Foreign Bible Society, through the publication and distribution of evangelical literature published in Malta.

Yet, for the British, the complex patchwork of communities in the Middle East would lead to competing, and sometimes, counterproductive goals from various segments within the Anglican church. While there were wings within the British government that desired to support the Jewish community in Palestine, there were those in the high-church elements of the Anglican church that desired formal relations and support of the Orthodox communities. In addition, there were appeals among British agents working in Syria for support of the Druze.[22] These conflicting goals of attempting to convert the Jews or the Muslims, and reforming the Orthodox or maintaining ecumenical relations with the Orthodox hierarchy, have continued to plague the Anglican church in the Middle East up to the present. The goals of the missionaries who engaged particular indigenous Christian confessions not only led them into conflict with the Muslim community and the Ottoman governors under charges that the schools and other activities were attempting to convert the local Muslims, but the leadership of the Orthodox churches saw the Protestants as sheep stealing. Ultimately, British support for missionary work in Jerusalem for both the evangelization among Jews and the reform of the Orthodox churches would lead to a joint British-German enterprise; the creation of a joint Lutheran-Anglican bishopric in Jerusalem and the establishment of a German Lutheran presence.

THE LUTHERAN-ANGLICAN BISHOPRIC

As we have already noted, many of the early CMS and LJS missionaries were Lutherans who had attended the Basel and Halle seminaries. These Lutheran Pietists would also become the primary resource for an Anglican office of bishop in one of the five great ancient sees: Jerusalem. This bishopric would become the center of ecclesiastical, ecumenical, and

---

22. See Churchill, *Druzes and Maronites*.

international cooperation and controversy. It would ultimately disrupt the sensitive balance of relationships between the religious communities in the City of David.

In 1826 John Nicolayson, originally from the Danish Lutheran church, became a naturalized British subject and took his ordination vows through the Anglican church in order to be sent out to Jerusalem by the LJS. Nicolayson spent his career within the Ottoman Empire evangelizing among the Jews. His first task was to build a Protestant church intended primarily for Jewish converts.[23] He began this work in the old city of Jerusalem with two other LJS missionaries by offering daily worship services in Hebrew and Sunday services in English, Arabic, and German. By 1849 Nicolayson was successful in getting permits to build a new church located near the Jaffa Gate opposite King David's Citadel. "Christ Church" would become the center of a small cadre of Jewish converts, as well as a small community of English and Germans. Each of these communities, however, held services separately in their own languages. The German congregation used the national United Lutheran-Reformed liturgy of Prussia and was served by German pastors who had not been ordained under the Anglican church. By 1860, a significant Arab congregation was made up of Greek Orthodox converts to Anglicanism. They requested the British consulate to build a new church, and by 1874 St. Paul's Church was consecrated.[24] The church, however, would become the focus of Muslim resentment. According to Islamic law and tradition, Jews and Christians, as *dhimmīs*, were forbidden from building new places of worship. The elevated status of the *dhimmīs* protected by a foreign Christian nation caused the ire of the traditional-minded Muslim leaders. As the status of indigenous Christians became more secure because of foreign support throughout the middle of the nineteenth century, Muslim resentment would continue to grow, leading, in part, to the massacres of Christians in Damascus in 1860.[25] Eventually, the German congregation followed the same path as the Arabic congregation and began worshiping on their own, this time on the site of the ruins of the hospice of the Knights of St. John, which had been given to the emperor of Germany by the Ottoman

---

23. Tibawi, *British Interests*, 13–15. See also Lieber, *Mystics and Missionaries*, 292–317.

24. Tibawi, *British Interests*, 164.

25. For a good introduction to the 1860 war see Fawaz, *Occasion for War*.

sultan in 1898.[26] This property would become the focus of the Lutheran presence in Jerusalem and the Holy Land, even to the present day.

Germany, in the middle of its own unification process during the middle of the nineteenth century, was interested in the possibilities of engagement in the Ottoman territories. It too saw the opportunities of advancing its own national interests and becoming involved in the European "Eastern Question." Frederick William IV (1795–1861), the king of Prussia, inherited both his father's piety and politics. His father, Frederick III, had united both the Lutheran and Reformed wings of the German church into one united German Evangelical Church in 1817. Frederick William dreamed of reviving the ideals of the great Holy Roman Empire. One avenue open to him was to secure a German presence in Jerusalem and thereby advocate for the rights of Protestants in Palestine. We are reminded that any European nation desiring to have a role in the "Eastern Question" during the early nineteenth century needed to have some leverage in the affairs of the Ottoman Empire through its minorities. King Frederick had heard of the success of the LJS project of establishing Christ Church in Jerusalem, and was hopeful that the possibility of a "united, undenominational, Protestant church" was at hand.[27] The king appointed Christian Bunsen, a member of the Prussian diplomatic corps who had studied Oriental languages in Paris and shared the king's views on the Protestant cause, to open up discussions with Canterbury about the possibility of creating a united Lutheran-Anglican bishopric.

Bunsen understood the situation in the Ottoman Empire very well. Given the well-entrenched *millet* system, the development of a legally recognized Protestant—or Evangelical, as they are generally known in the Middle East—community would be a difficult task. The ABCFM and later the Presbyterians, as well as the British LJS and CMS, continued to press Istanbul for recognition of the newly forming Evangelical community. It would not be until 1850, however, that the sultan issued a declaration recognizing the Protestants as a legal *millet*. However, unlike the Catholics and Orthodox, which had clearly defined hierarchical structures that could organize their own communities, the Protestants were a conglomeration of different Protestant traditions and national groups. The achievement of the recognition of a Protestant *millet* would

---

26. Tibawi, *British Interests*, 216.
27. Ibid., 45.

be difficult enough, there would be little chance of achieving any kind of German Protestant *millet*. Therefore, given the recent successes of the missionaries of the LJS and the CMS in the region, and given the fact that many of these missionaries were Germans, it was recommended to Frederick that the best possible course of action for the Lutherans would be for both Germany and Britain to formally work together and create a united Protestant church. This concept of a joint effort would, first and foremost, provide a positive witness to the Orthodox churches in the East regarding ecumenical relationships. Second, it would provide a united front against Roman Catholic missions in Palestine.[28] Third, the creation of a very important and powerful Christian community under the auspices of both Britain and Germany would give the two nations a great deal of leverage in dealing with the Ottoman Empire. Lastly, a church under a united bishopric would provide Frederick with the opportunity to create an Episcopal system, which the Prussian church did not have. (It is important to note that from the original conception of this mission, evangelization of the Muslim community, either directly or indirectly, was never an implicit or explicit goal.)

The time was ripe for such a development. In 1841 the parliament of England had instituted the right of the Anglican church to create bishoprics in foreign territories throughout the world. Because Prussia and Britain had helped to remove the Egyptians from Palestine and Syria, they were in good standing with the sultan: he owed them. In addition, there were important personalities in support of such a venture. The idea of reviving the old "See of St. James" as a Jewish Christian community filled the imaginations and fed the excitement of many evangelicals in England and Germany. To the LJS missionaries already on the ground in Palestine, it made sense in order to fulfill their objectives of creating and protecting a new community from among the Jews in Palestine. In addition, the fervor among many Anglican and German evangelicals for ecumenical partnerships was very high.

However, the scheme did have its detractors. The high-church wing of the Anglican church saw this development of establishing an Anglican bishopric in Jerusalem as an infringement on the traditional rights of the Greek Orthodox Patriarch of Jerusalem, one of the five great sees of Eastern Christianity. These detractors were also concerned about the

---

28. Hischfeld, "Some Findings," 264.

Prussian church's lack of an Episcopal system. They were not comfortable with the fact that the United Prussian Church did not have its roots within the historic episcopate. On the German side, there were those detractors from within the Pietist movement who saw the involvement of a state church project as a step backward for Christian missions. That being said, for most of the Lutheran Pietists already involved in the work of the CMS and LJS, the issue of ecclesiastical structures and orders were *adiaphora* [not central to the faith], and thus secondary to the overall goal of evangelizing the Jews. As far as the Lutherans were concerned, the ecclesiastical structure of the Anglican church was a helpful human tradition for the advancement of the gospel among the indigenous Ottoman subjects of Palestine, but it was not a theologically necessary institution for Christian salvation. Thus, they were willing to work under this state church even if this meant re-ordination in some cases. The early Anglican societies provided a missional structure for the Lutherans to carry on the work of the gospel that was missing in their own state churches. Their feelings about this, however, would change by the 1880s.

The issue of the proposed Lutheran-Anglican bishopric was not simply a church mission project; it was a political issue. The fact that an Anglican bishop was a member of Parliament and the House of Lords; and because it took an act of Parliament to push the venture forward, meant that this was an act of the British government. In addition, the project was also designed and supported by the king of Prussia and his diplomatic corps. The first vice consul of Prussia to the Ottoman Empire, Ernst Schultz, was extremely active in pushing the arrangement forward.[29] The creation of the joint bishopric was seen by the international community as a political maneuver to place Britain and Prussia in a positive situation to affect the status of specific Ottoman subjects, namely the Jews. In response to the agreement the French, Russians, and Austrians—the other major European powers of the day—formally objected to the foreign ministry office of the Ottoman Empire. Lastly, of course, there was grave concern by the Muslim governor that a foreign power would begin interfering with the religious minorities of the empire.

In any case, the British Foreign Minister Lord Palmerston ordered the British Ambassador in London to let the Ottomans know of the British

---

29. Ibid., 274.

decision to create the bishopric. It is worth quoting significant portions of this dispatch:

> ... in consequence of the communications which have taken place between the Prussian and the British Governments, and between Chevalier Bunsen, Envoy of the King of Prussia, the Archbishop of Canterbury, the Bishop of London and myself, it has been decided that a Bishop of the Church of England should be sent to Jerusalem, specially consecrated for the purpose of exercising his ecclesiastical function in Palestine, over such persons whether British or Prussian subjects, or others, who being of the Protestant faith may choose to place themselves under his spiritual care...
>
> Her Majesty's Government conceive that no special permission for this purpose will be required from the Porte. This bishop will like any other British or Prussian subject have aright to reside in any part of the Turkish dominions, and the spiritual functions which he will exercise will no way whatever interfere with the Mahometan [sic] subjects of the Sultan, and therefore they will be matters of which the Turkish Governments will have not right to take any cognizance whatever.[30]

The terms of this declaration clearly demonstrate the rise of British power in the region, or at least the British self-perception of their own power. That Palmerston saw no problem with the establishment of an Anglican bishop within the Ottoman Empire, and that the bishop could claim spiritual authority over any British, Prussian, or indigenous Ottoman Protestant, was once again to raise the issues of the Treaty of Küchück Kaynarja. Once again a foreign ruler, this time the monarch of England, as the head of the Anglican church, would through the bishop in Jerusalem affect the social-political structure of the Islamic empire. Palmerston, displaying a sense of arrogance, stated that the bishopric should not concern the sultan, as it did not have any designs to affect the Muslim population, but only had the intent of supporting the spiritual lives of British and Prussian subjects—as well as any Ottoman Jew who sought out the spiritual authority of the bishop. A dispatch from Prime Minister Palmerston to William Young, the first British vice-consul general in Jerusalem, stated that the bishop was "not to interfere into the religious concerns either of the Mahomedan, or the Christian subjects of the Porte [the Ottoman

---

30. Tibawi, *British Interests*, 48.

Foreign Ministry]; and not to attempt to make proselytes to the Church of England from either of these classes."[31]

According to classical Islamic law, however, the sultan was Muhammad's representative and the political ruler of *all* communities within the Islamic empire. Thus, the establishment of the Anglican-Lutheran bishopric in Ottoman lands, claiming authority over Ottoman subjects, was another example of the changing realities of power in the region and the collapse of the traditional Islamic worldview. The British Empire was able to run roughshod over the authority of the sultan, other European powers, and the Jewish community of Palestine as well. Thus, on September 14, 1841 Parliament passed the "Jerusalem Act," and by November the new bishop was heading toward Jerusalem aboard the Royal Navy frigate HMS *Devastation*. He was accompanied by both the British consul general from Beirut, as well as letters of introduction from the Archbishop of Canterbury to the prelates of the Eastern churches in Jerusalem. The proclamation was a *fait accompli*.

The Lutheran-Anglican bishopric organized by King Frederick, the Archbishop of Canterbury, and the British parliament was very much tilted toward Anglican polity and authority. According to Julius Richter, "Prussia enjoyed merely the honour of contributing £600 a year towards the salary of the bishop"![32] The agreement stated that the Archbishop of Canterbury and the Prussian sovereign would alternate turns in selecting a successor to the bishopric, while the Archbishop of Canterbury had full authority to veto the Prussian selection. In addition, the bishop would have to be ordained and consecrated according to Anglican orders by Anglican bishops. The bishop's primary oversight was to advance the conversion of Jews, "their protection, and to their useful employment."[33] In addition, the bishop would have spiritual authority over all Anglicans in Palestine, Syria, Chaldea, Egypt, and Abyssinia. As for the Lutheran-Reformed Germans, it is once again worth quoting the official statement of proceedings from Canterbury:

> Congregations, consisting of Protestants of the German tongue, residing within the limits of the Bishop's jurisdiction, and willing to submit to it, will be under the care of German clergymen, *ordained*

---

31. Ibid., 55.
32. Richter, *History of Protestant Missions*, 239.
33. Tibawi, *British Interests*, 84.

by him for that purpose; who will officiate in the German language, according to the forms of their national liturgy, compiled from the ancient liturgies, *agreeing in all points of doctrine with the liturgy of the English Church*, and sanctioned by the Bishop with consent of the Metropolitan [of Canterbury], for the special use of those congregations: such liturgy to be used in the German language only. Germans, intended for the charge of such congregations, *are to be ordained according to the ritual of the English Church*, and *to sign the Articles of that Church* [the 39 Articles]: and, in order that they may not be disqualified by the laws of Germany from officiating to German congregations, they are, before ordination to exhibit to the Bishop a certificate of their having subscribed, before some competent authority, the Confession of Augsburg.[34]

It is obvious that the joint bishopric was certainly not a "joint" venture. One has to ask the question of why the pious Prussian Lutheran king would accept such a humiliating agreement at the hands of the national British church. There are numerous reasons that allowed for this development in the 1840s. First and foremost, the ties between the two royal families were quite strong. Frederick was a member of the Hohenzollern family. They and the royal family of England, the Hanovers, were intermarried. Frederick and Queen Victoria of England were distant cousins and Victoria's daughter, also named Victoria, would ultimately marry Frederick's son, Frederick III. When their son William II was born in Berlin in 1859, a London theatre hall had an extra verse of "God Save the Queen" sung:

> *Hail the auspicious morn, To Prussia's throne is born a royal heir.*
> *May he defend its laws Joined with Old England's cause*
> *Thus win all men's applause, God save the Queen!*[35]

The second reason Frederick was willing to agree to the terms of the bishopric had to do with *realpolitik*. England was the supreme naval and military power of the day. Frederick was willing to ride the coattails of his cousin Queen Victoria for German purposes. His hope was to restore the glory of the Holy Roman Empire. Third, Frederick felt that having a state church with bishops claiming episcopacy back to the apostles would further the cause for the renewal of the Holy Roman Empire. It would only be a matter of time before the Germans had their own bishop claiming

---

34. Ibid., 84–85; emphasis added.
35. Palmer, *Kaiser*, 2.

apostolic episcopacy. This would provide an opportunity for Germany to garner some authority among the Eastern churches in a bid for resurrecting the ideals of the Holy Roman Empire. However, it was not to be.

Another prominent feature to be noted about the Jerusalem Act is the language utilized in reference to nationality. The text clearly identifies the confessional identity of the Lutherans with the German language and nation. Given the fact that the document was drafted by the British parliament with its own state church, this should not be surprising. It highlights, however, the common nature of Christian missions within the Ottoman Empire in the mid nineteenth century. The "Eastern Question" dictated that the churches of the various nations took on the identification of the imperial powers by virtue of administrative necessity, much to the frustration of the missionaries who had been working among indigenous populations before their own governments had arrived.[36] The missionaries, by virtue of their own nationalities, were treated as members of the particular *millet* of their own nation. In this regard, it is clear that the international context was moving more toward national missions. The fact that the first Prussian consul general arrived in Jerusalem only a year after the commencement of the joint Lutheran-Anglican bishopric is quite telling. Not only did the general public and the media of specific nations associate their missionaries with national honor, but also more importantly the Ottomans associated the missionaries with a particular nation, simply in order to fit them into the social structure of the *millet* system. German missionaries were mislabeled as *inglīzī* [English] because they were under the protection of the British crown. In addition, the common Arabic word for "Protestant"—*injīliyyūn* [Evangelical]—is very similar to the Arabic for "English"—*inglīzī*. Linguistically and politically Protestants were associated with Britain. It was British consular agents that would become the major protector of the Protestant community, regardless of denominational or national status.

The first bishop nominated by the Archbishop of Canterbury in 1841 for the joint Lutheran-Anglican bishopric was Michael Solomon Alexander. He was a German Jewish convert and former LJS missionary ordained within the Anglican church. Thus, his pedigree was perfect for the ideals of the "Jewish" see of St. James and the goals of the joint bishopric. There was a great deal of hope among the evangelical Anglicans

---

36. Gensichen, "German Protestant Missions," 184.

and Pietist Germans that this bishopric could be the beginning of the gathering in of the lost sheep of the house of Israel, and thus, the beginning of the end. However, the bishop would become involved in more than simply enticing Jewish converts. Because of the authority vested in the office of bishop, both ecclesiastical and political, the bishopric would have to contend with very difficult and conflicting loyalties.

In 1845 Bishop Alexander died. According to the joint agreement it was now up to the Prussian king to nominate the next bishop in Jerusalem. Frederick settled upon a former Basel seminary graduate and CMS missionary to Egypt and Abyssinia, Samuel Gobat (1799–1879). It is under the thirty-three year tenure of Samuel Gobat (1846–79) that the Lutheran-Anglican bishopric would challenge both the British and German ideals of national mission and identity. In fact, it was Gobat and his policies that would create distinctive Anglican and Lutheran communities. It is for this reason that neither country was able to support the bishopric after the death of Gobat in 1879. The Germans would ultimately withdraw their support by 1881.

Gobat, a French-speaking Swiss, was a graduate of the Basel seminary and ordained by the United Lutheran-Reformed Church of Baden. He had served with the CMS since 1825 in Egypt and Abyssinia. After he was selected, he returned from Malta to be re-ordained a priest and then consecrated a bishop in the Anglican church, according to the Jerusalem Act. Gobat, having worked with the CMS, was predisposed toward focusing on mission to the Oriental and Eastern Orthodox Christians. Thus, even before his arrival in Jerusalem there were concerns among some that he would begin proselytizing among the Greek Orthodox and move the bishopric away from its original purpose of evangelizing among the Jews. This is exactly what happened. When Gobat arrived in Jerusalem he had one congregation, consisting of forty or fifty communicants made up of a small foreign community and a handful of Jewish converts.[37] He quickly focused his attention on the those "seekers" among the Greeks who were interested in reading the Scriptures, and founded schools open to all regardless of religious confession, but aimed primarily at the large Greek Orthodox community.

Gobat claimed that there were dissatisfied members of the Greek Orthodox Church who miraculously petitioned him to provide services

---

37. Richter, *History of Protestant Missions*, 239.

for them in Arabic. These Greek Orthodox evangelicals now found a new association within Gobat's community.[38] He would not dissuade dissatisfied Orthodox from seeking sanctuary within the confines of the Protestant fold. The Archbishop of Canterbury, who ultimately supported this view, wrote in 1850:

> If Greek Christians, dissatisfied with the state of their Church, desire scriptural fellowship, and are imbued with the belief that the Anglican Church in doctrine and constitution doth answer to this condition, it were unreasonable to forbid the Bishop to afford to such Christians, his help and countenance. It were desirable, indeed, that congregations formed under these circumstances should be shepherded by likeminded priests of their original communion; if, therefore, the charge were undertaken by Anglican clergyman, this was to be looked upon merely as a measure of expediency, in order to preserve the seceders from complete spiritual destitution.[39]

Naturally, the Greek Orthodox patriarch was not thrilled with this new perspective; nor was Robert Finn, the new British consul general. Finn's father-in-law had originally been approached about being the first joint bishop, but declined in favor of Alexander who was a Jewish convert. Finn, and his wife, were very much interested in the work of LJS, and thus saw Gobat as betraying the intention of the bishopric. The two would ultimately become rivals during Finn's tenure in Jerusalem as the british consul.

Gobat's intention was to follow the method of "indirect evangelism," of encouraging the local Christians in order to bring about a revitalization of the ancient churches as a witness to the Muslim community. However, as happened in Lebanon, Syria, and Egypt among the missions of the Presbyterians and Congregationalists, Gobat found himself facing a growing number of interested Orthodox who desired to join the Protestant church and come under the bishop's care. They were not interested in becoming missionaries to the Muslims. Gobat then began organizing schools in Jerusalem and Nablus, in As-Salt (in Jordan), Bethlehem, and Jaffa, which created the nucleus of a new community. By 1874 these Greek Orthodox seekers would be organized into a new congregation, St.

---

38. Tibawi, *British Interests*, 93–94.

39. Ibid., 102. It should be noted that this quote by the archbishop is not found in any formal British records, but only in Gobat's autobiography, *Samuel Goba*, 292–93. Raheb also includes a German translation of this in "Die Evangelische Lutherische" 189.

Paul's, in Jerusalem. Gobat's decisions incensed the high church Anglican bishops who were sure Gobat had planned this all along charged him with proselytism. He responded to the charges, stating publicly:

> And now what am I to do? I have never wished to make converts from the old Churches, but only to lead to the Lord and to the knowledge of His truth as many as possible. From henceforth, I shall be obliged to receive into our communion such as are excluded for Bible-truth's sake from other Churches.[40]

In 1851 Gobat invited the CMS to come and work in Palestine to look after the schools he had organized, primarily among the (former) Greek Orthodox Palestinians. The CMS sent out an officer from England to check on the feasibility of such a request and ultimately decided that the time was right. They immediately sent out a number of Reformed-Lutheran Germans, one of whom was Frederick Augustus Klein, another graduate from the Basel seminary. Klein would go down in history as the discoverer of the famous ninth century B.C.E. Moabite Stone (which mentions the Israelites in a non-biblical text). His primary work, however, was as head of the CMS work in Palestine, directing the schools in Jerusalem, Bethlehem, Jaffa, and Nazareth.[41] Gobat's school system helped to develop a distinct Protestant, or Evangelical (*al-injīliyyūn*) identity in Palestine. By the beginning of the twentieth century, some fifty years after Gobat took over as bishop, the CMS had some fifty-four schools.[42]

As in previous years, German Lutheran Pietists proved to be the primary missionaries of the CMS. Two Württembergers that proved to be exceptional missionaries under CMS authority in Palestine were Christian Fallscheer and Johannes Zeller. Fallscheer worked in both Jerusalem and Nablus among both the Greek Orthodox and Muslims. In fact, he won the hearts and minds of the Muslim community, so much so that the Muslim leaders of Nablus carried Fallscheer's casket at his funeral.[43] Zeller, on the other hand, won the admiration of the local Greek Orthodox and Roman Catholic priests. Another important German Lutheran under the CMS was Theodore Friedrich Wolters. Previously working in Smyrna, Wolters was brought in to help organize the congregation in Jaffa.

---

40. Stock, *History of the CMS*, 2:148.
41. Tibawi, *British Interests*, 110.
42. Richter, *History of Protestant Missions*, 253.
43. Ibid., 244.

Upon the death of Gobat in 1879, it was the Archbishop of Canterbury's turn to appoint a new bishop. He appointed Joseph Barclay, a former LJS missionary as bishop, in hopes of returning the see to its intended purpose of focusing on the Jewish community in Palestine. However, times had passed the joint bishopric by. Even before Gobat's death, the community under the bishop's care was fractured into various groups with a wide variety of goals, all with different funding sources. The CMS and the LJS were completely separate institutions with different and sometimes competing projects. In addition, pressure from various wings of the Anglican church had pressured the bishop to focus upon bilateral relations with the Eastern prelates. And, with the arrival of more and more Germans, involved in their own private ministries, these new Lutherans were beyond the purview and authority of the Lutheran-Anglican bishop. The Arabic congregation in Jerusalem was holding an Anglican liturgy in Arabic, the English-speaking diplomatic community was holding services in English, while the growing German community held their own service in German. Thus, the bishop had very little power to control the growing and disparate Protestant community.

In addition, German support for the joint bishopric was waning. King Frederick passed away in 1861. The Lutherans had lost their central supporter of the joint bishopric. Without an heir, Frederick's brother, William I, took over the reigns of the empire. William did not share his brother's romantic ideals of the Holy Roman Empire. In addition, now under the central leadership of Prime Minister Otto Van Bismarck, Germans were feeling confident enough to establish their own national projects without British Anglican assistance. Thus, Bishop Barclay's untimely death only two years into his tenure spelled the death knell of the joint bishopric in 1881.

After Bishop Barclay's premature death it was the Prussian king's turn to nominate the bishop. However, because of the turn of events for Germany, the waning support for the bishopric both in Germany and Britain, and the fractured Protestant missionary community in Palestine, Emperor William I was slow to nominate a new candidate. Crown Prince Frederick III met with the Archbishop of Canterbury and let him know that there was considerable concern about the original conditions of the bishopric agreed to by his grandfather. The two major objections were to the archbishop's outright veto of any Prussian nominee, and the fact that the Lutheran pastors had to receive an Anglican ordination.[44] In Germany the issue of Anglican ordination had always been a contentious one. And yet, because of the fact that all Lutheran ordinands had to clearly subscribe to the Augsburg Confession, the authority of the joint bishopric was not questioned from a theological perspective but rather from a political one. As stated above, the orders of ordination had been *adiaphora* for the early Lutheran missionaries. Given the fact that the missionaries had to work among the ancient churches of the Middle East, the issue of ecclesiastical authority was paramount. The bishops of the ancient churches were more responsive to those who could claim to follow in an apostolic tradition. (Even among the evangelical churches of the Middle East today that take their roots from the Congregational and Presbyterian churches, the authority of their leadership is continually questioned, and the moderators of those churches have taken on themselves the trappings of Eastern prelates.) Thus, the Lutheran missionaries saw the purpose and advantage of being associated with a bishop.

In the end, it was the German political authorities that formally withdrew from joint bishopric in 1886. By that time a Lutheran presence was firmly established.[45] Lutherans no longer needed Anglican societies to function in the Middle East. The Lutheran missionaries and their projects had finally received national support and funding. This was vital for any type of work in the Ottoman Empire. In an era in which Jerusalem was taking on more importance among European evangelicals, as a rising power Germany could not afford not to stake its own claim and still maintain its reputation at the table of nations. It replaced the joint bishopric with the appointment of its own provost, who would now be responsible to the German government to coordinate all German missions.[46] The increasing number of German immigrants, pilgrims, and scholars to Palestine who had no connection with the CMS, LJS, or the joint Lutheran-Anglican bishop necessitated that the German government become more directly involved. By 1850, Germans began arriving in Palestine to take up their own homegrown missions and projects. They were outside the jurisdiction of the CMS or the joint Lutheran-Anglican bishop and had support and funding from German sources.

44. Tibawi, *British Interests*, 218.

45. For the correspondence between Germany and England on the conclusion of the joint bishopric see ibid., 217–19.

46. Raheb, "Die Evangelische Lutherische," 192.

The establishment of a new bishop in Jerusalem in the nineteenth century, supported by both the British and German crowns, would naturally have political consequences. The pietistic endeavors of the missionaries would also impact politics. The Lutheran-Anglican bishop, as any bishop, represented the authority of the church, and in this case both the British and German churches—and their crowns. Given the political nature of religious communities in the Ottoman Empire (and even today in many countries of the Middle East) the bishopric would affect the overall social-political landscape. It would affect the standing of all existing religious communities; Orthodox and Catholic, as well as the existing Jewish community.

The Lutheran-Anglican bishop, although given the mandate of creating a church from the Jewish community—which was very small—also served as the official Anglican and Prussian ecclesiastical authority in the area. The missionaries of the CMS that had been invited into Palestine by the bishop would ultimately have nothing to do with the bishopric and its mission. There was great confusion as CMS missionaries, being commissioned by an independent mission society of the church, suddenly found themselves under a bishop whose goal was different than their own and the important high church polity in Jerusalem for which they cared little. But, because of Anglican church polity, the bishop was the local Anglican authority over the territory. The work of the CMS among the Eastern churches led to charges that the Anglicans were sheep stealing. The bishop had to justify his work among Eastern Christians since this was not his original mandate by the Jerusalem Act. Thus, the concerns of the high church parties were justified, as the bishop in Jerusalem could not very well maintain positive ecumenical relations with the Eastern prelates when his missionaries were encouraging Orthodox members to join the Anglican church! Meanwhile the LJS missionaries continued their work in education and medical missions among the Jews. The CMS missionaries were primarily involved with the communities of the Eastern churches. At times there were tensions between the missionaries and the bishop over policies and decisions, as well as among their "surrogate" communities of the different nationalities (i.e., religious confessions).[47]

---

47. In 1890 Bishop G. F. P. Blythe would accuse the CMS missionaries in Palestine of proselytizing among the Greek Orthodox and so declared full control over all CMS projects and personnel in his diocese. This created a debate among the bishops in Britain, who held a conference and judged that the bishop had no right to take over an indepen-

Two corollary events came about as a result of the establishment of the bishopric *vis-à-vis* Anglican-Catholic relations. First of all, Bishop John Henry Newhouse, one of the important high church Anglican bishops who opposed the idea of the bishopric, ultimately left the Anglican church to accept the authority of the bishop of Rome. Although there were numerous issues involved in his famous decision to submit to papal authority, it was the decision of the British government and the Anglican church to undertake the new bishopric in Jerusalem which sent him over the edge.[48] The second issue involving the Roman Catholics was to revitalize their own Latin Patriarch of Jerusalem. They saw the new bishopric in Jerusalem as a challenge to their own ecclesiastical jurisdiction. Whereas the Franciscans had been granted important rights to the holy places in Jerusalem, they had no bishop. Thus, Joseph Valerga was consecrated the new Latin Patriarch in October 1847, restoring the office to Jerusalem for the first time since the patriarchate fell when the last crusader outpost of Acre was conquered by the Muslims in 1291. The joint Anglican-Lutheran bishopric re-antagonized Protestant Catholic relations.

THE DEVELOPMENT OF GERMAN INSTITUTIONS IN PALESTINE

Throughout the middle of the nineteenth century, a wave of interest in the Holy Land overcame Germany as it became possible for Germans to visit Palestine out of curiosity and scholarly interest. The idea of actually traveling to Palestine became possible in 1831 when Ibrahim Pasha invaded Palestine, then Syria, and annexed the territory in the name of the viceroy of Egypt. The Egyptians created a new infrastructure of administration and communication, and the region began to prosper. It now became safe and possible, in the estimation of many Christians from Germany, to travel to the Holy Land. By the time the Ottomans regained Syria from the Egyptians, along with help from the major European powers, Arab society had been opened up to the influences of the West. With the legal Ottoman *Tanẓīmāt* prescripts of the *Hattī Şerīf* of 1839 and the *Hattī Humāyūn* of 1856 declaring Jewish-Christian-Muslim legal equality, each European nation became involved in a patronage race to both support

---

dent mission organization. Blythe, however, continued to work at cross purposes with the remaining CMS missionaries. See Richter, *History of Protestant Missions*, 246–47.

48. Stock, *History of the CMS*, 1:422.

various indigenous communities and establish their own institutions. In addition, with the rise in the interest in biblical archaeology and biblical scholarship, especially among German scholars, Jerusalem was opened up to Western institutions searching for historical evidences of the Bible. The German Lutheran Institute for Ancient Science of the Holy Land was opened on property granted to the emperor until it was eventually moved to the site of the Augusta Victoria hospice on the Mount of Olives.[49]

Throughout the end of the eighteenth and the nineteenth century, the growth of higher biblical criticism among German scholars created an interest in studying first hand the lands of the Bible and in biblical archaeology. Interested scholars and their patrons began traveling to Jerusalem to seek out the historical roots of the Bible and investigate the "historical Jesus." F. A. Klein's discovery of the Moabite Stone in 1898 was part of this growing German fascination with the Holy Land. Modern methods of transportation, primarily the steamship, made it possible for interested scholars and travelers to visit the East. This facilitated German royalty in supporting the foundation of guesthouses, hospitals, and study centers for philanthropic purposes.[50] Thus, by the late nineteenth century, Germans were acquiring properties and undertaking projects on their own accord. The lands of the "Terrible Turk" had now given way to the "Holy Land," which was not to be re-conquered by the sword—but by the shovel.

But scholars were not the only ones interested in Palestine. The Pietists were still enamored with the Holy Land, but for spiritual reasons. In 1843 groups of Württemberg Pietist Lutherans from southwest Germany were beginning to migrate to Palestine in order to participate in the "Last Days." The Pietists of Württemberg developed a strong connection with the Holy Land. They had a deep desire and commitment to create Christian communities throughout the Holy Land "that would be an example and a source of light to their surroundings."[51] Oblivious to both Ottoman laws regarding the residency of foreigners in Ottoman territory and to the authority of the Lutheran-Anglican bishop, these small Christian communities simply settled in various areas of Palestine on their own accord. The influx of immigrants necessitated the need for a political arrangement between the bishop, the Prussian consul, and the

---

49. Rhein and Döring, *Jerusalem*, 189; Krüger, *Lutheran Church of the Redeemer*, 22.
50. Rhein and Döring, *Jerusalem*, 188–89.
51. Carmel, "C. F. Spittler," 256.

Turkish governor to relocate the Württemberg Lutherans to Russian territory, where other Germans had migrated years before.[52]

Another group of Pietist Germans that immigrated to Palestine in order to witness the second coming were the German millennialists known as the Templers. The Association for the Assembling of God's People in Jerusalem was established in 1854 by Christoph Hoffmann, a "talented but eccentric" Württemberg pastor who hoped to "collect the people of God in Jerusalem to prepare the way for the coming of the Kingdom of God."[53] Hoffmann interpreted the developments of the Crimean War (1854–56) as the beginning of the end for both the Ottoman Empire and the world. He led a group of three thousand Templers to Palestine in 1867, arriving in hopes of preparing the way for the return of Christ.[54] They settled in different communities in Haifa, Jaffa, and Jerusalem. King of Prussia William I was not particularly a religious person, but initially supported the Templers. Because they were German subjects, William saw their settlement in Palestine as furthering the cause for the rise of German power within the Ottoman Empire. He petitioned the Sublime Porte (the Ottoman foreign ministry office) to grant the Templers land where they could be organized into very effective colonies.[55] Once the particular religious views of the Templers became known, they proved to be somewhat of an embarrassment to the German government. Christoph Hoffmann's views were very controversial and would later cause him to be expelled from the Württemberg state church. The government then maintained its distance from the colonists until after German unification in 1871. By then there was growing pressure to support German colonies abroad, and the general German population saw the Templers as an already established German colony abroad. In 1877 Germany sent a small fleet to the eastern Mediterranean to demonstrate its willingness to protect German subjects in the Templer colonies.

Another assembly that saw the opening up of Palestine as a sign for mission work was the Pilgrims Mission. Christian Friedrich Spittler was sent in 1833 to develop a mission in the Holy Land similar to that of the Moravians, where committed missionaries would come and settle among

---

52. Tibawi, *British Interests*, 80.
53. Richter, *History of Protestant Missions*, 234.
54. Carmel, "German Settlers in Palestine," 443.
55. Rhein, Döring, et. al, *Jerusalem*, 29.

the Jews and Oriental Christians, providing for their own livelihood as local artisans; as matchmakers, carpenters or locksmiths, for example. They would then be a living witness to the evangelical faith. Spittler had been in communication with Samuel Gobat about these ideas when Gobat was still a CMS missionary in Egypt. Gobat was very supportive of the idea of sending a wave of Pietists to the Holy Land. In response to Spittler, he wrote that these "Christian workmen, craftsmen and peasants to the Holy Lands [would be] as salt to the earth and a light in the darkness . . . who would demonstrate true Christianity to the inhabitants through quiet work and good deeds."[56] It would not be until the re-establishment of Ottoman sovereignty in 1841 after the Egyptian affair that the possibility of these colonies would actually take shape. With the establishment of the Lutheran-Anglican joint bishopric and the Prussian consul general in Palestine, there would be sufficient support and protection for Germans to travel and settle in the Holy Land.

When Samuel Gobat was offered the post of the bishopric in 1846, Spittler saw this as a sign from God. His old friend to whom he had shared his visions of a German colony in the Holy Land was now the bishop over that precise territory. Thus, only five months after Gobat was offered the bishopric, two missionaries of the Pilgrims Mission sent out to Palestine with these formal instructions:

> Quietly establish a small German Protestant *Brüderhaus* in the form of a fraternal community, and to set up a warehouse of Bibles and Christian publications of every kind for the Orient . . . to be in closer touch with poor people, actually to live among them and to lead them to the Savior by word and example in every possible way. . .
>
> Only by a childlike and vital faith in the Lord, and by mutual trust, can the whole project and enterprise of establishing a German Protestant *Brüderhaus* in Jerusalem be accomplished. On this foundation alone will Salvation come and be triumphant. Our God and Savior, who always shows his love and lends his help to the weak and hears the prayers of his children, in They mercy help us in this. Amen.[57]

The German Pilgrims Mission's *Brüderhaus* would struggle throughout its twenty-four year existence in Jerusalem. The missionaries moved

---

56. Carmel, "German Settlers in Palestine," 260.

57. Ibid., 267–68.

into an apartment in the Old City, among the Armenians (which did not meet the missionaries' original expectations of living and working among the Jews of Palestine), and attempted to survive by the work of their own hands. This proved to be exceedingly difficult, as the standard of living in Turkish Jerusalem was not to the level of their homeland. They could not acquire the same materials for their own crafts, nor were they able to gain the confidence of the local populace who relied on their own well-established and preferred networks of skilled labor. The Pilgrims then began targeting the growing European population of Jerusalem for their business, which proved quite successful. This ultimately raised questions among the mission committee in Germany regarding the original goal of the missionaries as a quiet witness among the poor in Jerusalem. The board of the Pilgrims Mission began to think about other alternatives for the house. One option, suggested by Bishop Gobat, was to utilize the house as a training center for missionaries heading to Abyssinia (Ethiopia). Given Gobat's former role as a missionary to Ethiopia himself, this seemed to make sense. However, Spittler who was working from Germany could not oversee the work effectively, and once again this project pulled the society away from its original intention of providing a Christian witness to the local Jewish community. Because of the growing interest in the Holy Land, the idea was developing among supporters of the mission to develop the house into a modified guesthouse for Christians traveling to Jerusalem. The missionaries of the *Brüderhaus*, however, wanted nothing to do with this kind of ministry, and so the board sent out a new missionary to reorganize the house.

Johann Ludwig Schneller and his wife were sent out in 1854 to take up the responsibility of being the "house parents" of the *Brüderhaus*. Six new missionaries bound for Abyssinia accompanied them. But tensions between the Schnellers and the other missionaries prohibited them from developing a cohesive community. During his short time in the house, Schneller began to develop his own ideas about how the property could best provide for the poor in Jerusalem. The schizophrenic conception of the house and the relations between the German missionaries was strained enough that the Schnellers moved out of the house into their own apartment.

In 1857 Hermann Loewenthal arrived to take up a new role that Spittler now saw as the only option for the future of the *Brüderhaus*. With the foreign community continuing to grow in Jerusalem due to the opening of foreign diplomatic posts, Spittler now threw his energy into developing a "Mission Trade Association." The original intention of the trade center was to "allow Christian merchants who wished to put their training in commerce at the Mission's disposal to serve the Lord in their profession," which would provide a source of income for the mission.[58] The association, working from a large plot of property outside the walls of the Turkish Old City that had been previously purchased by Schneller, developed into one of the largest import-export firms in Palestine. As a commercial center it helped the various local and foreign Christian communities in purchasing and exporting primarily fruit and olive wood products, as well as importing European items desired by the foreign community.[59] This enterprise of the *Brüderhaus* had now taken it so far away from its original intention of working among the poor Jewish community of Jerusalem that even Spittler began to question its direction. With the establishment of the German community in Jerusalem the association had plenty of business and would continue to thrive off of the growing German expatriates. Recognizing the disparity in their vision for the *Brüderhaus*, the Pilgrims Mission committee released themselves from their property in 1870 and sold it to two of their own mission personnel, Frutiger and Duisberg, who continued on with the firm and developed a successful business. Spittler and the Mission committee were all too willing to release themselves from the problem that they themselves had created in their desire to have a successful mission post in Jerusalem when Schneller found a solution for a continued Protestant ministry. Sticking to his vision of working among the poor, the situation presented itself for Schneller to step forward and undertake one of the most successful German Lutheran mission enterprises in the Middle East.

As a result of civil war between the Druze and Maronites in Lebanon and Syria in 1860, Christians were massacred in the villages of Dayr al-Qamar and Zahle, as well as in Damascus. Although the 1860 civil war began as an inter-confessional dispute between the Druze and Maronites, as a result of the changing social-political power structure in Lebanon, the unrest spilled over into Damascus where the urban Sunni Muslim population was already disgruntled because of the recent reforms from Istanbul, such as the *Hattī Humāyūn* of 1856 declaring Christian-Muslim

---

58. Ibid., 278.
59. Ibid., 284.

equality of citizenship. Schneller, hearing of the massacres and of the untold suffering of the Christian community, traveled north to see what help he could offer. In Sidon Schneller found nine boys who had been orphaned in the massacre. He brought them back to Jerusalem and began to care for them. The orphanage became a major focus of the Pilgrims Mission, so much so that the Mission Trade Association became worried that its funds would be siphoned off to the new orphanage, and there was a great deal of tension between the two projects.

The orphanage was a huge success. Children at the orphanage were trained in a variety of trades; carpentry, pottery making, etc. Schneller added additional properties in northern Palestine and southern Lebanon, creating an agricultural school and farm, and eventually organizing the Lutheran congregation in Nazareth.[60] In addition to appeals by the Pilgrims Mission, Schneller sent out his own appeals for funds to help support the orphans. The orphanage functioned successfully up until World War I, when the Turks confiscated its properties. The British held the property during the Mandate period from 1920 until 1948, when it was then taken over by the Israeli government. The Israeli government eventually provided reparations to the mission for its loss of property and land. The Schneller orphanage was relocated to southern Lebanon in 1951 by Johann's grandson, Hermann Schneller, where it continues to function today, serving orphans "socially and vocationally underprivileged children regardless of their background, race, religion" or gender in southern Lebanon.[61]

The 1860 massacres in Lebanon and Syria provided an opportunity for deaconesses of Kaiserswerth to come to Jerusalem in order to help care for those tragically affected. The deaconess program, founded in 1836 by Reverend Theodore and Frederick Fliedner in Kaiserswerth, Germany, developed the earliest nursing schools and the most effective deaconess programs worldwide. (Florence Nightingale, the famous British nurse who served British troops in the Crimean War, visited the Kaiserswerth school in 1851 and utilized much of what she learned there in her own profession.) The Fliedners had first arrived in Jerusalem in 1851 at the invitation of Bishop Gobat and organized a hospice for pilgrims, as well

---

60. Haddad, "Lutheran Church in the Middle East," 120–21.
61. See the Johann Ludwig Schneller School Web site at http://www.jlss.org.

as a boarding school for girls, which was staffed by CMS workers.[62] The Fliedners and the Kaiserswerth deaconesses set up a children's hospital and a girl's home named "Talitha Cum," which was run by Fliedner's son-in-law, Rev. Disselhoff.[63] The Kaiserswerth deaconesses also began work in Beirut under the auspices of the Prussian Order of St. John, which was committed to the care of the sick and infirm. In 1887 the order turned over their property to the care of Syrian Protestant College, run by the American Presbyterians. This hospital would ultimately become the medical center of the American University of Beirut. In addition to the Kaiserswerth deaconesses, the Berlin Missionary Society also worked very closely with Gobat in Bethlehem and Beit Jala, ultimately taking over the administration of the CMS schools.[64]

In order to handle the growth of German mission programs whose financial support and interest was outside of the purview of the Anglican church, Bishop Gobat reached an agreement with the German missionaries in 1852 to divide Palestine into two spheres; north of Jerusalem would be the area allocated for the work of the British mission societies, while south of Jerusalem would be the area allocated for the work of the German missions. The administration of these German mission posts was then organized into an association called the Jerusalem Union. Ultimately, the union would oversee the work of the Arab congregations and schools that were primarily made up of former Greek Orthodox Arab Christians; in Bethlehem (1860), Beit Jala (1879), Hebron (1884), Beit Sahour (1900) and Jerusalem (1903).[65]

Ludwig Schneller, son of the famous the longtime Pilgrims Mission missionary Johann Schneller, was asked to take over as pastor of the Bethlehem congregation. He began collecting money from friends and contacts in Germany, and by 1887 he had begun to build "Christmas Church" in Bethlehem. The church received official approval from the sultan, who was asked by German empress Augusta Victoria to allow the

62. Rhein and Döring, *Jerusalem*, 187–88.

63. The name *Talitha Cum* comes from the Aramaic in Mark 5:41 (Richter, *History of Protestant Missions*, 202).

64. Tibawi, *British Interests*, 160.

65. Raheb, "Die Evangelische Lutherische," 190–91; Richter, *History of Protestant Missions*, 259. The Hebron post was closed shortly after WWII. These congregations would become four of the six congregations of the Evangelical Lutheran Church of Jordan and the Holy Land, the other two congregations being Rammallah and Amman.

church to be built as a favor to her. It was this church that would be the site of Israeli incursions and occupation of its premises in April 2002.⁶⁶

German Catholics also saw opportunities to support Christian witness and mission in the Holy Land. A Bavarian Catholic organization called "Custody for the Holy Land" was founded in 1843 to benefit the Church of the Holy Sepulchre, the traditional site of Jesus's death and resurrection. This was followed by the creation of the Association of the Holy Grave in 1855 to help support the work for what would be the newly resurrected Latin Patriarchate of Jerusalem. In the 1885 the German Catholics also established the Palestine Association of Catholics in Germany to help German Catholic interests. These two organizations joined together in 1895 to form the German Association of the Holy Land, which is still in operation today.⁶⁷ Because of the growing number of German Catholic pilgrims, the kaiser granted the German Catholic community a gift of land that was given to him by the sultan in 1899 for the purpose of building the Church of the Dormition on Mount Zion. The church was finally dedicated in 1910.⁶⁸

Prior to the 1870s, the German Catholics had no direct ecclesiastical or diplomatic support in the Holy Land. Frederick Willaim IV was a staunch Lutheran. During Frederick's reign it was the Austrian state that sought and encouraged German Catholic endeavors. The Austro-Hungarian Consulate opened in 1849 with the explicit mission of defending Austrian Catholic interests, protecting Catholic pilgrims and tourists, offering consular protection, supporting the property of the Holy Sepulchre, defending the Latin Patriarchate, as well as "officially" supporting the work of the Lutheran-Anglican bishop. Of course, such goals were impossible to accomplish in the highly charged confessional situation of Jerusalem. One could not publicly support both the Latin Patriarch and the Protestant bishop. The two had a very poor relationship and this permeated German Catholic and Protestant relations. Thus, the consulate had an impossible task.

In 1871, however, the German Catholics were brought under the full authority of William I, who was crowned "German Emperor." Unlike

---

66. For a very moving account of this occupation of the church see Raheb, *Bethlehem Besieged*.

67. See the Web site of *Deustcher Verein vom Heiligen Land* [The German association of the Holy Land] at http://www.heilig-land-verein.de/.

68. Elian, "German Interests and the Jewish Community," 428–31.

Frederick, William was moved more by national interests and honor than by faith. From the mid 1860s through 1871, the Prussian chancellor Otto von Bismarck had been orchestrating German unification, as the German Union added the important territories of Bohemia, Moravia and Austria. Thus, with the unification of Germany in 1871 the state was developing ideas of national-cultural missions abroad, as opposed to the purely ecumenical Pietist ideals that had originally helped to foster the concept of the joint Lutheran-Anglican bishopric.[69] Emperor William would begin supporting German Catholic endeavors in the Holy Land because they were his German subjects. Both Catholic and Protestant German missions would now have the full backing of the German Empire.

In 1878 Great Britain, Austria-Hungary, France, Germany, Italy, Russia, and the Ottoman Empire signed the Treaty of San Stefano as the result of the Russo-Turkish War, in which Russia sought to impose its right of the Treaty of Küchük Kaynarja to support the Orthodox Christians of the empire in the Balkans among the Bulgarians and Serbians. Article 62 of the treaty was an international mandate for the Ottomans to uphold the proclamations of 1839 and 1856. In other words, the international powers were forcing the Ottoman government to stand by its previous statements concerning the religious minorities, and thus, support the endeavors of the imperial powers. The article stated:

> The Sublime Porte having expressed the intention to maintain the principle of religious liberty, and give it the widest scope, the Contracting Parties take note of this spontaneous declaration. In no part of the Ottoman Empire shall difference of religion be alleged against any person as a ground for exclusion or incapacity in matters relating to the enjoyment of civil or political rights, admission to public employments, functions, and honors, or the exercise of the various professions and industries, in any locality whatsoever. The freedom and outward exercise of all forms of worship shall be assured to all, and no communions, or to their relations with their spiritual chiefs.
>
> Ecclesiastics, pilgrims, and monks of all nationalities traveling in Turkey in Europe, or in Turkey in Asia, shall enjoy the same rights, advantages, and privileges.
>
> The right of official protection by the Diplomatic and Consular Agents of the Powers in Turkey is recognized both as regards the

---

69. Farah, "Protestantism and Politics," 377.

above-mentioned persons and their religious, charitable, and other establishments in the Holy Places and elsewhere . . . .[70]

After the signing of the official treaty, the imperial powers were invited by the German Emperor to an international congress in Berlin that same year. It was here that Germany, following the unification of the German territories under Bismarck and fully confident in its own role among the imperial powers of Europe, invited the European nations to clarify their own imperial designs. The Congress of Berlin in 1878 would become the European agreement to divide up Africa into internationally recognized colonies. Gone were the days of riding British coattails!

Holding colonies in South-West Africa (later Namibia) and Tanganyika (Tanzania), Germany saw itself as a propagator of Christian civilization. More importantly for the German missionaries within the Ottoman Empire, the congress began, in the words of William H. Dawson, a "policy of peaceful penetration which served her so well."[71] Istanbul was now opened up to all kinds of German personnel: military, business, philanthropist, and religious. It was after this conference that Germany was willing to act on behalf of its subjects who had interests within the Ottoman Empire, not because of their religious undertakings or spiritual values, but merely because they were German subjects who were involved in a mission of the German nation.[72] In the eyes of Middle Eastern Muslims and Christians, however, there was no difference.

This rise of German power in 1878 was the final straw that would lead to the German withdrawal from the Lutheran-Anglican bishopric. Criticism had been growing for some time that the bishopric was a "betrayal of German interests."[73] Thus, being recognized internationally as a legitimate European power; holding foreign colonies as well as property within Jerusalem, Germany had now achieved its objectives of establishing itself in the Orient. The Templer colonies, once ostracized, now became the focus of the German public's desire for German glory and honor abroad. They had become a part of the development of German culture and presence in Palestine during the early part of the twentieth century. During World War II the British would turn these colonies into intern-

70. Mowat, *Select Treaties and Documents*, 83.
71. Dawson, *German Empire, 1867–1914*, 2:134.
72. Carmel, "Political Significance," 59.
73. Pittman, "Protestant Bishopric," 49.

ment camps for the German citizens living in Palestine, who were seen as possible collaborators with the Reich. Ultimately, these communities were "relocated" to Australia.

THE KAISER AND REDEEMER LUTHERAN CHURCH

In 1869 Crown Prince Frederick III visited Jerusalem on his way to Egypt for the international gala celebrating the opening of the Suez Canal. On the occasion of this visit the sultan of Istanbul, 'Abdul Aziz, granted the German Empire a gift of property in Jerusalem—the ruins of the hospice of the Knights of St. John. The German Emperor then authorized the process for the building of a Lutheran church in Jerusalem as well as a hospice for German pilgrims.

In 1888, William II took the royal seat as German Emperor after the death of his father. The stage was now set for the German Reich to display its authority and might in the great Imperial Age. On Reformation Day, 1898 Emperor William II and Empress Augusta Victoria, the granddaughter of Queen Victoria of England, dedicated the new Lutheran Church of the Redeemer in the Old City.[74] The event was one of great pomp and circumstance. In some ways, Frederick IV's grand romantic notions of Jerusalem of the medieval era had been fulfilled. Prussia, as part of the German union of states, now had a Lutheran church in Jerusalem built over the remains of the old site of the hospice of the Order of the Knights of St. John. One could not get more nostalgic for the Holy Roman Empire than that! This event was the crowning achievement of German national missions in Palestine.

On the same day as the dedication, William II took possession of another piece of property on the Mount of Olives. Here was built a hospice named in honor of his wife, Augusta Victoria. The Augusta Victoria Hospice was dedicated in 1910, together with the Dormition Abby for the German Catholics, and was intended to become a center for German pilgrims and visitors. However, only four years after its dedication the Ottomans impounded the property and utilized it for their purposes in the Great War. It was then taken over by the British during their occupation of Palestine. The property would ultimately be given over to the Lutheran World Federation in 1950, in whose hands the property rests today.

---

74. Neubert-Preine, *100 Jafre Evamgeosch-Lutherische Erlöserkirche*, 11.

By the late nineteenth century, as the fervor of German nationalism rose, German Lutherans had carved out territory of their own in Palestine through their own mission projects. There was great pressure from German supporters to withdraw from the Lutheran-Anglican bishopric and to allow German missions to stand on its own two feet. With the presence of German royalty and the establishment of the Lutheran Church of the Redeemer, Augusta Victoria, and the Church of the Dormition, the Germans had a vital presence in Jerusalem. However, the early days of Württemberg Pietists were now gone. William II was not interested in Jerusalem as a holy place, or even in converting Jews. He was, however, very much interested in the international prestige of German presence there. Given the role of the foreign nations in Jerusalem in the nineteenth century, it was vital that Germany maintain a presence there. Yet William II was more interested in another area of the Orient. He focused more of his attention on the massive and expensive "Berlin to Baghdad" railway. He saw this as the most important imperial project for Germany. It was this growing imperial relationship that tied Germany together with the Ottoman Empire in the years immediately preceding World War I.

In the midst of the intrigue of the "Eastern Question," from which German Lutheran mission projects benefited, their role in Palestine would continue to be tied to international politics and the affairs of the German Empire. Because of German imperialism in Europe, the occupying British forces impounded German property during World War I and German missionaries were suspect as agents of an enemy state. With British control of Palestine during and after World War II, German citizens were placed in internment camps, utilizing the Templers' colonies for such space until most of the German colonists were relocated to Australia. After the realities of the horrors of the Holocaust became known, German missionaries would lose a great deal of credibility, as members of a nation involved in atrocities against the very people to whom the early missionaries came to convert. Even if the German missionaries were not complicit in the Holocaust, simply by virtue of their nationality they were held liable. The German churches began to do all that they could to repair the relationship with the world Jewish community. But much like the Pietist-Scholastic debates of the late sixteenth and early seventeenth centuries, German Lutherans are still divided regarding matters of how to interpret the role of Judaism in the grand scheme of salvation history, and more specifically the State of Israel. On the one hand, some pietistic German organizations, although no longer interested in converting Jews, do see support for the State of Israel as a method of supporting the overall mission of Christ. Christian Zionism has become a popular theological position for many of the contemporary German Pietists who see the success of Israel as fulfillment of biblical prophecy. On the other hand, there are those German churches that have not supported the role of the Israeli occupation of Palestinian territories. Because of guilt over the Holocaust, however, they have had to rely on their counterpart Lutheran churches from Norway, Sweden, and the United States to make statements on issues of justice, especially when relating to Lutheran Palestinians. Contemporary German Lutheran missions in the Palestinian territories and the modern state of Israel must now take into account their relationship with the Israeli government before acting or speaking.

Once a distant mission post of the ABCFM in 1824, by the end of the nineteenth century Jerusalem had become the center of international activity. Lutheran Pietists originally came to Jerusalem interested in converting Jews. Some came with the explicit hope of witnessing the second coming of Christ. However, by the end of the century German interests had become more scholarly. The Pietists lost out to the scholastics and the humanists, as erudite study of the Holy Land overtook religious piety. The Scholars too would lose out to the politicians and statesmen, as international glory ultimately ended in the destruction of German designs. Yet, the early activity of the Lutheran Pietists, under the auspices of the Anglican mission agencies, did create an indigenous Arab Christian community, which would become both Anglican and Lutheran. These new "converts" came primarily from the ranks of the Greek Orthodox Church. In terms of the initial designs to convert Jews and Muslims through "indirect evangelism," however, the mission could be considered a failure. Neither Muslims nor Jews were in any considerable numbers enticed by the united, ecumenical Protestant church. This certainly was not due to the tireless efforts and work of the early missionaries, but was a result of international political movements and cultural forces beyond their control.

5

Early American Lutheran Views of Islam and Mission in Persia

The Shadow of the crescent falls on far-flung Moslem lands, And millions under Islam's yoke bow down to fate's demands; Through weary ages they have moved in silent hopeless night, Their fettered pilgrimage has missed the cross of radiant light.

Give us the will to dedicate our blood-bought lives to Thee, Till Mecca's sons rejoicing join the Son of Cavalry; And from the towers of the mosque this new call has been won: There is no God but Thou, O God; revealed in Christ the Son.

—Rev. W. F. Schmidt, 1955
Lutheran Orient Mission consecration hymn
for new missionaries

THE EARLY LUTHERAN PIETIST movement provided a wide array of individuals firmly committed to foreign missions who viewed the world much differently than did their forbearers. Whereas for Luther and the early Reformers fear of the "Terrible Turk" was clearly part the Reformation worldview, the Pietists viewed Islam within a much more secure world. By the beginning of the eighteenth century, the world was no longer in a bipolar struggle between Christendom and Islam; or in the Islamic reference, the battle between *Dār al-Islām* [the House of Islam] and *Dār al-Ḥarb* [the House of War]. Rather, with advent of new technology in sea travel, the development of the Enlightenment, and the subsequent Industrial Revolution, which resulted in a dramatic military advantage for Europe, by the beginning of the nineteenth century the world was a grand new adventure to be discovered and conquered. The possibilities of European advancement seemed endless. Thus, with the ascendancy of European empires and the relative ease of travel to Africa, Americas, and

South-East Asia, the "Sick Man of Europe" was no longer the nemesis it had once been. There was a newfound optimism in Europe.

The seventeenth century brought about not only a transformation in the balance of economic and military power in Europe, but intellectual power as well. The Reformation had opened up the opportunity for new interpretations of the faith and of the nature of revelation in general. Following closely on the heels of the Reformation, the Enlightenment brought forth successive waves of ideas about the Deity and his relationship with the world, completely separate from the authority of the church as an earthly institution. In other words, the Reformation had begun a process whereupon theological reflection was no longer the sole prerogative of the Roman Catholic Church and its official teachings. There was now space for theological and philosophical dissent.[1]

By the beginning of the eighteenth century, religion was a topic of philosophical enquiry in its own right. The concept of "natural religion," as opposed to "revealed religion," became a subject of curiosity among many Enlightenment thinkers. These Enlightenment ideas found their political end in the documents of the American and French Revolutions of 1776 and 1789, respectively, in which the Deity provided individual rights and abilities for humanity to engage in lifestyles for the public good outside the parameters of religious authoritarian institutions. In addition, the establishment of universities in Europe and North America allowed for the free exercise of philosophical and religious enquiry that gave rise to a wide variety of views on "revealed" and "natural" religion. The church was stripped of its authority by "natural religion."

As the world opened up to European expansion, the previously unknown world, with all of its interesting peoples and cultures, also became the object of speculation and inquiry. Non-Western religions, especially Islam, became the subject of academic study. Publications of Islamic texts, including translations of the Qur'ān, allowed Christians access to material that only a number of scholars in Europe had access to throughout the Middle Ages. The Dominican material on Islam that Luther had trouble accessing was suddenly supplanted by a wide assortment of information that became available for common consumption. Hundreds of works were published on the people, history, and religions of the Orient. Edward Gibbon's popular *The History of the Decline and Fall of the Roman Empire*,

---

1. For a helpful analysis of Enlightenment thought see Bosch, *Transforming Mission*, 264–67.

published between 1776 and 1788, is a classic example of the information to which European audiences were being exposed about the history of Islam and its Prophet.[2]

Whereas the Dominicans and Franciscans began Arabic and Islamic study centers in the medieval period for the purpose of training missionaries, the development of university chairs in Arabic and Islamic studies was for the pursuit of academic knowledge. This was part of the overall explosion in the thirst for knowledge among geographers, historians, philologists, scientists, and explorers in the age of Enlightenment. As early as 1632, a Chair of Arabic Studies was founded at Cambridge, followed by a similar chair at Oxford in 1636. These academic centers provided a wide assortment of images of the "Orient" for Europeans. For some, the centers of research would see the Orient and Islam as immoral and irrational compared to the moral heights of Christianity and the cultures of Europe and North America. Islam would be seen as a backward religion, revealing the more primitive aspects of human culture. In 1633 Andrew Du Ryer translated Robert of Ketton's old Latin version of the Qur'ān into French. Du Ryer's translation was subsequently translated into English in 1649. The editor of the text, Alexander Ross, introduced Mahomet (as he was known) and his religion as such:

> Good reader, the great Arabian imposter, now at last after a thousand years, is by the way of France arrived in England, and his Alcoran, or gallimaufry of errors . . . as full of heresies . . . hath learned to speak English. . . . so should the reading of this Alcoran excited us both to bless God's goodness towards us in this land, who enjoy the light of the gospel . . . as to admire God's judgments who suffers so many countries to be blinded and enslaved with this misshapen issue of Mahomet's brain.[3]

The language here is indicative of a particular genre of interpreting Islam. Works like *The True Nature of Imposture Fully Displayed in the Life of Mahomet* by Humphrey Prideaux in 1697 demonstrated the European Orientalist view of Islam of the time.[4] The Englishman George Sale, in the introduction to his 1734 English translation of the Qur'ān, wrote that in

2. See Gibbon, *Decline and Fall*, esp. chaps. 50–52.

3. Salem, "Elizabethan Image of Islam," 51. A new German edition of the Qur'ān was translated in 1694.

4. Prideaux, *Nature of Imposture*. For further reading on Orientalist views of Islam see Macfie, *Orientalism*; and Said, *Orientalism*.

reading "Alcoran" one would find "it so rude and incongruous a composure, so farced with contradictions, blasphemies, obscene speeches, and ridiculous fables."[5] Even with such a critique, the House of Commons denounced Sale's translation as a "subversive" work because of its relatively positive views of Muhammad and because Sale had the audacity to critique Prideaux's scathing charges against Muhammad.[6]

> [Muhammad] has given a new system of religion, which has had still greater success than the arms of his followers, and to establish this religion made use of an imposture; and on this account it is supposed that he must of necessity have been a most abandoned villain, and his memory is become infamous. But as Mohammed gave his Arabs the best religion he could, as well as the best laws, preferable, at least, to those of the ancient pagan lawgivers, I confess I cannot see why he deserves not equal respect, though not with Moses or Jesus Christ, whose law came really from heaven, yet with Minos or Numa, notwithstanding the distinction of a learned writer, who seems to think it a greater crime to make use of an imposture to set up a *new* religion, founded on the acknowledgment of one true God, and to destroy idolatry, then to sue the same means to gain reception to rules and regulations for the more orderly practice of heathenism already established.[7]

(It is interesting to take notice that in the post-9/11 era this genre has seen a renewal in popularity.[8])

Another category of interpreters of Islam during the eighteenth century went much further, and saw in Islam a humanistic religion that provided answers to the superstitious doctrines of Christianity.[9] These Orientalists, such as Carlysle, Savary, Sylvester, and Gibbon, would begin to see Islam in a new light. The story of Muhammad and his companions served as a positive example of a simple humanistic religion that enlisted all the positive elements of leadership and communal organization. Muhammad was made into the image of a great epic hero, much like those

---

5. Khalaf, *Cultural Resistance*, 212.

6. Toomer, *Eastern Wisedome and Learning*, 200. For Sale's comments on Muhammad's positive role in pre-Islamic society, see the "Preliminary Discourse" in his translation of *The Koran*, iii–iv.

7. Sale, *Koran*, iii–iv.

8. See, for example, Ansārī, *Psychology of Mohammed*; and Spencer, *Truth about Muhammad*.

9. Vander Werff, *Christian Mission*, 20–22.

of the Greek mythology. Simon Ockley, Professor of Arabic at Cambridge, produced *A History of the Saracens* in three volumes from 1708 to 1757, which was extremely popular and utilized throughout Europe and North America.

Closely related to this perspective was a trend that utilized the story of Muhammad as a thinly veiled attack on all religion, including Christianity. Many humanist and deist thinkers began to attack all forms of organized "revealed religion." Voltaire, for instance, used caricatures of Muhammad to provide a critique of all "revealed religion" as irrational.[10] This rational critique of the irrationality of Scripture led Thomas Jefferson to excise those passages from his own Bible that were not reasonable, which he published in his own gospel version entitled *The Life and Morals of Jesus*. Jefferson, as a lawyer, was also led to turn through the pages of the Qur'ān, looking for elements of natural law that could be applied to the newly forming United States.[11]

Evangelical Christians involved in missionary endeavors in India and the Middle East took part in this Orientalist view of Islam as well. The Anglican Edward Pococke (1604–91) and the Scottish Presbyterian Sir William Muir (1819–1905) both undertook the study of Arabic texts for an "objective" study of Islam, and contributed a great deal to our understanding of the origins of Islamic traditions.[12] But Christian missionaries had a vested interest in defending "revealed religion." Unlike the deists or the secular humanists, they were not willing to refute all revelation over against reason. They did, however, begin to apply the lessons of reason and objectivity to their interpretation of Islam.

THE UNREASONABLE RELIGION

Early American society was introduced to these images of Islam during the opening days of the Republic of the eighteenth century. We have already reviewed the common Orientalist literature that was being imported "across the pond," including the works of Knolles, Ockley, and Ross. In addition to these writings, however, Americans began to receive further negative images of the "Mohammedans," which were beginning to appear in American newspapers and circulars; such as the stories of

---

10. See ibid., 21.
11. Hayes, "How Thomas Jefferson Read the Qur'ān."
12. See Lewis, *Islam and the West*, 85–98.

the Barbary pirates, and shortly thereafter, direct commentary by newly planted American missionaries in the Middle East after 1819.[13]

As the new American nation emerged from its War of Independence, it was immediately plunged into an international crisis with the Barbary states (Algiers, Morocco, and Tunis) when pirates began plundering American merchant ships and taking captives. The economy of new Republic was held captive by the ransoms of petty despots along the North African coastline. Descriptions of the barbarous "Turk" and their culture became a mainstay of American printed media.[14] In addition, during 1820s the Greeks were in the midst of their own revolution of independence from the Ottoman Empire, which stirred a great deal of sympathy among Americans. Although the political struggles were sometimes seen as a war between Christianity and Islam, its primary point of reference for Americans was the role of Oriental despotism as manifested through Turkish culture and religion against the truth of Protestant Christianity as manifested through the pursuit of liberty and freedom in its republican form of government.[15]

For American Lutherans in the late eighteenth and early nineteenth century, however, the Orient and Islam were not very relevant issues to the burgeoning American Lutheran immigrant communities, as their energies were taken focused on organizing disparate immigrant Lutheran communities along the Eastern seaboard and in the newly forming Midwestern territories. In such a context, the Orient and Islam were simply off the radar screen of American Lutheranism. However, during this time American Protestantism was being swept by a wave a revivalism, and there was a growing interest in foreign missions. It was this period that gave rise to the development of the American Board of Commissioners of Foreign Missionaries, reviewed earlier. Samuel Simon Schmucker (1799-1873), who had established the Lutheran seminary at Gettysburg in 1826, and who had at one time been a missionary to the American frontier, was deeply invested in the growing interest in foreign missions. Only one year after the founding of the seminary he was the driving force

---

13. The first American Protestants to undertake a mission in the Middle East were Pliny Fisk and Levi Parsons, of the ABCFM. Their views of the "Mohammedan" became part of American evangelical views of the Orient. See Makdisi, *Artillery of Heaven* and "Reclaiming the Land"; and the classic study by Tibawi, *American Interests in Syria*.

14. See Allison, *The Crescent Obscured*.

15. Marr, *Cultural Roots of American Islamicism*, 10.

behind the establishment of a mission organization called the Evangelical Lutheran Society of Inquiry on Missions.[16] The Society was guided by the spirit of the revivals sweeping the United States, combining nineteenth century evangelicalism and American optimism.[17]

The Society met monthly and engaged in a number of activities, collecting funds for domestic and foreign missions, as well as corresponding with other seminaries and societies around the world. During their meetings time was given for discussions centered on one or two presentations made by members, faculty, or visiting missionaries. One of the active members who provided several presentations was a young seminary student named Lewis Eichelberger. Eichelberger (1801–59) was handpicked by Schmucker himself to join the Society because of his keen mind and strong piety, and was a prominent member during his time at the seminary.[18] At only the second meeting of the Society in April 1827, he gave a presentation on the role of missions toward the "Mohammedan" (the common and inaccurate Western Orientalist nomenclature for Muslim). This presentation is important in that it is the earliest American Lutheran systematic view of Islam.

The main thesis of Echelberger's presentation is clear from its title, "By What Arguments Can We Convince the Mohammedan of the Falsity of His Religion." The paper is an attempt to demonstrate to North American Protestants, by way of an objective and reasonable articulation of facts, the failings of Islam. His views, however, were not based upon primarily Islamic

---

16. The archives of the Society, housed at the Wentz Library of the Lutheran Theological Seminary at Gettysburg, provide a great deal of information on the formation of independent mission societies and the networks that were established through these societies in the early and middle of the nineteenth century. The archives include letters from the student mission societies at Andover Seminary, Princeton, the Basel Missionary Training Center in Switzerland, and the Berlin Theological Seminary (box 2, folders 3–4). This correspondence helps us to understand the strong networks among evangelical mission societies throughout Europe and North America during this period, and the important information and resources that were shared between organizations. The archives also demonstrate the role of Gettysburg in this network of ecumenical foreign missions, sending eleven graduates abroad between 1843 and 1891 (box 2).

17. "Preamble to the Constitution of the Evangelical Lutheran Society of Inquiry on Missions," Evangelical Lutheran Society of Inquiry on Missions archives, box 3. For early American evangelical missiological views see Bosch, *Transforming Mission*, 278, 298–99.

18. Eichelberger would go on to play a role in the work of the American Lutheran Church in the Carolinas, serving as one of the founding professors—and for awhile the only professor—of Southern Seminary during its time in Lexington and later at Columbia, South Carolina. See McCullough, *History of the Lutheran Church*, 234–36.

sources, but two published sources: *A Brief Outline of the Evidences of the Christian Religion* (1823) by Archibald Alexander, one of the leading figures of nineteenth century American Protestant theology; and *The Nature of Imposture Displayed in the Life of Mahamet* (1697), the classic British Orientalist text by Bishop Humprhey Prideaux, introduced above.[19]

Archibald Alexander (1772–1851) was a giant in early nineteenth century American Protestantism. He was the guiding force behind Princeton Theological Seminary, and well known to Samuel Schmucker. It is most likely that Schmucker recommended this work to Eichelberger. *A Brief Outline* was not primarily concerned with attacking Islam, rather it was written as a response to the challenge of the deist critique of revealed religion. Islam, however, figured into Alexander's argument about true and false revealed religion.

On several occasions Eichelberger quotes Alexander at length. In fact, the last section of his paper is entitled "The Evidences of the Truth," which is taken directly from Alexander's book. Here he follows Alexander's argument verbatim; that compared with Christianity and Christ, Islam and Muhammad cannot measure up. First, following an old medieval argument, Alexander states that Muhammad was never prophesied to appear in any pre-Islamic source, whereas Jesus fulfilled Old Testament prophecies.[20] Second, if one were to compare Jesus with Muhammad one would find the character of Muhammad wanting. Third, compared to the New Testament, the Qur'ān, in Alexander's view, is a jumble of confusing stories, lies, and contradictions. Fourth, while Jesus came and preached his message and gained converts, Muhammad had to resort to the sword to create a community of converts. Lastly, while Christianity as a religion has brought blessing to those countries that have followed the gospel, those countries that have followed the "artful imposter" wallow in despotism.[21]

In addition to *A Brief Outline*, we find numerous references to Prideaux's very popular biography of Muhammad, *The Nature of*

19. Alexander himself relies on Prideaux's work.

20. Both Alexander and Eichelberger, however, were apparently not aware of the longstanding Muslim response to this argument. The most prominent argument for the prediction of Muhammad in the Jewish and Christian Scriptures was developed by 'Alī al-Ṭabarī (785–860) in *Kitāb al-dīn w'al-dawla* [The Book of Religion and Empire]. The most common arguments developed regarding the foretelling of Muhammad focus on interpretations of Deuteronomy 18:15 and John 14:16; 16:7; and 26:15, 26. See Thomas, "Bible in Early Muslim Anti-Christian Polemi."

21. Alexander, *Brief Outline*, 171–80.

Imposture.²² Eichelberger does not directly quote from Prideaux; however, his language reflects much of the terminology and descriptions of Muhammad found in Prideaux. He utilized Prideaux's terms such as "the barbarous character" of the Muslims, and descriptions of Muhammad as the "deceiver," "licentious," "ambitious," and most importantly, the "artful imposter" of Arabia.

Eichelberger's paper uses basic Orientalist views to argue for the unreasonableness of Islam, and thus, the superiority of Christianity. Muhammad is described in the traditional style of Victorian Orientalism as the "imposter" who has taken bits and pieces from Judaism, Christianity, and Arab paganism in order to create his own religion.²³ In his bid for power, Muhammad has created a new religion in order to control the ignorant Arabians. Some of the earliest Christian polemic against Islam held that Muhammad had borrowed from a variety of Jewish and Christian sources. The medieval Latin tradition, which Luther inherited (as we saw in chapter 1), began to offer up interpretations of Muhammad's evil nature in deception and leading people astray. Orientalist works during the late eighteenth century then added to this characterization of Muhammad, adding descriptions of Muhammad's immorality and "licentiousness"— usually based around his sexual exploits. Eichelberger describes Muhammad as "licentious, ambitious, malevolent, and revengeful," and a "vile deceiver."²⁴ He then goes on to describe how the Muslims have taken on these attributes of their leader, which has lead to their "inferior" state.

Eichelberger moves on to describe the "inferior" state of the Arab Muslim, and then asks how one can convince a Muslim of the error of his or her ways. He provides five arguments as proof. First, he states that it is clear that religion by its very nature is to uplift and provide direction for humanity. It is the very nature of humanity, he argues, to be religious and therefore to pursue truth, progress, and freedom. That is the very essence of true religion. The Muslim, however, continues to live with "barbarous manners," stuck in ignorance, and thus subverting the divine spark of true religion. Muslim governments and "Alkoran" keep Muslims from experiencing "temporal prosperity." Muslims are ignorant, Eichelberger argues, because they come from a land "known only by the barbarous character

22. Edwin Wolf, *Book Culture*, 122.
23. For an example of the Western negative views of Muhammad's religious motives, see Setton, *Western Hostility to Islam*, 2–3.
24. See also Salem, "Elizabethan Image of Islam," 45–46.

of its inhabitants," while the Christian nations around it are "virtuous, enlightened and happy."[25] Thus, because of their immoral state, the teachings of Muhammad hold sway. In fact, the reason there have been so few conversions of Muslims to Christianity is because they are held in bondage to ignorance and are thus incapable of understanding the truth.

> Ignorance and Prejudice must determine its [Islam's] validity; and hence the reason why conversions from this sect to Christianity have been so extremely rare.[26]

Second, according to Eichelberger, reason declares that true religion and its adherents should exhibit the moral characteristics of its leader. Like other Orientalists, he focuses on Muhammad's "licentious indulgence." The pleasures of paradise as portrayed in the Qur'ān become a fixation of selfish and childish gain. Lustfulness is also a charge labeled at Muhammad because of his polygamy and his marriage to the young Zaynab, the former wife of his companion Zayid.

Third, true religion should provide for the development of a moral character and a hope for a better life. Islam, claims Eichelberger, does neither. Islam does not raise up the Muslim to a better life because it does not acknowledge hope for a better life. This is because it does not recognize sin, nor provide a remedy for sin. There is no assurance of salvation or a promise that in following the Prophet there will be any kind of promise of salvation. This is because the Qur'ān is—here he directly quotes Alexander—

> a confused and incongruous heap of sublime sentiments, moral precepts, positive institutions, extravagant and incredulous stories and manifest lies . . .[27]

Fourth, "Nothing can place Christianity in a more favorable light," Eichelberger says, "than contrasting it with the religion of Arabia."[28] Islam is the quintessential unreasonable faith given to flights of fancy. Muslims, as ignorant individuals, are easily fooled into believing in the stories of Muhammad's conversations with the angel Gabriel, the story of his night

---

25. Eichelberger, "By What Arguments."
26. Ibid.
27. Ibid.
28. Ibid.

journey to heaven and his standing before the throne of God. Christianity, on the other hand, demonstrates that

> The Saviour of mankind has not only exhibited an example of virtuous suffering worthy of imitation—He has not only pointed out the only way to reason and purchased the sinners' title to its inheritance by his meritorious death: but has confirmed and perfected his crucifixion by his glorious resurrection from the dead.[29]

Eichelberger certainly sees no logical problem in claiming that the miraculous revelations to Muhammad are "fanciful"; and yet, the virgin birth and Christ's resurrection are reasonable, despite the fact that these doctrines were used by numerous humanist Enlightenment thinkers as evidence of the unreasonableness of Christianity.

Eichelberger's last argument for the unreasonableness of Islam is based on his idea that the nature of humanity is to seek the truth, to come to the light. Those who have not or cannot understand the truth have somehow subverted their own true human nature, which seeks the truth. The proof of the reasonableness of Christianity is clear simply from the fact that the Christian nations are "virtuous, enlightened and happy." In fact, "The millions who now live and die in its [Islam's] belief never question" why they are in such a deplorable state. If they would simply reason with objectivity and without prejudice, they would certainly see themselves as living in darkness. Those who truly seek after God and simply accept faith in Christ receive a measure of grace that is "too simple even by the poor Moslem not to be apprehended."[30]

For eighteenth century Orientalists, and then for the mid nineteenth century Protestant missionaries in India and the Ottoman Empire, Islam was the epitome of the unreasonable religion, which could be overturned not only by logical argument, but also by demonstrating the progress of Western nations over Muslim peoples. Eichelberger, however, provides a particularly American perspective. Here, Western culture and government, supported by Protestant Christianity, were assumed to be the pinnacle of human achievement.[31] Only two years after this presentation Eichelberger would preach two important sermons, which were published, on the importance of the role of America in God's providen-

29. Ibid.
30. Ibid.
31. Schlorff, *Missiological Models*, 4.

tial plan.[32] Thus, the stability and progress of republican North America stood as a testament to the superiority of evangelical Christianity over and against Islam, whose adherents lived in backward and "barbaric" nations. Thus, what we find in Eichelberger's view of Islam is not only a European Orientalist tradition that ridiculed Islam, but the beginning of an American Orientalism that viewed Islam through the lens of North American republican society and culture. This perhaps is the most helpful aspect of Eichelberger's presentation on Islam in our understanding of Lutheran perspectives on Islam. Here is the kernel of what would become the North American Orientalist perspective on Islam, which would see the truths of Christianity as naturally expressed through the freedoms of North American society over and against the "falsity" of a "barbaric" Islam steeped in a culture of despotism.

Eichelberger was speaking to an American Mission society at Gettysburg Lutheran seminary. He was engaging those involved with or interested in foreign missions. One wonders how much impact his views had on the then current or future American Lutheran views of Islam or on missions to Muslim countries? This remains to be seen with further research. What can be said with certainty, however, is that Eichelberger was proposing a specific approach to Islam that was not unique. Like the Dominicans long before, he was proposing that reason be utilized to point out errors of one religion, while extolling the other. Comparing the greatest of Islamic scholars as "unworthy of a child who had just learned to read his Bible" (undoubtedly much to the amusement of his seminary audience), Eichelberger was clearly unaware of the centuries of Islamic scholarship on medicine, philosophy, and theology, of Ibn Sina (Avicenna) and Ibn Rushd (Averroes), which ultimately provided a philosophical basis for Thomas Aquinas and later Western Latin scholarship. He was also equally unaware of the Islamic reform movement that was at that very moment modernizing Islamic traditions in Egypt. And yet, his view of Islam adds the particularly American view of the superiority of, not only Christianity over Islam, but of North American republican society and Protestant culture over Oriental despotism in all its forms. If Eichelberger's views of Islam were formed from a distance, across cultural and geographic borders, what of those American Lutherans who did have first hand experience with Islam and Muslims?

32. Eichelberger, *Two Sermons*.

URUMIA, PERSIA

Most American Lutheran missionary societies began to develop after the formation of the General Synod in 1821. It must be remembered that the Lutheran immigrant communities of North America were themselves from the very beginning part of the European Lutheran mission. Most European Lutheran bodies viewed the colonies and the frontier zone of the expanding United States as a foreign mission field and sent pastors to work "in the fields." In the words of an early American Lutheran church historian, Edward Jacob Wolf, "The church here was born of the spirit of missions. Her life was nursed for years at the bosom of the mother churches of Europe."[33] Throughout the early nineteenth century, as most American Lutheran immigrant communities were struggling simply to organize themselves into functioning synods, there were few resources left over for foreign missions. But, the concept of mission was very relevant to these churches. Being born as a mission church, they felt the tug to extend the resources of Christian missionary activity. So, the Central Home Missionary Society at Mechanicsburg, Pennsylvania, the American Lutheran Missionary Society (ALMS) of the Ministerium of Pennsylvania, and the German Foreign Missionary Society were finally organized in 1835, 1836, and 1837, respectively.[34] The main focus of these societies was India, Liberia, and New Guinea.[35] Like the first Lutheran missionaries sent out by King Frederick IV of Denmark in 1706, the first American Lutheran missionary, C. F. Heyer, was sent to India. He was sent on behalf of the ALMS in 1841, and was followed a year later by Walter Gunn, who was supported by the General Synod.[36]

It was not until 1885, however, that the ALMS began working in the Middle East. In conjunction with the Germans, the American Lutherans began supporting the work among the Nestorians (members of the

---

33. E. J. Wolf, *Lutherans in America*, 497.

34. Ibid., 498. Laury, *History of Lutheran Missions*, 93–94, has slightly different dates. The GFMS would change its name in 1839 to the Missionary Society of the Evangelical Lutheran Church in the United States.

35. Laury, *History of Lutheran Missions*, 94–99. In addition to these societies, the United Synod of the Evangelical Lutheran Church in the North had missions in India, while the USELC in the South sent its missionaries to Japan. The Norwegian-American Hauge Synod and the Swedish Mission Covenant of America sent its missionaries to China, and the United Norwegian Lutheran Church in America sent personnel to Madagascar.

36. E. J. Wolf, 499–500.

Assyrian Church of the East) in Tabriz, in northwest Persia, and shortly thereafter among the Armenians.[37] Although the German Lutherans had arrived a year before any other agency, including the Anglican CMS and the American Presbyterians, the Germans would simply never be able to match the resources of these other mission societies. The German Basel Mission sent out Christoph Frederick Haas to Tabriz in 1833 as part of its expanding Caucasus Mission. There he opened a school for the Armenians. Friederich Edward Scheider and Christian Gottlieb Hoernle later joined him in 1834 and 1835, respectively. The mission post struggled, due to theological differences between the missionaries and the committee. With the large influx of British and American missionaries to Tabriz, the Basel Mission could not compete with the other mission societies, and so closed the school in 1837.[38]

Urumia, however, was chosen as a mission post first by the American Presbyterian missionaries, because it was the primary city of the Assyrian Church of the East. It was the main Christian center of northwest Persia, on the border between Persia, Turkey, Russia, Kurdistan, and Armenia. This land was also the border between the ancient kingdoms of Armenia, Assyria and Media.[39] It was a rugged area that had hundreds of villages comprised of Persians, Kurds, Armenians, Turkomen, and Assyrian Christians, who were all mostly illiterate. Thus, the Persian mission field provided the opportunity for "indirect evangelism" with Islam. The Presbyterian Nestorian Mission (first under the authority of the American Board of Commissioners for Foreign Missions and after 1871 under the auspices of the Presbyterian Church of North America) was to "enable the Nestorian Church, through the grace of God, to exert a commanding influence in the spiritual regeneration of Asia" among the Sunni and Shi'a Muslims, as well as the small number of remaining Jews and Zoroastrians.[40] The mission established an Assyrian presbytery in 1862.

---

37. The Assyrian church of the East has traditionally been called the "Nestorian Church," named after the patriarch of Constantinople, Nestorius, whose views were condemned by the Council of Ephesus in 431. Officially named the Assyrian Church of the East, the Assyrians have maintained that neither are, nor ever have never been, followers of the teachings of Nestorius. The classic historical text of the Assyrian Church of the East is Wigram, *Introduction to the History*. See also W. Shedd, *Islam and the Oriental Churches*.

38. Waldburger, *Missionare und Moslems*, 125–35, 153–79.

39. M. Shedd, *Measure of a Man*, 29.

40. PC-USA Board of Foreign Missions, *Century of Mission Work*, 2.

By 1869 a "Reformed Nestorian Church" was organized, which by 1907 included five thousand members. In addition, the Assyrian Presbyterians had as many as sixty-three schools in the surrounding area, with almost two thousand students.[41] During World War I, the Caucasus area was hotly contested between the Turks and the Russians. The occupation of the Azerbaijan province of Persia by Russian troops, and their subsequent withdrawal, led to the massacre of Assyrian Christians by Kurds and Ottoman troops in 1915, and by Armenians in 1917.[42]

Despite the hardships involved in dealing with the Russians and the Turks, the mission post was so successful that it began to attract the attention of other mission agencies. By the beginning of the twentieth century, Urumia was a major center not only for the Presbyterians, but also the Anglicans, Catholics (under the Lazarist order), Lutherans, and even the Russian Orthodox Church.[43] Among the Lutherans, there were at least four different mission agencies centered in Urumia: the Evangelical Association for the Advancement of the Nestorian Church, the Orientmission sent by the Germans; the predominantly Norwegian United Lutheran Church, and the Swedish Augustana Synod of the Americans.

The sudden influx of foreign institutions and schools created a new dynamic in the traditionally small and rural area of Urumia. Each mission society developed its own school, where their brightest and best graduates were then encouraged to go on for further study in the home country of the mission agency. There were high hopes that these Persian students could return as educated and enlightened Protestants to carry on the work of evangelizing the country. The creation of these avenues for Assyrians to travel to the West brought with it several problems. First, the work among the Assyrians created a great deal of resentment among the Kurds and the Turks, which would later lead to horrible atrocities. Second, the large number of mission agencies in the area led to compe-

---

41. Richter, *History of Protestant Missions*, 304–5.

42. For first hand missionary accounts of the massacres see M. Shedd, *Measure of a Man*. For the impact of the massacres on Presbyterian mission policy and in American foreign policy, see Grabill, *Protestant Diplomacy*, esp. 58–79.

43. Russian advances into the southern Caucasus and the central states of Asia prompted sections of the Assyrian church to seek protection under the Russian Orthodox Church after the Armenian massacres by the Turks in 1890s. The Nestorians feared similar episodes by the Kurds against them. Richter states that up to twenty-five thousand Nestorians joined the Russian Orthodox Church and fell under its jurisdiction (*History of Protestant Missions*, 310–12).

tition. The Presbyterians and the CMS had signed a comity agreement, recognizing each other's work and respecting the specific areas of each mission society. But the Lutherans and the British had difficulty getting along. In 1926 the Anglicans and Presbyterians held a conference in Tehran to share information and discuss matters pertaining to Protestant missionary work in Iran. However, there were no Lutherans from any mission society in attendance.[44] The missiologist Julius Richter offered his criticism of this type of missionary proliferation:

> Nestorian adventurers go to America and Europe, where, by touching stories and exaggerated descriptions of the work they are doing, they win the interest of credulous people. Then they return home with full pockets, and, with the continued support of the friends they have made, there enjoy the fruits of the "work" they have done in Christian countries. They open a few day-schools, build a chapel and engage a few Syrian helpers; they are now in a position to send glowing reports of their work to their easily satisfied friends in foreign lands.[45]

By the beginning of the twentieth centuries, numerous Assyrian priests or deacons who were associated with Lutheran mission programs began visiting Germany and the United States in hopes of gathering support from Lutheran churches for their own indigenous work. In 1881 the German Lutherans of the Hermannsburg Mission Society (HMS) began work in the Urumia district, when the Assyrian priest Pera Johannes traveled to Germany and befriended Friedrich Horning of Strasbourg. The Hermannsburg congregation, which had its own missionary training center, provided Johannes with financial support for five years, while he studied Lutheran doctrine and polity.[46] Louis Harms, pastor of the Hermannsburg church, gathered support among the congregations in the area and sent Johannes back to his village outside of Urumia to "disseminate Lutheran ideas in their small congregations."[47] Following this, two other Assyrians then came to study at Hermannsburg: Jaure Abraham in 1885, and Luther Pera (son of Pera Johannes) in 1905. All three worked

---

44. See PC-USA Board of Foreign Missions, *Mission Problems in New Persia*.

45. Richter, *History of Protestant Missions*, 314.

46. Laury, *History of Lutheran Missions*, 64–65; Fossum, "Lutheran Evangelization Work," 3.

47. Richter, *History of Protestant Missions*, 308.

on behalf of the HMS, combining both the ancient liturgy of the Assyrian Church of the East and Lutheran theology.

In the same way, the Augustana Synod, formed in 1860 by Swedish Lutheran immigrants in America, became involved in the work in Persia when a deacon by the name of Knanishu Morhatkhan struck up a relationship with the Swedish Lutherans working under the HMS. Morhatkhan's son, Joseph Knanishu, came to the U.S. to study at Augustana College in Rock Island, Illinois and returned to Persia as an ordained Lutheran pastor in 1902. A second Assyrian, Isaac Johannan, was educated at Augustana and also returned home to work.[48]

A similar situation occurred with the Ohio Synod when Baba N. Shabaz had attended one of the Lutheran schools in the Urumia district. He came to Ohio to complete his education at Capital University in Columbus, Ohio, was confirmed a member of Christ Church and attended Hamma Theological Seminary (now Trinity Lutheran Seminary).[49] Christ Church commissioned Shabaz as its own independent missionary, as the Ohio Synod had no such venture at the time. Shabaz returned to work in Soujbulak from 1902 till his death in 1934. He operated a school for thirty-two years, which Christ Church helped to fund. After his death the congregation decided to donate the remaining funds of the "Persian Mission Fund" to the American Lutheran Church Board of Foreign Missions for its work in India.[50]

In 1899 there had been some skeptical reports of the work in Urumia, and the HMS was showing signs of frustration. The Norwegian Americans that were supporting N. G. Malech and his work sent M. O. Wee of Luther Seminary, St. Paul, Minnesota to investigate. Upon his return he recommended that the synod discontinue its support of the mission, as it was being run "in an unorganized and entirely unsatisfactory manner. There has been a sad lack of system, oversight and control."[51] One of the short-term missionaries of the American United Lutheran Church who worked in Urumia with Malech from 1905 to 1908 was Ludwig O. Fossum (1879–1920). Fossum was ultimately dissatisfied with the mission work being done and left. He returned to the U.S., but he had committed

---

48. Fossum, "Lutheran Evangelization Work," 5.
49. Laury, *History of Lutheran Missions*, 98.
50. Grimm, *Centennial History*, 27.
51. Olson, 6.

himself to working among Muslims in "direct evangelism" rather than the "indirect evangelism" among the Assyrian Christians.[52]

LUTHERAN ORIENT MISSION

At the beginning of the twentieth century, Western civilization was confident in itself. The Enlightenment had led to the Industrial Revolution and to a new scientific revolution. Western civilization believed that it was at the pinnacle of human achievement. There was nothing the human intellect could not do—given enough time and resources. This confidence was felt throughout the Western church. As Western culture had a high opinion of the possibilities of human achievements, there was the general belief in the concept of "civiliatrice," cultivating a civilized culture—especially among those in the darkest places of Africa and Asia. Europe was at the height of the colonial era, and the Western church, even if not complicit with colonialist designs, was involved. Its missionaries, whether or not they so desired, were members of nations involved in the dangerous game of imperial politics. As nationalist feelings rose, support for national missions increased back home.

The positive belief in the creation of a new and better world proved to be a chimera, however, as the "Guns of August" destroyed the great ideals of the nineteenth century. As World War I ground out into a blood bath, it was clear that the possibilities of Western human achievement could also lead to its own destruction and demise. Intellect, science, and technology could be harnessed not only to protect and prolong life but also to end it. As a result of the horrors of the war, every aspect of European thought was affected. Existential pessimism took over, and the church felt its affects. As European Christians realized that their own cultures held dark sides, they became less confident in their own cultural and national missions. By the 1920s the church had abandoned its confident claim to "evangelize the world in this century." Rather, it became engaged in a fight for its own survival as fascism, communism and atheism began to surface within the cracks of national-religious honor.

German Lutheran missions in Palestine and the development of German posts in Egypt (in Cairo and northern Sudan) at the turn of the century left the Protestant Lutheran-Reformed church of the German Empire feeling secure and self-assured. With the catastrophe of World

---

52. Fossum, "Lutheran Evangelization Work," 8.

War I, however, the subsequent impounding of German property by the British in Palestine and Egypt, and finally the horrors of the Holocaust of World War II, German missions in the Middle East were ultimately left in shambles. The German expatriate communities of the Middle East fled, were forcibly relocated, or were humiliated, leaving the Middle East regretful of how their pietistic designs had been subverted by nationalism.

This was not the case for the American Lutherans, however. The American Protestant church was in the midst of the Social Gospel movement, which had begun in the 1880s. The American piety of individualism, progress, and "good, old fashioned" hard work—the Protestant work ethic—engendered a sense of service for the public good. With the publication of Walter Rausenbusch's *A Theology for the Social Gospel* in 1917, the American perspective was still one of positive engagement with the world. Rausenbusch's ideas were followed by those of the Niebuhrs, who encouraged Christian realism and engagement with the world. Thus, while European Christians were withdrawing from international engagements, Americans were just beginning! Led by Robert E. Speer and John R. Mott, mainline Protestant "liberalism" engaged the world with an American sense of positive activism.[53] Although Lutherans were somewhat involved in the general American mission enterprise, their role was curtailed by a general sensitivity toward German enterprises abroad. German Americans kept a low profile during the world wars. However, after World War II, and in response to the development work of the Lutheran World Federation, American Lutheran churches began to think about the Middle East as a possible field for some kind of mission work. Prior to that, there was only one foray by a lone American Lutheran mission agency into the Middle East, the Lutheran Orient Mission.

In 1910 Ludwig O. Fossum, former missionary of the HMS, and M. O. Wee, professor at Luther Seminary, attended the international World Evangelism Conference at Edinburgh. Although they had no formal role in the conference, a private conversation took place between John Newton Wright, one of the long time Presbyterians in Urumia, and German Lutheran representatives from the HMS and the Orientmission working among the Assyrians, as well as Dr. Robert Speer, the chair of the Edinburgh conference.[54] It was suggested that the American Lutherans

---

53. See Hutchison, *Errand to the World*.
54. Jensen, *God through the Shadows*, 14.

should take up the work among the Sunni Kurds, as no one was currently working among them. Although there had been missions to northern Persia among the Nestorians (the Assyrian Church of the East) and Armenian Orthodox by the Presbyterians and Lutheran mission agencies for some thirty-five years, there was no one working with the nearly four million Muslim Kurds. It was hoped that the Americans and German Lutherans could cooperate in this endeavor to undertake "direct evangelism." Thus, at the height of the colonial period and at the end of the great modern missionary age, with the world ready to erupt into the Great War, American Lutherans entered the Middle East to work directly with Muslims in northern Persia, among the Sunni Kurds.

At a meeting in Berwyn, Illinois in 1910, ten individuals representing six different American Lutheran synods (Norwegian Lutheran Church, United Lutheran Church, Augustana Lutheran Church, and the synods of Buffalo, Ohio, and Iowa) met to form the board of directors of the new Inter-Synodical Lutheran Orient Mission Society.[55] The name of the mission would later become simply the Lutheran Orient Mission (LOM). Its purpose was to work among the Kurdish population of "Kurdistan."[56] The Kurds lived in tribal communities in villages stretching from the eastern borders of present day Turkey, northern Iraq, eastern Iran and the state of Azerbaijan. Throughout the early days of the twentieth century this territory was continually disputed between the Ottoman Empire, the Russians, and Persia.

While most American mission agencies had developed the policy of "indirect evangelism," the Reformed Church in America's Arabian Mission and the LOM took it upon themselves to engage Muslims of the Middle East directly. The task for the LOM was to evangelize among Muslims guided by the underlying belief in the superior rationality of the Christian faith over a backward cultural system that degraded humanity. The closing address at the inauguration of the new mission combines the best of scholastic Orientalism and nineteenth century activist missionary thoughts on Islam:

> If we now leave the Mohammedans in their ignorance of the World's Saviour, that will be our sin. When, then, the Mohammedans fall

---

55. Olson, "Historical Sketch," 6.

56. I have used quotes around "Kurdistan," since it is a recognized area and referred to in the literature, but is not an officially recognized country.

upon us once again, if not by and with the sword, but win a corrupt Christian world by Moslem missionary activity, that will be our punishment, our death....

We must wake up, lest God again let the scourge fall upon a guilty church. God will not give His glory to another. He will not suffer the Creator and the creature to be confounded. If those who are appointed witnesses for the truth, and we thereby mean any and every Christian, clergy and layity [sic], if they forget, forsake or deny it, God will raise up witnesses from quarters the most unlooked for, and will strengthen their hands, and give victory to their arms, even against those who hear His name, but have forsaken His truth....

Islamism is an unreasonable religion, Christianity is reasonable. Islamism is against reason, Christianity above reason. The devotees of Islam have never had their soul cravings satisfied. It is Jesus who proclaims a parental King, unveils His glory... This heaven is not like Mohammed's consisting in sensuality, nay, eternal purity. Christ's kingdom triumphs over all....[57]

The LOM immediately began raising funds in order for Ludwig Fossum, its first missionary, to be sent out. By 1910 Fossum and his wife and their first of two daughters were preparing to go to "Kurdistan" along with Dr. and Mrs. E. Edman of the Augstana Lutheran Synod.[58] The Americans worked in partnership with the German HMS, establishing a mission station in Soujbalak, in the northwest corner of Persia. The Presbyterian missionary John Newton Wright suggested the site as a location suitable for work directly with the Kurds. This was also the location where Fossum had worked earlier with the Assyrians under the United Lutheran Church, so he felt secure in establishing a base there. The method of the work was to be twofold: medical work and direct pastoral evangelism. In a sincere letter Wright provided some advice to the fledging mission agency and laid the missiological groundwork for the Lutherans:

> Be careful not to let these two forms of service [medical and evangelism] get divorced the one from the other... The best way to combine these two agencies in the Soujbulak region is to have a hospital, strongly manned with a good surgeon and physician;

---

57. Jensen, *God through the Shadows*, 15–16.

58 Olson, "Historical Sketch," 7. Edman had spent twenty-one years in India under the work of the Central Missionary Society of the General Synod. He was also a graduate of Augustana Seminary, Rock Island (ibid., 18).

and where the ordained Missionary can hold private and public spiritual service with patients and their friends.

> Leave educational work for converts to develop later on. Let it follow rather than precede the development of the native church. Then when you have a Christian community, where the children need education, begin it; but with the view of training up Christian workers in the home and the church. No class of people are [sic] so hard to reach with the Gospel as those who have been educated by us in schools where the atmosphere is non-Christian, or even nominally Christian.[59]

This focus of the LOM was now going against the grain of prevailing Presbyterian and Lutheran mission, which included educational work. It is apparent that both Wright, a long time missionary of the Presbyterian work in Persia, and Fossum, who was not impressed with the previous Lutheran educational work in the region under Malech, believed that the policy of "indirect evangelism" would not be effective with Muslims, especially the Kurds. Thus, the LOM was now heading off into uncharted territory. Fossum can be credited as the first Lutheran missionary from an American Lutheran institution to work directly with Muslims.

The Fossums and the Edmans arrived in Soujbulak in the autumn of 1911 and began work immediately. Ludwig Fossum began holding worship services and eventually built a small chapel. After one year he reported to the board that there was an average attendance of thirty to forty persons, although it was not clear if these were Kurds or local Assyrian Christians. By 1912 Fossum had organized and established Bethel Kurdish Evangelical Lutheran Congregation. The annual report of 1915 stated that there were seventy-six members, "most of them native Christians."[60] Edman began work in a dispensary that was run out of several buildings the mission rented. He noted that in one year, from 1912 to 1913, over 2,275 individuals had been treated. With the arrival in 1913 of Augusta D. Gudhart, a nurse from Trinity German Evangelical Lutheran Church in Pittsburgh, the mission opened up an orphanage to care for the needy children of the surrounding area.

One of the major projects undertaken by Fossum was a translation of the Gospels of Luke and John into Kurdish. This was a laudable feat in

---

59. Jensen, *God through the Shadows*, 16–17.
60. Olson, "Historical Sketch," 13.

itself; but Fossum, a gifted linguist who already knew German, Syriac, and Turkish, actually had to first develop a written Kurdish language in order to do the translation, as Kurdish was only a spoken language at the time. He created an alphabet of twenty-eight Arabic characters and four Persian. Once this was completed, Fossum also wrote an English-Kurdish grammar and translated a Lutheran hymnal and Luther's Small Catechism.[61]

The missionaries of the LOM spent four years in Soujbulak, until they were forced to leave on account of hostilities between Russia and the Ottoman Empire over Russian occupation of the Caucasus. In 1910 the Russians had occupied much of the Caucasus, but by 1914 the Turks pushed eastward into Persia. What followed was two years of war and bloodshed as the Turks engaged the Russians who were supported by the Kurds. As the Turks moved forward into areas in which the Armenians and Assyrian Christians were living, general massacres began to take place. In 1915, the Turks moved into Armenia and conducted a genocide, killing anywhere from 800,000 to 1.5 million Armenians!

In April 1916 the Lutherans quickly left their mission compound for the safety of Tabriz because of Ottoman incursions into the area, moving in with the Presbyterians missionaries, who had also been providing a safe haven for the Assyrian Christians of the area. When they fled Soujbulak all LOM property was destroyed. Fossum was never to see Soujbulak again. For the rest of the LOM missionaries, it would be five years before they could return to rebuild the mission.[62]

After the World War I the Russians were in possession of most of the Caucasus region. The infrastructure was in shambles. Great Britain and the Allies in Paris were disputing the fate of "Kurdistan." Although, Britain wanted to maintain control of northern Persia for its oil depositories, it was not in a position to do so, having retrenched most of its military forces. But by the San Remo conference of 1922, "Kurdistan" was simply dropped from the discussion. Britain had helped put Reza Pehlavi on the Peacock

---

61. The Gospel of John has often utilized by Christians in Muslim countries as the sayings of Jesus and the lengthy narratives have often been well received by Muslim audiences. The esoteric nature of the Gospel, as opposed to the synoptics, has been popular with Sufis as well. The prominence of Jesus's healing ministry in Luke would fit well with the medical ministry of LOM.

62. For several accounts of the Turkish massacres among the Assyrians see W. Shedd, *Islam and the Oriental Churches*; and Shahbaz, *Rage of Islam*.

Throne of Persia, and Iran was granted sovereignty over its own district of Azerbaijan.[63] In addition, Britain created the new nation-state of Iraq from the previous Ottoman vilayets of Mosul, Mesopotamia, and parts of Aleppo. The newly formed Soviet Union now reclaimed the disputed territories of the Caucasus states of Armenia, Azerbaijan, and Georgia. The Ottoman district of "Kurdistan" simply ceased to exist. Its territory was divided into four sovereign areas: Iran, Iraq, the Soviet Union, and the new state of Turkey.

After the Armistice in November 1919, the LOM made plans for Fossum and Augusta Gudhart to return, along with several new missionaries, including Fossum's sister Alma, a registered nurse. (Mrs. Fossum and their two girls Otte and Esther did not return with him to Persia on account of her "mother's health." They would not see him again.) Because of the extremely poor conditions in the region, the Lutherans were only able to journey as far as Yerevan (now present day Armenia) before the Russians refused them further passage. Fossum and the other missionaries were then employed by the New York office of Near East Relief in the effort to help the Armenians recover from the atrocities and genocide inflicted upon them by the Turks during the war. It was at this time in Armenia, during a trip near Mount Ararat in 1920 to help communal negotiations between the Christian Armenians and the Sunni Kurds, that Fossum died from "exhaustion."[64]

The LOM was now without its primary leader and ideologue. Despite this loss, the rest of the missionaries, led by Pastor George H. Bachimont, pressed on and actually made it to Soujbulak in the spring of 1921. By the fall of the same year another tragedy struck the mission. The missionary compound was raided by Kurdish soldiers and Rev. Bachimont was killed. Once again the missionaries fled Soujbulak.

In 1924 Augusta Gudhart and Alma Fossum returned to Soujbulak, along with a Dr. Herman Schalk from Germany.[65] There the three continued to work for another eleven years, until the LOM was asked to leave Soujbulak by the Persian government. According to records from the missionaries themselves, their departure was not due to anti-missionary policy, but rather because the government was securing sites for military

63. Iran's northwest district is known as "Iranian Azerbaijan." This is distinct from the contemporary nation state of Azerbaijan.

64. Jensen, *God through the Shadows*, 21.

65. Ibid., 30.

operations and demanded that all foreigners leave the area. In a process of negotiation the government agreed to purchase the LOM buildings and property. Thus, after an unexpected change in plans, and after undertaking some swift reconnoitering, the mission decided to relocate to Arbil in the Kingdom of Iraq. From there they could continue to serve the Kurds. The situation in Arbil, however, was radically different from that of Soujbulak. In Soujbulak the missionaries were living and working among the rugged Kurdish tribesmen in a remote area. Arbil, by the 1930s, was bustling with activity. It was a proposed site of the Berlin to Baghdad railway and was also slated for a new airport. In addition, precious natural resources just had been discovered in the area, including the most important of all—oil. Because of the dramatic influx of diplomatic and business communities, the missionaries were no longer the only foreigners living among the Kurds. The Kurds and Arabs now had to contend with foreigners all living in their midst who had very dif-

MISSIONARIES
1950 - 1984

Rev. and Mrs. H. A. Mueller
Rev. and Mrs. Philip Mueller
Clarence Mueller
Rev. and Mrs. Earl Erickson
Ruth Mickelson
Sadiq Shammi — native

Dr. and Mrs. Richard Gardiner

FIGURE 2: LOM Staff, Arbil, Iraq, 1950

ferent agendas, and it was not always easy for them to understand what motives were driving each particular foreign community.

Although they were faced with a completely different context, the growing city of Arbil offered new opportunities. Because they were now within the Kingdom of Iraq it was possible to travel from Arbil to Damascus, and even to Beirut. This meant that the LOM was now able to bring in more literature for distribution from Christian publishing houses in Beirut. They took full advantage of the developing infrastructure by importing a new station wagon from the United States. This was to help the missionaries travel more effectively throughout the region and to help with Bible and pamphlet distribution, as well with opening up new mission posts further afield. They were aided in this by the addition of six new members from the U.S., the Rev. and Mrs. H. A. Mueller arrived in 1954, while Rev. and Mrs. Carl C. Ericksen and Mr. and Mrs. Phillip K. Mueller arrived in 1955. By 1957 two volunteer nurses, Ms. Orlaug Haarvik and Ruth Mickelson, as well as Dr. and Mrs. R. M. Gardiner, began working under the auspices of the LOM. The focus during this period was on evangelism through literature distribution and church planting, as well as the original medical work. The main station was in Arbil, where on Christmas Eve of 1956 they gathered 130 people. Another station was opened up in Mosul in 1956, and one in Shaqlawa in 1958. In fact, the period when the mission settled in Arbil, between the end of World War II and 1958, comprised the most stable years of the mission.

Suddenly, in July of 1958, the Ba'athists over threw King Faisal in an extremely bloody coup. In the autumn all of the foreign missionaries in Iraq were forced to leave. The LOM missionaries were already on their way back to the United States by the time the board of directors received word from them. The property and work of the LOM was left to just one of its Iraqi workers to carry it on, Sadiq Shammi. Shammi, born a Yazidi, converted to Christianity through the work of the Danish Lutheran Mission. He began working with the LOM upon its arrival in 1935, and by 1958 he and his wife were the only ones left to continue. They maintained weekly church services, pastoral visitation, and the running of a Christian bookshop. At one point the board of the LOM considered finding a way to ordain Shammi in the Lutheran church so that he could provide sacramental duties for the mission, but they ultimately decided against this as he had no thorough theological training or education. From 1958 until the middle 1980s this small ministry limped along, until it simply vanished. As the Iran-Iraq War dragged on from 1980 to 1988, the board simply lost all contact with Shammi and the small ministry in Arbil that LOM had started.[66]

With the removal of the Americans from Iraqi in 1958, the LOM took the opportunity to find another location to work among the Kurds in Iran. Continuing the focus on medical missions, Dr. Richard Gardiner, a former British army officer who had been working as a volunteer with LOM, along with his wife, found property in Gorveh, Iran. The board of LOM unanimously voted to call the Gardiners as full-time missionaries, and began fundraising for the hospital in Gorveh. In 1963 another missionary was called to the field; Rev. Paul E. Bungum accepted a call to serve as the administrator of the hospital. Ruth Bennett, who came to serve in the hospital as a nurse, joined him.

The hospital work continued until 1979 when, as a result of the Iranian Revolution, all foreign missionaries were forced to leave the country. Once again, the LOM was forced to start from scratch, having lost all of its property and holdings in Iran. Without any personnel among the Kurds, in either Iran or Iraq (with the exception of Sadiq Shammi), the board finally considered disbanding the society. Throughout the 1980s the LOM moved away from its intended goal of working with the Kurds—but still worked directly with Muslims. It sent Dr. William R. and Mrs. Scott to Bangladesh to help build a hospital in partnership with the World Mission Prayer League. In addition, the mission supported Marvin and Ina Johnson as evangelists in Cairo, Egypt. Marvin Johnson officially taught English at the American University in Cairo in order to obtain a valid visa, but they were privately involved in proselytism among Egyptian Muslims.[67]

In 1986 Rev. Marvin Palmquist, a former missionary to Tanzania, was asked by the LOM board to survey the field and suggest a new direction for the society. Palmquist befriended a Christian worker in Turkey working among the Kurds, Matthew Hand. The society decided to support some of the work of Hand, as it fulfilled the original objectives of the mission.[68] By the mid 1990s the society began a "Direct to the People" fund, which was established to assist Kurds in financial needs as a result

---

66. Oberg, *Messengers of God*.
67. Ibid., 82.
68. Hand, "Rev. Marvin Palmquist Inverview," 2.

of the dramatic social and political upheaval of the first Gulf War and the subsequent embargo of Iraq. After the initial fighting of Desert Storm, Kurdish separatists appealed to the United States to secede from Iraq, and Kurdish separatist rebels in eastern Turkey waged a guerilla war against the Turkish government. In addition to the severe political situation of the Kurds, several tragic earthquakes in the Caucasus left many Kurdish communities destitute. As a result of these events LOM orchestrated large scale fundraising efforts to provide relief. It was one of the only foreign agencies with local support and a long history among the Kurds, enabling it to work effectively. They began to employ local Kurds to oversee the "Direct to the People" fund in "Kurdistan."

The fund had two important foci: educational scholarships to help young Kurds through secondary and university education, and assistance for unsupported women and children. Ironically, neither of these projects involved evangelism of any kind. The first component goes directly against John Newton Wright's advice in 1910 not to undertake educational opportunities. In 1999 the LOM supported the "Reconciliation Walk," which corresponded with the nine hundredth anniversary of the First Crusade. Designed by Matthew Hand, the walk was an organized tour of Western Christians to the Middle East to engage in conversation with local leaders in order to apologize for the Crusades and to "address the bitter legacy of the Crusades" and a "clash of civilizations" mentality.[69] The LOM was still directly engaging Muslims, but times had certainly changed. Dialogue now was the order of the day!

Over it's almost one hundred years of existence, the LOM had been forced to change and transform itself over and over again. Initially, the mission began as a typical Lutheran mission; developing a compound of several western missionary families, organizing a congregation, supporting medical work, and developing the translation of Scripture and catechetical materials into the local language. By the 1990s the mission was made up of local Kurdish projects run by Kurds, with only one executive director working from the U.S. and one field director abroad, Matthew Hand. Having been forced to flee its work in 1916, 1921, 1935, 1959, and finally 1979, this mission which had dedicated itself to serving the Sunni Kurds has had to re-invent itself along the way. Throughout the years, however, the LOM continued to focus on medical issues and health care

---

69. Lutheran Orient Mission brochure, 2005.

Early American Lutheran Views of Islam and Mission in Persia 175

through either dispensaries, hospitals, or relief work. At the beginning of the twenty-first century, LOM projects included support of medical facilities, a carpet weaving project in Van, and a Kurdish relief and development fund. The lack of intentional spiritual activities, especially after the development of the educational scholarships, was cause for concern among its traditional supporters who expected Muslim conversions. In the May–June 2003 issue of the *Messenger*, LOM's newsletter, the concluding paragraph of a report about its scholarships program argues:

> Throughout the Middle East, Christianity is known mainly for the Crusades! Any act of Christian compassion is therefore a powerful form of evangelism. A scholarship given in the name of Christ preaches a thousand sermons, and far more powerfully than words alone. With this practical evidence of Christ's nature known, we then find that many Kurds are curious about the teachings of Christ and overtly ask to be taught the Gospel.
>
> Obviously, without any evidence of Christ's compassion, a sermon or tract would be seen as nothing more than an attack on Islam or Kurdish culture, in effect, turning the Good News into an insult. When evangelism is true, it comes with a compassionate heart, is not overbearing. It comes as Good News indeed![70]

The different missiological perspectives of the traditional support base within Lutheran communities in the United States, and the emerging development work of Matthew Hand, ultimately led to the disbanding of the LOM. In its place emerged Lutheran Mideast Development.[71]

The Middle East had changed dramatically since 1911 when the LOM took up its work in northwest Persia. As an institution associated with Americans, it was at some times viewed favorably by the Ottoman, Iranian, and Iraqi governments, while at other times the work was simply shut down, either because of the workers' foreign nationality or their role as missionaries. In each case, the LOM had to dramatically shift its methods of "direct evangelism." The projects of the mission also moved from missionary evangelism to the present method of supporting local Kuridsh development projects, and doing its part to foster positive relationships across borders.

---

70. Hand, "But Is it Evangelism?" 2.

71. See the *Lutheran Mideast Development* Web site: http://www.lutheran-mideast.org/index.html.

THE SOCIETY FOR THE PROMOTION OF MOHAMMADEN MISSIONS

Though the LOM was the only American Lutheran mission society to directly engage in evangelism toward Muslims in the Middle East at the beginning of the twentieth century, there was another society that supported such a move, and ultimately succeeded in helping the LCMS engage in such an endeavor. This was the Society for the Promotion of Mohammedan Missions (SPMM), organized by Henry Nau, a German born Missouri Synod pastor and missionary.

Nau, born in Marburg, Germany in 1881, emigrated to the U.S. and enrolled at Concordia Seminary in St. Louis, where he was ordained a pastor in the LCMS. His first call was to a mission posting in Krishnagiri, Madras, India, where he served from 1905 to 1914. With the outbreak of World War I, German missionaries and American Lutherans of German descent were looked upon with suspicion in British controlled territories. As in the case of Palestine and Persia, most of the German mission work had to be suspended or turned over to other agencies. Nau found himself facing a difficult decision: go back to the United States or to Germany. With most of his family in Germany, he decided to return there to serve as a hospital chaplain in Chemnitz. Following the war he moved to Halle, the home of the great Lutheran-Reformed Pietists, where he enrolled in the University of Halle-Wittenberg and received a doctorate in philosophy in 1920. From Halle, Nau returned to the United States when he was offered the position as president of Luther College, New Orleans. From 1920 until his retirement in 1950, Nau served as the president or administrator of several LCMS institutions, and would continue to serve in various roles overseas. Nau was thoroughly committed to the evangelization of Muslims, and was thus dubbed by the LCMS as their "first missionary to the followers of Mohammed."[72]

In the early 1930s, Nau served on a committee that was responsible for surveying the possibility of opening an LCMS mission post in Nigeria. After a visit to Nigeria he came back very enthusiastic about the possibility. He was then granted an eighteen-month leave of absence from Immanuel Lutheran College in Greensboro, North Carolina, where he was serving as president, in order to begin the mission.[73] Some twenty

---

72. Stade, "In Memoriam," 3.
73. Nau, *We Move into Africa*, xi–xii.

years later in 1951, Nau and his wife went back to the mission field once again, returning to India. This time he would be going to work directly with Muslims. After a short three-year term, Nau retired from service and returned to the U.S., where he continued to have an active role within the church until his death in 1956.

In 1944, while serving as president of Immanuel, Nau was the primary architect behind the development of a mission society of LCMS pastors and congregations called the SPMM. The primary goal of the mission society was to encourage the church to "carry on aggressive mission work among the Moslems," especially in those countries where work had not yet been begun.[74] He was tireless in his effort to generate both energy and financial support in order to open mission posts in Kurdistan, Somalia, Southeast Asia, and Lebanon. After years of meetings, submitting proposals, and raising funds, however, he was only successful in prompting the LCMS to begin work Lebanon (which we will look at in the next chapter). In reality, most of the funds raised for the society would ultimately go toward supporting the already established LCMS mission work in India.

As the head of SPMM, Nau created a journal, *The Minaret*, which became an effective tool for developing support within the LCMS for their work in Muslim countries. Published from 1945 to 1964, the journal was the mouthpiece for Nau and the LCMS missionaries working among Muslims, primarily those in working in India. As the general editor for eleven of its nineteen years, Nau provided articles aimed at introducing Islam to his North American constituents and offered information on the missionary work being accomplished at each specific site. Throughout the pages of *The Minaret*, Nau professed his desire for mission to the Muslim world. It is worth quoting Nau at length to catch both the style and tenor of language that articulates Islam as the greatest challenge from which the Church has shrunk:

> The Society for the Promotion of Mohammedan Missions is eager to see such a spirit revive in our midst. It wants to help set afire the watchmen of the Church. It wants to press home deep into the conscience of our people the conviction that the missionary obligation of the Church is not fulfilled so long as . . . souls redeemed with Christ's precious blood are passed by in the missionary endeavors of the Church. It wants to picture the world of Islam as being within the scope of the promises of the Gospel. . . .

---

74. Nau, "A Test and a Challenge," 1.

> The Moslem Mission problem should be approached not with fear and trembling, not with a palpitating heart, but with victory in the eyes and faith in the heart which will not shrink though pressed by many a foe, that, when in danger knows no fear, in darkness feels no doubt, that shines more bright and clear when tempests rage without.[75]

Mission to Islam was not like any other mission challenge for Nau. Much like Luther, Nau saw Islam as having a role to play in the God's ultimate ingathering of all of the nations. Pointing to Isaiah 60, he saw the prophecy of the nations coming to the light of the Lord as including the Muslims of the Middle East. Isaiah 60:6–7 reads:

> *A multitude of camels shall cover you, the young camels of Midian and Ephah; all those from Sheba shall come. They shall bring gold and frankincense, and shall proclaim the praise of the Lord. All the flocks of Kedar shall be gathered to you, the rams of Nebaioth shall minister to you; they shall be acceptable on my altar, and I will glorify my glorious house.*

According to Genesis 25:1, Midian and Ephaph were the sons of Abraham through Keturah. Further on in Genesis 25:13, Kedar and Nabaioth were children to Ishmael. Thus, for Nau, the Isaiah text, combined with Genesis 25, pointed to a clear sign that the Arabs, who take their ancestry from Abraham and Ishmael, will one day be brought into the fold of the faith. The references to these descendents

> are too specific and geographically too accurate to be limited to such generalization. They literally offer the hope of successful missions to the sons of Midian, Ephah, Sheba, Kedar and Nabaioth, and of missions to Moslems in particular, for these either are the physical descendants of the sons and grandson of Abraham, or they share the present faith of these descendants. These very definitely will have a place in the coming glory of the Lord and in the brightness of His rising. The fulfillment of this promise has been delayed only by the negligence of the Christian Church. But God will keep His promise![76]

Nau's views of Islam followed much of Western scholarship (and Luther himself!) that saw the development of Islam as a result of Muhammad's misconceptions of orthodox Jewish and Christian theol-

75. Nau, "A Life-Long Ambition," 4.
76. Nau, "The Wrong Appeal?" 3; also Nau, "Zeal without Knowledge," 5.

ogy. Nau argued that the heretical Jewish and Christian communities of Arabia were responsible for Muhammad's acceptance of a mutated Christianity.[77] In addition, Nau believed that Mohammad's rejection of the doctrine of the Trinity was also based upon a misreading of orthodox Christian beliefs from his own particular Arabian context. For example, Muhammad's conception of the Trinity was conceived of in the context of rampant Arab polytheism, which Muhammad clearly rejected. Thus, he associated the concept of "triune" with the Arab triad of Allat, Al-'Uzzá, and Manat. In addition, Arabs had held that the supreme deity had various offspring, or daughters. The language of the "Son" and Mary as "the mother of God," then, was understood in the context polytheism. The language utilized in the Qur'ān was that of human physical relations, which would be denied by orthodox Christianity.[78]

Nau saw the major difference between the Qur'ānic image of God and the God of the Bible as one of *pathos* versus *a-pathos*. For Nau, the God of Islam is "the loveless Allah, the religion of the lifeless creed, the religion of the degraded home."[79] The faith focuses heavily upon the will of Allah and does not understand the love of God for the world. God's will is supreme, and therefore leaves no room for human freedom or human responsibility. This then keeps Muslims in a state of moral depravity; God wills what God wills and humanity is left without any recourse. God's sovereignty reigns supreme and humanity must simply accept the consequences of God's actions. As a result of this *apathetic* view of God, Nau asserts, humans live in a mechanical universe and have no responsibility in their daily lives. Thus, if all responsibility is removed from the human, there is no concept of culpability for their actions. Not only does Islam have no concept of human accountability to God for sin, but also their religious system has no mechanism to develop social morality.[80] Much like the earliest Protestant missionaries of the ABCFM, Pliny Fisk and Levi Parsons, as well as Lewis Eichelberger, Nau understood Islam as keeping Muslims in a degraded state

---

77. Gall, "Allah," 8. For further examples of this argument see Bell, *Origin of Islam*. For recent examples of the "heresy" argument see Cragg, *Arab Christian*, 42–43; and Parrinder, *Jesus in the Qur'ān*, 135.

78. For an contemporary Muslim study of this issue of the sonship of Jesus in the Qur'ān, see Ayoub, *Muslim View of Christianity*, 117–33.

79. Nau, "Christianity and Non-Christianity," 6.

80. Otten, "Muslim Books of Revelation," 7.

of morality, where polygamy and violence were championed.[81] In Nau's view, the Muslim tendency toward violence is clearly demonstrated by the spread of Islam by "the scimitar, or the sword . . . In the war for their faith, and using the sword of steel."[82] Nau's Western evangelical views were carried on by the SPMM even after his death. Robert C. Stade, who became the editor in chief of *The Minaret* when Nau died, continued espousing these pejorative views of a violent Islam.

> Mohammedanism was born in violence and itself went on to conquer peoples and nations with violence. . .
>
> The sword, as a means of conquest and rule, became as much a factor in the rapid advance of Islam as were the fanatical fervor and disciplined rigidity of its religious system. Trade routes were raided, villages plundered, and tribe after tribe brought under subjection. [Meanwhile] Mohammed's fanatical followers . . . impart a religious fervor to dull unimaginative heathen.[83]

In contrast to Islam's Allah, Nau says, the God of the Bible is a God of love who undertakes the cross to redeem a lost humanity.

> As we think of the millions in Moslem lands to whom our hearts go out in sympathy because of their ignorance, their sinfulness, their utter need for the Savior—those other words of the apostle assume new meaning . . . We must meet the challenge of Moslem opponents neither by compromise and concessions nor by cowardice or silence, but by boldly proclaiming that the very heart of our religion, its life's blood, is the atonement wrought by Christ on the Cross. If we preach Christ crucified, risen again on the third day, and sitting on the Right hand of God, faithfully, fearlessly and warm-heartedly, He can very well turn this stumbling block into the very gate of heaven.[84]

For Henry Nau, only the preaching of the crucified Christ would drive a Muslim to understand his condition; that he or she is a sinful human being in need of transformation. And only in realizing this fact would there be recognition that only Christ, through the cross, can save. Thus, engaging Muslims through direct evangelism, preaching the Word pub-

81. See Khalaf, "Protestant Images of Islam, 211–30.
82. Nau, "The Scimitar," 12.
83. Stade, *The Minaret*, n.p.
84. Nau, "The Stumbling Block of the Cross," 3.

licly—either through sermons, literature, or even radio broadcasts, was the most effective and faithful way to undertake mission to Islam. His views would finally lead to the development of the LCMS's work in the Middle East. It is to this part of the Lutheran narrative that we turn to in the next chapter.

While Palestine was a central field for German Lutheran missions in the Middle East, Persia was primary for the Americans. For the American Lutherans, who worked in partnership with their German Lutheran compatriots, at least until the beginning of World War I, Persia would be the first arena of American Lutheran missions in the Middle East. Unlike with Palestine, the missionaries would have no national endowments to draw from. The United States was urged by Presbyterian missionaries to step in to create a U.S. mandate in order to protect the religious minorities of the Caucasus region—the Armenians, the Assyrians, and the Kurds, and although there was heavy pressure to do this, the U.S. administration ultimately decided not to join the imperial game.[85] Thus, missionaries in this region were left to their own designs and their own protection. Their mission posts were plagued by the calamities of World Wars I and II, Soviet occupation, the Iranian Revolution, and finally the Gulf Wars of 1991 and 2003. The American Lutherans had very few years in which they were not interrupted by war, bloodshed, and political turmoil.

Whereas most Protestant mission agencies (e.g., Anglican or Presbyterian) either worked for the reform of one of the ancient churches or supported their newly created evangelical churches which broke away from the mother churches, the American Lutherans were interested in "direct evangelism" among the Sunni Kurds, whose national lands straddled both Persia (Iran) and Iraq. The LOM has been the longest serving American Lutheran mission agency working in the Middle East, though its methods and strategies have changed over the years. As we will see in the next chapter, the American Lutheran denominations formally entered into the Middle East throughout the second half of the twentieth century; the LCMS in 1950, the ALC in 1960, and the LCA in 1962. However, as the missionaries of these denominations invested themselves in the cultures in which they were living, their mission would begin to focus on dialogue with Muslims rather than conversion.

85. See Balakian, *Burning Tigris*; Barton, *Turkish Atrocities*; Grabill, *Protestant Diplomacy*, esp. 140–206; and DeNovo, *American Interests*.

6

The American Lutheran "Conversation" with Islam

> *This task of Christians and Muslims and others coming together, attempting, in small but significant ways, to offer some of who we are to one another; this delicate task, like the changing of the seasons, needs to go on, and that's our intention, to go on bringing people together, to meet, to share, to listen, hoping that in the process, mutual respect and appreciation will spring to life and grow.... The practice, not the public display of religion; this is our hope and prayer.*
>
> —Harold Vogelaar, 2006

AT THE ANNUAL MEETING of the Southeastern District of the LCMS in 1946, the synod voted to pass on to the national convention a memorial that the church "should undertake an intensive mission program among Moslems as a fitting memorial to a century of blessings, and that this effort be begun in a virgin mission field, preferably Kurdistan."[1]

The Southeastern District was the heartland of the movement for the SPMM, and it was from here that the LCMS would be encouraged again to take up its "responsibility" of mission to "the sons of Ishmael." As a result of this resolution the board of LCMS World Mission would send Henry Nau to Iraq and Iran in 1950 to survey the possibilities. (Nau had already provided several surveys for the LCMS—of Puerto Rico in 1932 and Nigeria in 1935, and so was well qualified for the task.)[2] After spending time with LOM missionaries, Kurdistan was viewed as too risky. The LCMS settled on India, where Nau was ultimately sent for three years to work as the Missouri Synod's "first missionary to the followers of Mohammed."

---

1. Nau, "Where Shall We Go?" 1.
2. Nau would go on to work in Havana, Cuba at the request of the BFM as well, before his death in 1956.

On his way back from India in 1954, the board of World Mission once again asked Nau to undertake a "fact finding" mission throughout the Middle East in order to ascertain whether the church could begin work there. On this specific trip Nau journeyed throughout Egypt, Cyprus, Lebanon, Syria, and Transjordan (including Jerusalem). In Beirut, LCMS layman Carl F. Agerstrand, who like Nau had a strong desire to do ministry among Muslims, hosted him. Agerstrand, feeling a call to the Muslim world, packed up his things and left his home, bound for Beirut. He eventually garnered the support of the International Lutheran Laymen's League (ILLL), the most prominent mission auxiliary within the LCMS. It was Agerstrand who developed the concept of utilizing a media ministry for evangelism to Muslims in the Middle East.

THE "MIDDLE EAST LUTHERAN MINISTRY" (MELM) RADIO EVANGELISM

Carl Agerstrand was a successful businessman from Muskegon, Michigan. In 1948 he sold his business and moved to Beirut, compelled and "full of zeal to serve the Lord among the people" of the Middle East.[3] Agerstrand, using his personal finances, and following the path of Johann Schneller a little more than a hundred years before, opened up an orphanage in Mansouriyya, outside of Beirut. He wished to combine social work for the community with public preaching of the gospel. He then helped to develop two Lutheran congregations: Redeemer Lutheran Church in Ashrafiyya in 1956, and St. Mark's Lutheran Church in Sin al-Fil in 1960. However, Aagerstrand's primary interest was in radio evangelism. He arranged to have *The Lutheran Hour* broadcast in Arabic from a Beirut station on Christmas in 1950.[4] Thus the Middle East Lutheran Ministry (MELM) was born, whose goal was to "proclaim the Gospel message to the Arab-speaking people in the Arab world through the different mass media."[5]

The broadcasts, the heart of what would become the LCMS's ministry in the Middle East, would be very successful and continue weekly

---

3. Jahshan, "History and Background."

4. *The Lutheran Hour*, the longest running Christian radio broadcast, which began in 1930, is operated by the ILLL, an auxiliary of the LCMS. See the Web site at http://www.lhm.org.

5. "Long Range Objectives for MELM Mass Communications Department," 1978, MELM archives.

from Beirut until the outbreak of the Lebanese Civil War in 1975.[6] MELM broadcasted two fifteen-minute programs each month, plus a thirty-minute broadcast on the fifth Sunday of the month. In 1957 the ministry added a second program broadcast to the Middle East through Eternal Love Winning Africa (ELWA) from Monrovia, Liberia. The programs were written in Beirut, mailed to Monrovia, and then placed on the air from there. They consisted of Western-style hymns as well as a conversation between two individuals about religious topics. They were cancelled in 1967 due to "doctrinal differences" between MELM and ELWA.[7] From 1967 onward MELM was able to broadcast over Trans World Radio from Monte Carlo for fifteen minutes per week, and five fifteen-minute programs from Cyprus beginning in 1970. By 1964, MELM was also producing two twenty-five-minute programs for the LWF's Radio Voice of the Gospel from Addis Ababa. When the station was nationalized by Haile Selassie in 1977, the RVOG moved its broadcasts to Cyprus and increased the number of programs.

In the early 1960s MELM began to work in cooperation with the Near East Council of Churches (NECC), the association of Protestant denominations in the Middle East.[8] In 1963 the NECC, MELM, and the LCMS can to an agreement in order to create a radio studio at the property of Lutheran Church of the Redeemer in Jerusalem. Although the NECC could utilize the studio, MELM would administrate the program under the direction its own staff member, the Palestinian Moris Jahshan. However, progress on the studio was very slow. The preparations were ultimately interrupted by the 1967 War and the occupation of East Jerusalem by the Israelis. Although the studio itself was not damaged and could technically still function, the property was now under Israeli occupation. In order for programs to be aired they would have to be mailed to Jerusalem through the Israeli post. This put the NECC and MELM in a difficult situation, as they would be seen as collaborating with the occupiers. In the words of LCMS Middle East program director William Reinking, "in order to produce Arabic programs and send them out of the country some type of permission would have to be given by the Israeli

6. "Mass Communication in the Middle East," 1978, MELM archives.

7. Strengholt, "Gospel in the Air."

8. The NECC would formally become the Middle East Council of Churches in 1990 with the inclusion of the Oriental Orthodox churches, and, in 1984, the Eastern Catholic churches. See the MECC Web site: http://www.mec-churches.org.

government. This permission would be looked upon as cooperation on the part of the Lutheran Church with the Israeli government and could harm the Christian cause by increasing the suspicion of Arab Muslims regarding the Christians."[9] Wisely, the project was scrapped. However, Reinking proposed an alternative possibility for the studio. Hearkening back to the early Lutheran missionary roots in Palestine, he suggested the possibility of utilizing the studio to begin broadcasts in Hebrew. However, the issue of a Lutheran organization continuing to evangelize among Jews in a post-Holocaust environment was still a sensitive subject, and never gained support. The idea was dropped.

In addition to the radio broadcasts, MELM utilized several other types of mass media in order to evangelize among non-Christians and bolster the faith of Middle Eastern Christians from various church communities. By the 1960s, the cassette tape was becoming a very popular medium of mass communication. The cassette became not only a cheap and easy way for people to listen to their favorite music, but a tool used religious indoctrination as well, and it revolutionized the expression of religion in the Middle East throughout the late 1960s and 1970s. However, Christian missionaries were not the only groups to exploit this "modern" technology. Muslims began using cassettes as well, not only to listen to the chanting of the Qur'ān, but to sermons as well. Monologues of the Middle East's favorite Muslim preachers, like Sheikhs 'Abd al-Hamid Kishk, Muhammad Shar'awi, and Muhammed al-Ghazali from Egypt, helped export conservative Islamist views from Egypt around the Middle East. The Bible societies of the Middle East would also begin to utilize the cassette in the same format, publishing the Bible on cassette with a Qurānic style chant for general distribution.

MELM began developing *The Lutheran Hour* its own musical program for cassette distribution. Funding was secured to begin recording hymns sung by local choirs, as well as other Christian music, including traditional and contemporary Arab songs performed by popular Arab musicians. They then began to encourage the development of contemporary indigenous Christian songs in Arabic.[10] The music was not aimed at one particular denomination or community but for general consumption, especially for youth. Although clearly Christian, the music was pro-

---

9. Reinking, "Preliminary Report on the Situation in Jerusalem as It Is Related to the Proposed Lutheran Radio Studio," October 13, 1967, MELM archives.

10. "Mass Communication in the Middle East," 1978, MELM archives.

duced to be part of the general Arab cultural backdrop of the early 1970s that was riding the swell of pan-Arab nationalism. There was a concerted effort by this time to demonstrate that the churches of the Middle East were truly loyal to their Arab and Middle Eastern cultures, as opposed to being simply Western implants. A MELM brochure stated that the ministry

> is helping Arab Christians witness that they are just as Arab as any Muslim Arab – and that they have good news to share about Someone who came for Arabs and all men.[11]

Like the nineteenth century Arab literary renaissance [al-Naḥda], MELM found itself not only undertaking Christian evangelism in the Muslim world, but also helping to articulate an Arab or Middle Eastern Christian identity, fully rooted in the Christian faith and fully Arab in culture. MELM was encouraging the publication not of Arab literature, but Arab music. Ultimately, however, a programmatic focus on helping to encourage an Arab Christian identity in the modern Middle East would be too difficult a concept for the North American Lutheran constituency of the LCMS. By the late 1970s, there was grave concern from the board of the LCMS Foreign Mission as to the direction of the ministry, as it was not viewed to be "evangelical" enough. By 1978, however, MELM was also interested in moving into television programming. Plans were drawn up to begin using the LCMS's *This Is the Life* and the LCA's *David & Goliath* programs, dubbed into Arabic. However, the ongoing Lebanese Civil War prohibited further planning and implementation of this project.

The most popular program of MELM, however, was the Bible correspondence courses developed by *The Lutheran Hour*. In 1952 Agerstrand had begun utilizing "The Life of Christ" and "The Life of Saint Paul" which had been very popular in the United States. These courses were translated into Arabic and mailed out locally. The correspondence course format became one of the most popular programs of MELM in the Middle East, at one point claiming to have registered up to eighty-five thousand participants by 1973![12]

---

11. "Mission Through Media/Middle East," 1973, MELM archives.
12. Ibid.

THE LCMS MISSIONARIES—THE BEGINNING OF THE LANGUAGE OF "DIALOGUE"

Agerstrand developed the "Lutheran office" out of Beirut with the help of numerous Lebanese Christians, including Jad Hatem, Ibrahim Matter, Shehadah Awabdi, and Moris Jahshan, a Palestinian by birth. They not only helped with the translation of the radio broadcasts, but with all the ministries, including services at the two Lutheran chapels and additional prison ministry. Henry Nau's visit with Agerstrand in 1954 proved to be a vital success for Agerstrand's objectives and vision for the development of a Lutheran mission in the Middle East. After returning to the United States, Nau reported to the LCMS World Mission board that the media ministry begun by Agerstrand was well worth supporting, as well as theologically sound—it had already utilized material from *The Lutheran Hour*. However, the synod could not be pushed forward to commit to any formal support until 1959, when at its national convention in San Francisco the denomination finally passed a resolution to enter into the Middle East "to widen our approach to the Muslim," and began to raise money for personnel and programs.[13] Agerstrand then returned to the U.S. in 1958 to enroll in Concordia Seminary, Springfield, Illinois in order to undergo theological training for ordination in the Lutheran church. With Agerstrand's departure Moris Jahshan was appointed as the director of MELM. Jahshan would go on to be the longest serving member of the Lutheran ministry, serving from 1957 until his retirement in 2002.

In 1960 Rev. Agerstrand returned to Beirut and was accompanied by Edward Azzam. Walter Boss joined the two a year later in 1961. Azzam and Boss were given explicit instructions from their mission board to undertake a thorough study of the Middle Eastern context in order to ascertain the best method of mission work for the LCMS. By 1962 Azzam and Boss had surveyed the Arab world. Their report would dramatically change the role of the LCMS in the Middle East. Originally an independent mission organization led by the vision of one autonomous layman, MELM had now been suddenly and dramatically transformed into a ministry under the auspices of the board of the LCMS World Mission. The original intent of the Lutheran mission as envisioned by Agerstrand was to undertake evangelistic missionary activity by planting churches and developing the field of mass media (radio, cassettes, and television) for

---

13. Resolution 21 of the *Proceedings of the 44th Regular Convention*.

evangelization. However, the new incoming Missouri Synod missionaries found out that traditional methods of evangelism and church planting did not work well in the contemporary Muslim Middle East, especially in a predominantly Christian Lebanon, which included a wide variety of indigenous churches and foreign missionary communities. In addition to the historically and legally recognized indigenous churches of Lebanon, by 1957 there were 20 different Western missionary agencies working in Lebanon, with more than 250 Western missionaries.[14] The two missionaries found that the development of a Lutheran ministry for the purpose establishing Lutheran congregations would create "another fragment to an already fragmented church situation."[15] Given the plethora of mission agencies working in Beirut, and given the difficulties and sensitivities of the indigenous historic churches of the Middle East, the report recommended that the LCMS "not enter the Middle East as another Protestant church . . . but rather to be a ministry to the churches in the area."[16] They wrote:

> Here in the Middle East our church has experienced perhaps for the first time that a whole section of the world can and will lock its doors even to a sincere and well-intentioned mission approach . . . It does not suggest a promising future for our church in the Middle East. . . . We like to believe that the "closed doors of the Middle East" can become a springboard for a bolder Christian approach to Muslims in other parts of the world.[17]

As Azzam and Boss met with numerous Arab Christian leaders within Lebanon and throughout the region, it became clear to them that they would face incredible social and legal problems, not only from Muslim detractors, but also from the complex social-political *millet* system within Lebanon. The LCMS quickly found out, much like the many other Western Protestant missionary agencies before it, that communal identi-

14. Roland Miller, "Report on Lebanon," November 11, 1959, as cited in Meyer, "Middle East," 8. The historic churches of Lebanon that have legal recognition from the state include the Armenian, Assyrian Church of the East (Nestorian), Coptic, Greek, and Syrian Orthodox churches; the Catholic rites include the Armenian, Chaldean, Greek (Melkite), Latin, Maronite, and Syrian Catholic rites; while the Protestants are represented by a national evangelical council under which most Protestant denominations are included.

15. Meyer, "Middle East" 10.

16. Jahshan, "History and Background"; emphasis added.

17. Azzam and Boss, "Middle East Mission Survey," 2.c.1.

ties in the Middle East were firmly set, and that creating a relationship with one community often closed doors to another. The ancient churches were not at all excited about new opportunities for evangelizing among the Muslim community. One reason is the first time the Protestants came to the Middle East to evangelize among Muslims they ended up creating a Protestant community out of disillusioned Orthodox Christians! Thus, the Orthodox were worried that this new Lutheran movement would be no different, and up to that point it had seemed as if this was its intent. They saw the work of the Lutherans as simply another "Protestant invasion."[18] Second, the existing Protestant churches of Syria and Lebanon (the Congregationalists and the Presbyterians) were not likely to agree to further competition from within their own Protestant branch. For the Lutherans to actually develop recognized churches within Lebanon they would have to be granted that right by the head of the Association of Protestant Churches whose policy was that all new Christian ministries must be under the jurisdiction of already existing Christian denominations. Third, the member churches of the NECC were not about to be associated with a Western mission agency attempting to convert Muslims, as this would upset the carefully constructed but tenuous balance of Christian-Muslim relationships in the complex confessional setting of Lebanon and Syria—especially when the mission agency was from the United States, a strong supporter of the modern State of Israel. In other words, the local Arab, Armenian, and Greek churches were not very supportive of such an endeavor!

> To attempt any other way of entrance [into Lebanon and Syria], even if it were permitted, would brand us as a "fringe group" not recognized by the national churches (this has been the lot of the Seventh Day Adventitsts, Jehovahs Witnesses and to some extent the Southern Baptists.)[19]

The Missouri Synod Lutherans, not wanting to be thrown in with the Seventh Day Adventists or the Jehovah's Witnesses, heeded the report. Instead of church planting, they would continue to support indigenous ministries, primarily through the already existing radio ministry. In addition, Azzam and Boss encouraged the LCMS not to give up on its bold endeavors to evangelize among Muslims in other parts of the world.

18. Jahshan, "Middle East Lutheran Ministry," 29.
19. Azzam and Boss, "Middle East Mission Survey," 1.a.4.

The Azzam/Boss report did lead to the closing of all LCMS-supported ministries begun by Agerstrand; the two small Lutheran congregations, the prison ministry, and the small schools associated with the original orphanages were closed, and the evangelists who were employed were released from service. Only the mass media work and Bible correspondence courses were continued. The office of MELM was moved from the predominantly Christian side of East Beirut to Hamra, in the predominantly Muslim West Beirut, near the American University in Beirut, the Near East School of Theology, and the (Presbyterian) American Mission Press. This allowed for greater contacts within the artistic, educational, evangelical, and publishing communities, and provided more exposure for the ministry. The old offices in East Beirut were maintained as a chapel for English Language services.

Agerstrand, who had only recently returned from the U.S. fresh from ordination, now saw his ministry completely transformed. He was no longer in control of the work, nor of the goals of the ministry. More than likely very discouraged, if not angry, he returned to the U.S. and entered parish ministry. Azzam and Boss, who had concluded their work, soon followed him. This left only Moris Jahshan remaining from among the original workers of MELM. He would continue to serve as director of MELM, developing a staff of Lebanese and Palestinian Christians.

The LCMS, however, had not washed its hands of its direct work in the Middle East. It was committed to evangelizing among Muslims, but, unlike during the Agerstrand years, it decided to do so only in conversation with the indigenous church, specifically the NECC. Its next batch of missionaries, straight from seminary graduation, would dramatically transform the role of MELM. Dennis Hilgendorf and his family arrived in 1963, while John Stelling and his family came in 1965. Although they were technically "advisors" for the work being done by the Lebanese and Palestinian staff, the two new LCMS missionaries would help to develop the role of MELM from its traditional foreign missionary evangelistic role to a contextual Christian resource in the midst of various Middle Eastern Christian churches living in an Islamic context.

The original goal of MELM was captured in its mission statement: "Arabic speaking people understanding and sharing the love of God for all men in Christ." After their own survey of the needs and prospects of ministry in the Arab world, Hilgendorf and Stelling would write that "the goal of the Middle East Lutheran ministry simply stated is '*Christians and Muslims* understanding and sharing the love of God for all men in Christ.'"[20] The change in the wording of the mission statement would be a huge methodological shift for the focus of the ministry.

Hilgendorf had a degree in anthropology and had spent a year at Hartford Seminary studying Arabic and Islam at the Duncan Black MacDonald Center for the Study of Islam and Christian-Muslim Relations before being sent out to Lebanon. Stelling spent one year in the Arab Studies program at the American University of Beirut, and one year in Islamic Studies at McGill University in Toronto during a 1970–71 furlough. Thus, both missionaries were keenly aware of the Islamic context and the communal complexities of Middle Eastern society. Their initial education led them to begin thinking and planning for alternative forms of doing mission.

The Hilgendorfs (above) and Stellings (below) with friends.

FIGURE 3: LCMS Personnel, Beirut, Lebanon, 1973

20. Hilgendorf and Stelling, *People Who Need People*, 32.

First, MELM would no longer only produce transmissions of *The Lutheran Hour*, translate programs written in other countries, or write its own programs, but would seek to support and assist the faith of the historic churches in the Middle East in order to help them to carry out their missions. Thus, MELM began to work with the Maronite church, preparing radio programs for them, as well as to work more closely with the NECC. This was a variation on the "indirect evangelism" method employed by so many other Western missionaries. But rather than encouraging the churches to evangelize among their Muslim compatriots, the LCMS missionaries began to encourage Arab Christians and Muslims to engage in "dialogue" with one another. Stelling would write:

> We were committed to work together with established Christian churches in the Middle East to refer any interested correspondents who lived in their region to them. That included both Christians and Muslims. Our hope was that Christians would have contact with Muslims and be able to meet them, get to know them and to share with them on various levels. . . . So dialogue . . . would begin at the very basic level of talking to one another around common issues . . . being able to hear and understand and trust one another on those issues. Then would come the opportunity to talk about deeper issues including religion and for Christians to speak their understanding of Scripture and how their faith impacts their lives.[21]

This missiological shift would help to create a different language and vision about how to do mission as a Western Christian (and Lutheran) missionary society in the Middle East. Although the intent of the LCMS missionaries was basically the traditional ABCFM role of attempting to revive the ancient churches, their purpose was not simply to bring members over to the Protestant faith from Islam, but to help the people of the Middle East come together in a common culture which God in Christ had already sanctified. Unlike the ABCFM view of Rufus Anderson, where the American missionaries were instilling a sense of American Christian liberty and freedom, the LCMS missionaries of the 1970s were deeply committed to Arab and Middle Eastern culture. With this commitment came the same conundrum that indigenous Middle Eastern Christians face. As the Anglican Islamicist Bishop Kenneth Cragg once wrote, "The crux of Arab Christianity might be linguistically expressed; it is bound over to a

---

21. John Stelling, email to author, October 11, 2007.

language that is bound over to Islam."[22] That is, Middle Eastern Christians have always needed to find a way to accept that, while being descendents of some of the original Christians from Pentecost, they now live in and are part of a predominantly Islamic culture. The danger has always been that to thoroughly reject all trappings of Islamic civilization is to reject one's own cultural identity. If this was complex enough for indigenous Middle Eastern Christians, it was—and continues to be—very complicated for the average North American Christian, who is more often than not simply interested in gaining numbers of new converts to the faith.

The new missiological shift, however, could be seen in four distinct ways. First, MELM became firmly committed to indigenous Middle Eastern ecumenical relationships. Second, they were dedicated to an indigenous expression of the Christian faith, to be developed through their programming. Third, they would come to associate themselves with "the Arab cause" and the plight of the Palestinians. Lastly, they would encourage those around them, including the staff of MELM, to work for positive Christian-Muslim relationships.

Rather than working alone as in independent foreign mission agency in an already crowded mission depot, MELM became committed to working ecumenically with indigenous churches. In 1969 MELM helped form the Middle East Communication Fellowship (MECF), which encompassed the NECC and the American Southern Baptists' International Mission Board.[23] In addition, in 1973 MELM began a relationship with the Maronite church, providing airtime for Catholic programming, as well as helping to produce some of their work. As a part of this relationship the two missionaries sat on the Catholic Mass Communication Committee. Other ecumenical relationships included working with the local Greek Orthodox priest in the village of Enfe and supporting a joint Presbyterian-Latin Catholic initiative in Nabatiyya. These programs demonstrated that the American Lutheran missionaries were thoroughly committed to the Lebanese context and communities.[24] These relationships certainly did frustrate missionaries and the work of MELM, but their commitment to indigenous mission would not allow them to go it alone.

---

22. Cragg, *Arab Christian*, 31.
23. Strengholt, "Gospel in the Air."
24. "Mission with Christians/Middle East," n.d., MELM archives.

Second, the recording and distribution of indigenous Christian music helped to provide an authentically Arab Christian participation in a society seeking to find its identity in the early 1970s. During a time in which Lebanon was being torn apart by different spheres of influence (e.g., Pan-Arab nationalism, regional nationalisms, capitalism, Marxism, Islamic and Christian fundamentalism), causing it to suffer from an identity crisis, the conscious effort to foster Arab Christian music was a way to remind both Christians and Muslims that Christianity was not simply a Western faith brought by Protestant missionaries but uniquely Eastern and Arab. In some cases the music produced was even Arab religious music sung by Muslim artists. Thus, while there were dramatic pulls toward Westernization and Marxist socialism, MELM attempted to create space for a Middle Eastern Christian voice. The publications written for the LCMS during this time began to raise the issues of Arab Christian identity to a primarily midwestern Lutheran constituency that, like most Americans, had little, if any, knowledge of Christians in the Middle East.

Third, and directly related to the issue of general knowledge of the Middle East, came the concern for the plight of the Palestinians. Whereas most Americans saw 1948 and especially 1967 as the great miracle of the creation of the modern state of Israel, very few Americans seemed to understand the realities of the Palestinians, especially Christian Palestinians. Most Western churches, except those that had direct links to Palestinian churches, saw the Arab-Israeli issue through the lens of the modern state of Israel, not through that of the Palestinian Christians. The Six Day War of 1967 was the impetus for the development of contemporary Christian Zionism, which believes that support for the modern state of Israel is a duty for Christians in order to bring about the return of Christ.[25] As a result of the 1967 Six Day War and the Israeli occupation of the Old City of Jerusalem and the West Bank, however, more Palestinian refugees fled from their villages and lands into neighboring Lebanon, Syria, Jordan, and Egypt. Hilgendorf and Stelling were living in and among Palestinian refugees and displaced persons in Lebanon.

William Reinking, LCMS area program director to the Middle East, visited Jerusalem in October 1967 to assess the situation. He wrote:

> The Christians in the occupied areas feel that the Christian cause in the Middle East, and specifically in their own areas, has been

---

25. See Ruether and Ruether, *Wrath of Jonah*.

> hurt because of Western policy before, during and after the war ... When I would ask the question: what the churches in America could do to assist the churches in Jerusalem and the occupied areas at the present time? The answer was always given: "Stop supporting Israel."[26]

Lebanon was particularly affected by the plight of the Palestinians in 1967, as more Palestinian refugee camps sprung up along the southern border of the country, as well as in Beirut. Tensions between the Palestinians and the Lebanese grew, becoming the catalyst for the 1975–90 Lebanese Civil War.[27] But, the issue of the Palestinians was not only a national one, but a personal one. Several of MELM staff members, including the director, Moris Jahshan, were Palestinians.

In 1969, the Lutheran Council in the U.S.A. (an ad hoc committee of representatives from the denominations of the ALC, LCA, LCMS, and the Slovak Evangelical Lutheran Church) was meeting to decide just how American Lutherans could become involved in this very important and sensitive issue. They turned to Dennis Hilgendorf for guidance. The council invited Hilgendorf, who was on furlough in the U.S., to Detroit to present a paper on the Middle East. His presentation prompted the committee to think about the issues of "poverty, prejudice and power"; namely the issue of the Palestinian refugees and the role of the modern state of Israel as an occupier.

Speaking almost two years after the Six Day War while the state of Israel had continued to occupy East Jerusalem, the West Bank, the Gaza Strip, the Sinai Peninsula, and the Golan Heights, Dennis Hilgendorf directly addressed the issue of the occupation from "the underside"—the experience of the Palestinians:

> ... if the church is going to choose the "middle ground" of compromise [between Israel and the Palestinians], it has chosen the side of Israel, for in the Arab view their can be no compromise between an aggressor and his victims. And the church that thinks there can be a compromise should be honest enough to admit that it is an Israeli partisan, and having done that, it can then decide to follow that partisanship consistently or abandon it.
>
> If the church were to come this distance and then decide that the Israeli view is undemocratic, unjust, and fringing on fanatic

---

26. Reinking, "Preliminary Report," MELM archives.
27. Grafton, *Christians of Lebanon*, 136–37.

> tribalism and aggression . . . only then could it influence the Arab view which has, in its frustration, given voice to fanatic threats. Then it could work for a Palestine in which those Jews who wished to be part of a pluralistic society could live securely . . . [28]

Hilgendorf's words would prove to set the agenda for most of the later American Lutheran missionaries in the Middle East who would see the issues of war and land from the vantage point of the victims, be they Palestinian, Lebanese, Sudanese, or even Israeli. From this point onward the focus, at least as far as American Lutheran ministry in Beirut and Jerusalem was concerned, would be on issues of justice. This stance would be and continues to be highly controversial, as the mainstream American and German Lutheran traditions have continued to hold deep sympathies for Israeli Jews and their recent past.

The fourth area in which the LCMS missionaries challenged the Protestant missionary landscape in the Middle East was with the development of the language of "dialogue." After their arrival, fresh on the heels of the Azzam/Boss report calling for an LCMS withdrawal from the church planting, Hilgendorf and Stelling began to carve out their own niche. In a time in which Arab Christians were charged with being a "fifth column" for Israel and the West, and in which a wide array of nationalist platforms was seeking to pull Lebanon apart at the seams, MELM began to look at the bigger picture.

> We have learned that Christianity and Islam are built on monotheistic foundations, that "God" and "Allah" are simply two names for the same Being, although their perspectives may be somewhat different. We have also discovered, from talking to Arab Christians and Arab Muslims, that their spiritual and day-to-day concerns are very similar. Both Muslims and Christians need to see the other as an Arab friend, an Arab brother . . . They are all children of God.[29]

The explicit focus on helping Christians and Muslims to share and "dialogue" was a highly controversial subject. Even though MELM had not abandoned its evangelical views regarding the uniqueness of Christ, it was hoping to use religion as a way to find commonalities rather than to divide. This led MELM in 1972 to develop a course for the expressed purpose of dialogue, centered on the Arabic novel *City of Wrong*, by Kāmil

---

28. Hilgendorf, "Middle East," 16.1.1.
29. Hilgendorf and Stelling, *People Who Need People*, 32.

Ḥusayn.³⁰ Ḥusayn, a famous Arabic Muslim author, describes the events surrounding Good Friday from a Muslim perspective. According to the Qur'ān, Jesus was never crucified. The Arabic text of the Qur'ān, however, is not clear as to whether Jesus was hung on the cross and simply did not die, or whether he was never put up on the cross at all.³¹ Muslims throughout the ages have developed a wide variety of interpretations of this passage. Ḥusayn, in his novel, introduces both characters from the biblical story and from Christian tradition. He weaves a story around the intent of the people of the Jerusalem to crucify Christ, something he says both Christians and Muslims can agree upon. The theme of the novel focuses upon the dark side of humanity that seeks to subvert God's designs. It is a story well suited for a Christian-Muslim discussion, and that is just what MELM encouraged.

By 1974 Hilgendorf was beginning to think about new productions in the radio programs that could help foster this dialogue. He suggested new styles of presenting Christianity, such as chanting Scriptures similar to that of the Qur'ān, as well as by refraining from utilizing the traditional Christian terms "Trinity" and "Son of God," in order that Muslims would be more willing to listen to the theological concepts of the Christian faith.³² Hilgendorf even suggested using quotations from the Qur'ān on the air in order to help Muslims make connections between their own faith and Christianity. His ideas were flat out rejected by MELM director Morris Jahshan, who argued that "if we use the Koran, then we have to quote it, the sura and the verse. In other words we are confessing that the Koran is an inspired word of God."³³ The drive to provide positive engagement between different religious groups was not only theological controversial, but was getting much more difficult in the social-political climate of 1974. Tensions between religious and political communities of all different confessional groups were rising.

---

30. See the English translation of the work as listed in the bibliography.
31. See 4:157–58.
32. Strengholt, "Gospel in the Air."
33. Joyce, *Message to Islam*, 13, as cited in Strengholt, "Gospel in the Air."

THE CREATION OF THE "CONTACT AND RESOURCE CENTER" (CRC)

By the spring of 1975 civil war had broken out in central and northern Lebanon. MELM staff were evacuated to Cyprus, along with those of most other Christian organizations—including the NECC, now the Middle East Council of Churches (MECC). The Stelling family moved back to the U.S., and John Stelling traveled back and forth as the situation would permit. Dennis Hilgendorf, however, refused to leave Lebanon and continued to work in the midst of the developing civil war in Beirut.

By 1976 the Syrian army had entered the war, occupying parts of Lebanon. The country was very unstable and things were dangerous. It was clear that the situation would not get better in Beirut in the foreseeable future. Dennis Hilgendorf was committed to continue working for intercommunal dialogue with the conflicted Lebanese communities. Now, however, theological differences between Christians and Muslims took a back seat to the reality of the struggle for life on the streets of Beirut. He began focusing much of his time and energy to provide support for those young people tragically affected by the war. This led Hilgendorf and a young student, Agnes Wakim Dagher, to create the Contact and Resource Center (CRC) in 1978 to respond to the needs of Lebanese young people suffering physically, psychologically, and economically from the war. Although clearly a "Christian" project, the center was open to people of all confessions, and was not interested in proselytizing, but rather relief and development. The CRC would be one of the only social service agencies that would continue to function and provide services for those in need throughout the severest fighting of the war.

The LCMS World Mission board for was concerned about the situation in Lebanon. The radio ministry of MELM was still continuing, albeit very much scaled back. The ILLL continued to fund the work of MELM, but the LCMS board felt that this work could be carried on completely by Lebanese nationals, especially given that they had asked LCMS missionaries to leave the country for their own safety.[34] The LCMS had, for some time, tried to turn over whatever foreign ministries it could to indigenous Christian institutions, and it seemed as if the time had come. More importantly, however, the board did not fully support the direction in which Hilgendorf was going with the work of the CRC. So, in 1979 the board

---

34. John Stelling, email to author, October 11, 2007.

finally offered the two missionaries and their families the possibility of new mission posts in another Muslim country. Both families rejected the offers. From the perspective of the missionaries and the staff of the CRC, the LCMS was simply withdrawing its support of their work. From the perspective of the LCMS, however, the two missionaries had made "personal" decisions to resign from missionary service with the denomination. Stelling, who had for some time been struggling with a decision to move into another form of ministry, resigned from foreign mission service and accepted a position in hospital chaplaincy. Hilgendorf, however, refused to leave Lebanon and abandon his work. The Hilgendorf's were fully committed to life and ministry in Lebanon, and so they found themselves on their own in the middle of a civil war. As the war raged on the Hildgendorfs managed to continue working independently in Beirut with the CRC.

Between 1973 and 1976 the LCMS was involved in an internal denominational struggle centered on issues of biblical interpretation. Numerous faculty members at Concordia Seminary in St. Louis were charged with teaching false doctrine, primarily for utilizing modern historical-critical methods of interpreting the Bible. A split among faculty and students ultimately led to the development of a splinter denomination, the Association of Evangelical Lutheran Churches in America (AELC). Two former LCMS missionaries, Rev. Paul Strege and Rev. Jim Mayer, created an organization called the International Partners in Mission, which would allow AELC congregations and individuals to continue supporting Lutheran missionaries that had been part of the breakaway. The new mission agency was very supportive of the vision and work of the CRC and agreed to support the Hilgendorfs.

Fred Nuedoerffer, the foreign missions South Asia area director for the LCA, was also very interested in the CRC as well. As the Hilgendorfs were the only AELC personnel in the area, Neudoerffer took them under his wing and began to include them in the LCA programming that was just developing at the time. Contact was made through Bruce Schein, the first LCA missionary, who had earlier come to Beirut and worked with Hilgendorf in 1968. Schein encouraged Nuedoerffer to offer some kind of working arrangement with the Hilgendorfs. The Hilgendorfs were invited into the newly forming LCA missionary network, and to attend the annual personnel conferences held in Cyprus. Loosely affiliated with the LCA, Hilgendorf would continue to work as the director of the CRC until he succumbed to a heart attack in 1989, where the other co-founder of the center, Agnes Wakim Dagher, has continued as the director. Since 1988, and the dissolution of the AELC, the CRC has continued to receive both financial and programmatic support from the ELCA.

LCMS "CHURCH PLANTING"

With no American missionaries in the Lebanon, the LCMS continued to support MELM and serve as the primary donor (through the ILLL) for its continued Arab ministry. The policy of supporting indigenous Christian programs continued, as MELM sustained the radio broadcast of *The Lutheran Hour* over Trans World Radio from Monte Carlo and Cyprus. In 1992, however, the LCMS made a dramatic about face from its previous policies. The general convention of the denomination, which met in Pittsburg in July of 1992, passed a resolution to develop further evangelical opportunities among Muslims in the Arab World. With a clear directive from the denomination to develop explicit programs of evangelism, representatives for the LCMS met with MELM in Cyprus. There the MELM mission statement was significantly changed to reflect the new direction of the denomination:

> Middle East Lutheran Ministry, a ministry in partnership with the BFMS and the ILLL, serves the Arabic speaking world (both Christians and non-Christians) primarily in Morocco, Algeria, Egypt, Lebanon and Jordan. *Our mission calls for clear proclamation of the Gospel* via Radio, Video, T.V. BCC, Print and Evangelism. We will cooperate with local Christian churches where that is possible, and refer contacts to local Christian churches where that is feasible. *In certain defined areas of need, we will also train respondents / contacts in Lutheran leadership training and discipleship, so that they will plant a Lutheran church in their local community.*[35]

What is significant about this new mission statement was the insertion of the unambiguous phrase "clear proclamation of the Gospel." The previous years of "dialogue" were no longer part of the new focus. The previous work with LCMS mission personnel had left a bad taste in some mouths, regarding how exactly to do appropriate mission work among Muslims. There were some within the denomination who felt that "dialogue" with Muslims was simply a liberal agenda, which detracted from

---

35. Jahshan, "Middle East Lutheran Ministry," 32; emphasis added.

the purpose and core of evangelism. Thus, the new initiative was clear—the purpose was the "proclamation of the Gospel," as in the days of Henry Martyn and Karl Pfander when public bazaar preaching was encouraged as an appropriate method of evangelism.

Another significant addition to the mission statement was the specific goal of planting Lutheran churches. MELM was now beholden not only to cooperate with both the historic and national churches of the Middle East where "possible" or "feasible," but to actually create confessional Lutherans. This was Agerstrand's original model of mission. In order to do this, the director of MELM, Moris Jahshan then suggested to the LCMS World Mission board and the ILLL representatives that this would need "specialized people who know the Arabic language well, Lutheran theology, knowledge about Islam and Christianity and ability in Christian education . . ."[36] In other words, MELM would need either new Western mission personnel who were trained for longtime service in the Middle East or an Arab staff would need to be sent to Lutheran institutions in the West (presumably North America) for theological training. The board had already tried the former method, and re-sending new personnel would be risky. In addition, such an endeavor would not adhere to their missiological ideals of supporting indigenous ministries. Thus, while short-term LCMS missionaries might be sent to support ongoing work, there would be the need to find an appropriate Arab church worker in whom the denomination could invest. The LCMS continues to follow this strategy, with the goal of training and educating an LCMS Arab pastor or Muslim convert for the purpose of church planting. This mission policy will inevitably be faced with many of the same issues already dealt with by Azzam and Boss, as well as by Hilgendorf and Stelling. The legal status of Lutheran congregations poses a multitude of relationship issues, not only in the Muslim community, but from within the Christian *millet*, as we have already discussed above. In addition, new Lutheran converts from the Muslim community would create apostates from Islam whose livelihoods would be in jeopardy, and whose community would never be completely accepted by indigenous Arab and Armenian Christians due to cultural pressures and suspicions. The only alternative, in the end, will be to produce illegal house churches, similar to the Seventh Day Adventists, Jehovah's Witnesses, and other Pentecostal organizations that work underground.

36. Ibid., 36.

One clear byproduct of the new mission statement was the proliferation of printed material from MELM throughout the Middle East. In 1999 MELM would open up operations in Cairo. Through a small office in the Egyptian Presbyterian congregation of Fagalla Evangelical Church in the middle of Cairo, MELM has continued its mission of distributing Christian material, including Arabic translations of Luther's *Small Catechism*.

THE LCA "CONVERSATION WITH ISLAM"

By the late 1960s, the LCA, through its Division of World Mission and Ecumenism (DWME), was committed to entering into the Middle East in order to find a "wholly new approach to Islam." Much like what the LCMS was doing during the Hilgendorf/Stelling years, the LCA was interesting in developing a "conversation" with Muslims in the Middle East that did not simply seek to change their religious identity. In the words of Fred Neudorffer, the LCA secretary for South Asia and the Middle East, "Although we did have some contact with Islam in India, the Middle East represented an area about which our Church knew little or nothing. It remained a vast desert in terms of relationships, interest and mission." The intent was to make a completely new approach "in contact and relationships with Islam ... Arab Islamic peoples and religious leaders ... whereby the Gospel of love and freedom and hope could become a factor to assist in the changing role of peoples in the Middle East."[37]

The LCA called a young seminary graduate with a great deal of drive and focus, albeit brashness, to undertake a two year study of the Middle East in order to help the denomination develop its Middle East program. Bruce Schein was sent out in 1968 to Beirut where he undertook Arabic study, and then toured the Middle East while basing himself in Jerusalem. It was during this period in Beirut where Schein came into contact with Hilgendorf and Stelling, even helping to work on the *City of Wrong* project. Schein's experience and the final report of his tenure in Lebanon and Jerusalem was reflective of the Arab social movements of the times.

Prior to the Iranian Revolution of 1978–79, Marxist and socialist movements were predominant public forces in the Middle East. Arab nationalism in all its forms (e.g., pan-Arabism, Syrian and other particular regional nationalisms) was in its heyday, and became the driving force

---

37. J. F. Neudeorffer, "Report on the Middle East," September 1974, DWME archives, 16/1/1.

among young Arab idealists. The concepts of Arab nationalism had been developed in the early part of the twentieth century by the Syrian Sati al-Husri and, most importantly, the Greek Orthodox Arab nationalist ideologues George Antonius and Michel Aflaq. It was Aflaq, the founder of the secular Ba'athist Party in Syria, who developed a concept of Islam as a cultural legacy to which both Christians and Muslims could adhere as part of a social-political definition. Aflaq wrote:

> Is not faith in the regenerating power of Islam, and its ability to influence the spiritual and cultural destiny of mankind one of the basic tenets of the Ba'th Party? This is equally true of our belief in Islam both as a religion and a civilization for the Arabs, and in its being a vital factor in the modern Arab renaissance, as well as of our perception of its global dimensions in so far as it relates to the Muslim peoples of the Arab nation.[38]

Under the Arab Nationalist doctrines Islam was interpreted as a cultural pillar that gave identity to a people as they gained independence from European mandates, rather than concepts of *sharī'a* that would gain prominence in Islamic social-political discourse after the Iranian Revolution. Islam as a cultural pillar, however, was governed by the ideas of secular nationalism that laid the foundations for the Arab socialist movements of the 1960s and 1970s. The primary ideologue of Arab national socialism was the Egyptian president Gamal 'Abd al-Nasser.[39]

During the two years in which Schein was in the Middle East, significant events took place that would color his views of how the church might best engage with Muslims in the Arab nationalist context. First, in September of 1970, Yassir Arafat and his Fatah movement gained control of the Palestine Liberation Organization (PLO). The rise in power of the PLO, based on a secular nationalist platform, was part of the overall Arab nationalist trend. The PLO found its base among Palestinian refugees and displaced persons in the Kingdom of Jordan. However, these guerilla forces clashed with the Jordanian national army under the leadership of a young King Hussein. The events of Black September would force Arafat to relocate his liberation movement from Amman to Beirut. This was an intra-Arab clash of political ideologies, not religious zeal. Second, Hasan

---

38. Choueiri, *Islamic Fundamentalism*, 54.

39. See Abu-Rabi', *Contemporary Arab Thought*; Ajami, *Arab Predicament*; and Choueiri, *Arab Nationalism*.

al-Asad, a young colonel in the Syrian military establishment, led a coup and took firm control of the country of Syria. Syria would thus be gripped by an iron-fisted secular national socialist ideology. Third, Mu'ammar Ghaddafi seized control of Libya, declaring it the Socialist Peoples Arab Libyan Republic. Fourth, Yemen was in the midst of a brutal civil war, which led to the south declaring itself the People's Democratic Republic of Yemen. Fifth, Gamal 'Abd al-Nasser, the primary charismatic leader of the Arab world, died. The Arab world mourned his passing and vowed to carry forth his legacy of Arab socialism.

These events all prompted Schein to develop a model of mission to engage a society of young secularized nationalist students who were being blown by the winds of political change. By working in the "free space" of the classroom, Schein reasoned that religious teachers could engage students in conversation, allowing students to express themselves and search for answers to the social and ethical questions facing their communities. It was in the classroom that the missionary would be able to introduce the "freedom" of the gospel. Schein argued that the youth of the Arab world were lost. They were seeking for answers and identity in a world in which the traditional Islam of their parents could not provide answers to the highly charged political atmosphere of the Middle East. Looking around, the young people were attracted to political movements that seemed to be doing something. Schein would write: "Islam as such just is not the force that moves the times. It is the excuse, or the museum piece to be dusted off from time to time, or the part of the heritage to be understood as background for literature or cultural studies ... Islam is not the issue today."[40]

Although the origin of political Islam would have its roots in the 1960s, it had not taken firm root yet.[41] The genesis of radical Arab Islamist thought can be traced back to the defeat of the Arabs in the Six Day War of 1967. This war prompted great soul searching by the Arabs, whose honor had been smashed, and prompted much of the political upheaval of the 1970s. One of the answers to the defeat was an Islamist response that argued for the return to a pure Islamic state. This concept, seething under the surface in the West Bank and in Beirut, would not bubble to the surface until the success of the Iranian Revolution in 1979, and most

---

40. Schein, "Middle East."

41. See Chouieri, *Islamic Fundamentalism*; Abu-Rabi', *Intellectual Origins*; Mawṣilili, *Moderate and Radical*.

importantly with the Israeli invasion of Lebanon in 1982, when Hizb'allah would rise from the ashes of the Israeli invasion of Beirut. At the end of the 1960s, however, political Islam (in either its moderate or radical versions) had not made its appearance as a movement, and students were left to ponder how the socialist movements of the day would rescue them from despair.[42]

FIGURE 4: Bruce Schein, LCA Personnel, Larnaca, Cyprus, 1982

---

42. The most prominent work on the effect of the 1967 war on Arab thought is Ajami, *Arab Predicament* and *Dream Palace*.

In developing his plan for the LCA, Schein believed that it was an opportune moment for an American Lutheran mission. He proposed Jerusalem as the center for the LCA's mission in the Middle East and "ministry to Islam." There, at the center of the three monotheistic religions, the LCA would develop a team of highly specialized personnel who could interact with Muslims on every level of society. The "Schein-Neudoerffer plan" called for the appointment of an *educator*, who would engage students in a liberal arts style class setting, a *social worker*, who would respond to the social needs of Palestinian communities, a *pastor* based out of the Lutheran Church of the Redeemer who would serve as the chaplain of the English-speaking Lutheran community and help tourists and pilgrims engage Palestinians, an *Islamicist*, who would engage the local religious leaders in dialogue, and a *coordinator* of the team who would maintain relationships with local churches, agencies, and foreign institutions. The whole plan was intended to be "a conversation with Islam."[43] In 1975 the "Policy for the Middle East Program" was accepted by the DWME. This policy "would color and permeate all LCA activities in the Middle East [for] the development of a new and unique ministry related to Islam."[44]

Between 1970 and 1975, however, significant problems had arisen, both within the DWME itself and within the Middle East, that would necessitate changes to Schein's carefully crafted plan. First of all, how was the LCA to begin such a venture? This novel approach to Islam was based upon a presumption that the LCA would be free from ecumenical ties that might deter the team from undertaking its work. Looking back historically at the Presbyterians, the Anglicans, as well as the more recent problems of the Missouri Synod and their ties to indigenous churches, the LCA's approach necessitated freedom of association. Yet, one does not merely drop into a foreign country and set up house without legal permission, or without affecting the status quo of communal relationships. The days of Protestant missionaries wandering about the Ottoman Empire or the Arabian Gulf were long gone! Thus, the two avenues open to the LCA were through the Lutheran Church of the Redeemer in Jerusalem, under the authority of the German probst, and at the August Victoria property through the auspices of the Lutheran World Federation (LWF).

43. BWM minutes, November 9–11, 1970, LCA 28/1/1/1.

44. "Aims for the LCA Middle East Program," DWME minutes, October, 9–10, 1975, LCA 16/1/1.

The Probst welcomed an LCA pastor, although his activities would necessarily be curtailed because of a lack of space on the compound. But the probst had to be sensitive to both the Israelis and the local Palestinian Christian community. He was thus concerned about Schein's attempt to engage Palestinian Muslims and upset the delicate inter-faith balance. The LWF, for its part, was not exactly energetic in its response for the Americans to piggyback off the LWF. Neudoerffer had offered the services of Schein to be the program director of a possible new LWF study center at August Victoria. However, the Europeans were quite cold to the idea. Furthermore, the plan called for the recruitment of highly qualified people who would commit themselves to a long-term ministry, learning the language, religions, and cultures of the Middle East. Where were they to be found?

The easiest member of the team to recruit was the pastor. A pastoral search surfaced Dale Truscott, who was called and sent for a one-year term to serve as the pastor of the English language congregation of the Lutheran Church of the Redeemer. Charles Moline then replaced him in 1971 and served until 1977. Throughout Moline's tenure the concept of the congregation being a center of hospitality to tourists, pilgrims, and visiting groups developed. The congregation became a ministry in its own right, helping to interpret the context of the Middle East for short-term visitors. There was little time left over for engaging Muslim students.

The educator and social worker were still nowhere to be found, however. Finally, in 1974 a professor of literature, Dr. Evelyn Gus, would be called. She spent two years as the educator, interacting with students at Birzeit University on the West Bank. Unfortunately, she was placed at the university prior to any language instruction or training in Islamic studies, thereby hampering Schein's plan. Thus, the two individuals of the team who were on the ground working, the pastor and the educator, had no specialized training in either Arabic or Islamic Studies.

Meanwhile, Schein was sent to complete a Ph.D. in biblical studies at Yale. The intention was for him to return as the coordinator of the team. Yet, due to personality differences between Schein and the German probst, as well as with other LCA personnel, in addition to chronic health problems, Schein's role became much more diminished as time went on. He would end up not becoming the coordinator of the team, but rather a resource person to develop and lead biblical studies seminars for visiting Lutheran leaders from around the world. His role became less interactive with young Palestinian and Jordanian Muslim students, and more involved with expatriate visitors. This must have been extremely frustrating for him.

The most important issue for this plan to work, however, was the placing of the Islamicist. After all, the idea was an engagement with Islam! However, the Lutheran church had no programs in Islam and no personnel with such a background. Thus, the LCA turned to the Reformed Church in America (RCA), which had a long-established mission in the Arabian Gulf, dating from 1889.[45] The LCA and the RCA joined forces to call Harold Vogelaar, who had been serving as part of the Arabian Mission since 1963, currently in Oman. The agreement called for Vogelaar to pursue a degree in Islamic studies from Columbia University in New York. In 1972, after his residency coursework at Columbia, Vogelaar and his family moved to Cairo where he began to work on his dissertation. It was this move to Cairo that proved to have the major impact on Schein's intended plan.

HAROLD VOGELAAR

Harold Vogelaar has been one of the most important guiding forces in theological engagement with Islam within the LCA, the ALC and ELCA in the last twenty-five years of the twentieth century and beyond. Under Vogelaar's guidance, and through his relationship with numerous Islamicists, missiologists, mission personnel, and most importantly, Muslims—both within the United States and abroad, Vogelaar has made his mark on the Lutheran-Muslim encounter. For most of his career as an Islamicist, the LCA and the RCA jointly sponsored Vogelaar; during his work in Cairo, his time at the New Brunswick Theological Seminary in New Jersey, and finally during most of his time at the Lutheran School of Theology at Chicago (LSTC). In September 2006 the LSTC inaugurated a newly funded Center of Christian-Muslim Engagement for Peace and Justice, and also endowed the new Harold S. Vogelaar Chair of Christian-Muslim Studies and Interfaith Relations. This chair will ensure a continued presence of Vogelaar's ideals of Christian-Muslim encounter.

Vogelaar's roots in the conservative, rural Dutch Reformed community of Iowa seemed to have primed him for a missiological perspective similar to the Lutheran-Reformed Pietists who came through the Basel

---

45. For a very extensive and extremely thorough review of the Arabian Mission see Scudder, *Arabian Mission's Story*.

and Halle mission schools, like Karl Gottleib Pfander who engaged in apologetics and polemics with Islam; or that of the Dutch-American Missionary Scholar Samuel Zwemer, who founded the Arabian Mission in 1899.[46] Following in the path of Zwemer, Vogelaar undertook a life long journey of engagement with Islam. But, whereas Zwemer was intent on converting the heart of the Muslim world, Vogelaar carved his own niche. Through his encounters with Muslims in Oman, Bahrain, Egypt, and the United States, this conservative piety of evangelization for the purpose of conversion was transformed into a dialogical approach to Islam. Vogelaar described his transformation: "I had come to accept that for me Christian witness was the key element . . . Evangelism but not in the sense of pressing for converts, not proselytizing. Within the framework of friendship, we could talk on any subject, and did."[47] The key was the model of "friendship." Throughout his time in the Middle East, Vogelaar sought out Muslim sheikhs, not for the purpose of conversion, but for the intention of developing friendships. In the midst of those friendships, matters of daily life—including issues of faith—were discussed. The concept of "conversation with Islam" found its home in the invitation to a cup of tea where two *individuals* sat together to talk, rather than two representatives of faith traditions with longstanding antagonism between them.

The RCA committed itself to supporting Vogelaar's pursuit of a Ph.D. in Islamic studies at Columbia University. But in 1970 he was asked to return to Oman prematurely from Columbia to fill in for a colleague who was on furlough. While he was in Oman, Fred Neudorffer, the LCA director for foreign mission in South Asia, approached the RCA about the possibility of an arrangement whereby Vogelaar could be utilized by both mission boards. This arrangement proved agreeable to all parties, and in 1971 the Vogelaars were sent back to Columbia for another year of study fully supported by both the LCA and RCA, after which he would be relocated to Cairo. This Reformed-Lutheran relationship is no anomaly. As we have already noted, the Reformed and Lutheran wings of the Protestant Reformation have always worked closely in their mission work, especially in the Middle East. The mission schools of Basel and Halle produced Lutheran-Reformed Pietists who were the primary personnel to supply not only German mission agencies but also the Anglican CMS in

---

46. The classic biography of Zwemer is Wilson, *Apostle to Islam*. See also Wilson, "Legacy of Samuel M. Zwemer"; and Hubers, "Samuel Zwemer."

47. Boden, "Following Jesus," 10.

both Palestine and Egypt, respectively. The esteemed Anglican Islamicist Kenneth Cragg was working at the Anglican cathedral in Cairo, where Vogelaar would spend a number of years. The relationship struck between Cragg and Vogelaar would prove to be an important link in Lutheran-Islamic encounter.[48] Cragg introduced Vogelaar to the Islamic humanist scholar Kamel Ḥusayn, author of the aforementioned work *City of Wrong*. The two Islamicists gathered with Hussein for inter-faith conversations. Vogelaar also became very active in the Society of Religious Fraternity, a group of Christian and Muslim leaders who gathered monthly for meetings. These relationships opened Vogelaar to the possibilities of dialogue in which Christians and Muslims might be able to learn from each other about matters of faith. Thus, Vogelaar's vocation seemed to fit the early pattern of Lutheran-Reformed-Anglican relationships in the Middle East.

In his engagement with the Islamic tradition, Vogelaar found a helpful avenue into inter-faith dialogue through the image of Abraham as the "archetype of faith." The Abraham of Genesis and the Ibrāhīm of the Qur'ān provide both faith traditions with a rich shared witness to the one God. "What makes Abraham such an exemplary Muslim is that he was able to commit himself wholeheartedly to his Lord," as a *mukhlis* [sincere one] wrote Vogelaar.[49] This sincere belief "involves a *commitment* that is wholehearted, a *dependence* that is total, and a *gratitude* that is responsive to God's goodness and mercy."[50] Certainly, this is something that both Christians and Muslims can agree upon together in their respective faith lives, argues Vogelaar.

In this spiritual Christian-Muslim encounter, Vogelaar states that an earnest Christian attempt to see Muhammad and his message in its proper faith context (and not contemporary political rhetoric, or the "public display of religion") might help Christians deepen their own spirituality. "We have a place in our faith for Moses, but do we have any room for Muhammad? We use the Jewish Psalms devotionally, but is

---

48. It was through this relationship that Michael Shelley was introduced to Kenneth Cragg, who served as Shelley's Ph.D. examiner on his research of the Anglican missionary in Cairo. See M. Shelley, "Life and Thought"; idem., "Temple Gairdner"; and idem., "Al-Ghazali's Benign Influence." For further information on Cragg see A. D'Souza, "Christian Approaches"; Lamb, *Call to Retrieval*; and Quinn, "'Am I Not Your Lord?'"

49. Vogelaar, "Abraham the Archetype of Faith," 170.

50. Ibid., 172.

there any room in our devotional life for the *Fātiḥa* [the opening prayer of the Qur'ān]?⁵¹ Vogelaar asks why Christians cannot utilize the Qur'ān on their own terms as a bridge for their own spirituality.

> When it comes to the Prophet Muhammad, I always try to emphasize that his first mission was to overcome the power false deities had over his people, which he did by proclaiming the oneness of God. It was an arduous task for which he solicited the help of Jews and Christians whom he believed would be his allies in this struggle. Unfortunately, it didn't turn out that way. But it's nice to think the hope and expectation of that initial invitation may still be there as we confront the demons and false deities of our own day.⁵²

This view of Islam, discovered through a committed long-term relationship of engagement with Muslims, can certainly work in a pluralistic American society—where the abundance of ideas and religious beliefs is commonplace. In the Middle East, however, the social-political context is more complicated. The Center for the Study of Religion that Vogelaar founded at the Evangelical (Presbyterian) Theological Seminary in Cairo in the 1970s for the purpose of inter-faith dialogue did not last very long. Its views were considered too radical within the Egyptian Presbyterian community, especially during the 1980s, when Christian-Muslim relations were growing tense. With Sadat's open door policy [*infitāḥ*], the Muslim Brotherhood and its more radical offshoots began to carry the day as they began to respond to the growing gap between the wealthy and the marginalized middle class. Likewise, the Coptic Orthodox Church of Alexandria, Pope Shenouda III, began to exert a strong Coptic—some claimed "separatist"—identity. The evangelicals (the common term used for Protestants in the Middle East), small in number, were caught in the middle. They did not want to stir up the pot in a tense social-political context, and so were not willing to create a public display of religion themselves. Because religion in the Middle East concerns more than simply personal belief, but also social and communal belonging and loyalty, the ideas of gleaning spiritual gems from each other's religious traditions was simply too radical for most Egyptians. To see a positive sign within another's religious tradition would somehow be seen as criticizing one's

---

51. Vogelaar, "Christian Witness to Islam," 6, September 1977, DWME archives, 16/1/1.

52. Vogelaar, "Open Doors to Dialogue," 402.

own faith tradition, which would be anathema. Thus, while a Western Christian missionary might be free (especially according to Schein's plan) to engage with Muslims and participate in cutting edge dialogue, Christian Egyptians were not at liberty given the prevailing social pressures and religious sensitivities.

It was Vogelaar's relationship with Kamel Ḥusayn and other sheikhs in Cairo that enabled him to appreciate the idea that all religious systems help give "expression to the inner core of faith found in all people."[53] It was in Cairo that Vogelaar saw many opportunities for conversation with Islam. As the spiritual center of the Sunni Islamic world, al-Azhar University attracted Muslim students and scholars from around the world. In Cairo, he believed, the church would have access to the central nervous system of Sunni thought in the Arab world. In the words of Vogelaar,

> it was here where the church could have a closer look at Muslims, to discover where they are, to sense their frustrations, to feel their pain, their hurt, to understand their hopes and aspirations and so be better equipped to make our Christian witness a response to their deepest needs.[54]

While Bruce Schein's plan called for the LCA to be centered in Jerusalem, Vogelaar argued that the original LCA program had to be widened. Jerusalem would no longer serve as the center for Christian-Muslim dialogue, but rather Cairo. This would prove to be a wise move, as, with the beginning of the First and Second Intifadas in 1987 and 2000, respectively, American Lutheran involvement in the occupied territories would by necessity begin to focus more on issues of peace and justice rather than inter-religious dialogue. Thus, the tightly knit team concept was broadened to function as a network of people working in different cities of the Arab world. The shift from Jerusalem to Cairo, however, was not a change in policy—it was only implementation. The LCA's goal was still "reclamation and illumination of the Gospel of Jesus Christ within the Islamic tradition . . . [which] would color and permeate all LCA activities in the Middle East [for] the development of a new and unique ministry related to Islam."[55]

---

53. Vogelaar, "Religious Pluralism," 419.

54. Division for World Mission and Ecumenism minutes, March 18–21, 1981, LCA 28/1/1/1.

55. "DWME Policy for the Middle East Program," October 1975, LCA 16/1/1.

THE "CAIRO CONNECTION"

The LCA's move to Cairo became possible in 1974 when two small international congregations in Cairo, St. Andrew's United Church of Cairo in the heart of the city, and Maadi Community Church in a Cairo suburb, called Harold Vogelaar to serve as their pastor. From here he would begin his part of the mission of guiding Christian-Muslim encounter. Four important ministries developed in Cairo that would carve out the Lutheran niche in Egypt. First, a teaching ministry developed on different levels. The concept of offering month-long seminars on Islam for church leaders from around the world was developed. Centered first at St. Andrew's, and then later at the Presbyterian seminary when Vogelaar was invited to begin an Islamic studies program there, the LCA brought in a wide array of people from around the world to learn about Islam and Christian-Muslim relations from 1979 to 1984. Vogelaar tapped the resources of another Reformed Islamicist, Willem Bijlefeld, director of the Duncan Black Macdonald Center for Christian-Muslim Relations at Hartford Seminary and the editor of *The Muslim World*. (Bijlefeld would prove to have a tremendous impact on the development of Lutheran-Muslim engagement, not only in the Middle East but at ELCA institutions as well.)[56] Vogelaar was asked to teach courses in Islamic studies at the Egyptian Presbyterian Seminary in Cairo, and eventually moved there to be a full-time faculty member in 1978 until he returned to the U.S. The move to the seminary opened a door which the LCA and later the ELCA maintained, providing a professor to teach in the fields of the New Testament, church history, Arabic Christian literature, and Islamic studies.

The second important ministry in Cairo was that of the international congregations themselves. At first, the LCA had a pastoral role in the yoked ministry of both St. Andrew's United Church of Cairo and Maadi Community Church. After Vogelaar, David Johnson served in this capacity from 1978 until 1982, when Maadi Community Church sought out its own pastor. The Lutheran arrangement, however, has continued on at St. Andrew's to the present.

By 1979 the American Lutheran Church (ALC) was ready to step into the Middle East. Assisted by the LCA's work, the ALC offered to

---

56. Mark Swanson earned his MA in Islamic Studies under Bijlefeld at Hartford Seminary, and was profoundly affected by his thinking on the issue of Christian-Muslim relations. Bijlefeld was a visiting lecturer at both Luther Seminary and Lutheran School of Theology.

place a Lutheran pastor at the services of another developing international congregation, the Heliopolis Community Church.[57] The ALC then sent Michael Shelley, who had already served as a seminary intern at St. Andrew's several years before under Vogelaar, to serve as the pastor of Heliopolis until 1982, when he moved into full-time Arabic study. Oscar Kraft was then called to the Heliopolis congregation until 1986 when, like the Maadi congregation, it sought its own pastor outside the Lutheran denomination. Thus, in a country that had typically been Presbyterian territory, the American Lutherans had a hand in the development of three international congregations.

The international congregations (including the Lutheran Church of the Redeemer in Jerusalem) not only provided Word and sacrament ministry for Protestant expatriates from around the world, but also sought to help its members engage in the Middle Eastern context, including both the local Muslim and Christian communities. As Charles Moline had argued back in 1974, the educational opportunities that the international congregations could offer should stand on their own merits as valuable ministries for the church in the Middle East.[58] These congregations had a "mandate to assist . . . in a better understanding of the world of the Middle East."[59] This is exactly what they did, providing hospitality and educational opportunities, in addition to pastoral services, to expatriates living in both Israel/Palestine and Egypt.

The third area of ministry that became an important to the American Lutheran churches in the long-term development of their mission was the establishment of an internship program within the congregations. With Harold Vogelaar working as the pastor of two congregations, teaching at the Presbyterian seminary, and organizing the Cairo seminars, the workload became overwhelming. The ALC sent out the first Lutheran intern in 1976, Michael T. Shelley, who would return to Cairo to serve as pastor

---

57. The HCC was originally a joint venture between St. Andrew's and the Anglican diocese of Egypt and North Africa. Initially, Dean Bard, the LCA intern serving at St. Andrew's, worked with Canon Derek Eaton of All Saints Cathedral to offer services in the Heliopolis district of the city.

58. "The LCA English-speaking Ministry in Jersualem . . . Pastoral Perspective," 1974, LCA 16/1/1.

59. J. F. Neudoerffer, "Report to the Management Committee," DWME, March 18–21, 1981, LCA 16/1/1.

not only of Heliopolis Community Church in 1979, but St. Andrew's in 1988, as well.

It was through this internship program that theology students from both the RCA and the various Lutheran seminaries of the ALC/LCA/ELCA were placed for a one year term at St. Andrew's in Cairo and at Lutheran Church of the Redeemer in Jerusalem as well. The congregations helped train many pastors and teachers, and introduced them to the issues of Middle Eastern culture, history, and religion. Over a period of thirty years many seminarians came and cut their teeth in these internship programs, ultimately moving on to further work in the Middle East or other Muslim countries around the world, Christian-Muslim relations in the U.S., pastoral ministry, and social services. They have also gone on to provide key leadership roles to the church.[60]

In 1979, however, something happened that dramatically transformed the Lutheran ministry in Cairo to develop a fourth and unexpected niche of ministry. Under the direction of David Johnson at St. Andrew's, intern Stan Steele began a ministry for Ethiopian refugees who had fled their country and sought U.N. protection in Cairo during the rule of Mengistu Haile Mariam. What began as an attempt to provide some form of hospitality by having a tea house developed into a complex refugee ministry center, which has offered spiritual, financial, and educational programs to thousands of refugees from around the world. Initially, the refugee ministry of St. Andrew's served Ethiopians, but as the program became well known by refugee communities it began to serve Somalians and Sudanese throughout the turmoil in their respective countries.

What was so important about this ministry to refugees was that it came to embody all of the noble ideals of the Schein-Neudoerffer plan of "conversation with Islam," though quite unexpectedly. Throughout its existence the refugee ministry of St. Andrew's has grown, and the congregation has been challenged to find appropriate ways to programmatically respond to the needs of the refugees. But what made the small compound of the church much more important than its actual physical size was not

---

60. Another important intern was John Hubers, an RCA intern who served under Vogelaar (1980–81). He would go on to serve in the RCA in Oman (1986–91), Bahrain (1991–96), and as the RCA area program director for the Middle East and South Asia (2001–6), before beginning a Ph.D. program at LSTC. He is a founding member of the Institute for the Study of Christian Zionism. See the Web site Challenging Christian Zionism: http://www.christianzionism.org.

only the programming but the vision of its ministry. The majority of the refugees who were served at St. Andrew's were predominantly Muslim, and thus, the driving ethos of the community was daily inter-faith encounter.[61] Both Christians and Muslims were hired on as staff and worked together side by side. This vision of an inter-faith community was both a direct result of the LCA's commitment to have a "conversation with Islam" as well as the personnel whom it molded. Over the years St. Andrew's generated five formally trained Islamicists; Harold Vogelaar, Michael T. Shelley, Nelly Van Doorn-Harder,[62] Mark Swanson, and David D. Grafton all served at St. Andrew's in one form or another. This small church in the middle of Cairo would prove to have a profound affect on the ministry of the ELCA in regard to Islam. Each of these persons would go on to earn a Ph.D. in Islamic studies and serve at numerous institutions of the Lutheran church, including Valparaiso University, Luther Seminary, the Lutheran School of Theology at Chicago (where in September 2006 the Center of Christian-Muslim Engagement for Peace and Justice was inaugurated), and the Lutheran Theological Seminary at Philadelphia.[63]

Certainly, there were many other individuals who developed and contributed to the life of the refugee ministry and provided invaluable leadership other than the formally trained Islamicists. The pastors, interns, and coordinators of the refugee ministry have through the years provided their own stamp of leadership on this ministry. In addition, there were countless others—staff and volunteers, Christians and Muslims, Africans, Arabs, and Westerners—who gave of their time and energy to make St. Andrew's a community of inter-faith encounter. They are the ones who actually had to live out the daily encounter. It would be impossible to list all of these valuable servants who helped create an atmosphere in which

---

61. Although most of the Muslim refugees were from either the horn of Africa or sub-Saharan Africa, the program did serve others, including those from North Africa (Libya and Algeria) and the Balkans. At the time of this writing, the newest influx of Muslim refugees has been Shi'a Iraqis, having fled persecution from Sunnis as a result of the turmoil of the U.S.-led invasion of Iraqi in 2003.

62. Nelly van Doorn-Harder was sent to St. Andrew's in 1986 on behalf of the Dutch Reformed Church to serve as the director of the Joint Refugee Program, a united effort by both St. Andrew's and the Anglican All Saints' Cathedral. From 1994 until 1999 she served with the ELCA teaching at the Lutheran seminary in Yogyakarta, Indonesia, where she helped to form an inter-faith institute there. She has focused much of her research on women's issues; see *Women Shaping Islam*.

63. Boden, "Learning from One Another."

"the least of these" were provided honor and dignity. In fact, it is more appropriate to say that the community of St. Andrew's as a whole helped to create the vision of the ELCA Islamicists, as it fostered and supported the need and desire for deep reflection on Christian-Muslim relations.

"ENGAGEMENT" IN CONFLICT

Throughout the 1980s the ALC and LCA developed their ministries with the intent of engaging Islam. But for all intents and purposes, they simply responded to the needs of the local communities where they found themselves working. Throughout the 1980s the mission personnel lived out their lives in a variety of vocational enterprises within the largely Islamic culture and in relationship with the historic churches. The ideal of engagement with Muslims on a variety of levels became less a conscious part of the programming and more deeply part of the vocational responses to the dramatic changes in the region. The contexts of the West Bank were quite different than Cairo, and Beirut even more so! Thus, Schein's model lost all cohesiveness. Because the network of Lutherans was spread over at least three countries (four with the addition of Cyprus after 1991) and doing vary different tasks, the focus shifted from an overall direct "conversation with Islam" to a variety of responses engaging the local populations in areas of social ministry.

When Schein proposed the American Lutheran missiological agenda for the Middle East it appeared as if the secular politics of the day would support inter-faith conversation in the public sphere (at least in the classrooms of the universities). However, the decade of the 1980s had changed everything. The 1980s witnessed the rise of radical Islamic movements that gained popular support among Muslim communities throughout the Middle East. In October 1981, members of *al-Jihād*, a separatist branch of the Egyptian Muslim Brotherhood, gunned down Egyptian president Anwar Sadat on Egyptian public television. Al-Jihād then led to the development of a sustained radical Islamist movement in

Egypt throughout the 1990s, *al-Jamāʿat al-Islāmiyya*.[64] The Israeli invasion of Lebanon in 1982 helped create *Hizb'allah* the "Party of God," among the Shi'a community, which claimed to be a national resistance movement to expel Israel from Lebanese territory and then ultimately from Jerusalem itself.[65] Finally, the Intifada of the Palestinians that began surreptitiously in 1987 helped to birth the Palestinian Islamist organization *Hamas*.[66] All of these movements began their struggles either against the local nationalist governments in order to implement an Islamic ethos (in response to the predominant Arab nationalism), or to do battle with Israel for what they considered to be unjust occupation of Islamic land. The Lutheran missionaries viewed this time, however, not only as the radicalization of Islam, but as the politicization of religions. In other words, the 1980s was not only a time in which radical Islamist movements developed, but in which religious ideology in general began to supplant the secular ideologies that governed society in the 1960s and 1970s. For example, one could certainly talk about the radical ideology of the Maronites in Lebanon prior to the rise of the Islamist Shi'a militias. In Egypt, the development of the popularity of the Muslim Brotherhood and other radical Islamist organizations was by equaled by the politicization of the Coptic Church.[67] We might even add radical Christian Zionists, be they Middle Eastern or Western Christians, who would support the use of military violence to support the modern state of Israel for theological reasons.

Needless to say, the turbulent times of the 1980s made the concept of a benign conversation with secularized Muslim students very difficult, if not outdated. Rather than responding to a generation of young Arab Muslims who were searching for answers to the questions posed by nationalism, modernity, and Westernization, they [young Arab Muslims] began to retract into communities of conservative and radicalist Islamic ideologies. Schein in 1969 wrote, in a prophetic tone, that ". . . the main forces holding the younger generation [of Arabs] together are a lingering sense of family loyalty . . . When these are gone, one shudders to think of

---

64. For a helpful exposition of Egyptian Islamist movements see Kepel, *Roots of Radical Islam*.

65. See Jaber, *Hezbollah*.

66. See Abū ʿAmr, *Islamic Fundamentalism*; Hroub, *Hamas*; and Nüsse, *Muslim Palestine*.

67. "Planning Document for ELCA Middle East Ministry," February 6–10, 1987, DGM archives.

what will take place."[68] What Schein could not have foreseen was the development of a radical Islamic atmosphere that smothered all other forms of loyalty; familial, national, and individual.

Thus, the guiding concept of "conversation with Islam" became in reality a "conversation" with local communities (be they Muslim or Christian) who were dealing with the dramatic issues of the day: the development of religious and ethnic conservative communal identity, Soviet and American neo-imperialism, and Israeli occupation. As American Lutheran missionaries, together with the administrators of the ALC/LCA mission boards, gathered every year to reflect, plan, and develop objectives, it became clear that one could not merely plop down in the Middle East and begin a "conversation with Islam" without engaging the whole of Middle Eastern society in its complicated web of inter- and intra-communal relationships—social, political, and especially spiritual. Thus, the team truly did become a network of people living and working in quite different contexts.

For example, Hilgendorf's work in Beirut at the CRC became an all-consuming task as the Lebanese civil war was even further complicated by the Israeli invasion of 1982. The invasion and subsequent occupation of southern Lebanon dramatically transformed the war. After the invasion, the war degenerated into a grotesque reality of death that spawned the Sabra and Shatilla refugee camp massacres by the Christian Philangists (a Maronite militia). The Shi'a militias then turned on each other during the "Camp Wars" in the mid-80s. Even the U.S. military entered the foray by shelling Druze strongholds from its offshore naval batteries. This led to the distinct belief that the U.S. had chosen sides in the civil war by supporting the Maronite Christian-led government. It became clear to Palestinian guerrillas and Lebanese Shi'a that the American-Israeli-Maronite triumvirate was the true enemy. While the U.S. Administration saw its role as a neutral peace keeping force, it sent Marines into the quagmire. The bombing of the U.S. Marine barracks by a suicide bomber in 1983 left everyone feeling as if no one was safe in Lebanon.

Under the direction of Hilgendorf, however, the CRC did what it could to respond to these horrors. It kept its doors open to provide humanitarian assistance and financial loans to those wounded or disabled by the war. It was one of the only NGOs to stay open throughout the dark-

---

68. Schein, "Middle East."

est days of Lebanon's modern history. Most international organizations pulled out of Beirut during the Israeli invasion, including the MECC, which relocated to Cyprus. In the long run this meant that any future work the American Lutherans would be involved in with the MECC would now be based in Cyprus, another country for the network and another layer of difficulty in maintaining close relationships.

On the West Bank, support for the LWF Augusta Victoria Hospital thrust the American Lutherans into the midst of the Intifada. David Johnson, who had served as the LCA's pastor at St. Andrew's and Maadi Community Church from 1978 to 1982, returned in 1989 to serve as the LWF field director based in Jerusalem. Originally built as a hospice for visiting German Lutheran pilgrims, the hospital now became the only safe medical facility for Palestinians living in the West Bank within the Jerusalem area. Like the refugee ministry at St. Andrew's, both Christians and Muslims engaged each other in a "daily dialogue." Most of the staff working at the hospital were Muslim, necessitating that the hospital engage their workers not simply in an inter-religious theological dialogue, but in a dialogue that focused on the issues of communal justice for the sake of saving lives in the midst of the turmoil of the Intifada. Opportunities at the Friends School in Ramallah, as well the Lutheran schools of the Evangelical Lutheran Church of Jordan in the West Bank gave American Lutheran personnel the opportunity to interact with Muslims in ways in which Schein had anticipated.[69] Peter and Kathy Kapenga, another family with RCA roots (like the Vogelaars, and later the Scudders) whose family served with the American mission in the Arabian Gulf, worked with the Palestinian communities at the Friends School in Ramallah from 1977 through 2002. In addition, further opportunities for LCA and then ELCA work included assisting the local work of the Peace Center for the Blind, and a Greek Orthodox clinic in East Jerusalem.

But, work in such times would not come without a cost—as the church has always known. The first educator of the Schein plan, Dr. Evelyn Gus, was only in the field for two years and was never fully trained in either in Arabic or Islam. Her successor, Dr. Albert Glock, who joined the LCA team in 1976, proved to be quite different. Dr. Glock was an Old Testament scholar and archaeologist. An LCMS professor teaching at

---

69. When the ELCJ was recognized in 1959, East Jerusalem and the West Bank were part of the Kingdom of Trans-Jordan. The name was officially changed to the Evangelical Lutheran Church of Jordan and the Holy Land (ELCJHL) in 2005.

Concordia College in River Forest, Illinois, Glock was involved in biblical archaeology through the American School of Oriental Research (ASOR; the W. F. Albright Institute) in Jerusalem. He and his wife Lois and their children had been living in Jerusalem during dig seasons and returning to teach at Concordia during the academic school year. In 1969 Glock was asked to oversee the publication of reports of ASOR in Jennīn. His family resided full time in Jerusalem from 1969 to 1972, and again from 1973 to 1975. In addition to his publication work, Glock was invited to teach at Birzeit University as an adjunct where there was interest in developing a Palestinian archaeology program.

It was during this last period that Fred Neudoerffer met with Albert and Lois Glock. Evelyn Gus, the LCA educator at Birzeit, was having health problems and needed to return to the U.S. Thus the LCA was in need of another team member. In the words of Lois Glock, "It all fell into place."[70] Although Albert was initially not concerned with Christian-Muslim issues, both he and Lois were fully engaged with young Palestinians within the university setting. Glock fit the profile for a highly specialized educator fully involved with Muslim students. Thus, in 1976 they came under the wing of the LCA.

Al Glock became the primary force behind the establishment of the Palestinian archaeology department at Birzeit. The original idea had been put forward by another LCMS archaeology professor, Paul Lapp. The goal was to help Palestinians develop skills in order to help them "dig up" their own past rather than rely on either foreign or Israeli archaeologists to interpret the past. Dr. Glock's commitment to this work was highly controversial, however. On the one side, he was viewed with suspicion by people from his own denomination, his colleagues, and by the Israelis. Historical archaeology that dealt with the history of the inhabitants of Palestine had traditionally been filtered through the lens of biblical archaeology, limiting them to the role of the conquered "Canaanites." The concept of "the Land" as the inheritance of either Israelis or Palestinians has always been the cusp of the problem for those who saw the modern state of Israel as a fulfillment of biblical prophecy.[71] Yet, the debate over the right of the Jews to land has rested both on Old Testament promises as well as modern po-

---

70. Interview with author, October 26, 2007.

71. Prominent ot texts quoted to support the belief that "the Land" is irrevocably given by God to the Jews include Gen 15:18–21 and Deut 11:22–25; see also 2 Samuel 7:18–29 and 1 Kings 4:20–21.

litical movements and events.⁷² Glock felt that simply disregarding layers of history to get to the "biblical" stratum did a disservice not only to the Palestinians, but to the profession of archaeology as a whole. He wrote:

> Palestine's rich cultural past has been a focus of considerable archaeological activity. Much of this work has been done by western scholars in search of evidence to support and illustrate the Bible, perceived as a major source of western cultural values. In Palestine the result has been an alienation of the Muslim and Christian Arab population from its own cultural past.
>
> ... the "archaeological record," has been selectively used to document and sometimes to defend the version of the past required by Christian and Jewish Zionists to justify the present occupation of Arab Palestine.⁷³

Glock's chosen role of helping to provide the Palestinians with tools to interpret their own past, and thus direct their own future, was in the end a risky task.

On the other side, as a Protestant missionary, his position was viewed quite suspiciously by conservative Palestinian Muslim leaders, who saw him as a possible collaborator with the Israeli government. After 1967 all archaeological reports and permits needed to be obtained through the Israeli Department of Antiquities. Because of his need to work through legal channels with the Israeli government, and because of his role among prominent Palestinian leaders in the West Bank, he was never fully trusted by either side. On January 19, 1992 an unknown assailant gunned down Dr. Glock, making him the first American Lutheran missionary to be killed in the Middle East. His assassins have not been identified.⁷⁴

---

72. The most popular work to articulate Israeli claims for a Jewish state has been J. Peters, *From Time Immemorial*. Glock helped provide research for Elusa and Khālidī's *All That Remains*.

73. Glock, "Archaeology as Cultural Survival," 320–21.

74. The sensationalized version of this story can be found in Fox, *Palestine Twilight* and *Sacred Geography*. Fox's record seems to overstate issues and is very negative toward the church's role, especially the LCMS. For an obituary written by former students see Watson and Ziadeh, "Obituary: Albert Ernest Glock," 270–72. See Silberman, "Albert E. Glock."

THE ALC'S COMMITMENT

The presentation by Dennis Hilgendorf to the Lutheran Council in 1969, which encouraged the American Lutherans to begin thinking about the status of the Palestinians, was a small pebble that disturbed the whole pond. The ALC, a participant in the council, had no mission personnel in the Middle East during the beginning of the 1970s. There was a sincere interest to enter the region, but they had no idea of where to begin or what to do. John C. Westby, the area program director for Latin American operations, was given the responsibility for developing plans for mission work in the Middle East. The possibility of work in Yemen was first raised, but how would they begin?[75] With the help of Fred Neudoerffer, Westby set off for Yemen in October 1975 on a fact-finding mission. He met with various mission organizations working in Yemen, including the Church of Scotland Mission in Aden, as well as the Danish Lutheran Mission.[76] Upon returning to the U.S., Westby prepared a report for the board of the Division for World Mission with options for beginning medical mission work in Yemen. However, he counseled that beginning mission work in Yemen would be unlike any other mission work the ALC had ever done before! This would not be like their work among Muslims in India or Sub-Saharan Africa. In addition to the normal Middle Eastern prohibitions against proselytizing, it was clear that the new missionaries would be living under extremely harsh conditions (as Yemen was the poorest country in the Arab world). Although it was originally hoped that the first ALC missionaries to the Middle East would be able to provide a larger picture of issues in the Middle East for the American church, it quickly became clear that Yemen was not an average Arab country with its fingers on the pulse of the Arab world. Thus, the original proposal was scrapped.[77]

The ALC mission board was still committed, however, to some sort of engagement in the Middle East, but like most Americans it simply lacked knowledge and information about the Middle East and the Arab world in

---

75. Division for World Mission and Inter-Church Cooperation minutes, October 9–10, 1975, TALC 16/1/1/1.

76. See David D. Grafton, "Ion Keith-Falconer, Scholar-Missionary to Arabia: an appraisal of a method from the 19th century to Post 9/11." *Bulletin of Missionary Research*. Vol. 31, No. 3 (July 2007), 148–52.

77. John C. Westby, "Report on Trip to Yemen (October 13–26, 1975); TALC 16/1/1/1.

general.⁷⁸ The board then commissioned Dr. Edwin Schick, academic dean at Wartburg Theological Seminary, to prepare a study of the Middle East with the aim of helping the board make some decisions. The board was being introduced to an area of the world that posed serious missiological difficulties, which all previous Protestant mission agencies before them had to face: the presence of Jewish communities and ancient Orthodox churches, and the prohibition of proselytizing. Thus, by the end of 1977 it became clear that the only way the ALC would be able to get involved in the Middle East was with the help of the LCA and their personnel already on the ground. Westby once again asked Nuedoerffer to help set up a trip, this time to Beirut, Jerusalem, and Cairo, in the spring of 1978. Following this trip, Westby provided a detailed report of the possibilities of mission in the region. He proposed several opportunities for the church to consider, including placing personnel in Israel with the Norwegian Mission to Israel to work among Israeli Jews in Haifa.⁷⁹ This opportunity, however, would mean that the ALC would close itself off to any conversation with the Arab world. In the highly charged political atmosphere, they would be perceived to be on the side of Israel.⁸⁰ A similar proposal was made to the LCA by board member Dr. George Lindbeck in October 1979. Lindbeck wrote a report to the Board criticizing what he saw as the LCA personnel's tendency to live in a "West Bank box," falling victim to "polarization rather than rising above it." He argued that the "need for reconciliation demands attention both to Jewish relations and to Muslim relations" by placing personnel in positions to work with Jewish Israelis. The LCA personnel formally responded to this report by claiming that dialogue models used in the West do not work in Jerusalem (e.g., Jewish-Christian dialogue is not merely a theological conversation in the West Bank). They concluded: "Dr. Lindbeck's assertion of a connection—for the Christian—of attitudes toward the Arab-Israeli conflict with attitudes towards religious Judaism, this seems ultimately to lead to the charge that those who are in any way critical of the policies of the state of Israel are anti-Semitic. This kind

---

78. Division for World Mission and Inter-Church Cooperation minutes, March 23–26, 1977, TALC 16/1/1/1.

79. The Norwegian Lutheran Mission to Israel had been working directly with Jews since the 1844, originally formed as the Friends of Israel.

80. "Missions in the Holy Land: Reflections Prompted By a Stay in Jerusalem, February to July, 1979," October 1979, LCA 16/1/1; and "Response to Dr. George Lindbeck," January 5, 1980, LCA 16/1/1.

of politicization of religion has to be rejected, together with the political use to which theology and theologians are often put by persons on both sides of the conflict. There is certainly a great need for the discussion of this concern, particularly with respect to the meaning of 'land.'" Thus, like the situation offered in Yemen, a placement within Israel would limit the ability of their missionaries to provide information on the rest of the Arab world.

The ALC had a deep commitment to enter in the region, whether working among Eastern Christians or Muslims, but they did not have any clear goals. So, without any clear objectives, the ALC committed itself to place two people "in the Arab/Islamic world ... to be engaged in an intensive study program in the Arabic language and Islam, with no guarantee as to the kind of ministry which finally will be available."[81] It is clear that the leadership of the ALC really had no idea what they were getting themselves into! They were walking into a situation blind. That being said, they pulled out all of the stops to invest into an area of the world they knew virtually nothing about, but were committed to engaging. Thus, they allocated money and resources to provide for the training of new personnel to enter the Middle East and encounter the Islamic world simply for its own sake. At the outset there was no plan or goal other than investing time and money to place families in the region for long-term service.

Michael and Joanne Shelley were called in 1979 as the first ALC missionaries in the Middle East. Michael had served as the pastoral intern at St. Andrew's and Maadi Community Church under Harold Vogelaar (1976–77). This time Shelley was asked to serve as the part-time pastor of a newly organized international congregation in Heliopolis, a suburb of Cairo, while he studied Arabic. He served there until he left to undertake full-time study of the Arabic language. After completing his Ph.D. at the University of Birmingham in 1988, he returned to become the full time pastor of St. Andrew's from 1988 until 1998, and then the first director of graduate studies at the Presbyterian seminary from 1998 to 2003.

The second intern the ALC sent to Cairo would also go on to provide vital leadership in the growing ALC work in the region, as well as in future work of the ELCA. Mark Brown came to serve with Harold Vogelaar at Maadi Community Church and St. Andrew's as an intern in 1980–81. After graduation from Luther Seminary in St. Paul, Minnesota, Brown would

---

81. Division for World Mission and Inter-Church Cooperation minutes, March 29–31, 1978, TALC 16/1/1/1.

return to the Middle East. He spent one year of study at the Centre for the Study of Islam and Christian-Muslim Relations at Selly Oak Colleges and one year at the Kelsey Language School in Amman. By 1984 he was in the West Bank working with the Kapengas at the Friends School, and serving as an assistant pastor at one of the Evangelical Lutheran Church in Jordan (now the Evangelical Lutheran Church in Jordan and the Holy Land [ELCJHL]) congregations, the Evangelical Lutheran Church of Hope in Ramallah. In 2001 Brown returned to the U.S. to become Assistant Director of the Lutheran Office for Governmental Affairs (LOGA), where issues of peace and justice for Palestinians (both Christian and Muslim) were raised through political channels. Brown would serve under the director of LOGA, Russ Siler. Siler would step down as director and take a call from the ELCA Division for Global Mission (DGM) to become the pastor of the English-speaking congregation of the Lutheran Church of the Redeemer in Jerusalem in 2003. (The strong connection between LOGA and the Palestinian/Israeli conflict ensured that the issue would come before the ELCA through the LOGA office.) Brown would eventually come back to the West Bank as the LWF representative based at the Augusta Victoria Hospital, a post held previously by David Johnson.

MARK THOMSEN AND THE ALC'S "FOCUS ON ISLAM"

The Shelleys and Mark Brown (later with his family) would go on to fulfill the initial desire of the ALC by undertaking years of service in the Middle East and by providing "expertise in Arabic [language and culture] and in the world of Islam, and the historical and political situation of the Middle East."[82] Their role in the Middle East was supported and fostered by a missiological vision being developed first in Minneapolis during the final years of the ALC and then in Chicago during the first years of the ELCA. In 1982, Mark Thomsen was called by the board of the Division for World Mission and Inter-Church Cooperation of the ALC to serve as its director until the inception of the ELCA, where he continued on as the director for the Division for Global Mission until 1996. Thomsen was firmly committed to a Lutheran agenda of coming to terms with Islam, socially, theologically, and missiologically, and was able to build upon the work begun by Fred Neudoerffer. Although Neudoerffer was the architect

---

82. "Report and Evaluation of DWMIC Participation in Mission in Middle East throughout 1983," TALC 16/1/1/1.

of the modern American Lutheran model of engagement with Islam in the Middle East, it was Thomsen who engaged in theological reflection and the missiological implications of that encounter.

As a former missionary in northern Nigeria, Thomsen was well acquainted with the issues related to Christian mission in an Islamic context. After graduating from Trinity Theological Seminary in 1957, Thomsen was called as a missionary of the ALC to northern Nigeria. There he served as the principal of the Lutheran Pastors School in Lamurde, and then as professor of theology at the Theological College of Northern Nigeria, in Bukuru, until 1966. After earning a doctorate in theology from Northwestern University in 1971, Thomsen went on to teach at Blair College, Luther Northwestern Seminary, and finally at Lutheran School of Theology at Chicago. Thomsen was well suited to lead the denomination in a discussion on the implications of encounter with Islam.

In 1983, he organized a Task Force on Christian Witness to Muslims, comprised of Lutheran scholars from various theological institutions, and began an "in-depth study of ways in which the confession of the Triune God can be articulated in our time so as to convey faithfully and meaningfully the message of the New Testament in a Muslim context."[83] By 1986 the task force published its study, *God and Jesus: Theological Reflections for Christian-Muslim Dialog*.[84] The document demonstrated that the ALC was treading on new ground. Other than the distinguished Dutch Reformed Islamicist Willem Bijlefeld, who was working at Duncan Black MacDonald Center for Islamic Studies of Hartford Seminary, the major contributors to the taskforce were theologians or biblical scholars—not Islamicists. (Bruce Schein, the architect of the 1969 LCA engagement with Islam was slated for participation in the task force, but unfortunately had to withdraw due to health problems, and died shortly thereafter in 1986.) The ALC at this point then had no Lutheran scholars trained in Islamic studies. It would not be until 1988 that the American Lutheran church would have its first Islamicist in Michael T. Shelley. (It is surprising, however, that Harold Vogelaar from the RCA, the first Islamicist called by the LCA, was not included in the task force.)

---

83. Division for World Mission and Inter-Church Cooperation minutes, October 26–28, 1983, TALC 16/1/1/1.

84. Thomsen, "God and Jesus." For a recent reference to this work see M. Swanson, "The Trinity in Christian-Muslim Conversation."

Throughout his tenure with the ALC and the ELCA, Thomsen worked to develop a missiology for the church based upon a theology of the Cross, where to be a disciple of the God who reveals himself in the crucified Christ is to enter into a "cruciform" mission. He would later write that the very nature of the God of the crucified Christ entails that the church in its mission must shed all desires or intentions of control or power and fully enter into the lives of those who are hurting and broken. We are to reflect the life of the "suffering-with-us-God" by fully participating in the "brokenness and pain of the human community."[85] The church is called to "passionate involvement in human brokenness and suffering . . . to participate in the messianic struggle for life in the midst of death . . . [to be involved in a] call to vulnerability."[86] The church then is to abandon all efforts of social or political control and be a prophetic voice in the world. Reflecting the divine will to restore wholeness and healing means that we are to cross the boundaries of even religious divides by becoming deeply involved in the lives of those from other faith traditions. Therefore, by fully engaging the world we will become fully invested in the various contexts in which the church finds itself—and one of these is the Muslim community and the Middle East.

After the Iranian Revolution of 1979 and the kidnapping of American embassy personnel by Iranian students, the lack of in-depth knowledge of Islam became a major concern for North Americans. As the political climate of the Middle East became more prominent in the American media throughout the 1980s, as the Lebanese Civil War heated up and more American hostages were taken, the church in the U.S. in general, and the Lutheran Church in particular, was not in a position to adequately assess the role of the church in the tense climate of the Middle East. Thus, the ALC committed itself to providing resources to train a new order of what Mark Thomsen called "Lutheran Jesuits," who would be thoroughly trained in Islamic and Middle Eastern studies.

By 1989 Thomsen's theological reflection had led the ELCA to develop its *Commitments for Mission in the 1990's*.[87] This document provided a priority for the ELCA to recruit and train people for service among Muslim communities. Commitment four (of nine) was to "witness

---

85. Thomsen, *The Word and the Way*, 85.
86. Ibid., 80.
87. Ibid., 14–19.

to people of other faiths" through "mutual conversations and interfaith dialogue."[88] That, combined with a commitment to "seek to alleviate suffering and empower the weak and advocate for righteousness, justice and peace," led to the ELCA's programs in East Jerusalem and the West Bank being considered a high propriety. St. Andrew's refugee ministry was also seen as a place where both solidarity with the suffering and ongoing dialogue with Muslims could continue.

To underline this commitment for direct conversation with Islam, the DGM commissioned former a Missouri Synod Lutheran missionary to India, Roland E. Miller, to undertake a two-year study to propose to the ELCA a holistic "Focus on Islam."[89] Miller's four hundred-page document was a guideline for proposals on how the ELCA might maximize some of its on-going missions among Muslims and augment areas in which it was not engaged; as well as develop educational programs for the congregations in the United States in the area of witness to the Muslim community.[90] As far as the Middle East was concerned, Miller proposed that the ELCA should go back to its mission roots and focus on relating to "'Muslims at all levels through proclamation of the Gospel, service, and dialogue' [and that this] be seen as the central purpose of Middle East ministry"[91] In addition to enhancing some of the important ministries in Cairo, Lebanon, and the West Bank, Miller proposed several new mission opportunities. The first was to revive the old Samuel Zwemer missionary training center, or "Cairo Study Centre," at the Evangelical Presbyterian Seminary, which commenced in 1912 and ran until Zwemer left Cairo for Princeton Seminary in 1929. Harold Vogelaar's month-long seminars on Islam during the 1980s were of the same mold, albeit on a dialogical model as opposed to an evangelical one. The second proposal was to develop opportunities for reconciliation in Iraq (in the immediate aftermath of the first Gulf War), and, following in the footsteps of the LOM, to begin work among the Kurds.[92] Ultimately, however, no major initiatives were put into place in the Middle East. There were no major changes to the

88. Ibid., 13 and 16, respectively.

89. Miller served with several LC-MS missionaries in India and was a frequent contributor to *The Minaret*, the journal of the Society for the Promotion of Mohammedan Missions.

90. Miller, "Planning Proposal," 4.

91. Ibid., 226.

92. Ibid., 141–56.

FIGURE 5: Harold Vogelaar and Mark Swanson, LCA Personnel, Larnaca, Cyprus, 1982

network of activities going on, either in Beirut, Cairo, Jerusalem, or the West Bank. However, two other major proposals that *were* acted upon would have enormous benefits for the ELCA Middle East mission.

In terms of helping the church to "Focus on Islam" on the national level, Miller had proposed that at least two seminaries of the ELCA become "interested in generating trained workers for the engagement with Muslims, and moved to place the study of Islam within formal learning rubrics."[93] This proposal would lead to the establishment of two very important centers. In 1993, Luther Theological Seminary in St. Paul, Minnesota formally established a master's program in Islamic studies. Roland Miller would be appointed as director until 1998, when Mark Swanson replaced Miller upon his retirement. Swanson had also served as an intern in Cairo under Harold Vogelaar from 1979 to 1980. After graduation from Gettysburg Seminary he returned to Cairo in 1981 and taught full-time at the Presbyterian seminary from 1984 until 1998, when he then moved to Luther Seminary.[94] Under Swanson's guidance, the Islamic studies program at Luther was to become a training ground for students who would be going out to serve in Muslim communities in a variety of ministries, either within the United States or abroad. Swanson's focus on medieval Arabic Christian theology has provided deep and invaluable resources for the church's continued theological reflection on encounter with Islam.[95]

Swanson, one of the "Lutheran Jesuits," had been sent to the Pontifical Institute for Arabic and Islamic Studies in Rome, and was granted his doctorate in 1992. Both Mark and Rosanne Swanson served together with the LCA and the ELCA from 1981 until 1998. Rosanne had also served under Vogelaar as the first Lutheran female intern at St. Andrew's, from 1982 to 1983, and was probably the first female ever ordained into the ministry in Egypt, being ordained at St. Andrew's in 1994.[96]

The other seminary that took Miller's proposal to heart was the Lutheran School of Theology at Chicago (LSTC). Harold Vogelaar had been invited to teach Islamic studies at LSTC throughout the 1980s during his sabbaticals in the U.S. However, in 1990 he was called as the visiting Professor of World Religions to help the seminary focus on Islam. Throughout this time he developed extensive networks with Muslim communities in the Chicago area, throughout the U.S., and abroad. In

---

93. Ibid., 45.

94. Swanson was under a call from the LCA from 1981. He began two years of Arabic language study in Cairo and one year of Islamic studies at Hartford Seminary in the U.S., before commencing full time work as a professor at the Presbyterian seminary.

95. See especially Swanson's "Beyond Prooftexting" and "Cross of Christ"; and Grypeou, Swanson, and Thomas, *Encounter of Eastern Christianity*.

96. Lani Hill-Alto of the RCA was actually the first female pastoral intern to serve at St. Andrew's (1975–76). She was followed by the Lutherans Rosanne Swanson (1982–83), Janine Mathison (1993–94), and Elyse Nelson-Winger (2000–1).

addition, Mark Thomsen joined the faculty in 1996 after his retirement as the director for DGM in 1996. In the fall of 2003, Michael T. Shelley also came to LSTC. LSTC was taking advantage of those resources who had been thoroughly trained abroad and applying them at the seminary in the multi-confessional context in Chicago and the U.S.

In the fall of 2006 the LSTC inaugurated a bold new program, unveiling its Center of Christian-Muslim Engagement for Peace and Justice. Vogelaar, instrumental in developing the vision for the center, began as the director for its first year of existence until his retirement.[97] In 2007 Shelley was appointed as its director, while Mark Swanson, who had been called from Luther Seminary, was appointed as the first Harold S. Vogelaar Professor of Christian-Muslim Studies and Inter-faith Relations, and then became the associate director of the center. Both of these seminary programs at Luther and LSTC were results of the Miller proposals in 1991, and ultimately have their roots going back to Schein's proposals in 1969 encouraging the Lutheran Church to engage Islam.

Another major proposal of Miller's that was taken to heart by the ELCA was the development of missionary training programs on Islam. The first of these was offered for newly appointed missionaries in 1992 in Kenosha, Wisconsin. Since then, the DGM has held a wide variety of educational opportunities for mission personnel going out to work in Muslim communities. The "Islam component" continues to be a part of all mission personnel training, although its format has changed over the years.

When Roland Miller presented his proposals for a "Focus on Islam" at the beginning of the 1990s, he stated that the ELCA was "ill-prepared to engage in this mission" to Islam.[98] There were not enough personnel or resources committed to this task of engaging Islam, he wrote. In a mere ten years, by September 2001, the ELCA would have to ask itself whether it had heeded Miller's warnings and prepared itself in the previous decade. At the turn of the twenty-first century, the ELCA was well situated with trained Islamicists, pastors, and church workers with a background in Islamic studies and experience working with Muslim communities. These individuals would be needed by an American society that was wrapped in fear and anxiety as a result of 9/11 and the American-lead War on Terror.

---

97. See Boden, "Mark Swanson Joins LSTC."
98. Miller, "Planning Proposal," 1.

THE ELCA ACCOMPANIMENT AND THE ELCJHL

In 1975 the LCA went out of its way to avoid local ecclesiastical relationships, especially with the Palestinian Lutheran church, which was very much tied to its German Lutheran commitments. This was done intentionally, in order to free themselves up from any formal ecclesiastical relationships that might tie their hands from engaging with the local Muslim community. By 1984, the new LCA secretary for the Middle East area, Warner W. Luoma, was critical of this policy and began seeking ways to place personnel with indigenous Christian institutions. With the establishment of the ELCA and its DGM, going it alone was no longer an option. By 1987 the ALC/LCA personnel stated to the newly-emerging ELCA that they were "committed to witness—with and through indigenous Christian people, churches, institutions, and agencies."[99] With the development of the new Lutheran denomination, the Evangelical Lutheran Church in America, these practices would become church policy.

The guidelines for ministry in the ELCA directed the church to abide by the concept of *accompaniment*, the "walking together in Jesus Christ of two or more churches in companionship and in service in God's mission."[100] This model, developed from the context of South America, sought to escape the charges of Western missionary imperialism or colonialism by allowing the indigenous church to speak for itself. Missionaries could no longer assume to set the agenda. Mission was to be generated by the indigenous church in its own context, and the ELCA would *accompany* the indigenous church as it set its own agenda. The concept recognized the realities of world Christianity as a predominantly "Two-Thirds World" church; and for this the architects are to be congratulated for their vision.

In the Middle East, however, this missiological guideline would begin to hamper "conversation with Islam" as it had been originally conceived, and put restraints on the Neudoerffer-Schein plan as a novel approach to Islam. The ELCA was now committed to being sensitive and respectful of the context of the indigenous Christians of the Middle East. For good or bad, it would no longer be possible to create independent relationships with the Middle Eastern Muslim community, but only through their contacts within the local Middle Eastern churches. Formal relationships with

---

99. "Planning Document for ELCA Middle East Ministry," February 6–10, 1987, DGM archives.

100. ELCA Division for Global Mission, "Global Mission," 6.

Muslims in Lebanon would be dependent upon the offices of the MECC. The Islamic studies program at the Evangelical Theological Seminary in Cairo was now subject to the Presbyterian Synod of the Nile's views of evangelism and inter-faith relations (which were quite conservative in outlook). In the West Bank, the interest in conversing with Muslims would be guided by the overarching concern for the issues of peace and justice for the Palestinians, through the contacts of the ELCJHL. On the one hand, the "conversation" would be geared toward the practical issues of how Christian and Muslim Palestinians could address the issues of the Israeli occupation. This was a positive factor. On the other hand, however, it meant that American Lutheran mission personnel were asked to focus on the occupation. This was especially true after the "Peace Not Walls" program passed by the General Assembly of the ELCA in 2005.[101] The issues, as far as the Jerusalem and West Bank ministries were concerned, were focused on advocacy and human rights. These issues, in and of themselves, justify commitment on behalf of the ELCA. In terms of encountering Islam, however, the focus became quite minimal, primarily because the issues of the occupation were of a much more critical nature.

The issue of responsibility to the local church here is the paramount problem. In Schein's proposal, relationships with the local church were frowned upon, precisely so that the Americans would be freed up to engage Muslims on their own. The Luoma and GM21 guidelines, however, stated that all activity needed to be developed in agreement with the local church. From a bi-lateral church perspective, the policy has worked well. What this meant for the American Lutheran missionaries, however, was that the development of mission in the Middle East was handled through administrative channels—from Chicago to Jerusalem, or Chicago to Beirut. Between the 1990s and the 2000s, there was a dramatic shift in how mission policy would be developed and implemented in the Middle East. On the one hand, the implementation of the "accompaniment" model provided indigenous Christians in the Middle East with access not only to missionaries, or messengers who relayed information back to church headquarters, but directly to the top of the mission board and the presiding bishop himself. On the other hand, for those missionaries who had been accustomed to actually developing Middle East policy, as they

---

101. See the "Peace Not Walls" Web site: http://www.elca.org/Our-Faith-In-Action/Justice/Peace-Not-Walls.aspx.

FIGURE 6: ELCA personnel, Larnaca, Cyprus, 1992

had done for years in the LCA and ALC, it was easy to feel as if the focus of their work was becoming obsolete. In some ways it was.

In addition, the development of the companion synod relationships meant that the focus of ELCA involvement was directed primarily, but not exclusively, to the only indigenous Middle Eastern Lutheran church, the ELCJHL. These synodical relationships accelerated in 2002 with the Israeli occupation of the Christmas Lutheran Church in Bethlehem, and the building of the separation wall between Israeli and the Palestinian community, which had involved the illegal expropriation of Palestinian land. The Southeast Michigan and New England Synods of the ELCA provided integral support to the ELCJHL by sending delegations of its bishops, pastors, and laypeople. In addition, ELCA members of prominence (congressional representatives, lobbyists, business persons, etc.) were encouraged to take part in travel programs to see for themselves what life was like for Palestinians in the occupied territories, and, echoing the words of Dennis Hilgendorf from years past, to "make a choice." Thus, the choice was made by the American Lutheran church to fully engage in the Middle East in the issues of poverty, prejudice, and power.

8

Conclusion

An American Lutheran view of Islam in the Middle East in "Pax Americana"

THE LUTHERAN TRADITION HAS had a symbiotic relationship with the Middle East ever since the sixteenth century. The expression of Luther's apocalypticism and the success of the Lutheran princes at the expense of Charles V were encouraged by the general fear of the Turkish Islamic empire at the very door of central Europe. To some extent, the success of the Reformation can be attributed to the social-political context dominated by fear of the "Terrible Turk." After the Ottoman threat dissolved, Europe began to expand beyond its cultural, political, and religious boundaries. While European merchants sought easier ways to bypass the expensive tariffs in transporting their goods through Ottoman lands, European explorers sought opportunities by sea to enlarge their nations' empires. This era of European expansion and the decline of the Ottoman Empire helped create a more congenial climate for travelers—including missionaries.

The first Western missionaries to the "Orient" were the Dominicans and Franciscans. Their mission was to bring the Orthodox churches back into the Roman fold; only a few of these brave mendicants focused their attention on Islam. The earliest days of Protestant mission to the Middle East were no different. Peter Heyling and his friends attempted to bring the light of the gospel to those Oriental Christians who they saw as suffering from ignorance of the true evangelical faith. Since that time, Lutheran missionaries have engaged various communities of the Middle East; Jewish, Christian, and Muslim. On the larger landscape of Protestant missions, Lutheran missions did not have a very large role to play in impacting Middle Eastern society compared to that of the

Anglicans, Congregationalists, and the Presbyterians. These denominations developed fairly successful Protestant communities, primarily from among Orthodox converts. The Lutheran presence in the Middle East, conversely, has always been small and scattered. Other than the German Lutheran activities in Palestine in the 1860s, which established an indigenous Palestinian Lutheran church, Lutherans have been satisfied with helping the small-scale mission work of other mission organizations and supporting local social service projects (i.e., orphanages, hospitals, hospices, etc.). Its personnel have represented a wide array of theological positions, served a variety of different mission societies, and pursued various goals; from the conversion of Jews and Muslims, on the one hand, to the development of dialog with Islam, on the other.

In most cases, Lutherans have not worked in the Middle East in isolation. They have instead occupied themselves with ecumenical projects to further their objectives. Be it through Lutheran, Reformed, Anglican or Presbyterian mission societies, Lutherans have continually worked with other ecumenical partners. Although the original LCA plan in the Middle East called for no direct links to indigenous churches in order to free up American Lutherans to engage Muslims without being entangled in local church politics, this proved nearly impossible to accomplish. In Palestine the ELCJHL became the primary reference for Lutheran work. The ELCA has provided both personnel and funding to assist the ELCJHL in its own ministries, especially with its school system. In addition, the ELCA has become heavily involved in numerous ecumenical organizations that seek to address the issue of peace and justice in Israel/Palestine, including Churches for Middle East Peace.[1] In Lebanon, the ELCA has provided a scattering of personnel both in the offices of the MECC and as professors at the Near East School of Theology. In addition to personnel, the ELCA continues to provide financial support to the CRC.

In Egypt, however, the Lutherans have maintained some sense of independence. Even so, the American Lutheran church has worked directly in conjunction with the mission of Evangelical Theological Seminary in Cairo, the theological institution of the Egyptian Presbyterian Synod of the Nile. At a very early stage in American Lutheran engagement in Egypt, relationships were established with the Coptic Orthodox Church. From 1979 until 1989 Lutherans had personnel teaching at the Institute

---

1. See their Web site: http://www.cmep.org/.

of Coptic Studies. The most prominent site of American Lutheran work, however, has been at the congregation of St. Andrew's United Church of Cairo. As a Scottish Presbyterian church built during the height of British occupation, and now under the legal ownership of an independent congregation made up of foreigners, the congregation has never truly fit the model of "accompanying" an indigenous church. Nevertheless, the ELCA has assisted this congregation in its work, especially with its African refugee population. Lastly, the Cairo Islamicists Shelley, Swanson, and Grafton all maintained an active presence among the Roman Catholic Comboni fathers. From 1991 through 2007 these Lutherans provided courses and lectures on Islam and Christian-Muslim relations at the Dar Comboni Center for Arabic and Islamic Studies, for Catholic and Protestant church workers who were in the process of training for long-term service in a Muslim majority country.

Thus, it has been through the Lutheran ability to work ecumenically in Palestine and Egypt with the Reformed and Presbyterians, Anglicans and Catholics, and to some extent the Orthodox, that Lutheran work developed in the Middle East. These relationships underline the reality that Lutherans in the Middle East have utilized ecumenical relationships for the purpose of furthering mission. In the first instance, this was because German Lutherans were organically joined to the Reformed wing of the Reformation through the Lutheran-Reformed unification. Secondly, the Lutheran Pietists saw "mission" as the overall goal in the Middle East, and had no qualms about working with other denominations or structures. In fact, the Pietists saw church order as *adiophora*, to the extent that they were willing to undergo secondary Anglican ordinations in order to work under the CMS. Lastly, by the time the ALC arrived in the region in 1979, it was one of the latest of the Western denominations to engage in the region, and had no choice but to work ecumenically.

Throughout the twentieth century, Lutherans have had a more dramatic impact on the Middle East through their development and relief work rather than through direct missionary activity. The LWF, Lutheran World Relief (LWR), and Lutheran World Hunger Appeal have all provided continuing aid to communities in need, including Palestinians, Kurds, Iraqis, and Sudanese. Since its beginning in 1947 the LWF and LWR assistance has certainly been the largest Lutheran activity in the Middle East in terms of financial resources and support, a story which has been largely left out of this narrative. This is a story that needs to be told in its own right.

MISSION IN "*PAX AMERICANA*"

American Lutherans are facing a particular challenge at the beginning of the twenty-first century. Much like the specter of the "Terrible Turk" that hung over the Europe in the sixteenth century, Americans are faced with a similar fear from the same region. Since Americans watched in horror as the smoke billowed from the Twin Towers before they collapsed, the image of the "Terrible Turk," now in the guise of the "radical Muslim terrorist," has arisen anew. In some ways, not much has changed for Lutherans.

Luther's writings, taken in the context of Imperial-Ottoman relations, provide an important commentary on our contemporary views of the "Other" across borders. Times of extreme anxiety or distress often bring about the desire to demonize the "Other." Complex external international relations and multi-faceted internal social problems can often be too overwhelming, leading a nation to blindly attempt to justify its own cause. It is easier that way. Luther continues to admonish us to beware of forgetting our own sins in the midst of extreme international social-political pressure. The demons do not only reside without, but also within. Vain attempts at self-preservation can only lead to destruction. The answer to such vanity and sin is not to blame the "Turk," but to always first look inward.[2]

Regardless of one's views of the military and political responses to 9/11, the reality of American imperial presence is now felt by Middle Easterners who view "Amrika" not only as the only remaining superpower, but as a world empire seeking domination.[3] "*Pax Americana*," the image of an American cultural, economic, political, and now military empire, is viewed as a negative presence in the Middle Eastern social conscience. Many Middle Eastern Muslims see the struggle against "*Pax Americana*" as a necessary defense against cultural and military invasion.

In response to the attacks of 9/11, President Bush uttered that regrettable word: "crusade." We are involved in "this crusade, this war on

---

2. *WA* 53:396; as cited in Williams, "Erasmus and the Reformers," 348.

3. The most prominent and helpful articulation of this is Khalidi, *Resurrecting Empire*.

terrorism," he said.[4] In American culture the term has a positive, moral connotation. To be on a crusade implies holding the high moral ground for some moral or ethical cause. In Middle Eastern culture (Christian, Jewish, or Muslim), "crusade" simply brings to life the memory of that horrible period of history in which Western "pilgrims" slaughtered their way through local populations to establish European colonies and connotes the foreign occupation of their lands.

For many people of the Middle East, the events of 1948, 1967, 1991, and 2003 are clear examples of Western imperial expansion and the continuation of the historic Crusades. Daily media throughout the Middle East supports this imperial image. In 2003 the U.S. and its allies invaded Iraq under the pretense of self-defense. Very few newspapers of the Middle East saw things that way, however. The popular understanding was that the U.S. was on another Crusade—this time not for holy places, but for oil and power. American foreign policy, from their perspective, has only seemed to support such a claim.

In 1984 the *USS New Jersey* became the first naval vessel to fire on foreign targets since the Vietnam War, shelling Druze positions in Lebanon at the request of Maronite militias. Although the U.S. Administration argued that it was neutral in the Civil War, the action supported the belief that the U.S. had already sided with the Christian Maronite government. In 1987, the U.S. re-flagged eleven Kuwaiti oil tankers during the Iran-Iraq War in a move to provide a continued supply of oil through the Straits of Hormuz. This seemed to support the view that while the U.S. was willing to allow Iraq and Iran to duke it out, it would make sure that the flow of oil continued unharmed through the Persian Gulf.[5] In 1991, Desert Shield was thrown together for the military defense of Kuwait and Saudi Arabia. It was this event that prompted Osama Bin Laden to issue his famous *fatwa* against the "Crusaders and Jews" who were occupying the lands of the two Islamic holy places, Mecca and Medina (a reference to the fact that there were American soldiers still present in Saudi Arabia seven years after the first Gulf War).[6] Finally, the invasion of Iraq and the awarding of billion dollar contracts to American firms for the "rebuilding" of the Iraqi oil industry has been interpreted on the "Arab street" as proof that there

4. White House, Office of the Press Secretary, "Remarks by the President."
5. See Brands, *Into the Labyrinth*, 193.
6. See Lewis, "License to Kill." See also Lawrence, *Messages to the World*; and Kelsay, "Bin Laden's Reasons."

is a definite American agenda in the Arab Muslim Middle East. And, of course, we have not even touched on the issue of the Israeli-Palestinian conflict, concerning which Arabs continually point to the U.S.'s double standard of allowing Israel to occupy land, but not Iraq. For the people of the Middle East there was clearly a link between the two issues over the occupation of land: one has been allowed to continue, the other was systematically and militarily destroyed. While the Bush administration utilized rhetoric arguing that 9/11 was the result of those who hate America because it is a land of freedom, prior to the "War on Terror," no such rhetoric could be found among Islamic radicalists. From the perspective of the Middle East—from moderates, conservatives, and radicals—the issue has always been about American foreign policy decisions.

The events of 9/11 and the subsequent "War on Terror" have no doubt changed the world. The effects of the war of Bin Laden and Bush have been felt throughout the world, and there are many victims; especially the people whose lands have been occupied, scarred, and whose lives have been irrevocably torn asunder. One community that has been radically affected are Middle Eastern Christians. They have been hard pressed to prove their national and ethnic loyalties, much like American Lutherans of German decent during World War II. In places like Palestine, Syria, Lebanon, Egypt, and especially Sudan, indigenous Christians have often been charged with being in league with the Westerner. The fallout of the war in Iraq has been the complete destruction of the indigenous Chaldean community![7]

The work of Western Christian missionaries and church workers in the Middle East—regardless of intent (i.e., to educate, develop, or proselytize)—like all Middle East mission work before, is now being impacted by international conditions over which they have no control. This was the case with the Presbyterian missions in Lebanon and Syria in 1860 and 1975 when civil war broke out, and in Armenia and Persia during the Turkish genocides of the late nineteenth and the early twentieth centuries. It was the case for the German Pietists who were rounded up by the British in Egypt and Palestine and deported. Even for those who have undertaken altruistic, faithful, and supportive ministries to the indigenous peoples around them, their work has often been wiped away by international events beyond their control. Issues of politics and power

---

7. See Taneja, *Assimilation, Exodus, and Eradication*.

have always been at play, and Western missionaries have either tried to use them to their advantage or have become its victims. It is no different with American missionary endeavors today. On the one hand, conservative evangelical organizations have utilized "*Pax Americana*" for their own purposes. Numerous Christian organizations exploited Amman, Jordan as a staging post for their own invasion once Baghdad fell to the American forces. They rushed in to save souls in the midst of the chaos. The same could be said for Christian evangelical work in Afghanistan.[8] On the other hand, where American mission workers have tended to be critical of their own government's actions and policies, as citizens of their country of origin they have been and will continue to be negatively affected by international politics. As a result of the contemporary international incidents in the Middle East, American church mission projects have been hampered, pastoral and social care activities have been limited, and personnel have been removed for fear of violence directed against them. Although the local communities, be they Jewish, Christian, or Muslim, have often provided safety and encouragement for American personnel (who more often than not have sincere sympathies with the indigenous people), the mere guilt by association as American citizens has created tensions in those local communities.

Middle Eastern society at large has been very negative, even vitriolic, in its response to U.S. foreign policy. This has put pressure on those Christian communities that do associate with American programs. On the larger scale, those Arab governments attempting to uphold their collective agreements with Washington have bent over backwards to provide protection for Americans and American economic interests. This has usually taken the form in the increased presence of local gendarmes, and restrictions in the areas to which Americans can travel, in order to "protect" them. When American church workers do travel, the local communities for which they are working often feel pressure from their own governments who are suspicious of these local informal relationships. In other Middle Eastern states that are not close allies with the U.S. (e.g., Libya, Iran, Syria, etc.), guilt by association is transferred even to the local Christian community with which American mission personnel may associate. This is an age-old problem.

---

8. See Grafton, "Is It Time."

Most mainline Protestant churches and mission agencies that have been in the Middle East longer than the American Lutherans have struggled with how to respond to the social-political problems in the region. For example, the PC-USA and the RCA have been involved in internal struggles over the theological issues of Christian Zionism and Israel's occupation of the West Bank and Gaza Strip.[9] There is a deep divide within these churches, as those with dispensationalist perspectives see the state of Israel's presence as the fulfillment of biblical prophecy, while others have sought to uphold biblical models of justice in viewing the Palestinian cause.[10] No church is more conflicted than the Anglican church over these matters of who to identify with—should it support the indigenous Anglican Arab church or the Jewish Israelis, both of whom it helped create? The active personnel from the CMS (of England, Australia, and New Zealand), with their focus on conservative evangelism, have struggled with the British Episcopal hierarchy and the American Episcopal Church, who have tended to focus on peace, justice, and inter-faith reconciliation.[11] Even the Mennonites, who have played a prominent pro-Palestinian role through the activism of the Mennonite Central Committee and Christian Peacemaker Teams in the West Bank, have been impacted by a socially conservative constituency suspicious of any political involvement.

AMERICAN LUTHERANS, PALESTINIAN LUTHERANS, AND THE MODERN STATE OF ISRAEL

Since the beginning of the second Intifada in the fall of 2000, and with the subsequent horror of 9/11, American Lutherans have been quickly drawn into the issues of the Middle East. The occupation of ELCJHL property, the Dar al-Kalima school and the Christmas Lutheran Church, in the spring of 2002 brought the Palestinian/Israeli conflict into the

---

9. After much debate in the 2004 General Synod, the RCA received John Hubers's paper "Christian Zionism" as a study guide for congregations. The PC-USA also accepted a "Resolution on Confronting Christian Zionism" at its 2004 General Assembly. The Web site Challenging Christian Zionism, organized by Hubers, provides the Web page "Churches Speak Out, " an overview of official church statements addressing Christian Zionism.

10. See Grafton, "Survey of the Use of Scripture."

11. One of the most prominent Anglicans to deal with this issue has been Colin Chapman; see his book *Whose Promised Land?*

forefront of national church life.[12] American Lutherans were now faced with the particular predicament of having to respond not only to another international crisis in the Middle East, or simply another news bulletin about Arab terrorists, but a crisis dealing with the reality of Palestinian Lutherans—indigenous Arab Lutherans—caught up in the quagmire of the conflict and occupation in Palestine.[13] The use of the terms "Arab" and "Lutheran" in the same sentence to describe Palestinians was a surprise to many North American Lutherans, who perhaps offered the question, "There are Arab Lutherans?"

Whereas initially Lutherans undertook mission in the Middle East to proselytize to Jews, and Muslims and reform Orthodox Christians, the predominant theme since Hilgendorf's presentation to the Lutheran Council in the U.S.A. in 1969 has been "justice." The occupation of the ELCJHL properties prompted immediate action by several wings of the ELCA, all seeking to address the situation: the Division for Global Mission, the Division for Church and Society, through LOGA, the Office for Ecumenical and Inter-Religious Relations, the companion synods of New England and Southeast Michigan, and the conference of bishops who sent delegates to Jerusalem as demonstrations of the ELCA's solidarity and "accompaniment" with the Palestinians and the ELCJHL. Since 2002 there has been a sincere and concerted effort to re-focus the ELCA constituency on the issue of Palestine/Israel through the lens of justice, and subsequently to address the issues biblical interpretation of "the Land" as it relates to the particular theology of Christian Zionism. The ELCA's 2005 "Churchwide Strategy for Engagement in Israel and Palestine" has as its design to "contribute to the wider movement for peace with justice in the Middle East."[14] This strategy has led to public pronouncements from the presiding bishop of the ELCA in taking a stand on the injustice of the Israeli separation wall.[15] Within the U.S., this dramatic transformation of Lutheran perspectives on Arab Christians has also raised the importance of Arab Lutheran ministries lodged within the Commission for Multicultural Ministries, which struggles to find a voice.[16]

12. ELCA News Service, "Israeli Troops Reoccupy" and "Israeli Soldiers Release."
13. See Raheb, *Bethlehem Besieged*.
14. ELCA, "Churchwide Strategy."
15. Hanson, "Letter from Presiding Bishop."
16. ELCA News Service, "ELCA Council."

Responding to the Israeli/Palestinian crisis necessitates not only a social response, but a unique ecclesiastical and theological one as well. The Lutheran engagement in Israel/Palestine has differed from other ELCA relief responses, such as medical missions to Afghan tribesmen or food shipments to Rawandan refugees. In the case of Israel/Palestine there are several other important dynamics. First and foremost, there is the question of the modern state of Israel and the sensitivities of German Lutherans and Roman Catholics *vis-à-vis* their past history in the Holocaust. Neither the Vatican nor the German Lutheran churches wish to be labeled as supporting anti-semitism or reliving all of its past horrors— and rightfully so! The German propst of the property of the Lutheran Church of the Redeemer in Jerusalem must be extremely careful in his public statements regarding the state of Israel and its actions. The issue of guilt over the Holocaust cannot wholly explain all Lutheran actions in response to issues in the Middle East, but neither should it be overlooked in contemporary German-American Lutheran communities. The most recent ELCA publications on Jewish-Christian relations states: "The recognition that Hitler could not have succeeded without the church's 'teaching of contempt' towards Jews and Judaism over the centuries has led to Christian soul-searching."[17] This must especially be noted along with the 1994 statement by the ELCA "to the Jewish Community" apologizing for Luther's tract *On the Jews and Their Lies*.[18] In addition, as we have already noted, many of the first Lutheran Pietists to go to the Middle East focused on evangelizing among Jews. Early mission societies focused their mission toward the Jewish communities of Palestine and Egypt. This culminated with the consecration of the first Anglican-Lutheran bishop in Jerusalem, Michael Solomon Alexander, a convert from Judaism. Thus, the Lutheran presence in Palestine must reckon with its past in terms of targeting Jews for evangelization, an extremely sensitive topic in Israel today.

The second important issue necessitating a unique response to the Israeli/Palestinian conflict is the perception of biblical dispensationalists, Christian Zionists, and pseudo Christian Zionists that the establishment of the modern state of Israel is the fulfillment of biblical prophecy. Dispensationalists see the capture of the old city of Jerusalem by the Israelis in 1967 as the fulfillment of Old Testament prophecies and the necessary

---

17. Trice and LaHurd, "Windows for Understanding."
18. ELCA, "Declaration." See also ibid., 9–10.

catalyst to kick-start the events interpreted in the book of Revelation that will bring about Christ's return.[19] Christian Zionists are those who have undertaken political platforms to support Israel in order to bring about Christ's return—for some, the opportunity for all Jews to accept Christ as the Messiah. Since the Six Day War of 1967, popular American Protestant piety has dramatically and violently moved toward a millennialist view of events in the Middle East. This theological position, however, is also held by many pseudo Christian Zionists. These are the many mainline Protestants—including members of the ELCA and LCMS—who would not adhere to biblical millennialism or dispensationalism in its pure sense if not for a strong trend of biblical illiteracy. In other words, most mainline Protestants have not been given adequate tools necessary for articulating a different biblical interpretation of the current conflict. To put it simply, for most mainline Christians, the fact that the Old Testament is about the "Israelites," and because there is a modern state of "Israel" made up of Jews, there naturally must be a connection in which God has chosen a side.[20] It just seems to make plain sense.

The third issue necessitating a response to the Israeli/Palestinian issue is the general anxiety in American society regarding Arabs and the Middle East as the origin and haven of terrorism. American society has deep-seated fears and anxieties regarding the Middle East. The images of the blindfolded Iranian and Lebanese hostages, the bombing of the Marine barracks in Lebanon, and the images of the Twin Towers have seared themselves into the collective emotional psyche of America. Like most Americans, American Lutherans have been somewhat slow to digest the issues of the Middle East.[21] There is a general confusion among Americans as to why "those people hate us when all we are trying to do is help them?" Such honest and yet naïve responses have failed to heed Luther's warnings about the necessity of looking inward during a crisis. Unlike the Wilsonian refusal to undertake a political mandate for Armenia after World War I, American involvement in the Middle East since 1948 has never been solely about altruistic goals, but economic and political "national interests."

19. A very good review of American millennial views can be found in Weber, *On the Road to Armageddon*.

20. See Hafften, "Challenge the Implications"; Grafton, "American Cultural Roots"; and R. Smith, "A Lutheran Response."

21. See Sudilovsky, "Saving Lives, Creating Peace."

Lastly, with all of contemporary Middle Eastern politics in mind, there has been a very important legacy of Jewish-Lutheran theological dialogue. The investment that has been made, and the great strides taken in this relationship, has prompted the Lutheran-Jewish relationship to focus on theological matters, rather than focusing on the contemporary issues of justice and the situation of Palestinian Lutherans.[22]

All this being said, the current focus on indigenous Lutherans in the Middle East has provided an important opportunity for North Americans Lutherans to look anew at the Middle East, this time more attentive to the realities and complexities of the context; its people and their religions, rather than through the sound bytes of a two minute segment on the nightly news. With all these dynamics pulling at the American Lutheran psyche it is quite remarkable that the 2005 ELCA general assembly was able to pass its *Churchwide Strategy for Engagement in Israel and Palestine*. This resolution utilized many of the longstanding relationships between the American Lutheran Church and the ELCJHL and LWF. The leadership of the ELCA Divisions for Church and Society, Global Mission, and Ecumenical Relations worked tirelessly to convince an American constituency that had been bombarded with media images of the Palestinian "Terrible Turk." The fact that several mainline churches along with the ELCA, including both the PC-USA and RCA, have recognized that the Israeli-Palestinian conflict is much more complicated than simply an "Islamic threat" or the extension of "anti-Semitism" is quite telling—suggesting that the wheel may be slowly turning toward supporting a just settlement.

Still, although the issue of Israel/Palestine is vital to many of the issues in the contemporary Middle East, it is not the only issue with which to deal. As the LCA found out very early in its planning process, the Middle East is a big place. Ramallah is not San'aa. Cairo is not Muscat. Beirut is not Soujbulak. While the focus on Palestine has centered on the issues of justice, there are other issues, primarily Islam itself. This work has set out to provide a narrative of the historical roots of the American Lutheran engagement in the Middle East with a special focus on Islam. It is this issue with which we will conclude the narrative.

---

22. See ELCA, "Guidelines for Lutheran-Jewish Relations."

A LUTHERAN THEOLOGICAL RESPONSE TO ISLAM IN THE MIDDLE EAST

At the end of the nineteenth and beginning of twentieth century, the height of Western Protestant missionary era, the Middle East posed a particular missiological dilemma for mission agencies, unlike any other region of the world. The Middle East is home to the three great monotheistic faiths. Missionaries were faced with the particular problem of providing explicit rationale for their missiological agendas in the region. In the case of mission to the Jewish community, Romans 9–11 prompted mission societies to think carefully about how Christians should relate to the Jewish community, especially in and around the Holy Land. Another big missiological question for Protestant missions in the Middle East, however, was how to justify evangelizing among Eastern and Oriental Christian communities. The early American missionaries were quite vitriolic in their attacks on the superstitions of the Christians of the East. And yet, they were still Christians, even if only nominally so from the perspective of the pious missionaries. The debate over how to treat the Orthodox was quite severe, especially within several quarters of the Anglican community that saw the establishment of the Lutheran-Anglican bishopric in Jerusalem as an affront to the authority of the ancient churches. Mission agencies in the Middle East have been forced to clarify their relationship with these churches, especially with the rise of the MECC, which now includes all three families of Christian communities.

The Jewish and Christian communities aside, the Muslim community posed the most difficult missiological challenge. Not only was the Middle East the center of the Islamic world (in terms of its historical and theological identity), it was the only major religion to come *after* Christianity. Thus was raised the question, "If Muslims have been able to hear the true gospel over the centuries why have they not followed?" There are, of course, explicit rejections of Christian doctrine by Islam in its own texts.[23] For many missionaries the issue was clear: Muslims have heard of Christ and have rejected him. Therefore, the onus is on them and their explicit rejection; only repentance of this rejection will suffice. For others, looking deeply into the history of Christian-Muslim relations in

---

23. See the following verses from the Qurʾān addressing specific Christian doctrines: the Trinity, 4:171; the divinity of Christ, 5:116; 19:35, 88–93; and the Crucifixion, 4:157–58.

the early medieval period and the social-political context of the Middle East, the answer has not been so clear. There have been those who have asked, "Have they really heard the 'true gospel' or has it been acculturated in Western trappings and been misrepresented, especially through the experience of the Crusades?" In the 1980s American Lutherans involved with mission to Islam in the Middle East began to look back at the Middle Eastern Christian engagement with Islam. Was there a clue for contemporary Christian-Muslim engagement to be found among the Christians of the Middle East who have been carrying on this dialogue since the seventh century, completely within the sphere of Middle Eastern culture? This led some to utilize dialogical models of mission rather than the early nineteenth century methods of public debate and preaching. These missionaries were interested in actually listening to what Muslims had to say; not only about their own faith, but also about how they perceived Christianity. As American Lutherans entered into the Middle East they eagerly took on this missiological challenge. They were committed to asking difficult questions about how to do mission in the region. The 1986 document *God and Jesus*, published by the Division for World Mission of the ALC, was a very important endeavor to begin the reflection on Islam. The fact that as the ALC began this task when they had no Lutheran Islamicist is very instructive for the present.[24] The ALC's utilization of biblically and theologically trained scholars to write a document on Islam underlines the Lutheran intention of framing the discussion of Islam within a larger model—an appropriately Lutheran confessional model. Dr. Mark Thomsen's 1993 publication, *The Word and the Way of the Cross: Christian Witness among Muslim and Buddhist People*, has been one of the most important attempts by American Lutherans to address the issue of Islam within a larger confessional-theological context: the Word. Firmly committed to an encounter with and response to Islam in the early 1980s, but without any adequate personnel resources at the time, Thomsen set about to create those long-term resources.

In the 1990s several important works on Islam were published by long-time LCMS missionaries in India, such as Ernest Hahn's *How to*

---

24. At the time of the development of the document the only Lutheran-trained Islamicist was Roland Miller, a member of the Lutheran Church of Canada serving with the LCMS. It should be remembered that Willem Bijlefeld was Dutch Reformed and Harold Vogelaar was RCA (although he was not a member of the panel), and that Bruce Schein held a Ph.D. in New Testament, not Islamic studies.

Respond to Muslims and Roland Miller's *Muslim Friends: Their Faith and Feeling*.[25] Most recently, Miller's *Muslims and the Gospel: Reflections on Christian Sharing* has provided a post-9/11 voice to the conversation. These works are interested in helping North Americans engage in theological reflection on Islam in a thoughtful and honest way, but are still deeply concerned with upholding the theological differences between the gospel of God in Jesus Christ, and Islam. The focus on the theme of "friendship" and the commitment to inter-faith relationship is to be appreciated.

Yet, in response to the upheavals of the Middle East in the 1980s and 90s, when the American Lutheran mission in the Middle East was in its prime, the church was never able to fully harvest the fruits of its ministry. The knowledge and skill of those in the field of the Middle East were never adequately utilized within the American church at large—where they were needed most. Other than the resources listed above, there were no other statements or studies on Islam published by the ELCA or the LCMS as denominations during this time. For the ELCA, this was due to several factors. First and foremost, as a genuine interest in Islam was taking shape through the vision of Mark Thomsen, the Lutheran church went through major institutional transformations. By 1988 the Lutheran denominations were diverted from the possibilities of further engagement with Islam because of institutional necessities. The formation of the new ELCA and its early years stalled any new endeavors, as the church simply tried to develop its own identity and role.

Second, Thomsen was not able to convince the denomination that the vision of theological reflection on Islam and interaction in the Middle East was vital to the life of the American church. On the national Lutheran scene, Islamic studies continued to be pushed aside by debates about confessional identity, ethical issues, and ecumenical agreements. Thomsen's vision of engagement with Islam had not convinced a tradition that values serious confessional reflection that there is an important calling to respond to the challenges of Islam; for social, political, ethical, and most importantly, theological reasons—in their own right.

For North American Lutherans, the issues of the Middle East, as important as they are for the world and for American security and foreign policy, played a minor roll next to the intra-Lutheran debates of ecumenical orders (i.e., *Called to Common Mission* and the WordAlone Network)

---

25. We might also add to this list of introductions to Islam by Lutherans, Martinson, *Islam: An Introduction for Christians*.

and sexuality studies. These topics had all but consumed the energy, drive, and vision of the church. Thus, the general assembly of the church had been exhausted by its own moral and confessional discussions before it could address matters of the day affecting American society: international occupations, terrorism, the biblical hermeneutics supporting Christian Zionism, and theological reflection on Islam.

The third factor that diverted an American Lutheran "conversation with Islam" in the Middle East was the ELCA's focus on "accompaniment" as a part of its global vision. The diversion was not intentional, but unfortunately became a byproduct of Lutheran work in the Middle Eastern context. The issue of accountability (which the "accompaniment" model aims toward) is certainly a proper and vital marker of relationships in a post-colonial world. The Western church, by all rights, is no longer to set the agenda for its companions. On the issue of an American-Islamic engagement, however, it is evident that Americans have very different needs when encountering Islam than their Middle Eastern Christian brothers and sisters. Coming from their own context, Americans operate on a much more open field in terms of addressing the issues of pluralism, dialogue, and encounter than contemporary Middle Eastern Christians. Thus, while the American Lutheran church is free to develop the program of engaging Islam in the U.S.—to encounter and develop relationships with the North American Muslim community through seminaries, study centers, church colleges, and even in its local congregations—in the Middle East, as in other places in the world, it must work within the parameters of the indigenous church and its own particular views and feelings about Islam and Muslims. In a post-9/11 world, and in an era of *Pax Americana*, in which the U.S. occupies Iraq and has numerous active military bases around the region, American society is desperately in need of developing its knowledge of Islam and the Middle East for reasons of international responsibility. Middle Eastern Christians often have very different needs than Western churches in terms of engaging Islam. Middle Eastern Christians often need to focus on the issues of minority rights, civil society, and even foreign occupation (be it Israeli, Syrian, Turkish, or even American), and Americans can participate in that conversation. American Christians, however, in their conversation with Islam, have the need to focus on the role of women in society, freedom of religious expression, and most importantly, issues of violence.²⁶ As a church, the ELCA has not been able to engage directly with the center of the Islamic world on its own terms for the sake of its own constituency. The imbalance has not been for lack of interest or desire, but due to the models and structures with which the church has worked.

For the LCMS the unfortunate censoring of the Rev. Dr. David Benke for the public inter-faith meeting at Yankee Stadium on September 23, 2001 highlights the problems of inter-faith conversation.²⁷ The LCMS understands itself to be a confessionally Lutheran church that proclaims the gospel of Christ supported by the faithful witness of the Augsburg Confession. This orthodox Lutheran stance has prohibited the denomination, unfortunately, from engaging in conversations with a multitude of partners (Jews, Muslims, and other Lutherans). Recent works by Adam S. Francisco, professor at Concordia Theological Seminary in Fort Wayne, Indiana, have provided another Lutheran voice to the topic as of late. However, in the opinion of the author, these outspoken views detract from any necessary theological, social, and political conversation needing to take place in the current *Pax Americana*.²⁸ The denomination must realize the necessity for American Lutherans to reflect on the effects of *Pax Americana* in the Middle East as part of its engagement with Islam, which must reflect the reality of *power* and *politics*, and not only *piety*.

In an era of *Pax Americana* in the Middle East, perhaps the American Lutheran church can utilize its own resources, both in terms of relationships with indigenous Middle Eastern institutions and its own specially trained personnel, to have the Middle Eastern church "accompany" it for the sake of "peace in God's world." If, in the words of Mark Thomsen, we are to be followers of this "suffering-with-us" God, then the choice is clear. Engagement is crucial, especially in areas where Muslims have misheard the gospel of the crucified Christ, either because of previous or current Western Christian association with the political and military powers of the world. In the post-9/11 world, where the centers of power have espoused or utilized Christian images and language for the sake of

---

26. The issue of women in Islam is particularly interesting here. Quite often, many new church workers or visitors to the Middle East are surprised to find out that many of the issues of gender are just as prominent among the Christian communities as they are among the Muslim communities.

27. Cooperman, "New York Lutheran Leader Suspended."

28. See Francisco, *Martin Luther and Islam* and "Luther, Lutheranism."

power (even the utilization of power for "self defense"), it is imperative that the church dialogue with Muslims who have misheard the Christian witness to the God of Jesus Christ through the language of "Crusade" rather than "crucifixion."

Perhaps in this context we could utilize the gifts of the indigenous Middle Eastern churches to help the American church address questions within our own context. Rather than participating in neo-imperialism, such an initiative could prove to be another possible model of "accompaniment"; where the indigenous Middle Eastern church can "accompany" the Western church in its engagement with Islam. Europeans and Americans are in need of understanding the complex social-political issues of the Middle East that have contributed to discontent among Arab Islamic radicals and, more importantly, have created sympathy among average Muslims in the Middle East, who have called for some kind of change in the international social-political order. This issue is now more important than ever. The 2003 invasion of Iraq has placed the U.S. in a new frame of reference for Middle Easterners—especially Middle Eastern Muslims—who see "Amrika" as an imperial force. The image is certainly much more than simple rhetoric or propaganda from Bin Laden. It is an accepted paradigm by many.

To ask the indigenous Middle Eastern church to "accompany" the American church on its path to engage in "conversation with Islam" in the Middle East—that we might be able to address our own concerns related to the "War on Terror," U.S. occupation of Iraq and Afghanistan, immigration, pluralism, and inter-faith dialogue—would be a healthy step in living out two sides of the relationship of "accompaniment." There are important questions, however, concerning how to balance the needs of both American and Arab Lutheran churches without losing the critical edge of advocacy, peace, and justice, as well as the focus on inter-faith relationships. In addition, there will be the need to balance the American Christian-Muslim dialogue with the Christian-Muslim dialogue in the Middle East. Lastly, there is always the issue of Jewish-Lutheran dialogue *vis-à-vis* the social-political issues of Palestinian Lutheran justice. This is indeed a difficult balancing act, but one that must be undertaken. As an American church in the current age of empire, it is our responsibility.

Perhaps the opportunity for harvesting Thomsen's visions is now at hand. Luther Seminary's Islamic studies program (established in 1994) has been a major accomplishment, providing an avenue for seminary students and lay leaders to engage in academic encounter with Islam. Graduates of the center have gone on to serve in congregations and communities and to provide models for dialogical ministry with Muslim communities around the world. The Center of Christian-Muslim Engagement for Peace and Justice of the Lutheran School of Theology at Chicago, opened in 2006, will hopefully play a vital role in the continued expression of "conversation with Islam." This center will have the opportunity to tap the resources of the work that was developed by the individuals who in the 1980s and 90s helped to birth "conversation with Islam" in the Middle East. In addition, in September 2007 the ELCA Ecumenical and Inter-Religious Relations released online a helpful resource for congregations, entitled "Windows for Understanding: Jewish-Muslim-Lutheran Relations."[29] This primer should prove to be a very helpful tool in helping American Lutherans to begin to wade through the issues of pluralism in North American, and faith and politics in the Middle East. The question will be how these North American resources can be applied not only in local relationships, but also in international relationships—the driving concern of this narrative. Lastly, in October 2007 the presiding bishop of the ELCA, Mark Hanson, made a public response to Muslim leaders around the world who had sent out a general letter entitled "A Common Word." The Muslim epistle was intended to engage church leaders in a genuine dialogue. Hanson's favorable response and creation of a task force to formally respond to the topic will provide a great opportunity to open doors toward further American Lutheran-Middle Eastern Muslim dialogue.[30]

Lutherans have always been very intent on driving to the important theological heart of social-political issues, in order to ask the tough theological questions over what is really at stake in any particular issue. Social advocacy concerns have been and continue to be a very important part of the Lutheran vision and work in the Middle East. The development and relief work of LWF/LWR has continued to provide vital assistance to people in Palestine, Lebanon, Iraq, Afghanistan, and the Sudan. Yet, in regard to the Middle East there is a vital need to address missiological issues within the larger context of contemporary movements in Islam, the "War on Terror," and especially the consequences of the American

29. Trice and LaHurd, "Windows for Understanding."

30. ELCA News Service, "ELCA Presiding Bishop Responds." See also the Web site of A Common Word, which contains both the official letter and responses: http://www.acommonword.com/.

invasion of Iraq in 2003. Perhaps we are driven by our atavistic memory, which has labeled the Muslim as the "Terrible Turk," or by the fear of association with Luther's anti-Semitic tract, or even by the anxiety of being labeled "un-American." If Lutherans remind themselves of their Lutheran heritage in relation to the Middle East and Islam, and utilize the experience of their denominations since 1969, they might be able to forge new responses to Islam for our own contemporary American circumstances and provide a broader voice not only for American society, but for international reflection as well. With American society still feeling anxiety from 9/11, caught up in the "War on Terror," committed to military engagement in Afghanistan and Iraq, and involved in the issues of the Israeli-occupied territories, the opportunities for American Lutherans to engage in conversation with Muslims in the Middle East not only from "across the borders" but "along the borders" are now abundant and necessary. We cannot erase the borders, which are social-political as well as theological, but perhaps we can step a bit closer to the edge to speak "along with," as opposed to "across from," one another. In the Middle East where *power* and *politics* are just as real as *piety*, such a move is vital to the witness of the gospel.

Appendix

American Lutheran Personnel in the Middle East (1950–2003)

Throughout the history of Lutheran Missions in the Middle East there have been many individuals who have been part of the missionary endeavor. This list records only those individuals who have been formally under contract or call by a Lutheran church mission board (LCMS/LCA/ALC or ELCA) during the period from 1950 to 2003. It does not include the many volunteers who have served in a variety of capacities. (This information has been taken from previous records, including annual denominational yearbooks. The dates correspond to the dates of call or service under the denomination, and not necessarily the dates of service in the specified country.) This record is not intended to uphold the traditional stereotype that it has only been Western missionaries who have brought the true evangelical gospel to the people of the Middle East. Rather, it is merely to recognize those individuals and families who have received a call from their particular denominations and left their own cultures and countries to serve abroad.

The first section lists long-term personnel by geographic area served, years served, sending denomination, ministry function, and receiving institution (if any). The second section lists area program directors by the denomination under which they served, indicating the years each served in such capacity. The final section lists interns grouped by geographic area served, giving their respective years served and sending denominations.

LONG-TERM PERSONNEL

Beirut

- Carl Agerstrand (1950–63), LCMS, evangelism, pastoral ministry, MELM
- Edward Azzam (1961–63), LCMS, pastoral ministry, MELM
- Walter Boss (1961–63), LCMS, pastoral ministry, MELM
- Denis and Ellen Hilgendorf (1962–79), LCMS, evangelism, MELM; (1979–89), AELC, social work, CRC
- John and Kathryn Stelling (1965–79), LCMS, evangelism, MELM
- Austra Reinis (2002–4), ELCA, education, NEST
- Tom Scudder (1999–2005), ELCA/RCA, communication, MECC*

Cyprus

- Johnathan and Marian Frerichs (1991–93), ELCA, communication, MECC
- Lew and Nancy Scudder (1994–2004), ELCA/RCA, communication, ecumenism, MECC*

Jerusalem/West Bank

- Lydia Reich (1953–55), ULCA, nurse, Augusta Victoria Hospital
- Bruce Schein (1968–81), LCA, coordinator, education, Jerusalem
- Dale Truscott (1970–71), LCA, pastoral ministry, Redeemer Lutheran, Jerusalem
- Charles and Karla Moline (1971–77), LCA, pastoral ministry, Redeemer Lutheran, Jerusalem
- Evelyn Guss (1972–74), LCA, education, Birzeit University, West Bank
- Al and Lois Glock (1976–92), LCA, education, Birzeit University, West Bank
- Nancy Hill (1974–76), LCA, West Bank

* Served with the RCA-AM and seconded to the ELCA.

Appendix 259

- John and Pamela Lundblad (1977–84), LCA, pastoral ministry, Redeemer Lutheran, Jerusalem
- Peter and Kathy Kapenga (1976–2002), LCA, education, Friends School, West Bank
- Mark and Susanne Brown (1982–91), ALC/ELCA, education, MECC; pastoral ministry, ELCJ/HL, Jerusalem; (2004–current), ELCA, administration, LWF
- David and Mary Ann Johnson (1989–97), ELCA, administration, LWF, Jerusalem
- Tillman and Marsha Bergmann (1984–93), LCA, pastoral ministry, Redeemer Lutheran, Jerusalem
- John and Barbara Melin (1994–97), ELCA, pastoral ministry, Redeemer Lutheran, Jerusalem
- Susan and Michael Thomas (1998–2002), ELCA, pastoral ministry, Redeemer Lutheran, Jerusalem
- Mary Jensen (2002–4), ELCA, communication, ELCJ/HL, Jerusalem
- Russ and Anne Siler (2002–6), ELCA, pastoral ministry, Redeemer Lutheran, Jerusalem
- Andy Willis (2003–5), ELCA, education, ELCJ/HL, West Bank

Cairo

- Harold and Neva Vogelaar (1972–88), LCA/RCA*, pastoral ministry, education, ETSC, RCG, AUC; (1985–86), LCA/RCA*, pastoral ministry, International Cong. Bahrain
- David and Mary Ann Johnson (1978–82), LCA, pastoral ministry, MCC/St. Andrew's
- Paul and Lrna Bhai (1979–82), LCA/RCA, evangelism, CMS
- Michael and Joanne Shelley (1979–2003), ALC/ELCA, pastoral care, HCC/St. Andrew's; education, ETSC
- Timothy Matyi (1979–82), LCA, education, Institute of Coptic Studies

- Mark and Rosanne Swanson (1984–98), LCA, education, ETSC; pastoral ministry, St. Andrew's
- Oscar and Shirley Kraft (1982–86), ALC, pastor, HCC
- Joseph and Martha Rittman (1982–84), LCA, education, Institute of Coptic Studies
- Ken and Charlene Johnson (1983–86), LCA, pastor, St. Andrew's
- Peter and Kathy Kapenga (1983–84), LCA, education, Institute of Coptic Studies
- Neal and Anette Stixrud (1987–89), LCA, ecumenism, Coptic Orthodox Church
- Heather Brown (1992–94), ELCA, social work, St. Andrew's
- Peter and Shannon Vogelaar (1998–2001), ELCA/RCA, social work, St. Andrew's
- David and Karla Grafton (1999–2006), ELCA, Inter, pastor, St. Andrew's; education, ETSC
- Dick and Lynn Alhusen (2001–7), ELCA/RCA, social work, pastor, St. Andrew's
- Mark Nelson and Marcie Horner (2003–5), ELCA, pastor, St. Andrew's

MIDDLE EAST AREA PROGRAM DIRECTORS
(during periods investigated in this work)

LCMS
- Bill Reinking (1966–74)
- Otto Heintz (1974–77)
- Allan Buckman (1977–90)
- Roger Roegner (1990–95)

LCA
- Fred Neudoerffer (1969–84)
- Warner Luoma (1984–87)

ALC

- John Westby (1972–79)
- David Nelson (1979–87)

ELCA

- Carol Birkland (1988–91)
- David Nelson (1992–97)
- Said Ailabouni (1998–2006)

INTERNS

Jerusalem

- Craig Koester (1978–79), LCA
- Barbara Rasmussen (1983–84), LCA
- Mary Jensen (1986–87), ALC
- Daniel Whitener (1986–87), LCA
- Dale Sylte-Wilson (1988), LCA
- John Calhoun (1993–94), ELCA
- Beth Maeker (1995–96), ELCA
- Amy Jo Mathias (1996), ELCA
- Heather Matthias (1998–99), ELCA

Cairo

- Mike Shelley (1976–77), ALC
- Dean Bard (1978–79), LCA
- G. Stanley Steele (1979–80), LCA
- Mark Swanson (1979–80), LCA
- Mark Brown (1980–81), ALC
- Thomas Johnson (1981–82), LCA
- Rosanne Swanson (1982–83), LCA

- Paul Harder (1989–90), ELCA
- Kevin Massey (1990–91), ELCA
- David Grafton (1991–92), ELCA
- Douglas Cox (1992–93), ELCA
- Janine Mathison (1993–94), ELCA
- Christian Holleck (1994–95), ELCA
- Elyse Nelson Winger (2000–2001), ELCA
- Philip Martin (2001–2), ELCA

Credits

Matthias Gerung Woodcut, "Turks Slaughtering Christians: The Pope Pursuing the Poor," (1548). Walter L. Strauss, *The German Single-Leaf Woodcut 1550–1600,* vols. 1–3 (New York: Abaris Books, 1975), v. 1, 305.

Lutheran Orient Mission Staff, Arbil, Iraq, 1950. C.C.A. Jensen and Einar J. Oberg, *The Messengers of God: The Mission to Kurdistan and Neighboring Areas.* Lutheran Orient Mission Society, 1950, p. 87.

Lutheran Church-Missouri Synod Personnel, Beirut, Lebanon, 1973. Dennis Hilgendorf and John Stelling, *People Who Need People*, Beirut, Lebanon, 1973, p. 33.

Bruce Schein. American Lutheran Church—Lutheran Church in America Personnel, Larnaca, Cyprus, 1982 and 1992. Picture in possession of author used by permission from photographer David Johnson.

Harold Vogelaar and Mark Swanson. American Lutheran Church—Lutheran Church in America Personnel, Larnaca, Cyprus, 1982 and 1992. Picture in possession of author used by permission from photographer David Johnson.

ELCA personnel, Larnaca, Cyprus, 1992. Picture in possession of author, used by permission of author.

Bibliography

LUTHER'S WRITINGS ON ISLAM

D. Martin Luthers Werke. Kritische Gesamtausgabe. Vols. 2, 30, 51. Weimar: H. Böhlau. 1883–2001. Online: http://fig.lib.harvard.edu/fig/?bib=000182121. [*WA*]

Luther's Works. Vols. 22, 31, 32, 34, 43, 46, 48, 49, 54. St. Louis: Concordia Pub. House; Philadelphia: Fortress, 1955–1986. [*LW*]

Appeal for Prayer against the Turk (1541). LW 43: 211–41 German: *Vermahung zum Gebet wider den Türken,* WA 51:585–625.

Explanation of the Ninety-Five Theses (1518). LW 31:76–251.

Heerpredigt wider den Türken [Army sermon against the Turk] (1529). WA 30/2:160–97.

Libellus de ritu et moribus Turcorum [Tract on religion and customs of the Turks] (1530). WA 30/2: 205–8. English translation in Sarah Heinrich and James Boyce, "Martin Luther—Translations of Two Prefaces on Islam: *Preface to the* Libellus de ritu et moribus Turcorum (1530), and *Preface to Bibliander's Edition of the Qur'ān* (1543)," WW 16 (1996) 250–66.

Martini Lutheri Doctoris Theologie et Ecclesiastis ecclesiae Wittenbergensis in ALCORANUM Praefatior [Preface to Bibliander's translation of the Qur'ān] (1543). WA 53:569–72. English translation in Heinrich and Boyce.

Verlegung des Alcoran Bruder Richardi, Prediger Ordens [Preface and translation of *Confutatio Alcorani seu legis Saracenorum*] (1542). WA 53:272–396.

On War against the Turk (1529). LW 46: 161–204. German: *Vom Kriege wider die Türken,* WA 30/2:107–48.

ARCHIVES

Board for World Mission (1962–72) and Division for World Mission and Ecumenism (1972–87) of the Lutheran Church in America. ELCA Archives: 16/1/1; 28/1/1/1; 28/12/3. ELCA Headquarters, Elk Grove Village, IL. Online: http://www.elca.org/Who-We-Are/History/ELCA-Archives.aspx.

Board for World Missions (1960–72) and Division for World Mission and Inter-Church Cooperation of the American Lutheran Church (1973–87). ELCA Archives: TALC 14/1; 16/1/1/1; 16/6/4/1. ELCA Headquarters, Elk Grove Village, IL. Online: http://www.elca.org/Who-We-Are/History/ELCA-Archives.aspx.

Division for Global Mission (1988–2003) of the Evangelical Lutheran Church in America. ELCA Archives: 24/16/1. ELCA Headquarters, Elk Grove Village, IL. Online: http://www.elca.org/Who-We-Are/History/ELCA-Archives.aspx.

Evangelical Lutheran Society of Inquiry on Missions archives. Wentz Library, Lutheran Theological Seminary at Gettysburg, Gettysburg, PA.

Middle East Lutheran Ministry (1959-79), Board for World Mission of The Lutheran Church—Missouri Synod (1962-92). Department of Archives and History: 3.137.9. Concordia Historical Institute, St. Louis, MO. Online: http://chi.lcms.org/.

YEARBOOKS

Statistical Yearbook of the Lutheran Church—Missouri Synod (1922-92). St. Louis, MO: Concordia Pub. House, [1922-92].

Yearbook, Evangelical Lutheran Church in America (1988-2003). Minneapolis: Pub. House of the ELCA, 1988-2003.

Yearbook, Lutheran Church in America (1962-84). Philadelphia: Board of Pub. of the LCA, 1962-84.

Year Book of the American Lutheran Church (1961-87). Minneapolis: Augsburg Pub. House, 1961-87.

UNPUBLISHED REPORTS

Azzam, Edward, and Walter Boss. "Middle East Mission Survey." LCMS Board for World Mission, Beirut, 1962.

———. "A Manual for the Middle East Interfaith Mission Program." LCMS Board for World Mission, Beirut, 1963.

ELCA Division for Global Mission. "Global Mission in the Twenty-First Century." DGM strategic planning document, 2000.

Hilgendorf, Dennis. "The Middle East." Study paper prepared for the mission conference of the LCA Division of Mission Services, March 24-27, 1969.

Jahshan, Moris A. "History and Background about the Middle East Lutheran Ministry." 1970.

———. "Middle East Lutheran Ministry Mission Strategy." MELM report to the LCMS Board for World Mission, 1992.

Miller, Roland E. "Planning Proposal for a Focus on Islam." ELCA Division for Global Mission, Chicago, 1991.

Schein, Bruce. "The Middle East." LCA report, 1969. LCA archives, 16/1/1.

Shelley, Michael T. "Beginnings of Protestant Missionary Activity in the Near East." Unpublished paper, n.d.

Swanson, Mark N. "Area History: American Lutheran Mission Work in Egypt, 1970-1986." Unpublished paper, 1987.

Thomsen, Mark, editor. "God and Jesus: Theological Reflections for Christian-Muslim Dialog." ALC Division for World Mission and Interchurch Cooperation, Minneapolis, 1986.

ARTICLES AND BOOKS

Abū 'Amr, Ziyād. *Islamic Fundamentalism in the West Bank and Gaza: Muslim Brotherhood and Islamic Jihad*. Indiana Series in Arab and Islamic Studies. Bloomington: Indiana University Press, 1994.

Abu-Ghazaleh, Adnan. *American Missions in Syria: A Study of American Missionary Contributions to Arab Nationalism in 19th Century Syria*. Brattleboro, VT: Amana, 1990.

Abu-Rabi', Ibrahim M. *Contemporary Arab Thought: Studies in Post-1967 Arab Intellectual History*. Sterling, VA: Pluto, 2004.

———. *Intellectual Origins of Islamic Resurgence in the Modern Arab World*. SUNY Series in Near Eastern Studies. Albany: State University of New York Press, 1996.

Ajami, Fouad. *The Arab Predicament: Arab Political Thought and Practice Since 1967*. New York: Cambridge University Press, 1992.

———. *The Dream Palace of the Arabs*. New York: Vintage Books, 1999.

Alexander, Archibald. *A Brief Outline of the Evidences of the Christian Religion*. Princeton, NJ: Borrenstein, 1825.

Alighieri, Dante. *The Inferno of Dante: A New Verse Translation*. Translated by Robert Pinsky. New York: Farrar, Straus, and Giroux, 1994.

Allison, Robert J. *The Crescent Obscured: The United States and the Muslim World, 1776–1815*. New York: Oxford University Press, 1995.

Anderson, Rufus. *History of the Missions of the American Board of Commissioners for Foreign Missions*. Boston: Congregational Pub. Society, 1875.

Ansārī, Masūd. *Psychology of Mohammed: Inside the Brain of a Prophet*. Washington, DC: Mas-Press, 2007.

Antonius, George. *The Arab Awakening: The Story of the Arab National Movement*. New York: Capricorn, 1946.

Aquinas, Thomas. *Summa Contra Gentiles*. Notre Dame: University of Notre Dame Press, 1975.

Armstrong, Karen. *Holy War: The Crusades and Their Impact on Today's World*. New York: Anchor, 2001.

Austin, Allan D. *African Muslims in Antebellum America: Transatlantic Stories and Spiritual Struggles*. New York: Garland, 1997.

Ayoub, Mahmoud. *A Muslim View of Christianity: Essays on Dialogue*. Edited by Irfan A. Omar. Maryknoll, NY: Orbis, 2007.

Badr, Habib. "American Protestant Beginnings in the Middle East (1820–1865)." *Theological Review* 14 (1993) 63–86.

———. "The Protestant Evangelical Community in the Middle East: Impact on Cultural and Societal Developments." *International Review of Mission* 89 (2000) 60–69.

Bainton, Roland Herbert. *Here I Stand: A Life of Martin Luther*. Nashville: Abingdon, 1978.

Balakian, Peter. *The Burning Tigris: The Armenian Genocide and America's Response*. New York: HarperCollins, 2003.

Barber, Benjamin R. *Jihad vs. McWorld*. New York: Ballantine, 1996.

Barton, James. *Turkish Atrocities: Statements of American Missionaries on the Destruction of Christian Communities in Ottoman Turkey, 1915–1917*. Ann Arbor, MI: Gomidas Institute, 1998.

Bell, Richard. *The Origin of Islam in Its Christian Environment: The Gunning Lectures*. London: Macmillian, 1926.

Bengio, Ofra and Gabriel Ben-Dor, editors. *Minorities and the State in the Arab World*. Boulder, CO: Rienner, 1990.

Benigni, Umberto. "Sacred Congregation of Propaganda." In *The Catholic Encyclopedia*, vol. 12. New York: Appleton, 1911. Online: http://www.newadvent.org/cathen/12456a.htm (July 12, 2008).

Bennett, Clinton. "The Legacy of Karl Gottlieb Pfander." *International Bulletin of Missionary Research* 20 (1996) 76–81.

Bibliander, Theodore. *Machumetis Sarracenorum principis vita ac doctrina omnis, quam & Ishmahelitarum lex, & Alcoranum dicitur.* Basel: J. Oporinus, 1543.

Boden, Jan. "Following Jesus: Harold Vogealaar's Faithful Journey." *The Epistle*, Winter 2006, 9–11.

———. "Learning from One Another." *The Epistle*, Summer 2006, 4–5.

———. "Mark Swanson Joins LSTC Faculty." *The Epistle*, Summer 2006, 2–3.

Bohnstedt, John W. *The Infidel Scourge of God: The Turkish Menace as Seen by German Pamphleteers of the Reformation Era.* Transactions of the American Philosophical Society, n.s., 58/9. Philadelphia: American Philosophical Society, 1968.

Bonner, Anthony, editor and translator. *Doctor Illuminatus: A Ramón Llull Reader.* Princeton: Princeton University Press, 1994.

Bosch, David J. *Transforming Mission: Paradigm Shifts in Theology of Mission.* American Society of Missiology 16. Maryknoll, NY: Orbis, 1999.

Braaten, Carl E. *The Apostolic Imperative: Nature and Aim of the Church's Mission and Ministry.* Minneapolis: Augsburg, 1985.

———. *The Flaming Center: A Theology of the Christian Mission.* Philadelphia: Fortress, 1977.

———. *Principles of Lutheran Theology.* Minneapolis: Augsburg, 1983.

Brands, H. W. *Into the Labyrinth: The United States and the Middle East 1945–1993.* New York: McGraw-Hill, 1993.

Burgess, Andrew S. *In the Land of Pagodas, Temples and Mosques.* Minneapolis: Augsburg, 1945.

———, editor. *Lutheran Churches in the Third World.* Minneapolis: Augsburg, 1970.

———, editor. *Lutheran World Missions: Foreign Missions of the Lutheran Church in America.* Minneapolis: Augsburg, 1954.

Burigny, M. de. *The Life of the Truly Eminent and Learned Hugo Grotius.* London: A. Millar, 1754.

Carmel, Alex. "C. F. Spittler and the Activities of the Pilgrims Mission in Jerusalem." In *Ottoman Palestine 1800–1914: Studies in Economic and Social History*, edited by Gad G. Gilbar, 256–84. Leiden: Brill, 1990.

———. "The German Settlers in Palestine and Their Relations with the Local Arab Population and the Jewish Community, 1868–1918." In *Studies on Palestine During the Ottoman Period*, edited by Moshe Ma'oz, 442–65. Jerusalem: Magnes, 1975.

———. "A Note on the Christian Contribution to Palestine's Development in the 19th Century." In *Palestine in the Late Ottoman Period: Political, Social, and Economic Transformation*, edited by David Kushner, 302–8. Leiden: Brill, 1986.

———. "The Political Significance of German Settlement in Palestine: 1868–1918." In *Germany and the Middle East, 1835–1939: International Symposium, April 1975*, edited by Jehuda L. Wallach, 45–71. Jahrbuch des Instituts f[umlaut over u]ür Deutsche Geschichte 1. Tel Aviv: Tel Aviv University, 1975.

Challenging Christian Zionism. "Churches Speak Out on Christian Zionism and Left Behind Theology." Online: http://www.christianzionism.org/churchesN.asp (February 15, 2009).

Chapman, Colin Gilbert. *Whose Promised Land?: The Continuing Crisis over Israel and Palestine*. Grand Rapids: Baker, 2002.

Choi, David. "Martin Luther's Response to the Turkish Threat: Continuity and Contrast with the Medieval Commentators Riccoldo da Monte Croce and Nicholas of Cusa." Ph.D. diss., Princeton Theological Seminary, 2003.

Choueiri, Youssef M. *Arab Nationalism—A History: Nation and State in the Arab World*. Malden, MA: Blackwell, 2000.

———. *Islamic Fundamentalism*. Washington, DC: Pinter, 1997.

Christensen, Jens. *The Practical Approach to Muslims*. Blackwood, Aus.: New Creation, 2001.

Christensen, Torben, and William R. Hutchison, editors. *Missionary Ideologies in the Imperialist Era, 1880-1920: Papers from the Durham Consultation, 1981*. Denmark: Christensens Bogtrykkeri, 1982.

Churchill, Charles H. *The Druzes and Maronites under the Turkish Rule from 1840 to 1860*. Middle East Collection. New York: Arno, 1973.

Cocchia, Rocco da Cesinale. *Storia delle missioni dei Cappuccini*. Vol. 3. Paris: P. Lethielleux, 1867-73.

Colbi, S. P. *A History of the Christian Presence in the Holy Land*. London: University Press of America, 1988.

Coles, Paul. *The Ottoman Impact on Europe*. London: Thames & Hudson, 1968.

Cooperman, Alan. "New York Lutheran Leader Suspended: Synod Seeks Pastor's Apology for Praying with 'Pagans' after Sept. 11 Attacks." *Washington Post*, July 6, 2002.

Courbage, Youssef, and Philippe Fargues. *Christians and Jews under Islam*. Translated by Judy Mabro. London: Tauris, 1997.

Cracknell, Kenneth. *Justice, Courtesy and Love: Theologians and Missionaries Encountering World Religions, 1846-1914*. London: Epworth, 1995.

Cragg, Kenneth. *The Arab Christian: A History in the Middle East*. Louisville: Westminster John Knox, 1991.

———. "Being Made Disciples—The Middle East." In *The Church Mission Society and World Christianity, 1799-1999*, edited by Kevin Ward and Brian Stanley, 120-43. Studies in the History of Christian Missions. Grand Rapids: Eerdmans, 2000.

———. *Muhammad and the Christian: A Question of Response*. Oxford: OneWorld, 1999.

Curtis, Edward E. *Islam in Black America: Identity, Liberation, and Difference in African-American Islamic Thought*. Albany: State University of New York Press, 2002.

Cutler, A. "The 9th Century Spanish Martyrs' Movement and the Origins of Western Christian Missions to the Muslims." *Muslim World* 55 (1965) 321-39.

Daniel, Norman. *Islam and the West: The Making of an Image*. Oxford: OneWorld, 2000.

Davis, Moshe, editor. *Holy Land Missions and Missionaries*. America and the Holy Land. New York: Arno, 1977.

Davison, Roderic H. *Reform in the Ottoman Empire, 1856-76*. Princeton: Princeton University Press, 1963.

Dawson, William Harbutt. *The German Empire, 1867-1914, and the Unity Movement*. Vol. 2. Hamden, CT: Archon, 1966.

DeBurigny, M. *The Life of the Truly Eminent and Learned Hugo Grotius*. London: A. Millar, 1754.

DeNovo, John A. *American Interests and Policies in the Middle East, 1900-1939*. Minneapolis, University of Minnesota Press, 1963.

Detole, Teodosio Somigli di S. *Etiopia Francescana*. Vol. 1. Florence: Quaracchi, 1928.
Diouf, Sylviane. *Servants of Allah: African Muslims Enslaved in the Americas*. New York: New York University Press, 1998.
Doorn-Harder, Pieternella van. *Women Shaping Islam: Indonesian Women Reading the Qur'an*. Urbana: University of Illinois Press, 2006.
D'Souza, Andreas. "Christian Approaches to the Study of Islam: An Analysis of the Writings of Watt and Cragg." *Bulletin of the Henry Martyn Institute of Islamic Studies* 11 (July–December, 1992) 33–80.
D'Souza, Diane. "Evangelism, Dialogue, Reconciliation: A Case Study of the Growth and Transformation of the Henry Martyn Institute." *Muslim World* 91 (2001) 155–84.
Durant, Will. *The Reformation: A History of European Civilization from Wyclif to Calvin, 1300–1564*. The Story of Civilization 6. New York: Simon & Schuster, 1957.
"Egypt." In *World Christian Encyclopedia*, edited by David B. Barrett, 1:250. 2nd ed. New York: Oxford University Press, 2001.
"Egypt." In *The World Factbook*. Washington, DC: CIA, 1981–. Online: https://www.cia.gov/library/publications/the-world-factbook/geos/eg.html.
Eichelberger, Lewis. "By What Arguments Can We Best Convince the Mohammedan of the Falsity of His Religion." Paper presented to the Society of Inquiry on Missions, Lutheran Theological Seminary at Gettysburg, 1827. Gettysburg Theological Seminary archives, box 1, folder 4.
———. *Two Sermons on National Blessings and Obligations*. Winchester: Samuel H. Davis, 1830.
Eklund, Emmet E. *Peter Fjellstedt: Missionary Mentor to Three Continents*. Studia Missionalia Upsaliensia 36. Rock Island, IL: Augustana Historical Society, 1983.
El-Cheikh, Nadia Marie. *Byzantium Viewed by the Arabs*. Harvard Middle Eastern Monographs 36. Cambridge: Harvard University Press, 2004.
Elder, E. E. *Vindicating a Vision: The Story of the American Mission in Egypt, 1854–1954*. Philadelphia: Board of Foreign Missions of the United Presbyterian Church of North America, 1958.
Elder, John. *History of the American Presbyterian Mission to Iran: 1834–1960*. N.p.: Literature Committee of the Church Council of Iran, 1960.
Elian, Mordechai. "German Interests and the Jewish Community in Nineteenth Century Palestine." In *Studies on Palestine During the Ottoman Period*, edited by Moshe Ma'oz, 423–41. Jerusalem: Magnes, 1975.
Elmusa, Sharif S., and Muḥammad 'Alī Khālidī. *All That Remains: The Palestinian Villages Occupied and Depopulated by Israel in 1948*. Edited by Walid Khālidī. Washington, DC: Institute for Palestine Studies, 1992.
Erikson, Erik H. *Young Man Luther: A Study in Psychoanalysis and History*. London: Faber, 1958.
Ernst, Carl W. *Following Muhammad: Rethinking Islam in the Contemporary World*. Chapel Hill: University of North Carolina Press, 2003.
Esposito, John L., editor. *The Islamic World: Past and Present*. 3 vols. New York: Oxford University Press, 2004.
ELCA. "Churchwide Strategy for Engagement in Israel and Palestine." ELCA pre-assembly report, 2005. Online: http://www.elca.org/~/media/Files/Our%20Faith%20in%20Action/Justice/Peace%20Not%20Walls/StrategyFull.ashx (July 12, 2008).

———. "Declaration of the Evangelical Lutheran Church in America to the Jewish Community." ELCA Church Council statement, April 18, 1994. Online: http://archive.elca.org/ecumenical/interreligious/jewish/declaration.html (July 12, 2008).

———. "Guidelines for Lutheran-Jewish Relations." Draft adopted by the ELCA Church Council, November 16, 1998. Online: http://archive.elca.org/ecumenical/interreligious/jewish/guidelines.html (July 12, 2008).

ELCA News Service. "ELCA Council Moves Ethnic-Ministry Strategies Forward." News release, April 14, 2005. Online: http://www.wfn.org/2005/04/msg00155.html (July 12, 2008).

———. "ELCA Presiding Bishop Responds to Letter from Muslim Leaders." News release, October 12, 2007. Online: http://archive.elca.org/ScriptLib/CO/ELCA_News/encArticleList.asp?article=3749 (July 12, 2008).

———. "Israeli Troops Reoccupy Bethlehem Lutheran School." News release, March 11, 2002. Online: http://www.wfn.org/2002/03/msg00087.html (July 12, 2008).

———. "Israeli Soldiers Release Lutheran Pastor in Bethlehem." News release, April 4, 2002. Online: http://www.wfn.org/2002/04/msg00072.html (July 12, 2008).

Evans, Richard J. *The Coming of the Third Reich*. New York: Penguin, 2004.

Farah, Caesar E. "Protestantism and Politics: The 19th Century Dimension in Syria." In *Palestine in the Late Ottoman Period: Political, Social, and Economic Transformation*, edited by David Kushner, 320–40. Leiden: Brill, 1986.

Fargues, Philippe. "The Arab Christians of the Middle East: A Demographic Perspective." In *Christian Communities in the Arab Middle East: The Challenge of the Future*, edited by Andrea Pacini, 49–56. New York: Clarendon, 1998.

Fawaz, Leila Tarazi. *An Occasion for War: Civil Conflict in Lebanon and Damascus in 1860*. London: Tauris, 1994.

Feuerhan, Ronald. "The Roots and Fruits of German Pietism." In *Pietism and Lutheranism*, edited by John A. Maxfield, 50–74. The Pieper Lectures 3. St. Louis: Concordia Historical Institute, 1999.

Fischer-Galati, Stephen A. *Ottoman Imperialism and German Protestantism, 1521–1555*. Harvard Historical Monographs 43. Cambridge, Harvard University Press, 1959.

———. "Ottoman Imperialism and the Lutheran Struggle for Recognition in Germany, 1520–1529." *CH* 23 (1954) 46–67.

———. "The Turkish Question and the Religious Peace of Augsburg." *Sudost-Forschungen* 15 (1956) n.p.

Forell, George W. "Luther and the War against the Turks." *Church History* 14 (1945) 256–71.

Fossum, L. O. "Lutheran Evangelization Work in Persia and Kurdistan." Paper presented at the Second General Inter-Synodical Evangelical Lutheran Orient Mission Conference, Berwyn, IL, 1910.

Fox, Edward. *Palestine Twilight: The Murder of Dr Albert Glock and the Archaeology of the Holy Land*. London: HarperCollins, 2001.

———. *Sacred Geography: A Tale of Murder and Archeology in the Holy Land*. New York: Metropolitan, 2001.

Francisco, Adam S. "Luther, Lutheranism, and the Challenge of Islam." Paper prepared for the Concordia Theological Symposia, Fort Wayne, IN, 2007. Online: http://www.ctsfw.edu/events/symposia/papers/sym2007francisco.pdf (July 12, 2008).

———. *Martin Luther and Islam: A Study in Sixteenth-Century Polemics and Apologetics*. History of Christian-Muslim Relations 8. Leiden: Brill, 2007.

Frazee, Charles A. *Catholics and Sultans: The Church and the Ottoman Empire, 1453–1923.* London: Cambridge University Press, 1983.

Friedenthal, Richard. *Luther: His Life and Times.* Translated by John Nowell. New York: Harcourt Brace Jovanovich, 1970.

Friedmann, Yohanan. *Tolerance and Coercion in Islam: Interfaith Relations in the Muslim Tradition.* Cambridge Studies in Islamic Civilization. Cambridge: Cambridge University Press, 2003.

Friesen, LeRoy. *Mennonite Witness in the Middle East: A Missiological Introduction.* Elkhart, IN: Mennonite Board of Missions, 2000.

Fromkin, David. *A Peace to End All Peace: Creating the Modern Middle East, 1914–1922.* New York: Holt, 1989.

Fry, George C. "Islam in Review." *Lutheran Theological Journal* 15 (1981) 142–44.

Gairdner, W. H. T. *The Reproach of Islam.* London: Young People's Missionary Movement, 1909.

Gall, John D. "Allah." *The Minaret* 5, no. 2 (1949) 8.

Gaudeul, Jean-Marie. *Encounters and Clashes: Islam and Christianity in History.* Vols. 1, 2. Rome: PISAI, 2001.

Gensichen, Hans-Werner. "German Protestant Missions." In *Missionary Ideologies in the Imperialist Era, 1880–1920: Papers from the Durham Consultation, 1981,* edited by Torben Christensen and William R. Hutchison, 181–90. Denmark: Christensens Bogtrykkeri, 1982.

Gibbon, Edward. *The Decline and Fall of the Roman Empire.* New York: Random House, 2003.

Gidney, W. T. *The History of the London Society for the Promoting Christianity Amongst the Jews from 1809 to 1908.* London: LSPCAJ, 1908.

Glock, Albert. "Archaeology as Cultural Survival: The Future of the Palestinian Past." In Kapitan, Tomis. *Archaeology, History, and Culture in Palestine and the Near East: Essays in Memory of Albert E. Glock.* ASOR Books 3. New York: Scholars, 1999.

Gobat, Samuel. *Samuel Gobat Bishop of Jerusalem: His Life and Work, a Biographical Sketch.* London: Nisbet, 1884.

Gomez, Michael Angelo. *Black Crescent: The Experience and Legacy of African Muslims in the Americas.* New York: Cambridge University Press, 2005.

Goodwin, Jason. *Lords of the Horizons: A History of the Ottoman Empire.* London: Vintage, 1999.

Grafton, David D. "American Cultural Roots of Christian Zionism." Paper presented at the Fellowship of the Middle East Council of Churches, Amaan, Jordan, March 31, 2006.

———. *The Christians of Lebanon: Political Rights in Islamic Law.* London: Tauris, 2004.

———. "Is It Time for a New Mission Paradigm in the *Pax Americana*?" *Cross-Currents in Theology* 32 (2005) 348–54.

———. "A Survey of the Use of Scripture in the Current Israeli-Palestinian Conflict." *Word and World* 24 (2004) 29–39.

Grabill, Joseph L. "Missionary Influence on American Relations with the Near East, 1914–1923." *Muslim World* 58 (1968) 43–56, 141–54.

———. *Protestant Diplomacy and the Near East: Missionary Influence on American Policy, 1810–1927.* Minneapolis: University of Minnesota Press, 1971.

Grimm, Hilmar. *Centennial History of Christ Lutheran Church.* Bexley, OH: Pfeifer, 1978.

Grisilis, Egil. "Luther and the Turks." *Muslim World* 64 (1974) 180–93, 275–91.

Gritsch, Eric W. *Born-Againism: Perspectives on a Movement*. Philadelphia: Fortress, 1982.
Grotius, Hugo. *The Truth of the Christian Religion*. Edinburgh: Thomas Turnbull, 1819.
Grypeou, Emmanouela, Mark Swanson, and David Thomas, editors. *The Encounter of Eastern Christianity with Early Islam*. History of Christian-Muslim Relations 5. Leiden: Brill, 2006.
Gutzler, Michael D. *Lutheran Salzburgers and Muslim African Moors: The Earliest Evidence of Lutheran-Muslim Interaction in North America*. Berkeley: Three Trees, 2006.
Haddad, S. B. "The Lutheran Church in the Middle East." In *Lutheran Churches in the Third World*, edited by Andrew S. Burgess, 116–31. Minneapolis: Augsburg, 1970.
Ḥaddād, Yvonne Yazbeck, and Wadī Zaydān Ḥaddād, editors. *Christian-Muslim Encounters*. Gainesville: University Press of Florida, 1995.
Hafften, Ann E. "Challenge the Implications of 'Christian Zionism.'" *Journal of Lutheran Ethics*, February 2003, n.p. Online: http://archive.elca.org/ScriptLib/dcs/jle/article.asp?aid=60.
Hahn, Ernest. *How to Respond to Muslims*. St. Louis: Concordia, 1995.
Hallencreutz, Carl F. "Church-Centred Evangelism and Modernization—Emphases in Swedish Missions 1880–1920." In *Missionary Ideologies in the Imperialist Era, 1880–1920: Papers from the Durham Consultation, 1981*, edited by Torben Christensen and William R. Hutchison, 62–74. Denmark: Christensens Bogtrykkeri, 1982.
Hamilton, J. Taylor. *A History of the Missions of the Moravian Church during the Eighteenth and Nineteenth Centuries*. Bethlehem, PA: Times, 1901.
———, and Kenneth G. Hamilton. *History of the Moravian Church: The Renewed Unitas Fratrum*. Bethlehem, PA: Interprovincial Board of Christian Education, Moravian Church in America, 1967.
Hand, Matthew. "But Is it Evangelism?" *The Messenger* 92, no. 3 (2003) 2.
———. "Rev. Marvin Palmquist Inverview." *The Messenger* 92, no. 1 (2003) 2.
Hansen, Bruno Dødker. *Blandt muslimern I Kamalun*. Copenhagen: G.E.C. Gad, 1987.
Hanson, Mark S. "Letter from Presiding Bishop Mark Hanson to Jewish and Muslim Leaders." Public message, August 15, 2005. Online: https://archive.elca.org/bishop/messages/m_0508letter.html.
Ḥarūb, Khālid. *Hamas: Political Thought and Practice*. New York: Institute for Palestine Studies, 2000.
Hayes, Kevin J. "How Thomas Jefferson Read the Qur'ān." *Early American Literature* 39, no. 2 (2004) 247–61.
Herodotus. *The Histories*. Vol. 3. London: Heinemann, 1921–24.
Hess, Lawrence. "Capuchin Friars Minor." In *The Catholic Encyclopedia*, vol. 3. New York: Appleton, 1908. Online: http://www.newadvent.org/cathen/03320b.htm.
Hilgendorf, Dennis, and John Stelling. *People Who Need People*. Beirut: Middle East Lutheran Ministry, [1967].
Hischfeld, Yair. "Some Findings on Prussian and Ottoman Policies in Palestine During the 1840s Based on the Writings of Dr. Gustav E. Schultz, the First Prussian Vice-Consul to Jerusalem 1842–1851." In *Palestine in the Late Ottoman Period: Political, Social, and Economic Transformation*, edited by David Kushner, 263–79. Leiden: Brill, 1986.
Hitti, Philip Khuri. *History of the Arabs*. 10th ed. New York: Macmillan, 2002.
Hoeberichts, J. *Francis and Islam*. Qunicy, IL: Franciscan, 1997.
Hogg, Rena L. *A Master-Builder on the Nile: Being a Record of the Life and Aims of John Hogg, D. D., Christian Missionary*. New York: Revell, 1914.

Holmio, Armas K. E. *The Finnish Missionary Society, 1858–1950*. Hancock, MI: Finish Lutheran Book Concern, 1950.

The Holy Qurʾān. Transated by Abdullah Yusuf Ali. Medina: The Presidency of Islamic Researches, Ifta, Call and Guidance, 1990.

Hopwood, Derek. *The Russian Presence in Syria and Palestine, 1843–1914: Church and Politics in the Near East* Oxford: Clarendon, 1969.

Hourani, Albert Habib. *Arabic Thought in the Liberal Age, 1798–1939*. New York: Cambridge University Press, 1983.

———. *Islam in European Thought*. New York: Cambridge University Press, 1993.

Housely, Norman, editor and translator. *Documents on the Later Crusades, 1274–1580*. Macmillan Documents in History. Basingstoke, UK: Macmillan, 1996.

Hoyland, Robert, editor. *Muslims and Others in Early Islamic Society*. The Formation of the Classical Islamic World 18. Aldershot, UK: Ashgate, 2004.

Hubers, John. "Christian Zionism: A Historical Analysis and Critique." Paper submitted to the RCA General Synod, 2004. Online: http://images.rca.org/docs/synod/ChristianZionism.pdf.

———. "Samuel Zwemer and the challenge of Islam: From Polemic to a Hint of Dialogue." *International Bulletin of Missionary Research* 28 (2004) 117–21.

Hurewitz, J. C. *Diplomacy in the Near and Middle East: A Documentary Record*. Vol. 1. Princeton: Van Nostrand, 1956.

———. *The Middle East and North Africa in World Politics: A Documentary Record*. 2 vols. New Haven: Yale University Press, 1975.

Ḥusayn, Muḥammad Kāmil. *City of Wrong: A Friday in Jerusalem*. Translated by Kenneth Cragg. Oxford: OneWorld, 1996.

Hutchison, William R. *Errand to the World: American Protestant Thought and Foreign Missions*. Chicago: University of Chicago Press, 1987.

Hutton, J. E. "Moravian Missions in Moslems." *Moslem World* 14 (1924) 125–30.

Imber, Colin. *Ebu's-Suʿud: The Islamic Legal Tradition*. Jurists—Profiles in Legal Theory. Stanford: Stanford University Press, 1997.

İnalcık, Halil, and Cemal Kafadar, editors. *Süleymân the Second and His Time*. Istanbul: Isis, 1993.

Jaber, Hala. *Hezbollah: Born with a Vengeance*. New York: Columbia University Press, 1997.

Jefferson, Thomas. *The Life and Morals of Jesus of Nazareth*. Mineola, NY: Dover, 2006.

Jenkins, Paul. "The Church Missionary Society and the Basel Mission." In *Church Mission Society and World Christianity, 1799–1999*, edited by Kevin Ward and Brian Stanley, 43–65. Studies in the History of Christian Missions. Grand Rapids: Eerdmans, 2000.

———. "Villagers as Missionaries: Wurtemberg Pietism as a 19th Century Missionary Movement." *Missiology* 8 (1984) 425–32.

Jensen, C. C. A. *God through the Shadows: History with Comments of the Lutheran Orient Mission Society*. Hamilton, OH: LOMS, 1950.

Joyce, Raymond H, editor. *Message to Islam: Report of Study Conference on Literature, Correspondence Courses & Broadcasting in the Arab World, Including Panel Discussions on Communicating the Gospel to the Muslim*. Beirut: Muslim World Evangelical Literature Service, [1969].

Kedar, Benjamin Z. *Crusade and Mission: European Approaches toward the Muslims*. Princeton: Princeton University Press, 1988.

Kelsay, John. "Bin Laden's Reasons." *Christian Century*, February 27–March 26, 2002, 26–29.
Kepel, Gilles. *The Roots of Radical Islam*. London: Saqi, 2005.
Kerr, Malcolm H. *Islamic Reform: The Political and Legal Theories of Muammad 'Abduh and Rashīd Riḍā*. Berkeley: University of California Press, 1966.
Khalaf, Samir. *Cultural Resistance: Global and Local Encounters in the Middle East*. London: Saqi, 2002.
———. "Protestant Images of Islam: Disparaging Stereotypes Reconfirmed." *Islam and Christian-Muslim Relations* 8 (1997) 211–29.
Khālidī, Mustafá, and 'Umar Farrūkh. Resurrecting Empire: Western Footprints and America's Perilous Path in the Middle East. Boston: Beacon, 2004.
———. al-Tabshīr wa-al-istiʿmār fī al-bilād al-ʿArabīyah [Evangelism and imperialism in the Arab world]. 2nd ed. Beirut: al-Maktabah al-ʿAṣrīyah, 1957.
Kinkel, Gary S. *It Started with Zinzendorf: A Mission Study Then and Now*. N.p.: Moravian Church in America, 1996.
Kittelson, James M. *Luther the Reformer: The Story of the Man and His Career*. Minneapolis: Fortress, 1986.
Kramers, J. H. "Tanzimāt." In *Encyclopedia of Islam*, 10:200–209. 2nd ed. Leiden: Brill, 2000.
Krüger, Jürgen. *Lutheran Church of the Redeemer, Jerusalem*. Translated by Rebecca Wright von Tucher. Regensburg: Schnell & Steiner, 1997.
Lamb, Christopher A. *The Call to Retrieval: Kenneth Cragg's Christian Vocation to Islam*. CSIC Studies on Islam and Christianity. London: Grey Seal, 1997.
Latourette, Kenneth Scott. "Colonialism and Missions: Progressive Separation." *Journal of Church and State* 7 (1965) 330–49.
———. *A History of the Expansion of Christianity*. Vol. 3. Grand Rapids: Zondervan, 1970.
Laury, Preston A. *A History of Lutheran Missions*. Reading, PA: Pilger, 1905.
Lawrence, Bruce, editor. *Messages to the World: The Statements of Osama Bin Laden*. Translated by James Howarth. London: Verso, 2005.
Lequien, Michel. *Oriens christianus, in quatuor patriarchatus digestus quo exhibentur ecclesiae, patriarchae, caeterique praesules totius Orientis*. Vol. 2. Paris: n.p., 1740.
Leuthold, Steven. "The Book and the Peasant: Visual Representation and Social Change in German Woodcuts, 1521–1525." *Printing History* 17, no. 2 (1995) n.p. Online: http://art.nmu.edu/stevenleuthold/personal/book_peasant.html.
Lewis, Bernard. *The Emergence of Modern Turkey*. London: Oxford University Press, 1961.
———. *Islam: From the Prophet Muhammad to the Capture of Constantinople*. New York: Oxford University Press, 1987.
———. *Islam and the West*. New York: Oxford University Press, 1993.
———. "License to Kill." *Foreign Affairs* 77 (Nov/Dec 1998) 14–19.
———. *The Middle East: A Brief History of the Last 2,000 Years*. New York: Scribners, 1995.
———. *The Muslim Discovery of Europe*. New York: W. W. Norton, 1982.
———. *What Went Wrong?: Western Impact and Middle Eastern Reponse*. London: Weidenfeld & Nicolson, 2002.
Lieber, Sherman. *Mystics and Missionaries: The Jews in Palestine, 1799–1840*. Salt Lake City: University of Utah Press, 1992.

Lindsey, Hal. *The Everlasting Hatred: The Roots of Jihad.* Murrieta, CA: Oracle House, 2002.

Locke, John. *The Reasonableness of Christianity with a Discourse of Miracles and a Part of the Third Letter Concerning Toleration.* Edited by I. T. Ramsey. Stanford: Stanford University Press, 1997.

Loewenwich, Walther von. *Luther's Theology of the Cross.* Translated by Herbert J. A. Bouman. Minneapolis: Augsburg, 1979.

Löffler, Klemens. "Pope Leo X." In *The Catholic Encyclopedia*, vol. 9. New York: Appleton, 1910. Online: http://www.newadvent.org/cathen/09162a.htm.

Lohse, Bernard. *Martin Luther: An Introduction to His Life and Work.* Translated by Robert Schultz. Edinburgh: T. & T. Clark, 1987.

Lose, G. W. *Lutheran Foreign Missions.* Columbus, OH: Lutheran Book Concern, 1897.

Ludolphus, J. *A New History of Ethiopia, Being a Full and Accurate Description of the Kingdom of Abessinia.* London: Samuel Smith, 1682.

Lueking, F. Dean. *Mission in the Making: The Missionary Enterprise among Missouri Synod Lutherans, 1846–1963.* St. Louis: Concordia, 1964.

Maalouf, Tony. *Arabs in the Shadow of Israel: The Unfolding of God's Prophetic Plan for Ishmael's Line.* Grand Rapids: Kregal, 2003.

Macfie, A. L. *Orientalism: A Reader.* New York: New York University Press, 2001.

———. "Were the Magi from Persia or Arabia?" *Bibliotheca Sacra* 156 (1999) 423–42.

Makdisi, Ussama. *Artillery of Heaven: American Missionaries and the Failed Conversion of the Middle East.* Ithaca, NY: Cornell University Press, 2008.

———. "Reclaiming the Land of the Bible: Missionaries, Secularism, and Evangelical Modernity." *American Historical Review* 102 (1997) 680–713.

Mansoori, Ahmad. "American Missionaries in Iran: 1834–1934." Ph.D. diss., Ball State University, 1986.

Maʿoz, Moshe. *Ottoman Reform in Syria and Palestine, 1840–1861: The Impact of the Tanzimat on Politics and Society.* Oxford: Clarendon, 1968.

Marr, Timothy. *The Cultural Roots of American Islamicism.* New York: Cambridge University Press, 2006.

Marsden, George. "Evangelical and Fundamental Christianity." In *The Encyclopedia of Religion*, edited by Mircea Eliade, 5:190–97. New York: Macmillian, 1987.

Marshal, David. "Christianity in the Qur'ān." In *Islamic Interpretations of Christianity*, edited by Lloyd Ridgeon, 3–29. New York: St. Martin's, 2001.

Martinson, Paul Varo, editor. *Islam: An Introduction for Christians.* Translated by Stefanie Ormsby Cox. Minneapolis: n.p., 1994.

Marty, Martin. *Martin Luther.* New York: Penguin, 2004.

Masters, Bruce Alan. *Christians and Jews in the Ottoman Arab World: The Roots of Secularism.* Cambridge Studies in Islamic Civilization. London: Cambridge University Press, 2001.

Mawṣililī, Aḥmad. *Moderate and Radical Islamic Fundamentalism: The Quest for Modernity, Legitimacy, and the Islamic State.* Gainesville: University Press of Florida, 1999.

McAmis, Robert Day. "Toward a Lutheran Mission to Muslims in the United States." *Concordia Journal* 24 (1998) 234–49.

McCullough, Paul, editor. *A History of the Lutheran Church in South Carolina.* Columbia: South Carolina Synod of the LCA, 1971.

Meinardus, Otto F. A. "De Petro Heylingo." *Zeitschrift des Verins fur Lubeckische Geshichte und Altertumskunde* 68 (1988) 139–57.

———. "Peter Heyling, History and Legend." *Ostkirchliche Studien* 14 (1965) 305–26.
———. "Peter Heyling in the Light of Catholic Historiography." *Ostkirchliche Studien* 18 (1969) 16–22.
Merkley, Paul Charles. *The Politics of Christian Zionism, 1891–1948*. London: Routledge, 1998.
Meyer, Herbert C. "The Middle East." *The Minaret* 17, no. 2 (1962) 8–10.
Michaelis, Johann Heinrich. *Sonderbarer Lebens-Lauff Herrn Peter Heylings, aus Lübec, und dessen Reise nach Ethiopien*. Halle: Wäysenhauses, 1724.
Miller, Gregory J. "Luther on the Turks and Islam." In *Harvesting Martin Luther's Reflections on Theology, Ethics, and the Church*, edited by Timothy J. Wengert, 185–203. Lutheran Quarterly Books. Grand Rapids: Eerdmans, 2004.
Miller, Roland E. *Muslim Friends: Their Faith and Feeling, an Introduction to Islam*. Concordia Scholarship Today. St. Louis: Concordia, 1996.
———. *Muslims and the Gospel: Bridging the Gap, Reflections on Christian Sharing*. Minneapolis: Lutheran University Press, 2006.
Montgomery James A. *Arabia and the Bible*. Philadelphia: University of Pennsylvania Press, 1934.
Mowat, R. B., editor. *Select Treaties and Documents to Illustrate the Development of the Modern European States-System*. Oxford: Oxford University Press, 1915.
Mulholland, Kenneth B. "From Luther to Carey: Pietism and the Modern Missionary Movement." *Biliotheca Sacra* 156 (January–March 1999) 85–95.
Nau, Henry. "Christianity and Non-Christianity Are On the Move." *The Minaret* 6, no. 4 (1951) 6.
———. "A Life-Long Ambition." *The Minaret* 1, no. 4 (1946) 4.
———. "The Scimitar." *The Minaret* 3, no. 4 (1948) 12.
———. "The Stumbling Block of the Cross." *The Minaret* 4, no. 4 (1949) 3.
———. "A Test and a Challenge." *The Minaret* 2, no. 4 (1947) 1.
———. *We Move into Africa: The Story of the Planting of the Lutheran Church in Southeastern Nigeria*. St. Louis: Concordia, 1945.
———. "Where Shall We Go?" *The Minaret* 2, no. 3 (1946) 1.
———. "The Wrong Appeal?" *The Minaret* 3, no. 1 (1947) 3.
———. "Zeal without Knowledge." *The Minaret* 4, no. 2 (1948) 5.
Neill, Stephen. *A History of Christian Missions*. The Pelican History of the Church 6. New York: Penguin, 1964.
Nestingen, James Arne. *Martin Luther: A Life*. Minneapolis: Augsburg, 2003.
Neubert-Preine, Thorsten. *100 Jafre Evamgeosch-Lutherische Erl[umlaut over o]öserkirche in Jersualem*. Jerusalem: Commercial, 1998.
Noll, Mark A. *America's God: From Jonathan Edwards to Abraham Lincoln*. New York: Oxford University Press, 2002.
Nuovo, Victor, editor. *John Locke and Christianity: Contemporary Responses to* The Reasonableness of Christianity. Key Issues 16. Bristol: Thoemmes, 1997.
Nüsse, Andrea. *Muslim Palestine: The Ideology of Ḥamās*. Amsterdam: Overseas Pub. Association, 1998.
Oberg, Einar J. *The Messengers of God: The Mission to Kurdistan and Neighboring Areas*. N.p.: Lutheran Orient Mission Society, 1985.
Oberman, Heiko Augustinus. *Luther: Man between God and the Devil*. Translated by Eileen Walliser-Schwarzbart. New Haven: Yale University Press, 1989.

Olson, Norman I. "Historical Sketch of the Lutheran Orient Mission." Unpublished paper, Luther Theological Seminary, St. Paul, Minnesota, 1951.
One Hundred Years, Being the Short History of the Church Missionary Society. London: CMS, 1898.
Otten, Henry J. "The Muslim Books of Revelation." *The Minaret* 5, no. 4 (1950) 7.
Pacini, Andrea, editor. *Christian Communities in the Arab Middle East: The Challenge of the Future*. New York: Clarendon, 1998.
Padwick, Constance Evelyn. *Henry Martyn: Confessor of the Faith*. London: SCM, 1922.
Palmer, Alan. *The Kaiser: Warlord of the Second Reich*. New York: Scribner's, 1978.
Parrinder, Edward Geoffrey. *Jesus in the Qur'ān*. Oxford: OneWorld, 1995.
Patrides, C. A. "'The Bloody and Cruell Turke': The Background of a Renaissance Commonplace." *Studies in the Renaissance* 10 (1963) 126–35.
Pearson, J. D. "al-Kur'ān." In *Encyclopedia of Islam*, 5:400–432. 2nd ed. Leiden: Brill, 1998.
Peters, Joan. *From Time Immemorial: The Origins of the Arab-Jewish Conflict over Palestine*. New York: Harper & Row, 1984.
Peters, Paul. "The Fruits of Luther's Mission-Mindedness." *Wisconsin Lutheran Seminary Quarterly* 67, no. 1 (1947) n.p. Online: http://www.wlsessays.net/node/1838.
Pfander, Carl Gottlieb. *The Mîzânu'l Ḥaqq ("Balance of Truth")*. Rev. by W. St. Clair Tisdall. London: Religious Tract Society, 1910.
Pittman, Lester Groves. "The Protestant Bishopric in Jerusalem and the Eastern Question, 1841–1875." M.A. thesis, University of Virginia, 1992.
PC-USA. "Resolution on Confronting Christian Zionism." Resolution of the 216th General Assembly, 2004. Online: http://www.pcusa.org/worldwide/israelpalestine/christianzionism.htm.
PC-USA Board of Foreign Missions. *Mission Problems in New Persia*. Beirut: American Press, 1926.
———. *A Century of Mission Work in Iran (Persia): 1834–1934*. Beirut: American Press, 1936.
Prideaux, Humphrey. *The Nature of Imposture Fully Displayed in the Life of Mahamet*. London: W. Rogers, 1697.
Prior, Michael. *Zionism and the State of Israel: A Moral Inquiry*. New York: Routledge, 1999.
Proceedings of the 44th Regular Convention of the Lutheran Church—Missouri Synod (1959). St. Louis: Concordia Pub. House, 1959.
Quinn, Frederick. "'Am I Not Your Lord?' Kenneth Cragg on Muslim-Christian Dialogue." *Journal of Muslim Minority Affairs* 26 (2006) 127–33.
Raheb, Mitri. *Bethlehem Besieged: Stories of Hope in Times of Trouble*. Minneapolis: Fortress, 2004.
———. "Die Evangelische Lutherische Kirche in Palästina und Jordanien." In *Dem Erlöser der Welt zur Ehre: Festschrift zum hundertjährigen Jubiläum der Einweihung der evangelischen Erlöserkirche in Jerusalem*, edited by Karl-Heinz Ronecker, 183–200. Leipzig: Evangelische Verlagsdanstalt, 1998.
Railton, Nicholas M. *No North Sea: The Anglo-German Evangelical Network in the Middle of the Nineteenth Century*. Studies in Christian Mission 24. Leiden: Brill, 2000.
Rennstich, Karl, "The Understanding of Mission, Civilisation and Colonialism in the Basel Mission." In *Missionary Ideologies in the Imperialist Era, 1880–1920: Papers from the Durham Consultation, 1981*, edited by Torben Christensen and William R. Hutchison, 94–103. Denmark: Christensens Bogtrykkeri, 1982.

Rhein, Ernst, and Johannes Döring et al. *Jerusalem: Geshcichte einer Gemeinde.* Jerusalem: n.p., 1990.

Richter, Julius. *A History of Protestant Missions in the Near East.* London: Revell, 1910.

Ruether, Rosemary Radford, and J. Herman Reuther. *The Wrath of Jonah: The Crisis of Religious Nationalism in the Israeli-Palestinian Conflict.* Minneapolis: Fortress, 2002.

Rupp, Gordon. "Luther against 'The Turk, the Pope, and the Devil.'" In *Seven-Headed Luther: Essays in Commemoration of a Quincentenary, 1483-1983,* edited by Peter Newman Brooks, 255-73. Oxford: Clarendon, 1983.

Saeed, Abdullah. "The Charge of Distortion of Jewish and Christian Scriptures." *Muslim World* 92 (2004) 419-36.

Said, Edward W. *Orientalism.* New York: Vintage, 1979.

Salama, Adeeb Naguib. *Al-Kinīssa al-īngīliyya fī masr: 1854-1980.* Cairo: Dar al-Thaqafa, n.d.

Sale, George, translator. *The Koran, Commonly Called the Alcoran of Mohammed.* Springfield: Brewwer, 1865.

Salem, Elie. "The Elizabethan Image of Islam." *Studia Islamica* 22 (1965) 43-54.

Schattschneider, David A. "Pioneers in Mission: Zinzendorf and the Moravians." *International Bulletin of Missionary Research* 8 (April 1984) 63-67.

Scherer, James A. *Gospel, Church and Kingdom: Comparative Studies in World Mission Theology.* Minneapolis: Augsburg, 1987.

———. *. . . That the Gospel May Be Sincerely Preached throughout the World: A Lutheran Perspective on Mission and Evangelism in the 20th Century.* Geneva: LWF, 1982.

Schirrmacher, Christine. "The Influence of German Biblical Criticism on Muslim Apologetics in the 19th Century." Paper for the *festschrift* for Rousas John Rushdoony, 1997. Online: http://contra-mundum.org/schirrmacher/rationalism.html.

Schlorff, Sam. *Missiological Models in Ministry to Muslims.* Upper Darby, PA: Middle East Resources, 2006.

Schmutz, Rebecca. *All Africa Consultation on Christian Theology and Strategy for Mission.* Geneva: LWF Dept. of Church Cooperation, 1980.

Schwoebel, Robert. *The Shadow of the Crescent: The Renaissance Image of the Turk (1453-1517).* New York: St. Martin's, 1969.

Scudder, Lewis III. *The Arabian Mission's Story: In Search of Abraham's Other Son.* The Historical Series of the Reformed Church in America 30. Grand Rapids: Eerdmans, 1998.

Setton, Kenneth Meyer. "Lutheranism and the Turkish Peril." *Balkan Studies* 9 (1962) 133-68.

———. *Western Hostility to Islam and Prophecies of Turkish Doom.* Memoirs of the American Philosophical Society 201. Philadelphia: American Philosophical Society, 1992.

Shahbaz, Yonan H. *The Rage of Islam: An Account of the Massacres of Christians by the Turks in Persia.* Piscataway, NJ: Gorgias, 2006.

Shaheen, Jack G. *Reel Bad Arabs: How Hollywood Vilifies a People.* New York: Olive Branch, 2001.

Shahîd, Irfan. *Rome and the Arabs: A Prolegomenon to the Study of Byzantiym and the Arabs.* Washington, DC: Dumbarton Oaks Research Library, 1984.

Sharkey, Heather J. *American Evangelicals in Egypt: Missionary Encounters in an Age of Empire.* Princeton: Princeton University Press, 2008.

———. "Arabic Antimissionary Treatises: Muslim Responses to Christian Evangelism in the Modern Middle East." *International Bulletin of Missionary Research* 28 (2004) 112–18.

Shedd, Mary Lewis. *The Measure of a Man: The Life of William Ambrose Shedd, Missionary to Persia*. New York: Doran, 1922.

Shedd, William Ambrose. *Islam and the Oriental Churches: Their Historical Relations*. Students' Lectures on Missions, 1902–3. Philadelphia: Presbyterian Board of Publication and Sabbath-School Work, 1904.

Shelley, Michael T. "Al-Ghazali's Benign Influence on Temple Gairdner." In *A Faithful Presence: Essays for Kenneth Cragg*, edited by David Thomas and Clare Amos, 201–18. London: Melisende, 2003.

———. "The Life and Thought of W. H. T. Gairdner, 1873–1928: A Critical Evaluation of a Scholar-Missionary to Islam." Ph.D. diss., University of Birmingham, 1988.

———. "Temple Gairdner of Cairo Revisited." *Islam and Christian-Muslim Relations* 10 (1999) 261–78.

Showalter, Nathan D. *The End of a Crusade: The Student Volunteer Movement for Foreign Missions and the Great War*. ATLA Monograph Series 44. Lanham, MD: Scarecrow, 1998.

Silberman, Neil Asher. "Albert E. Glock (1925–1992): A Remembrance." In *Archaeology, History, and Culture in Palestine and the Near East: Essays in Memory of Albert E. Glock*, edited by Tomis Kapitan, 1–10. ASOR Books 3. Atlanta: Scholars, 1999.

Sizer, Stephen. *Christian Zionism: Road Map to Armageddon?* Leicester: InterVarsity, 2006.

Slomp, Jan. "Calvin and the Turks." In *Christian-Muslim Encounters*, edited by Yvonne Yazbeck Ḥaddād and Wadīʿ Zaydān Ḥaddād, 126–42. Gainesville: University Press of Florida, 1995.

Smith, Jane. "French Christian Narratives Concerning Muhammad and the Religion of Islam from the Fifteenth to the Eighteenth Centuries." *Islam and Christian-Muslim Relations* 7 (1996) 47–62.

———. "Old French Travel Accounts of Muslim Beliefs Concerning the Afterlife." In *Christian-Muslim Encounters*, edited by Yvonne Yazbeck Ḥaddād and Wadīʿ Zaydān Ḥaddād, 221–41. Gainesville: University Press of Florida, 1995.

Smith, Robert O. "Luther, the Turks, and Islam." *Currents in Theology and Mission* 34 (2007) 351–64.

———. "A Lutheran Response to Christian Zionism." Paper presented to the ELCA Conference of Bishops, San Mateo, CA, March 2008. Online: http://www.elca.org/~/media/Files/Our%20Faith%20in%20Action/Justice/Peace%20Not%20Walls/Lutheran%20Response%20to%20Christian%20Zionism.pdf.

Southern, R. W. *Western Views of Islam in the Middle Ages*. Cambridge: Harvard University Press, 1962.

Spartalis, Peter James. *Karl Kumm: Last of the Livingstones, Pioneer Missionary Statesman*. Bonn: Kultur und Wissenschaft, 1994.

Spencer, Robert. *The Truth about Muhammad: Founder of the World's Most Intolerant Religion*. Washington, DC: Regnery, 2007.

Stade, Robert C. "In Memoriam." *The Minaret* 11, no. 3 (1956) 3.

———. *The Minaret* 12, no. 12 (1957) n.p.

———. "Rev. Marvin Palmquist Inverview." *The Messenger* 92, no. 1 (2003) 2.

Stanley, Brian. *The Bible and the Flag: Protestant Missions and British Imperialism in the Nineteenth and Twentieth Centuries*. Downer's Grove, IL: InterVarsity, 1990.

———, editor. *Christian Missions and the Enlightenment*. Studies in the History of Christian Missions. Grand Rapids: Eerdmans, 2001.

Stein, K. James. *Philipp Jakob Spener: Pietist Patriarch*. Chicago: Covenant, 1986.

Stock, Eugene. *The History of the Church Missionary Society: Its Environment, Its Men and Its Work*. Vols. 1, 2. London: CMS, 1899.

Stoeffler, F. Ernest. *German Pietism during the Eighteenth Century*. Studies in the History of Religions, Supplements to Numen 24. Leiden: Brill, 1973.

Stolle, Volker, editor. *The Church Comes from All Nations: Luther Texts on Mission*. Translated by Klaus Detlev Schulz and Daniel Thies. St. Louis: Concordia, 2003.

Strabo. *The Geography of Strabo*. Translated by Horace Leonard Jones. 8 vols. London: Heinemann, 1917–33.

Strauss, Walter L. *The German Single-Leaf Woodcut, 1550–1600: A Pictorial Catalogue*. Vol. 1. New York: Abaris, 1975.

Strengholt, Jos M. "Gospel in the Air: 50 Years of Christian Witness through Radio in the Arab World." Ph.D. diss., University of Utrecht, 2007.

Sudilovsky, Judith. "Saving Lives, Creating Peace." *The Lutheran*, July 2005, 42–44.

Swanson, Mark. "Beyond Prooftexting: Approaches to the Qur'an in Some Early Arabic Christian Apologies." *Muslim World* 88 (1998) 297–319.

———. "The Cross of Christ in the Earliest Arabic Melkite Apologies." In *Christian Arabic Apologetics during the Abbasid Period, 750–1258*, edited by Samir Khalil Samir and Jørgen S. Nielsen, 115–45. Studies in the History of Religions 63. Leiden: Brill, 1994.

———. "The Trinity in Christian-Muslim conversation." *Dialog* 44 (2005) 256–63.

Swanson, Swan Hjalmar. *Foundation for Tomorrow: A Century of Progress in Augustana World Missions*. Minneapolis: Board of World Missions, Augustana Lutheran Church, 1960.

Taneja Preti. *Assimilation, Exodus, and Eradication: Iraq's Minorities Communities Since 2003*. London: Minority Rights Group International, 2007. Online: http://www.minorityrights.org/download.php?id=280.

Tappert, Theodore G., editor and translator. *The Book of Concord: The Confessions of the Evangelical Lutheran Church*. Philadelphia: Fortress, 1959.

Thomas, D. "The Bible in Early Muslim Anti-Christian Polemic." *Islam and Christian-Muslim Relations* 7 (1996) 29–38.

Thompson, A. C. *Moravian Missions: Twelve Lectures*. New York: Scribner's, 1882.

Thomsen, Mark W. *Christ Crucified: A 21st Century Missiology of the Cross*. Minneapolis: Lutheran University Press, 2004.

———. "Christian Mission within the Muslim World." *Word and World* 16 (1996) 194–212.

———. *The Word and the Way of the Cross: Christian Witness among Muslim and Buddhist People*. Chicago: Division for Global Mission, ELCA, 1993.

Tibawi, A. L. *American Interests in Syria, 1800–1901: A Study of Educational, Literary and Religious Work*. London: Oxford University Press, 1966.

———. *British Interests in Palestine, 1800–1901: A Study of Religious and Educational Enterprise*. London: Oxford University Press, 1961.

Tolan, John Victor. *Saracens: Islam in the Medieval European Imagination*. New York: Columbia University Press, 2002.

Toomer, G. J. *Eastern Wisedome and Learning: The Study of Arabic in Seventeenth-Century England.* Oxford: Clarendon, 1996.

Trice, Michael and Carol LaHurd. "Windows for Understanding: Jewish-Muslim-Lutheran Relations." ELCA booklet, September 1, 2007. Online: http://www.elca.org/ecumenical/interreligious/images/primer_09.01.07_rev.pdf.

Tritton, A. S. *The Caliphs and Their Non-Muslim Sujbects: A Critical Study of the Covenant of 'Umar.* London: Oxford University Press, 1930.

———. "Non Muslim Subjects of the Muslim State." *Journal of the Royal Asiatic Society* 70 (1928) 485–508.

UN Development Programme. *Arab Human Development Report 2002: Creating Opportunities for Future Generations.* New York: United Nations Publications, 2002. Online: http://www.pogar.org/publications/other/ahdr/ahdr2002e.pdf.

U.S. Copts Association. "Guide: Christians in the Middle East." Online: http://www.copts.com/english1/index.php/2005/12/15/guide-christians-in-the-middle-east/.

Valleskey, David J. "Luther's Impact on Mission Works." *Wisconsin Lutheran Seminary Quarterly* 92 (1995) 96–123.

Vander Werff, Lyle L. *Christian Mission to Muslims: The Record, Anglican and Reformed Approaches in India and the Near East, 1800–1938.* William Carey Library Series on Islamic Studies. Pasadena: William Carey Library, 1977.

Vogelaar, Harold. "Abraham the Archetype of Faith: 'There Is No God but God!'" *Word and World* 16 (1996) 169–72.

———. "Listening to Arab Voices." *The Lutheran*, June 2003, n.p.

———. "Open Doors to Dialogue," *Muslim World* 94 (2004) 397–403.

———. "Religious Pluralism in the Thought of Muhammad Kāmil Hussein." In *Christian-Muslim Encounters*, edited by Yvonne Yazbeck Ḥaddād and Wadī' Zaydān Ḥaddād, 411–25. Gainesville: University Press of Florida, 1995.

Waldberger, Andreas. *Missionare und Moslems: Die Basler Mission in Persien, 1833–1837.* Basel: Basileia, 1983.

Wansleben, J. M. *Brief Account of the Rebellions and Bloodshed, Occasioned by the Anti-Christian Practices of the Jesuits and Other Popish Emissaries in the Empire of Ethiopia.* London: n.p.: 1679.

Warneck, Gustav. *Outline of the History of Protestant Missions from the Reformation to the Present Time.* New York: Revell, 1902.

Watson, Andrew. *The American Mission in Egypt, 1854 to 1896.* Pittsburgh: United Presbyterian Board of Publication, 1904.

Watson, Patty Jo, and Ghada Ziadeh. "Obituary: Albert Ernest Glock, 1925–1992." *American Antiquity* 59 (1994) 270–72.

Weber, Nicholas. "Pope Pious II." In *The Catholic Encyclopedia*, vol. 9. New York: Appleton, 1910. Online: http://www.newadvent.org/cathen/12126c.htm.

Weber, Timothy P. *On the Road to Armageddon: How Evangelicals Became Israel's Best Friend.* Grand Rapids: Baker Academic, 2004.

Wengert, Timothy J., editor. *Harvesting Martin Luther's Reflections on Theology, Ethics and the Church.* Lutheran Quarterly Books. Grand Rapids: Eerdmans, 2004.

Wheatcroft, Andrew. *Infidels: The Conflict between Christendom and Islam, 638–2002.* London: Penguin, 2003.

White House, Office of the Press Secretary. "Remarks by the President upon Arrival." Press conference news release, September 16, 2001. Online: http://www.whitehouse.gov/news/releases/2001/09/20010916-2.html.

Wigram, W. A. *An Introduction to the History of the Assyrian Church, or The Church of the Sassanid Persian Empire 100–640 A.D.* London: Society for Promoting Christian Knowledge, 1910.
Williams, George Huntston. "Erasmus and the Reformers on Non-Christian Religions and *Salus Extra Ecclesiam.*" In *Action and Conviction in Early Modern Europe: Essays in Honor of E. H. Harbison,* edited by Theodore K. Rabb and Jerrold E. Seigel, 319–70. Princeton: Princeton University Press, 1969.
Wilson, J. Christy. *Apostle to Islam: A Biography of Samuel M. Zwemer.* Grand Rapids: Baker, 1952.
———. "The Legacy of Samuel M. Zwemer," *International Bulletin of Missionary Research* 10 (1986) 117–21.
Wolf, C. Umhau. "Luther and Mohammedanism." *Muslim World* 31 (1941) 161–77.
Wolf, Edmund Jacob. *The Lutherans in America: A Story of Struggle, Progress, Influence and Marvelous Growth.* New York: J. A. Hill, 1889.
Wolf, Edwin. *The Book Culture of a Colonial American City: Philadelphia Books, Bookmen, and Booksellers.* Oxford: Clarendon, 1988.
Wolf, Luther Benaiah. *After Fifty Years, or An Historical Sketch of the Guntur Mission of the Evangelical Lutheran Church of the General Synod in the United States of America.* Philadelphia: Lutheran Publication Society, 1896.
Yamauchi, Edwin M. *Persia and the Bible.* Grand Rapids: Baker, 1990.
Yeor, Bat. *The Decline of Eastern Christianity under Islam: From Jihad to Dhimmitude, Seventh-Twentieth Century.* Madison, NJ: Fairleigh Dickinson University Press, 1996.
———. *The Dhimmi: Jews and Christians under Islam.* Translated by David Maisel et al. Madison, NJ: Fairleigh Dickenson University Press, 1985.
———. *Islam and Dhimmitude: Where Civilizations Collide.* Translated by Miriam Kochan and David Littman. Madison, NJ: Fairleigh Dickinson University Press, 2002.
Zirinsky, Michael. "American Presbyterian Missionaries at Urmia during the Great War." Paper for the Iran Chamber Society, n.d.
Zwemer, Samuel Marinus. *Raymond Lull: First Missionary to the Moslems.* New York: Funk & Wagnalls, 1902.

PERIODICALS

The Messenger (formerly *Lutheran Orient Mission Newsletter*)
The Minaret (newsletter of the Society for the Promotion of Mohammaden Missions)

WEB SITES

Answering Christianity. http://www.answering-christianity.com/ac.htm.
Answering Islam: A Christian-Muslim Dialog. http://www.answering-islam.org/.
Challenging Christian Zionism. http://www.christianzionism.org.
Churches for Middle East Peace. http://www.cmep.org/.
A Common Word. http://www.acommonword.com/.
Deutscher Verein vom Heilgen Lande [The German Association of the Holy Land]. http://www.heilig-land-verein.de/.
Evangelical Lutheran Church in America. http://www.elca.org.
Institutum Judaicum Delitzschianum. http://egora.uni-muenster.de/ijd.

Johann Ludwig Schneller School. http://www.jlss.org.
Lutheran Church—Missouri Synod. http://www.lcms.org/.
Lutheran Hour Ministries. http://www.lhm.org.
Lutheran Mideast Development (formerly Lutheran Orient Mission Society). http://www.lutheran-mideast.org/index.html.
Lutheran World Federation Jerusalem (Augusta Victoria Hospital). http://www.lwfjerusalem.org.
Middle East Council of Churches. http://www.mec-churches.org.
"Peace Not Walls." http://www.elca.org/Our-Faith-In-Action/Justice/Peace-Not-Walls.aspx.

INTERVIEWS AND PERSONAL CORRESPONDENCE

Ailabouni, Said (ELCA)
Albrecht, Mark (LOM)
Azzam, Edward (LCMS)
Birkland, Carol (ELCA)
Boss, Walter (LCMS)
Brown, Mark (ALC/ELCA)
Buckman, Allan R. (LCMS)
Glock, Lois (LCA/ELCA)
Jahshan, Moris (MELM)
Jensen, Mary (ALC/ELCA)
Johnson, David (LCA/ELCA)
Kapenga, Peter (LCA/ELCA)
LaHurd, Carol (ELCA)
Nelson, Mark (ELCA)
Scudder, Louis R. III (RCA/ELCA)
Shelley, Michael (ALC/ELCA)
Smith, Robert (ELCA)
Stelling, John (LCMS)
Swanson, Mark (LCA/ELCA)
Thomsen, Mark (ALC/ELCA)
Tomeh, Nuhad (CRC)
Vogelaar, Harold (RCA/LCA/ELCA)
Wakim-Dagher, Anges (CRC)

Index

Abraham, Jaure, 162
Abyssinia, 70n24, 82, 124, 127, 137
accompaniment, 233, 234, 245, 252, 254
   See also ELCA
Adiaphora, 18, 122, 131
Aflaq, Michel, 203
Age of Discovery, 63, 105
Agerstrand, Carl, 183, 186, 187, 190, 201
   See also Lutheran Church-Missouri Synod
Ahmadiyya, 14
Alexander, Archibald, 154
Alexandria, 70, 71, 72, 84, 112, 211
American Evangelicals, 1, 9
   See also Missionary Societies; American Board of Commissioners of Foreign Missionaries
   See also Rufus Anderson
American Lutheran Church (ALC), 9, 12, 163, 181, 195, 208, 213–15, 217, 219, 223–28, 233, 235, 239, 248, 250
American Mission Press, 190

American Orientalism, 158
American School of Oriental Research (ASOR), 221
American United Lutheran Church (ULC), 163
American University of Beirut, 140, 191
Anderson, Rufus, 6, 9, 88, 192
Anglican Church, 95, 128
   Archbishop of Canterbury, 123, 124, 126, 128, 130
   Lutheran-Anglican Bishopric, 123, 124, 126, 128, 130
   See also Missionary Societies; Church Missionary Society
Antonius, George, 91, 203
Apology of the Augsburg Confession, 46
The Apology of al-Kindī, 104, 105n111
Aquinas, Thomas, 62, 65, 67, 100, 158
   See also Contra Gentiles
Arab Christians, 13–15, 91, 140, 186, 192, 196, 245
Arabia, 2, 14, 36, 68, 92, 104, 155, 156, 179, 223, 241

Titles of published works, as well as foreign or transliterated words are listed in *italics*. Those foreign words that have been adopted as part of normal English language usage are listed by their anglicized form. This includes all proper names and nouns.

Index

Arabic Studies, at Cambridge and Oxford, 149, 151
Arab-Israeli conflict, 194, 224
    See also Occupied Territories; Six Day War
Arab socialism, 194, 203, 204
Arab World, 183, 187, 190, 200, 204, 212, 223–25
    Definition of, 13, 14
Arafat, Yasser, 203
Armenians, 3, 160, 161,
    Apostolic Catholicos of Cilicia, 15
    Armenian Catholic Patriarch, 15
    Armenian massacres, 109, 161, 169–70, 219
Arbil, 171–73
Armenian Orthodox Church, 3, 79, 88, 15, 92, 99, 137, 166, 169, 170, 181
Association of American Evangelical Lutheran Churches (AELC), 199–200
    Jim Mayer, 199
    Paul Strege, 199
Association for the Assembling of God's People in Jerusalem, 135
    See also Templers
Association of the Holy Grave, 141
Assyrians, 16, 161, 162, 165, 167, 169, 181
    Assyrian Church of the East (Nestorians), 160, 161, 166, 188
    Reformed Nestorian Church, 161
Augsburg Confession, 11, 17, 46, 72, 77, 78, 131
Augusta Victoria Hospital, 220, 226
Augustana Synod, 161, 163

Azerbaijan of Persia, 14, 99, 161, 166, 170
Azzam, Edward, 187–90, 196, 201

Bachimont, George H., 170
Balkans, 42, 44, 66, 108, 142, 216
Barclay, Joseph, 130
    See also Anglican Church; Lutheran-Anglican Bishopric
Beirut, 84, 87, 91, 124, 140, 172, 183, 184, 187, 188, 190, 191, 195, 196, 198, 199, 202–5, 217, 219, 220, 224, 230, 234, 248
Belgrade, 42
Berlin to Baghdad railway, 145, 171
Bethlehem, 1, 128, 129, 140, 141, 235, 245
Bible, translations of,
    Arabic Van Dyck, 88
    Kurdish, 168
Bibliander, Theodore, 34–37, 57, 58
Bijlefeld, Willem, 213, 227, 250
Bin Laden, Osama, 241, 242, 254
Birzeit University, 207, 221
Bishop Markos, 72, 73, 81
Blumhardt, C. G., 78, 79
Boss, Walter, 187–90, 196, 201
British East India Company, 85
British Parliament, 225, 226
    Act of Jerusalem, 225, 226
Brown, Mark, 225, 226
Bulaq, 71
Bunsen, Christian, 120, 123
Bush, George, 240, 242
    "War on Terror," 232, 242, 254, 255
al-Bustani, Butrus, 88
    See also Bible translations, Arabic Van Dyck

Cairo, 12, 71, 72, 73, 81, 82, 84, 86, 91, 164, 173, 202, 208–17, 224, 225, 229, 230, 231, 234, 238, 239, 248
  See also St. Andrew's United Church
Capital University, 163
Capuchins, 70, 71, 72, 74
Cardinal Bakocz of Hungary, 48
Carey, William, 60, 83
Carlowitz, treaty of, 66, 90
Caucasus, 78, 79, 81, 107, 160, 161, 169, 170, 174, 181
Centre for the Study of Islam and Christian-Muslim Relations, 226
Charles V, 20, 40, 43, 44, 46, 47, 58, 237
  See also Holy Roman Emperor
Christ Church, Jerusalem, 119, 120, 163
Christendom, 4, 21, 22, 29, 47, 51, 60, 108, 147
Christian-Muslim Dialogue, 212, 254
  See also Bishop Kenneth Cragg; Harold Vogelaar
Christian Zionism, 85, 146, 194, 215, 244, 245
Christmas Lutheran Church, 235, 244
Christopher Columbus, 62, 163
Church of the Holy Sepulchre, 116, 141
Churches for Middle East Peace, 238
The City of Wrong, 196, 202, 210
  See also Kamil Ḥusayn
Clement VII, 42, 46
Commitments for Mission in the 1990's, 228
Concordia Seminary, 176, 187, 199
Confutatio Alcorani, 34, 58
  See also Ricoldo De Montecroce
Congregatatio de Propaganda Fide, 11
Congress of Berlin (1878), 143
Contact and Resource Center (CRC), 198–200
Contra Gentiles, 62, 66
  See also Thomas Aquinas
Coptic Orthodox Church, 70, 211, 238
Cragg, Bishop Kenneth, 179, 192, 193, 210
Crimean War, 116, 135, 139
Crusades, 3, 48, 49, 94, 105, 174, 175, 241, 250, 254
"Custody for the Holy Land," 141
Cyprus, 24, 183, 184, 198, 199, 200, 205, 217, 220, 230, 235

Dagher, Agnes Wakim, 198, 200
Damascus Massacres (1860), 119, 138
Danish Lutheran Church, Aden, 12, 93, 223
  See also Missionary Societies, Danish Church Mission
Danke, John Henry, 81
Dannhauer, John Konrad, 75
Dār al-Ḥarb, 147
Dār al-Islām, 147
Dar al-Kalima School, 244
  See also Christmas Lutheran Church
Delitzsch, Franz, 85
De Montecroce, Ricoldo, 34
Diet of Augsburg, 46, 65
Diet of Speyer, first, 42, 43
Diet of Speyer, second, 44
Diet of Worms, 43, 44, 46
Dietrich, A. H., 79
dhimmīs, 110, 111, 111n2, 119,
dīn wa dawla, 111

Dominicans, 3, 6, 61, 62, 68, 69, 100, 149, 158, 237
Dormition Abby, 141, 144, 145
Druze, 14, 15, 109, 118, 138, 219, 241
Duke Ernest the Pious of Gotha, 76, 77

Ecumenical Patriarch of Constantinople, 111, 160n37
Edinburgh Missionary Conference (1910), 11, 84, 165
Edman, Dr. and Mrs. E., 167, 168
Edomite, 32
Egypt, 4, 9, 13–16, 18, 40, 61, 66, 67, 70–74, 76, 81, 82, 88, 95, 108, 109, 124, 127, 128, 136, 144, 158, 164, 165, 173, 183, 185, 194, 200, 209, 210, 213, 214, 218, 231, 238, 239, 242, 246
    Invasion of Syria and Palestine, 112, 113, 115, 133
    See also Ibrahim Pasha, Muhammad Ali
Eichelberger, Lewis, 153–58, 179
Eigilsson, Oluf, 24
Enlightenment, 1, 6, 67, 80, 100, 106, 115, 147–49, 157, 164
Erasmus, 32, 35, 49, 65, 98, 240
Eternal Love Winning Africa (ELWA), 184
Ethiopian refugees, 215
    See also St. Andrew's United Church of Cairo
Evangelical Alliance, 18, 94
Evangelical Lutheran Church in America (ELCA): xii, 9, 200, 208, 213, 215–17, 220, 225–34, 238, 239, 245–48, 251–55

    Churchwide Strategy for Engagement in Israel and Palestine, 245
    Division for Global Mission, 226, 233
    Lutheran Office for Governmental Affairs (LOGA), 226, 245
    Ecumenical and Inter-Religious Relations, 245, 255
    "Peace Not Walls" campaign, 234
    See also accompaniment
Evangelical Lutheran Church of Jordan and the Holy Land (ELCJHL), 220
Evangelical (Presbyterian) Theological Seminary in Cairo, 211
    The Center for the Study of Religion, 211
    See also Harold S. Vogelaar
Extra ecclesium nullas salus, 64–66

Fallscheer, Christian, 129
Fasilides, 72, 73
Ferdinand of Austria, 41, 42, 43, 44, 45, 55
    See also Hapsburgs
Finn, Robert, 128
Fisk, Pliny, 87, 114, 152, 179
Fjellstedt, Peter, 95–98
fliegenschrift, 25
Fossum, Alma, 170
Fossum, Ludwig O., 163–68
Francis I of France, 21, 40, 42, 44, 46, 47, 115
Francis, St., 61
Franciscans, 6, 61, 71, 117, 133, 149, 237
Francisco, Adam S., 10, 33, 34, 52, 55, 64, 187, 253
Francke, Augustus Herman, 17, 74, 77, 78, 80
    See also Halle

Frederick IV of Denmark, 77, 78
Frederick William III, 17
Frederick William IV, 120, 159
French Revolution (1789), 148
Friends School in Ramallah, 220, 226

Gardiner, Dr. and Mrs. R. M., 172, 173
General Synod, 94, 159, 167, 244
German Association of the Holy Land, 141
German Lutheran Institute for Ancient Science of the Holy Land, 134
Germany, 10, 11, 22, 25, 27, 29, 31, 40, 42, 43, 45, 46, 48, 51, 53, 54, 55, 57, 63, 69, 78, 79, 81, 94, 95, 116, 119, 120, 121, 125, 126, 130, 131, 133–35, 137, 139, 140, 141–43, 145, 162, 170, 176
  German Catholics, 141, 144
  German Princes, 49
  German Pietists, 92, 146, 242
  Saxony, 42, 45, 52, 55, 80
  See also Swabians, Württemburg
George of Hungary, 33, 34
Georgievicz, Bartholomaeus, 32, 69
Gerung, Matthias, 22, 23
Gettysburg Lutheran Seminary, 152, 153n16, 158, 245
  See also Missionary Societies, Evangelical Lutheran Society of Inquiry on Missions
Gibbon, Edward, 148, 149, 150
Glock, Albert and Lois, 220, 221, 222
Gobat, Samuel, 73, 127, 128, 129, 130, 136, 137, 139, 140
  See also Anglican Church, Lutheran-Anglican Bishopric
Gog and Magog, 30, 32, 53
Gradin, Arvid, 81
Great Awakening, 1, 6, 83, 93
Greek Orthodox Church, 96, 146
  Ecumenical Patriarch of Constantinople, 111
  Greek Orthodox Patriarch of Jerusalem, 121
Greek War of Independence, 87
Gregory XV, 62
Grotius, Hugo, 67, 68, 69, 70
  The Truth of the Christian Religion, 67–69
Gudhart, Augusta D., 168, 170
Gus, Evelyn, 207, 220, 221

Halle, 17, 18, 77, 78, 80, 83, 85, 94, 118, 176, 209
  Oriental College, 77, 78
Hamas, 218
Hamma Theological Seminary, 163
Hand, Matthew, 173–75
Hanseatic League, 69
Hanson, Bishop Mark, 245, 255
Hapsburgs, 58, 66
  See also Charles V, Holy Roman Empire
Harms, Louis, 162
Hartford Seminary, 191, 213, 227, 231
  Duncan Black MacDonald Center for Islamic Studies, 191, 213, 227
  See also The Muslim World
Hattī Humāyūn, 116, 133, 138
  See also Ottoman Empire, *Tanzīmāt*
Hattī Şerīf, 133
  See also Ottoman Empire, *Tanzīmāt*

Heliopolis Community Church, 214, 215
Herodotus, 2
Herrick, George, 91
Herrnutt, 80
Heyer, C. F., 159
Heyling, Peter, 69–74, 82, 96, 237
Hijaz, 40
Hilgendorf, Dennis, 190, 191, 194–99, 201, 202, 219, 223, 235, 245
  See also Contact and Resource Center, Missionary Societies, Middle East Lutheran Ministry (MELM)
Hilten, Johann, 31
Hizb'allah, 205, 218
Hocker, Frederck William, 81, 82
Hoffmann, Christoph, 135
Holocaust, 145, 146, 165, 185, 246
Holy Land, 1, 8, 11, 48, 49, 87, 107, 109, 111, 113, 115, 117, 119, 120, 121, 123, 125, 127, 129, 131, 133, 134–46, 220, 224, 249
Holy Roman Emperor, 20, 40, 41, 44, 47, 57
  See also Charles V
Holy Roman Empire, 3, 8, 10, 41, 42, 45, 50, 61, 125, 126, 130, 144
Hungary, 33, 34, 42, 43, 48, 50, 55, 142
Ḥusayn, Kamil, 61, 196

Ibadi, 14
Ibrahim Pasha, 112–14, 133
"indirect evangelism," 89, 128, 160, 164, 166, 168, 192
infitāh, 211
inglīzī, 126, 129
al-Injīl, 110
injīliyyūn, 126
Intifada, 218, 220, 244

Iran, 14, 15, 16, 162, 166, 170, 173, 181, 182, 241, 243
  Gorveh Hospital, 173
  Hostage Crisis (1979–1980), Iranian Revolution (1978–1979), 173, 181, 202, 204, 228
  Reza Pehlavi, 169
Iran-Iraq War (1980–1988), 173
Iraq, 14, 15, 166, 170–74, 181, 182, 229, 241, 242, 252, 254–56
  First Gulf War (1990–1991), 174, 181, 229, 241
  Kingdom of Iraq, 171, 172
Isaac Johanan, 163
Islam, 3–6, 10–14, 20, 21, 24–27, 30–39, 48, 51, 52, 55, 57, 58, 61–64, 67, 68, 69, 70, 73, 86, 88, 89, 92, 97–100, 102–6, 111, 116, 147–63, 165–67, 169, 171, 173, 175, 177–83, 185, 187, 189, 191–93, 195–97, 199, 201–9, 211, 212, 213, 215–21, 223, 225–35, 237–39, 248–56
  Dialogue partner, 86, 174, 181, 192, 196, 197, 200, 206, 210, 212, 224, 229, 230, 232, 252, 254, 255
  "Missionary problem," 11
Islamic Studies, 191, 207, 213, 227, 231, 239
Israel, modern state of, 2, 4, 15, 84, 85, 127, 145, 146, 189, 194, 195, 196, 214, 218, 221, 224, 225, 238, 242, 244–48
Istanbul, 42–44, 47, 54, 55, 105, 111, 114, 120, 138, 143, 144

Jaffa, 119, 128, 129, 135
Jashshan, Moris, 184, 187, 190, 195, 201
al-Jamā'at al-Islāmiyya, 218
janissaries, 66

Jerusalem, 11, 12, 70, 72, 84, 87, 114, 116–24, 126–41, 143–46, 183, 184, 185, 194–97, 202, 206, 212, 214, 215, 218, 220, 221, 224, 226, 229, 230, 234–46, 249
Al-Jihād, 117
Joachim of Brandenburg, 4, 31, 39, 54
Johannes, Pera, 162
John Frederick, 55
John of Saxony, 42, 45
Jordon, Kingdom of,
  King Hussein, 203
  See also Palestinian Liberation Organization (PLO), Black September
Jefferson, Thomas, 151
Jehovah's Witnesses, 189, 201
Jesus, 8, 26, 28, 36, 38, 56, 65, 69, 77, 81, 82, 97, 101, 103, 104, 134, 141, 150, 151, 154, 167, 169, 179, 197, 209, 212, 227, 233, 250, 251, 254
Jessup, Henry, 89
Jews, 2, 7, 10, 13, 15, 16, 18, 19, 32, 36, 37, 39, 52, 62, 65, 75, 84, 85, 86, 87, 88, 89, 110, 111, 114, 115, 117, 118, 119, 121, 122, 124, 127, 132, 136, 137, 145, 146, 160, 185, 196, 211, 221, 224, 238, 241, 245, 246, 247, 253
  Ashkenazi and Sephardim, 16
Johnson, David, 213, 215, 226
Jowett, William, 86, 87, 118

al-Kairānawī, Rahmatullāh Ibn Khalīl al-'Uthmānī, 101
Kaiserswerth Deaconesses, 139, 140
Kapenga, Kathy and Peter, 220
Klein, Frederick Augustus, 129, 134

Knanishu, Joseph, 163
Kraft, Oscar, 214
Küchük Kaynarja, treaty of, 66, 115, 116, 142
  See also Russian Empire
Kurdistan, 160, 166, 167, 169, 170, 174, 177, 182
Kurds, 12, 13, 160, 161, 166–75, 181, 229, 239
  Bethel Kurdish Evangelical Lutheran Congregation, 168
  "Direct to the People" Fund, 187, 188
  See also Missionary Societies, Lutheran Orient Mission (LOM)

Latin Catholics, 115, 116
  Latin Catholic Patriarch of Jerusalem, 15
League of Cognac, 42, 44
Lebanese Civil War (1975–1990), 5, 184, 186, 195, 228, 241
Leo X, 40, 50
  Exsurge Domino (1520), 50
Levant, 4, 113, 114
Lindbeck, George, 224
"literary evangelism," 90, 91, 95
Lord Palmerston, 117, 122, 123
  See also British Empire
Lübeck, 69, 70
Luoma, Warner, 233, 234
Luther College, Greensboro, N.C., 176
Luther, Martin, 4, 10, 11, 17, 20–64, 68, 69, 75, 76, 79, 82, 84, 97, 98, 147, 148, 155, 162–65, 169, 176, 178, 202, 213, 216, 225, 227, 231, 232, 237, 240, 246, 247, 253, 254, 256
  Apocalypticism, 6, 29, 30, 31, 32
  Appeal for Prayer against the Turks (1541), 28, 54, 55

292 Index

Luther, Martin (cont.),
   Army Sermon (1529), 30, 55–57, 63
   Explanation of the Ninety-Five Theses (1518), 50
   "Lord Keep Us Steadfast in Thy Word," 28
   95 Theses, 10, 39
   On the Jews and their Lies (1543), 259
   On War against the Turk (1529), 30, 51, 53, 57, 68
   Preface and translation of *Confutatio Alcorani seu legis Saracenorum* (1542), "Table talks," 25, 27, 30, 36, 37, 50
   View on Crusade, 48–55
   View of Islam, 33–39
   View of the Qur'ān, 36–39
   View of the "Terrible Turk," 22, 24–27, 55–58
   See also Evangelical Lutheran Church in America (ELCA)
Lutheran Church in America (LCA), 9, 12, 159, 181, 186, 195, 199, 202, 205–40, 248
   Division of World Mission and Ecumenism (DWME), 202, 206, 211, 212, 214
Lutheran Church—Missouri Synod (LCMS), 9, 173, 176–86, 188–98, 206, 229
   World Mission Board, 187, 198, 201
   See also Missionary Societies, Middle East Lutheran Mission (MELM)
Lutheran Church of the Redeemer, Jerusalem, 134, 184, 206, 207, 215, 226
Lutheran Council in the U.S.A., 195, 223
The Lutheran Hour, 183, 185, 186, 200
Lutheran-Jewish Dialogue, 248
Lutheran Pietism, 6, 17, 18, 74, 79, 80, 82, 106
Lutheran Orient Mission (LOM), 9, 93, 147, 165–82
Lutheran Orthodoxy, 17
Lutheran School of Theology at Chicago, 216, 227, 231, 255
   Center of Christian-Muslim Engagement for Peace and Justice, 208, 216, 232, 255
Luther Seminary, St. Paul, 163, 165, 213, 216, 225, 231, 232, 254
   Islamic Studies Program, 231, 254
Lutheran Theological Seminary at Philadelphia, 216
Lutheran World Federation (LWF), 144, 165, 184, 206, 207, 220, 226, 239, 248, 255
Lutheran World Hunger Appeal, 239
Lutheran World Relief (LWR), 239, 255
Lutherans, 7, 8, 11, 12, 16, 18, 43, 46, 71, 74–86, 94, 95, 107, 118, 121, 122, 126, 130, 131, 134, 135, 145, 152, 158–70, 176, 181, 189, 195, 201, 214, 217, 220, 223, 231, 238–40, 242, 244, 245–48, 250, 251, 253, 255, 256
Lutheran-Anglican Bishopric, 123, 124, 126, 128, 130
Lutheran-Reformed United Evangelical Church, 12, 119, 127, 164, 176, 208–10, 239
Pietists, 17, 18, 59, 61, 63, 65, 67, 69, 71, 73–81, 83, 85, 87, 89, 91, 92–101, 103, 105–7, 118, 122, 129, 134, 136, 145–47, 176, 208, 209, 239, 242, 246
   See also Halle, Philipp Jacob Spener, Württemburg

Maadi Community Church, 213, 220, 225
Malech, N. G., 163, 168
Mamluks, 66
Mandeans, 13, 15, 16
Morhatkhan, Knanishu, 163
Margrave George of Brandenburg, 45
Maronite Church, 192, 193
Martyn, Henry, 85, 86, 89, 201
Matthew III, 72
Mehmed II, 31
Meinardus, Otto, 69–73
Melancthon, Philipp, 32, 46
   See also Apology of the Augsburg Confession
Mennonites, 244
Merklin von Waldkirch, Balthasar, 44
   See also Hungary
The Messenger, 175
Middle Ages, 48, 148
Middle East, 40, 59, 60–99, 101, 103, 105, 107, 108, 109, 111, 115, 118, 120, 131, 132, 138, 139, 151, 152, 159, 165, 166, 174–76, 178, 181, 183–96, 200–219, 222–30, 233–35, 237–56
   Geography, 15
   Origin of the term, 13
Middle East Council of Churches, 184
   See also Near East Council of Churches
Middle Eastern Christians, 2, 89, 115, 185, 192, 193, 242, 252
Miller, Roland E., 229, 231, 232, 250n24, 251
   "Focus on Islam," 229–32,
millet system, 93, 111, 114, 116, 117, 120, 121, 126, 188, 201
The Minaret, 177, 180, 229
Missionary Societies,

American Board of Commissioners for Foreign Missions, 6, 9, 87–89, 91, 94, 108, 120, 146, 152, 160, 179, 192
American Lutheran Missionary Society of the Ministerium of Pennsylvania (ALMS), 94, 159
American Southern Baptists' International Mission Board, 193
Baptist Society for the Propagation of the Gospel amongst Heathen, 83
Basel Missionary Society, 78–80, 153n16
Brüderhaus, 136–138
Central Home Missionary Society, 159
Church Missionary Society of the Anglican Church (CMS), 7, 9, 78, 84, 86, 87, 93–96, 99, 101, 105, 109, 117, 118, 120–22, 127, 129, 130–33, 136, 140, 159, 160, 162, 183, 194, 195, 209, 239, 244
Church of Scotland Mission Society, 84
Danish Church Mission, 12
Danish Lutheran Society for Missions to Israel, 84
Edinburgh and Glasgow Mission Society, 84
Evangelical Association for the Advancement of the Nestorian Church, 161
Evangelical Lutheran Society of Inquiry on Missions, 153
Evangelical Missionary Society of Dresden, 77
Finish Missionary Society, 84

Missionary Societies (cont.),
  German Foreign Missionary
    Society, 159
  Hermannsburg Mission Society
    (HMS), 124, 162, 163, 165,
    167
  International Lutheran
    Layman's League (ILLL),
    183, 198, 200, 201
  Jewish Missionary Association,
    84
  Leipzig Missionary Society, 78
  London Jewish Society (LJS),
    84, 93, 109, 114, 117–22,
    126, 128, 130–32
  London Missionary Society, 84
  Lutheran Orient Mission
    (LOM),
  Middle East Lutheran Ministry
    (MELM), 183–202
  Orientmission, 161, 165
  Pilgrims Mission, 135–40
  Society for the Propagation
    for Christian Knowledge
    (SPCK), 83
  Society for the Promotion of
    Mohammedan Missions
    (SPMM), 176–81
  Society for the Propagation of
    the Gospel (SPG), 83
  Society of Israel's Friends, 84
  Svenska Missions Sällskapet, 95
Mission Trade Association, 138,
  139
Moabite Stone, 129, 134
  See also Frederick Augustus
    Klein
Mohacs, battle of, 32, 43, 51, 55,
  57, 69
  See also Hungary
Moline, Charles, 207, 214
Moravians, 16, 81, 82, 96, 135
  See also Zinzendorf
Mosul, 170, 172

Mott, John R., 165
Mount Lebanon, 109, 115
Muhammad, 2, 14, 25, 26, 31–39,
  56, 68, 69, 100, 103–5, 110,
  111, 113, 124, 150, 151,
  154–57, 178, 179, 185, 210,
  211
  Dante's *Inferno*, 25
Muhammad Ali, 113
Muir, William, 151
  See also Orientalists
mukhlis, 210
Müntzer, Thomas, 26, 52
The Muslim Brotherhood, 211,
  217, 218
The Muslim World, 213
  See also Hartford Seminary
"Muslim World," 177, 183, 186, 209
  Mohammedans, Mahometans,
    86, 87, 89, 99, 151, 166
  Moors, 4, 65
  Shi'a, 14, 15, 160, 218, 219
  Sunni, 14, 15, 16, 109, 138, 160,
    166, 170, 174, 181, 212
  umma, 62
Muslims, 3–8, 11, 12, 14–19,
  32–34, 38, 39, 48, 51, 61–69,
  77, 79, 81–89, 91–93, 96,
  97, 99, 100, 102–5, 110, 111,
  113, 118, 128, 129, 133, 143,
  146, 155, 156, 158, 160, 164,
  166, 168, 173, 174, 176–85,
  188–94, 196–98, 200, 202,
  203, 206–12, 216–18, 220,
  223, 225, 227, 229, 230, 234,
  238, 240, 245, 249, 250–56
musta'mīn, 112

al-Naḥda, 91
Napoleon, 66, 67
al-Nasser, Gamal 'Abd, 203, 204
Nau, Henry, 176–80, 183
Navarino Bay, battle of, 66

Near East Council of Churches (NECC), 184, 189, 190, 192, 193, 198
  See also Middle East Council of Churches
Near East Relief, 170
Near East School of Theology, 190, 238
Nestorians, 12, 36, 159, 161, 166
  Assyrian Church of the East, 160, 188
Neudoerffer, Fred, 199, 206, 207, 214, 215, 221, 223, 226, 233
  See also Lutheran Church in America (LCA)
New Brunswick Theological Seminary, 208
Newhouse, John Henry, 133
Nicholas of Cusa, 69
Nicolai, Philip, 75
Nicolayson, John, 119
  See also Anglican Church, Lutheran-Anglican Bishopric
North Africa, 13, 84, 152, 200, 204, 214, 216, 243
Norwegian Lutheran Church, 159, 166

Occupied Territories (Gaza, Golan Heights, Sinai, West Bank), 1, 84, 194, 195, 204, 207, 217, 220, 222, 224, 226, 229, 230, 234, 244
Ockley, Simon, 151
  See also Orientalists
October War (1973), 4, 46, 133, 185, 192, 194, 198, 206, 212, 217, 221, 223, 224, 227, 255
Oman, 14, 208, 209, 215
Orient, 2, 6, 7, 9, 13, 61, 67, 68, 77, 107, 113, 136, 143, 145, 147–49, 152, 165, 166, 174, 237

Oriental Orthodox, 6, 15, 66, 70, 75, 79, 184
  See also Armenian Orthodox, Coptic Orthodox
Orientalists, 67, 106, 150, 156, 157
Organization of Arab Petroleum Exporting Countries (OAPEC), 4
Ottoman Empire, 9, 10, 13, 20, 21, 31, 33, 40, 57, 62, 66, 67, 90–92, 106–23, 126, 131, 132, 135, 142, 143, 145, 152, 157, 166, 169, 206, 237
  "Eastern Question," 92, 108, 116, 120, 126, 145

The Porte, 123, 135, 142
  "Sick Man of Europe," 108, 112, 148
  See also Suleiman the Magnificent, *Tanẓīmāt*
Pagans, 63, 65, 86
Palestine, 9, 11, 18, 85–88, 106, 107, 110, 112–24, 129–45, 164, 165, 176, 181, 185, 196, 203, 210, 214, 218, 221, 222, 238, 239, 242, 245, 246, 248, 255
Palestinian Archaeology, school of, 222
Palestine Association of Catholics in Germany, 141
Palestinian Liberation Organization (PLO), 203
  Black September, 203
Palmquist, Marvin, 173
Pan-Arab Nationalism, 186, 194
Parsons, Levi, 87, 114, 152, 179
"Pax Americana," 12, 237, 240, 243, 252, 253
  Invasion of Iraq (2003), 216n61, 241, 254–56
People of the Book, 110, 111
Pera, Luther, 162

Persia, 2, 12, 76, 79, 81, 86, 88, 99, 101, 107, 108, 111, 147, 149, 151, 153, 155, 157, 159–79, 181, 242
Persian Empire, 2
Peter the Venerable, 35, 61, 104, 105
Pfander, Karl Gottlieb, 59, 62, 99, 100–5, 109, 201, 209
The Balance of Truth, 101, 105
Philip of Hesse, 42, 45
Pius II, 48
Pluetschau, Heinrich, 77, 78
Pockocke, Bishop Andrew,
Presbyterians, 84, 86, 91, 109, 117, 120, 128, 140, 160–62, 165, 166, 169, 189, 206, 238, 239
Presbyterian Church of North America, 160
Presbyterian Church-United States of America (PC-USA), 160, 162, 244, 248
See also American Mission Evangelicals, American Mission Press
Prideaux, Humphrey, 149, 150, 154, 155
Proselytism, 79, 88, 89, 129, 132n47, 139, 173, 198, 209, 223, 224
Protestants, 16, 18, 46, 58, 60, 62, 65, 80, 116, 118, 120, 124, 126, 152, 153, 161, 188, 189, 211, 247
Prussia, 113, 114, 119–25, 135, 144
House of Hohenzollern, 125
Order of St. John, 140
polis, 8

Al-Qaeda, 99
Queen Victoria, 125, 144
See also British Empire
Qur'ān (Koran), 26, 36, 150, 197
Musa, 110

Translations of, Alexander Ross, 35, 149, 151
Andrew Du Ryer, 149
George Sale, 35, 149, 150
Robert of Ketton, 35, 149

Reconquista, 61
Redeemer Lutheran Church in Ashrafiyya, 183
Reinking, William, 184, 185, 194, 195
Reformed Church in America, 9, 92, 166, 208
Arabian Mission, 9, 92, 93, 208, 209
Renaissance, 4, 35, 48, 49, 58, 91, 97
Republic of Lebanon, 15
Richter, Julius, 10, 79, 95, 124, 127, 129, 133, 135, 140, 161, 162
Robert of Ketton, 35, 149
Rome, 3, 11, 29, 30, 31, 33, 39, 40, 42, 44, 47–51, 58, 63, 64, 65, 70–72, 133, 231
Russian Empire, 66, 79
Alexander I, 79
Russo-Turkish War, 142

Sadat, Anwar, 211, 217
See also infitāh
St. Andrew's United Church of Cairo, 213–17, 220, 225, 229, 231, 239
St. Mark's Lutheran Church in Sin al-Fil, 183
St. Paul's Church, Jerusalem, 119
Saracens, 3, 4, 31, 49, 105, 151
Origin of the term, 3
Schein, Bruce, 199, 202–8, 212, 215, 217–20, 227, 232–34
See also Lutheran Church in America (LCA)
"Schein-Neudoerffer plan," 206, 215

Schmucker, Samuel Simon, 152, 153, 154
Schneller, Johann Ludwig, 139, 140
  See also Missionary Societies, Pilgrims Mission
Schneller, Johann Ludwig, 137, 138, 139, 140, 183
Schöen, Erhard, 22
Selim the Grim, 39, 40
Selim III, 113
September Eleventh (9/11), xi, 5, 150, 223, 232, 240, 242, 244, 251–53, 256
Seventh Day Adventists, 189, 201
Shabaz, Baba N., 163
Shammi, Sadiq, 172, 173
Shelley, Joanne, 225
Shelley, Michael T., 81, 210, 214, 216, 225, 227, 232, 239
Shenouda III, 211
Siler, Russ, 226
Sitavatarok, treaty of, 66
  See also Russian Empire
Six Day War (1967), 85, 194, 195, 204, 247
Slovak Evangelical Lutheran Church, 195
Smyrna, 86, 87, 95, 96, 97, 129
Social Gospel Movement, 165
Societé d'Egypte, 67
Song of Roland, 3, 21, 41, 105, 188, 229, 231, 232, 250, 251
Soujbulak, 163, 167–71, 248
Spain, 4, 8, 21, 31, 32, 40–42, 48, 61, 62
  Spanish Armada, 62
Speer, Robert E., 165
Spener, Philipp Jacob, 17, 74, 75, 77, 80
Spittler, Christian Friedrich, 134, 135, 136, 137, 138
  See also Pilgrims Mission
Stelling, John, 190–99, 201, 202
  See also Missionary Societies, Middle East Lutheran Ministry (MELM)
Student Volunteer Movement, 94
Sudanese refugees, 16, 196, 215, 239
  See also St. Andrew's United Church of Cairo
Suez Canal, 108, 144
Suleiman the Magnificent, 42, 66, 111
Swabians, 79
Swanson, Mark, 213, 216, 227, 230, 231, 232, 239
Swanson, Rosanne, 231

Tabriz, 160, 169
  See also Persia
Tanẓīmāt, 113
  See also Ottoman Empire
al-Tawrāt, 110
Templers, 135, 145
"Terrible Turk," xii, 4, 21, 22–27, 40, 42, 45, 57, 58, 63, 66, 67, 106, 134, 144, 237, 240, 248, 256
Thirty Years War, 60, 69
  See also treaty of Westphalia
Thomsen, Mark, 226–28, 232, 250, 251, 253, 254
Tranquebar, India, 74, 77
Truscott, Dale, 207
Türckenbiechlin, 25
Turks, 4, 10, 21, 22, 24–34, 37–40, 42, 43, 45, 47–52, 54, 55–58, 63, 69, 75, 105, 139, 161, 169, 170

'ulemā', 66, 112
United Lutheran-Reformed Church of Baden, 127
United Lutheran-Reformed Church of Prussia, 119, 120, 122

United States, 4, 6, 13, 14, 92, 93, 116, 146, 151, 153, 159, 162, 172, 174–76, 181, 186, 189, 208, 209, 229, 231
   Barbary Wars, 152
   War of Independence, 87, 152
   Invasion of Iraq (2003), 216n61, 241, 254–56
   Mandate for Armenia, 139
   As the new Promised Land, 1
   Republican culture, 151, 152, 158
   See also "Pax Americana"
Ursinus, John, 75
Urumia, Persia, 160, 161, 162, 163, 165

Valerga, Joseph, 133
   See also Latin Catholics
Valparaiso University, 216
Van Doorn-Harder, Nelly, 216
Van Dyck, Cornelius, 88
Vatican, 8, 246
Vienna, 4, 22, 24, 30, 33, 43–47, 51, 53, 66
   Siege of 1529, 22, 24, 44–47
Vogelaar, Harold S., 182, 208–16, 225, 227, 229, 230, 231, 232, 250
Voice of the Gospel, 184
Von Dorne, Hieronymus, 42, 70, 72
Von Welz, Baron Justinian Ernest, 77

Wadi Natrun, 70, 71
Wansleben, John, 70, 71, 73, 76, 96
Warneck, Gustav, 10, 59
Wee, M. O., 163, 165
Wendt, Michael, 32
Westby, John, 223, 224
Westphalia, treaty of, 43, 60, 107, 115

William I, 17, 120, 125, 130, 135, 141, 144, 145
William II, 17, 125, 144, 145
Wittenberg, 30, 34, 39, 60, 75, 76, 80, 176
Wolf, Edward Jacob, 159
Wolf, Joseph, 84
Wolters, Theodore Fredrich, 129
World War I, 13, 139, 143, 145, 161, 164, 165, 169, 172, 176, 181, 242, 247
World War II, 143, 145, 165, 172, 242
Wright, John Newton, 105, 165, 167, 174
Württemberg, 17, 18, 79, 96, 99, 129, 134, 135, 145

Yazidi, 15, 172
Yemen, 12, 204, 223, 225
Young, William, 21, 123

Zaremba, Felician, 79
Zeller, Johannes, 95, 129
Ziegenbalg, Barthalomew, 77, 78
Zinzendorf, Ludwig von, 17, 18, 80, 81, 244
Zionism, 85, 110, 146, 194, 215, 244, 245, 252
Zoroastrians, 16, 111, 160
   See also Persian Empire
Zwemer, Samuel, 62, 92, 209, 229
   See also Reformed Church in America
Zwingli, Ulrich, 32

www.ingramcontent.com/pod-product-compliance
Lightning Source LLC
Chambersburg PA
CBHW071233230426
43668CB00011B/1411